CHRYSANTHEMUMS
Year-Round Growing

CHRYSANTHEMUMS
Year-Round Growing

Barrie Machin

and

Nigel Scopes

BLANDFORD PRESS

Poole   Dorset

First published 1978

Copyright © 1978 Blandford Press Ltd
Link House, West Street,
Poole, Dorset, BH15 1LL

ISBN 0 7137 0885 9

Printed in Great Britain by
Butler & Tanner Ltd, Frome and London

Colour plates printed by Woodwards of Bath

Contents

CONTENTS

PART FOUR FACTORS AFFECTING GROWTH AND FLOWERING

APPENDICES

Foreword

For generations the art of horticulture depended on the keen observation of master craftsmen who, by trial and error, devised successful methods for growing a wide range of first-class plants. In those days, labour was cheap, well trained and plentiful, and the spirit and conditions of the times encouraged painstaking work. By paying meticulous attention to detail, and by nearly always doing the right thing, in the right way and at the right time, gardeners and growers of the old school produced extremely good fruits, vegetables and flowers in their proper seasons, as ordained by nature.

However, times have changed. Labour is increasingly scarce and expensive, and often poorly trained, and the problem is how to grow good plants cheaply with a very much smaller labour force than used to be available.

One approach is to study the environmental factors such as temperature, feeding and watering. Then, having ascertained the precise levels of these factors at which plants grow best, one has to produce those conditions automatically and with certainty, so that control of the environment is not dependent on the judgement of relatively unskilled labour. This really amounts to taking the 'flair' out of plant handling, and transferring all vital decisions from the operative to the management level. A good deal of progress is being made along these lines, and the recommendations in this book show how far progressive growers can now control conditions.

Nevertheless, environment is not the only aspect worth careful study. A more accurate knowledge of what happens inside the plant itself can also point the way to improved methods of production. Indeed, in some cases a knowledge of plant physiology can show how the grower can even improve on nature in a way that was not dreamed of in traditional horticulture. One of the outstanding examples of such an approach is in the control of flowering. Every gardener is aware of the stately succession of the seasons, in which various species flower in regular order each year. If asked why snowdrops bloom in the winter, raspberries in summer and chrysanthemums in autumn, the old gardener—if he deigned to reply at all to so foolish a question—would have said it was their nature to behave in that way. Plant physiologists, whilst accepting this reply, have shown that the 'natural' sequence of growth is, in fact, the result of specific plant responses to the combination of external factors, such as temperature and daylength, which have characterized the weather in which the plants have grown.

Such knowledge at once opens up novel prospects of altering the plant's response by growing it in other environments. Year-round chrysanthemum production provides a good example of the type of behaviour that can thus be induced, once the underlying nature of the plant's response to environmental factors is understood. Control of plant behaviour on a commercial scale by altering the environment, was the main novelty described in the first edition of this book. This was probably the most important development in horticulture of the present century, but was followed by another breakthrough of equal excitement, based on the possibility of altering the behaviour of plants by the application of chemical growth regulators. The combination of plant control by both environmental and chemical means has been rapidly applied to the commercial production of chrysanthemums, in a way that was beyond our wildest dreams even twelve years ago.

It is the principle of the scientist to study the fundamental principles of environmental control and the detailed physiology of the plant. The findings of science are then recorded in a variety of specialist publications, which are not readily accessible to the busy grower, who is mainly interested in the day-to-day problems of his business. In any case, some of these findings are not too readily understandable, except by other workers in the same field of research. There is thus a pressing need for the appropriate scientific data to be brought together and interpreted in everyday terms, to show how new knowledge may be used in the business of producing plants for market.

In this book Dr Machin and Dr Scopes have tackled the task of showing how high-quality chrysanthemums of all types can be produced, at an economic rate, all the year round, with long stems for cutting or short stems as dwarf pot plants. It is a complex business, involving a clear understanding both of the environment and of the chrysanthemum plant. The authors are to be thanked for their initiative, both in writing the book and in revising it so thoroughly. It is a particular pleasure to write this preface since Dr Machin was one of my own students at the University of Nottingham School of Agriculture, Sutton Bonington.

J. P. HUDSON
Ex-Director, Long Ashton Research Station,
University of Bristol, England

Introduction

The florists' chrysanthemum (*Chrysanthemum morifolium* Ramat) is primarily a long-night plant (usually but incorrectly called a shortday plant) and cannot normally form flower buds when the daylength exceeds $14\frac{1}{2}$ hours or develop them when it exceeds $13\frac{1}{2}$ hours. Hence, the chrysanthemum is traditionally regarded as an autumn flower. However, with simple lighting or blackout systems, daylength (nightlength) can be altered and the flowering time precisely controlled.

The chrysanthemum is grown throughout the world by amateurs, often under the auspices of specialized chrysanthemum societies. It is also the most popular florist's flower, with hundreds of millions of stems being sold every year in North America and Europe alone; there is no alternative to rival its popularity.

Chrysanthemums owe this popularity with the consumer to the range of form and colour of flowers available and to their excellent keeping qualities when cut.

The chrysanthemum plant has been intensively studied by scientists and growers for many years. As a result of control over growing conditions by environmental manipulation, fertilizing, and the use of growth-regulating chemicals, crops can now be produced to precise schedules at any time.

The ability to produce chrysanthemums the year round depends on an understanding of the complex interactions between the plant and its environment; the better these are understood the higher quality will be the finished product. Such an understanding, together with a sound knowledge of management and marketing techniques, should ensure the continued success of the chrysanthemum crop despite increasing production costs.

Part One of this book studies in detail the factors of the environment and their individual and combined effects on the plant. An understanding of the theory and principles will enable the reader to use more readily Parts Two and Three.

Part Two concerns itself with raising plants, and describes the methods of breeding new varieties, growing the stock and rooting the cuttings. Not least are the problems of plant health. Although mainly of specialist interest, the principles apply to every plant that is grown for its flowers.

Part Three describes the practical techniques of growing the crop, and discusses in detail the methods of husbandry used in large production units. We feel that the book is noteworthy in that the most recent production techniques (for example the direct shortday planting system) are included. In addition to daylength and temperature control, the effects of watering and feeding have been studied in detail in view of their importance in the production of the quick-growing, good-quality crops that are a feature of the new methods.

In Part Four, the effects of all the environmental factors on the chrysanthemum plant are considered in full, and much of the research work covering the subject is discussed. A study of this section will serve to explain the reasons behind the practical techniques recommended. This will enable the grower to put his own facilities to the best possible use, and the student of the chrysanthemum to delve as far as he can within the present frontiers of knowledge.

Acknowledgements

We are very sorry that Mr Sidney A. Searle has decided to retire from authorship of this book, but we are grateful for his continued interest and helpful criticisms of the manuscript.

We would like to thank Mr George Sheard and Miss Marion Ebben for their considerable contribution to Chapters 2 and 10 respectively. The book has been enhanced by the drawings of Maurice Bone and photography of Peter Fiske, and their help is gratefully acknowledged.

We are grateful for constructive criticism of manuscripts which have been provided by Mr P. Adams, Dr K. E. Cockshull, Dr M. Hollings, Dr F. A. Langton, Mr M. S. Ledieu, Dr R. Menhenett, Dr R. Nicholls, Dr C. Payne, Dr G. W. Winsor and Dr C. R. Worthing.

We also wish to acknowledge the assistance given to us by the following: Mr P. S. Fox, Mr J. R. Frampton and Mr L. J. Kitchen all of Framptons Nurseries Ltd; Mr J. D. Abbott of DCK Nurseries; Mr J. Turner and Mr D. Wilding of Southdown Flowers Ltd; Mr A. E. Canham of Reading University; Dr N. W. Hussey, Mr G. Grimmett and Miss A. Paul of the GCRI; Mr S. G. Gosling of the National Chrysanthemum Society; and Mr R. Potter of ADAS.

We wish to record our thanks to Mr A. Graham Sparkes of Perifleur Ltd, for helpful criticism and permission to publish results of work carried out at Perifleur Ltd, and Dr D. Rudd-Jones for allowing the GCRI staff to participate in this book.

Finally, this work could not have been undertaken without the patience and understanding of our wives.

Felpham, England　　　　　　　　　　　　　　　　　　　　　　　　　　　　　Barrie Machin
May 1978　　　　　　　　　　　　　　　　　　　　　　　　　　　　　　　　Nigel Scopes

ACKNOWLEDGEMENTS FOR ILLUSTRATIONS

The Glasshouse Crops Research Institute: Figs 8, 11–13, 15–17, 21, 22, 24, 25, 35–41, 43–45, 49–52, 58, 59; Plates 2–5, 7–18, 21–23, 25, 26.
The National Chrysanthemum Society: Figs 9, 10, 42.
Framptons Nurseries Ltd: Plate 19.
DCK Nurseries: Plate 27.
Perifleur Ltd: Fig. 46; Plates 7, 10, 11 and 12.
Crown Copyright: Fig. 53.

PART ONE

Controlling the Environment

1 The Root Environment

The environment in a greenhouse may conveniently be considered in two parts—the conditions in which the roots of the plant grow, or the substrate environment, and the aerial environment in which the stem, leaves and flowers develop.

Substrate is a term used to refer to any media in which the plant roots fulfil their two primary functions, that of supporting the plant and of absorbing water and nutrients. Many different types of substrate have been used both experimentally and in commerce for the production of chrysanthemums. They range from various types of peat, sand, gravel, wood bark, leaf mould and combinations of all these substances with each other or with soil to form different types of compost. Some of the more important compost formulations may be found in Appendix 5. Also, a number of synthetic products such as foam plastic (polystyrene, urea formaldehyde or polyurethane) have been used successfully in composts and these are likely to become progressively more important as supplies of the naturally occurring products, particularly peat, are exhausted. However, for most growers, now and for some considerable time in the future, soil will remain the predominant substrate for the production of year-round chrysanthemum crops.

For this reason the factors of the environment affecting the roots of the plant are considered in relation to soil as the main constituent of the substrate, but it should not be forgotten that the main principles discussed apply equally to the other substrates mentioned above.

SOIL

The soil must be regarded as a highly complex living mass. In addition to the mineral matter constituting the bulk of the soil, all soils contain some organic material or humus, upon which the bacterial life in the soil depends. Soil air and soil water complete the main constituents of the top soil, or soil mantle, in which the plants are grown. It is this complex material that supports the plant, accommodates its roots and provides the moisture and nutrients needed for its growth and development.

Type

To qualify as soil it is generally accepted that the particle size must not exceed 2 mm* in diameter.

There are a great number of differing soil types, often with considerable variations over comparatively short distances, but the mineral matter in all soils is made up of only three components: sand, silt and clay, originally derived from the rocks upon which the top soil rests, or conveyed by the physical action of ice, water or wind. The proportion of these constituents determines the soil type, a light soil having a large proportion of sand and a heavy soil being mainly clay. However, a considerable proportion of the other constituents will generally be found in each type (Fig. 1).

The division of soils into types depends, therefore, upon the mineral particles present in the soil and upon the proportion in which the particles of different sizes occur in it. The main divisions which may be recognized are sand (particle size 2·0 to 0·05 mm), which is gritty, silt (0·05 to 0·002 mm), which feels silky, and clay (less than 0·002 mm), which feels sticky to the touch. If none of these characteristics is present when the soil is moulded in the hand, then the soil is said to be a loam. Sandy soils may be further sub-divided into (*a*) coarse sand, (*b*) medium sand, (*c*) fine sand and (*d*) very fine sand, depending on the size of the grains present.

* See Appendix 8 for full details of metrication scheme used in this book.

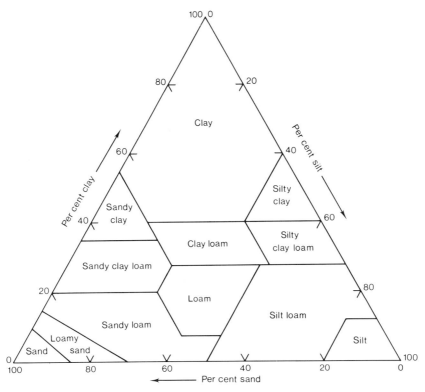

Fig. 1 The composition of the textural classes of soils used by the United States Soil Survey. (From Russell, 1973.)

Profile

If a trench is dug in the soil and the vertical wall face examined, it will be seen that the soil consists of a series of layers or horizons gradually changing in colour, until the raw material of the subsoil is reached. This succession of horizons, known as the soil profile, is of considerable importance because both this and the nature of the subsoil will have a great effect on the conditions in the surface layers and therefore upon the behaviour of the plant. The soil profile will show the depth of the top soil which is usually about 15 to 30 cm and its nature will very largely determine the degree of aeration and rate of drainage. In many cases, variations in soil profile can account for differences in crop performance on what would otherwise be considered similar soils.

The layers of the soil in which movement of air and water is impeded, such as those below the level of the winter water-table, are recognized by gley symptoms. Soluble iron is washed down through the soil and on reaching these levels it gives up its oxygen, and the iron combines with the sulphur present in the decaying vegetation. These compounds take on a bluish or greenish colour and may occur locally from depths of about 45 cm in conditions of poor aeration and bad drainage. In extreme cases, an iron pan forms and seriously impedes drainage into the subsoil (Russell, 1973).

Plant Nutrients

From the combination of mineral and organic matter, air and moisture, and the activities of the soil bacteria, the plant obtains the water and food it needs. The essential major nutrients supplied in the soil solution consist of nitrogen, in the form of nitrates, phosphorus compounds (phosphates) and potassium salts (potash) as

3

well as magnesium and sulphur, often in the form of magnesium sulphate. The trace elements, such as iron, manganese, boron, copper, molybdenum and zinc, are also required.

Lime, in the form of calcium carbonate, provides a small amount of food, and is also needed for its beneficial effect on the soil structure and on bacterial activity—and to neutralize the effect of acids. All these elements are present in the majority of soils, although they may not occur in the correct proportion for balanced plant growth.

Base Exchange Capacity

The organic matter and clay mineral components of soil, known as colloids, contain many small positive and negative electrical charges which hold acidic ions (anions) and basic ions (cations) respectively. Fertilizers added to the soil also contain anions such as nitrate and phosphate, and cations such as sodium, potassium and magnesium, which may interact with the exchangeable ions held by the soil colloids. If, for example, ammonium sulphate is added to a soil, the ammonium ions enter the exchange complex and replace an equivalent amount of a base held by the colloidal particles. If this base is calcium, as is usual, the calcium is washed out of the soil together with the sulphate anions. The ammonia is then nitrified by soil bacteria and the nitrate ions produced enter the soil solution and are neutralized again by more calcium ions. This calcium nitrate may then be either leached out of the soil or, if the nitrate is taken up by the plant roots, the remaining calcium ions are free to re-enter the exchange complex.

Thus the application of large quantities of ammonium sulphate, owing to the resultant leaching of calcium, leads to acidity in the soil unless the loss of calcium is made good by the addition of lime.

SOIL AIR

Soil air is an important factor if good crops are to be grown. Russell (1973) writes: 'Since the roots of most crops can only function actively if they have an adequate oxygen supply, there must be present in soils mechanisms or processes which allow the transfer of oxygen from the atmosphere to the soil organisms and plant roots, and of carbon dioxide from there to the atmosphere at rates adequate to meet the needs of the crop.'

Since the soil is porous, gases can diffuse through it and soil air differs little in composition from the atmosphere above it, except for the far greater amount of carbon dioxide which it contains. A further difference is that the air in fertile soil is always at 100 per cent relative humidity, that is to say, it is always fully charged with water vapour.

While the supply of gases both above and below the soil surface is obviously vital, the importance of the composition of the soil air probably needs the greater emphasis. In cultivating the soil, the grower has to produce conditions which will remain favourable to a ready supply of oxygen to the roots during the life of the crop, and which will permit the release of other gases from the soil. In nature, cultivations are mostly vertical, being the work of earthworms and plant roots, and with an adequate humus supply at the soil surface, result in good soil aeration and good soil structure. Human cultivations are usually horizontal, especially where mechanized, and there is thus a danger that panning will impede the free flow of gases into and out of the soil, and the passage of water and water vapour through the soil.

Pore Space

In addition to differences in the chemical and physical composition of soils, the pore space and thus aeration will vary. This depends on the type, treatment and degree of compaction, and some soils will be able to transfer water by capillary conduction to plant roots faster than others. The volumes of water and air in a soil are inversely related. Clay soils will not allow water to pass freely and the small pores will soon become saturated, leading to anaerobic conditions. Conversely, very sandy soils will allow water to pass straight through and very little moisture can be retained in the large pore spaces.

In field soils, the pore space can be about 60

per cent of its volume, whereas in a pure sphagnum peat, pore space may be as high as 95 per cent. Pore space in greenhouse soils should be maintained, by good cultivation and the addition of humus, at between 75 and 90 per cent to allow for good aeration with adequate water retention.

A diagrammatic representation of the physical nature of a soil is shown in Fig. 2.

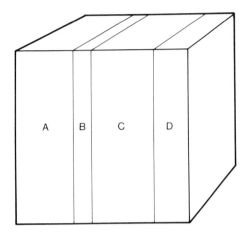

Fig. 2   A diagrammatic representation of a soil.

ABCD   Represents the soil–water–air system
A   Solids (for peat this is about 5 per cent and for agricultural soil is about 40 per cent)
BCD   Represents the total pore space
B   Water present but unavailable to plants even when they are wilting.
C   Pores that contain water or air, depending on the moisture content.
D   'Air capacity' pores that drain freely immediately after watering. Should be about 10 per cent in a potting compost. (From Bunt. 1976.)

SOIL MOISTURE

Water is a basic requirement in the substrate. Indeed, in the nutrient film technique of production (page 119), water in which nutrients are dissolved is the substrate itself. With plants grown in soil and other more conventional substrates a thorough understanding of the relationship of water to plant growth is essential for successful cropping. Apart from foliar feeding (page 77), chrysanthemums take in the elements of nutrition dissolved in soil water through their roots by the process of osmosis. The optimum availability of soil moisture is interdependent on many of the factors discussed in this chapter.

Moisture Deficit

The calculation of water loss from a soil has been an important step in the understanding of irrigation control (page 71).

The calculation of potential transpiration presupposes an ample supply, or more exactly, a readily available supply of water to the roots at all times. It also assumes that during any period water is readily available, and that the roots are able to meet the full transpiration demands of the plant under all weather conditions. As the soil moisture deficit increases, however, the soil reaches a state at which extraction of water by the plant ceases to be easy. When availability of soil water becomes limiting to the aerial parts of the plant, the plant must limit its transpiration, and the calculation of potential transpiration no longer refers to the actual water loss from the soil. Water uptake is at the optimum rate only so long as the soil moisture status is at or near the field capacity.

Moisture must be maintained in the shallow layers of the soil if the maximum transpiration and rate of growth are to be sustained, because of the rapid exhaustion of the readily available water in immediate contact with the roots. The rate of replenishment of water in the root area depends to some extent on the ability of the soil to transfer water by capillarity to the roots of the plant. This movement of soil water takes place through the soil pore space and the rate and amount of movement will be related to the size and continuity of the pores and to such factors as the suction gradient and the viscosity of the water.

The point at which the declining soil moisture commences to limit transpiration will depend in part on the soil type, the limited moisture in sandy soils being more readily available at first, but the transition from wet to dry in these soils is found to be much sharper than in the heavier soils. From all the available evidence it would seem certain that a sensible reduction in the transpiration rate will have commenced with all crops by the time about 40 to 50 per cent of the available water has been removed from the root zone, and that this reduction may have an adverse effect on the development and subsequent quality of the foliage and flowers. Since water movement in a drying soil is very slow, the transpiration rate of most crops would probably fall off very abruptly in some soils before this quantity of available water had been removed. Salter (1954) found a marked reduction in the growth rate and in the water uptake of tomato plants where irrigations were delayed until 35 per cent of the available water had been depleted, compared with a crop irrigated at 5 per cent depletion. It is well known that plants are often temporarily unable to meet heavy transpiration demands made upon them, and even during average summer conditions the moisture content of the leaves is depleted by day owing to the lag in water uptake, and wilting results.

When soil moisture becomes limiting, different plants have different mechanisms for keeping their leaves from heating and drying up. Once this mechanism is invoked, the removal of water from the soil will probably vary with different varieties of plants and with the stage of growth. The rate of reduction of both transpiration and growth may vary with the type of crop. Penman (1952) states that for some plants the growth rate decreases when the roots have to work against even small suctions in the soil, while others appear to be unaffected over a wide range of suction.

Where a crop is only partially covering the ground, or where it is well spaced in cultivated soil, less water than the calculated amount of potential transpiration will be needed because the plant can draw to a certain extent upon the reserves under the bare soil around it. The difference in its water need compared with that of a full-cover crop is not great, however, because wet bare soil loses water faster than does vegetation until the top few inches are dry (after which the losses from bare soil are arrested). The soil moisture deficit caused by evaporation from fallow soil would rarely exceed about 25 mm, but this could be a material factor with a newly planted crop.

Effect of Temperature and Other Factors

Other factors affect the availablity of water to the plant. Kramer (1934) found that lowering the temperature of the soil directly decreased the absorption of water in two ways: first, by its physical effects, chiefly increased viscosity of the water and decreased vapour pressure, which result in a slower movement of water from soil to root; and second, by its physiological effects on the permeability of the root cells. Soil temperature also affects root growth and hence the amount of absorption. Low soil temperatures, leading to poor root action and thus to reduction in the water uptake rate, are known to lead to difficulties on very bright days when the plant is temporarily unable to meet the heavy transpiration demand made upon it. The ability of soils to hold water against gravity increases, however, as their temperature is decreased.

With young plants the frequency of watering has to be increased owing to the small root range, and as the root range increases it is important to know, when deciding on the soil moisture reserve, the depth of soil from which the crop can draw its water supply at any particular time.

SOIL TEMPERATURE

When considering soil temperature, a number of factors have to be borne in mind:

1 The temperature of the shallow layers at about 8 am normally differ very little from the minimum temperature in those layers.

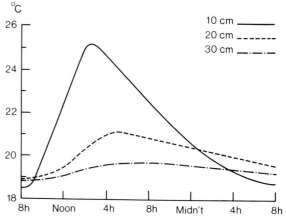

Fig. 3 In Britain, differences between soil temperatures in shallow layers are least about 8 am. Diurnal range in a greenhouse on a sunny August day.

6

2 The differences between the temperature at all levels down to about 30 cm are least at about 8 am and increase during the day as the surface warms up (Fig. 3).

3 When warming up in the early season, the temperature of the soil will normally be greatest in the shallow layers, and will decrease with depth.

4 There is a correlation between the temperature of the shallow soil and that of the air close above it; the two are interdependent because at the interface the temperatures are the same.

It is therefore impossible, in the early stages of growth, and where the soil is warmed from the surface, to maintain substantially different temperature regimes in the soil and the air in which the plants are growing. Under natural conditions the temperature of the air is maintained essentially by the ground.

To ensure that the minimum temperature needed in the soil has been reached when a greenhouse is to be planted, the earth thermometer reading at about 8 am must be used. This reading may be taken as the minimum of the top 30 cm. Below about 60 cm the temperature of the soil in the early season will invariably be below this value under the usual conditions in the heated house, and the difference will increase sharply with depth. After a cold winter this may be a material factor, particularly in houses that have been unheated for any length of time before planting, because the cold subsoil may have an unduly depressing effect on the temperature of the surface layers. This might be felt when the leaves of the growing plants shade the soil surface from the warming effect of solar radiation as the season progresses. Moreover, the plant roots grow down into the subsoil and may be adversely affected by the low temperature.

Temperature Requirement

The most reliable guide to the temperature needed in the soil is provided by reference to air temperature data in view of the known correlation that normally exists between the temperature of the air and that of the shallow layers of the soil. Searle (1954) has shown for example, that where an average night air temperature of 15·6° is required, the minimum soil temperature at 30 cm depth, read at 9 am, should be about 17·2° in January, rising to 19·4° by mid-June. The average night air temperature refers to the period from sunset to sunrise, and is best found from thermographs exposed in the plant rows.

These approximate figures may be used as a guide where soil warming equipment is available. With this equipment there is the possibility that soil temperatures at the depth of the heating medium may be raised above the optimum. This applies especially in the early season when a relatively high soil temperature would tend to maintain the air temperature of the microclimate above that required for plant development. Since the heat is injected at the depth of the heating medium, and not at the surface, a slightly higher soil temperature than that quoted above would appear to be in order, provided this did not release more nitrate from the soil than would be needed for balanced plant growth (page 77).

Temperature Gradients

In addition to the vertical gradient, other gradients in soil temperature are normally found in heated houses under commerical conditions. With sloping ground high ends are usually warmer than the centres and low ends of houses, but this would depend in part on the layout of the heating system. With blocks of north–south houses, the soil temperature of the outside houses is normally lower than that of the inside houses, and is lower near the sides than in the centre in the early season.

The measurement of the temperature of the shallow layers of the soil presents little difficulty. Angle and protected straight stem earth thermometers are used for depths down to about 23 cm, and for 30 cm and below the Symons steel tube and other types of thermometer are available.

If inserted to the depth, or immersion, for which they are intended to be used, earth thermometers will give accurate readings at all times of the day and night.

Soil Warming

For soil warming a satisfactory method is found in some greenhouses of laying small-bore heating pipes (30 mm steam pipes or 50 mm hot water pipes) on the surface of the ground. This system has the advantage of heating the soil from the surface downwards in a natural manner. With the hot water pipes, the temperature may be closely controlled by modulating the temperature of the circulating water.

Where the heating medium is buried in the soil, the selection of the correct depth for this medium is essential. Shallow laying of electric heating wires or of steam or hot water pipes is more certain to raise the temperature of the upper soil; deeper laying may result mainly in warming the subsoil. If, however, the heating grid is laid at a shallower depth, the reduced temperature difference upwards is counterbalanced by the shorter thermal path.

With the comparatively gentle application of heat from electric heating wires, the injection by night, with the object of partially arresting the natural fall in soil temperature during the dark hours, appears to represent a satisfactory use of electricity during the period when it is most readily available.

In benches, the use of electricity for soil warming has given satisfactory results, because, the even temperatures maintained throughout enable economies to be effected in space heating. Good results have also been obtained in small houses, especially where the area of warmed soil is enclosed above at night by glass or plastic frames. Electric soil warming systems for horticultural purposes have been described by Canham (1964).

With any system of direct soil warming, whether the heating element be laid in or on the soil, a profound effect on the soil moisture status may be expected. This is especially the case where heat is injected into the soil and the natural temperature gradient in the soil becomes partially inverted. Under these conditions, water vapour losses may be considerable, and must be anticipated when calculating the moisture requirements of the crop.

2 The Aerial Environment

Plant growth and development are affected by four main factors of the aerial environment: light, air temperature, carbon dioxide concentration and water vapour pressure deficit. With light, both the amount and daily duration are especially important, the former being related to the production of assimilates in photosynthesis the latter to the control of flowering. The quality of light, that is the part of the light spectrum the plant is capable of receiving and utilizing, varies according to the time of day and affects plants accordingly. Air temperature determines the rate of growth and affects the flowering response, while carbon dioxide concentration governs the rate of photosynthesis. Water vapour pressure deficit is more popularly thought of as relative humidity. As the deficit increases the plant is put under stress and photosynthetic assimilation reduced.

Accurate control of these factors is necessary if year-round production is to be successful and commercially profitable. The precise timing necessary under commercial conditions requires the manipulation of daylength throughout the year by artificial lighting or blackout. This means that for practical purposes the year-round crop must be grown under cover in houses which have good light transmission and well-designed heating and ventilating systems. They should be constructed to give maximum utilization of the growing area and facilitate the automatic operation of blackout and materials handling systems.

LIGHT
Amount of Light

The growth of all higher plants is governed by the process of photosynthesis, in which the plant combines carbon dioxide from the air with water obtained from the soil to form sugars.

The energy for the process is provided by the light which falls on the leaves and which is absorbed by the leaf pigments, particularly chlorophyll. These sugars have to be converted into more complex plant-building materials such as cellulose and proteins. The extra energy needed for this is supplied from the re-conversion of some of the sugars to carbon dioxide and water in the presence of oxygen during the process of respiration.

Respiration is a continuous process but as photosynthesis cannot occur during darkness the level of carbon dioxide rises at night in a closed structure such as a greenhouse. In the early morning when the light level is low some photosynthesis occurs and uses some of the excess carbon dioxide. But as light increases, the rate of carbon dioxide uptake in photosynthesis will equal the rate of output in respiration. This instant, when the carbon dioxide level around the plant remains constant and when plant weight neither increases or decreases because photosynthesis and respiration are balanced, is known as the *light compensation point*. For chrysanthemums approaching maturity in a year-round programme, this occurs at a light intensity of about 4000 lux (lx), or about an hour after sunrise with a clear sky in spring. Above this level of light, the rate of photosynthesis increases with intensity until at very high light intensities photosynthesis becomes limited by the availability of carbon dioxide.

Light Transmission and Greenhouse Design

Lawrence (1950) showed that plants require about 1·5 MJ/m²/day (page 14) of photosynthetically active radiation to maintain reasonable growth. From mid-December to mid-January the average daily light integral outdoors in southern England is only about 0·8 MJ/m²/day. This is further reduced in a greenhouse by the opaque structural material and transmission losses. Chrysanthemums require about 1·25 MJ/m²/day during the initial shortday period to en-

Fig. 4 A well-sited widespan house with no trees or high hedges in the immediate vicinity to obstruct light in the winter.

sure satisfactory growth and development. In Britain, from November to February, plant growth is directly proportional to the light integral and it is essential that when crops such as chrysanthemums are grown in greenhouses light transmission is as high as possible (Fig. 4).

Light intensity is dependent on the altitude of the sun:

Solar attitude	15°	30°	45°	60°	90°
Illumination (lx × 10³)	27	59	91	113	135

Solar altitude varies with latitude, season and time of day. The noon altitude in degrees, for latitudes between 45° and 60°N are set out in Table 1.

The presence of cloud also affects the intensity of illumination. With a completely overcast sky with sheet cloud, illumination may be no more than half that of a clear sky and is often as low as one-third. Average values of cloud amount and sunshine for Meteorological Office weather and climatological stations covering Britain are available and published in the Climatological Atlas.

Light may be direct or diffuse. The diffuse component is important as more than half the total light in each month throughout the year is diffuse. On days with thin or broken cloud, and notably with cumulus cloud, the reflected light from the whole sky will be a considerable part of the whole and will enter the greenhouse from all angles.

The location of a greenhouse will markedly affect the ambient light conditions. A grower can gain advantage from a southerly location, proximity to the coast and areas with good visibility and sunshine records. In Britain, it becomes increasingly difficult to maintain a year-round production programme the further

TABLE 1 Solar Altitude at Noon in Degrees

Latitude	Jan	Feb	Mar	Apr	May	Jun	Jul	Aug	Sep	Oct	Nov	Dec
45° N	24	32	42	54	64	68	67	59	48	37	27	23
50° N	19	27	37	49	59	63	62	54	43	32	22	18
55° N	14	22	32	44	54	58	57	49	38	27	17	13
60° N	9	17	27	39	49	53	52	44	33	22	12	8

north the location. This is illustrated by the concentration of production in the southern and south-eastern counties and the very few holdings with year-round programmes in the northern counties and Scotland:

TABLE 2   Distribution of Year-Round Chrysanth Crops Expressed as Percentages of Total Area of Production

County	Cut flowers	County	Pots
West Sussex	20·3	West Sussex	15·9
Hampshire	15·6	Hampshire	13·4
Essex	6·6	Surrey	8·0
Kent	5·3	Essex	6·9
Hertford	5·2	Cumberland	5·5
Devon	5·0	Norfolk	4·8

The transmission of direct sunlight is affected by three factors: orientation, the amount of opaque structural material and roof geometry.

East–west orientation of a single span greenhouse increases the transmission of direct light in winter by about 50 per cent and is the most important single factor in improving winter light (Fig. 5). Opaque structural members are necessary to support the roof and carry the glazing, and to give the greenhouse strength and stability against wind and snow loading, but they should be as small as possible. The almost universal use of steel and aluminium sections in modern greenhouses reduces opaque structural material to the lowest level consistent with adequate design. Roof geometry is important as it affects the transmission of light by the transparent envelope. When light strikes clean glass at an angle of 90° about 90 per cent of the light is transmitted. More light is reflected and less is transmitted as the angle approaches 60°, at which point reflection in-

Fig. 5   A modern east–west single span aluminium and steel-framed greenhouse.

creases rapidly and the proportion transmitted declines.

In mid-winter, when the elevation of the sun at noon in southern England is about 16°, the greatest admission of light to a greenhouse at that time would be through a south-facing side or roof slope at an angle of about 74°. The elevation of the sun varies with the time of day and with time of year and it is not possible to maintain a situation which is best for all conditions. Nevertheless, a single span house with a long, steep, south-facing side is best placed to transmit maximum direct solar radiation in winter. Roof slope has litttle affect on transmission of direct sunlight on houses oriented north–south, provided the slope is between 20° and 40°. The transmission of diffuse light is not affected by orientation or sun elevation.

Recent work at the Efford Experimental Horticulture Station (EHS) (Anon., 1977) has compared three types of glasshouse

(a) 20 m single clearspan with a conventional roof

(b) 20 m single clearspan with a Mansard type roof

(c) 3·2 m multispan Venlo.

One unit of each of these three types was built with east–west orientation and compared with a multispan Venlo unit oriented north–south. Each unit was approximately 0·1 hectare (ha) in size, the clearspans being 56 × 20 m and the Venlo multispan blocks 31 × 32 m. Measurements of light transmission were made over three years. These showed that on overcast days, when all the light was diffuse, there was little difference in transmission between the four units, but on bright sunny days there were marked differences. The two east–west clearspan houses gave 8 per cent better transmission than the east–west Venlo block from November to January but the position was reversed in summer. The Mansard roof was marginally better than the conventional but not sufficiently to warrant further consideration. In mid-winter the light transmission of the east–west Venlo was 8 per cent better than the north–south Venlo block. The affect on crop production was recorded over a period of eight years and in 1975 and 1976 year-round chrysan-

themums were the test crop. Crops flowered more quickly in those units oriented east–west, the single widespan being better than the multispan Venlo unit. The widespan houses produced up to 23 per cent better quality sprays in mid-winter but the advantage disappeared with crops flowering after mid-April.

TABLE 3   Percentage Transmission of Photosynthetically Active Radiation

	Widespan east–west	Venlo north–south 0·4 ha block
Diffuse light	74	70
Direct sunlight Equinox	65	61
Direct sunlight winter	70	51
Total light Equinox	68	65
Total light winter	72	60

Table 3 shows the order of difference in the best and worst combinations of design and orientation in modern greenhouses, based on earlier work at the National Institute of Agricultural Engineering (NIAE). Compared with the above, older timber houses built in 10 m spans have percentage transmission values as follows:

0·4 ha block north–south	30
single span 10 m by 50 m north–south	40
single span 10 m by 50 m east–west	60

Uniformity of light distribution in winter in east–west Venlo houses is marred by ridge and gutter shadows, nevertheless they are overall better than similar houses north–south. Considering light transmission, widespan houses oriented east–west offer the best conditions in the critical winter period. With multispan blocks, it is better to construct them east–west rather than north–south.

GREENHOUSE CONSTRUCTION

Steel and aluminium are now almost exclusively used for greenhouse construction in Britain, steel for the main load-bearing members, aluminium for the cladding. Timber is now rarely used as a constructional material. Initially, the change from timber to metal was stimulated by the high strength/size ratio of metal sections, particularly aluminium which can be extruded in complicated profiles. Light transmission is improved by the reduction in size and number of structural members and the properties of metal allow the construction of wider spans. Use of metal has also reduced maintenance and in recent years metal has become cheaper than timber in initial cost. Steel is invariably hot-dip galvanized, the sections being treated after fabrication.

The principles of greenhouse construction are discussed in detail in leaflets published by the Agricultural Development and Advisory Service (Appendix 2).

Greenhouses can be covered in plastic as an alternative to glass. Rigid sheet plastics are all more costly than glass and none is superior in performance. Most are inferior in light transmission and durability. Houses clad with thin film, usually polyethylene (polythene), are less costly than glass-covered houses, but they have a high risk of wind damage, require regular replacement of the skin and present problems of humidity control and ventilation. Though advantageous for some crops, they are not recommended for year-round chrysanthemum production in Britain, considering the high financial investment in the crop and the accurate programming demanded.

OTHER CONSIDERATIONS IN DESIGN

No greenhouse production unit should be built without full consideration of the crop to be grown. This is particularly true in the case of specialist year-round chrysanthemum cut flower or pot plant production. It is essential to get maximum use of the productive area and this is affected by the size and layout of beds or benches and pathways. Path width must be related to path function and whether paths provide a working stage or simply provide access. Where houses are benched as for pot production (Fig. 48), path width is related to bench height, the lower the bench the narrower it is possible to make the path. It is increasingly important to consider materials handling in greenhouses and in this respect the handling of flowers is a difficult problem. Light crop-spanning gantries, overhead runways and mono-rails (Fig. 38) offer possible solutions but they are much easier to incorporate if considered in the initial planning.

The choice of greenhouse type is dictated by economic considerations. Wide clearspan houses give the best light transmission in winter, offer the greatest flexibility and freedom of choice in layout and facilitate mechanization. They are more costly to build, more costly to heat and less efficient in the utilization of land. At the other extreme, multispan Venlo blocks are lowest in building costs, give good winter light transmission, better utilization of land and are more efficient to heat but the 3.2 m module imposes unacceptable limitations on flexibility and mechanization. The 3.2 m Venlo has too many technical disadvantages for year-round chrysanthemum production but wide single spans of 20 to 30 m are now too expensive to build. Under present conditions in Britain, the best compromise between cost and design is to build multispan blocks with east–west orientation choosing a span between 7 and 15 m.

SUPPLEMENTARY LIGHTING

In the latitudes of Britain (50° to 60° N), the natural daylight is insufficient to maintain adequate growth of chrysanthemums between November and February. Even in the most favourably oriented house with clean glass or polythene only about 60 per cent of natural light will be admitted.

The grower can, however, supplement natural light during seasons of low light intensity by the use of high illuminance lamps which, although expensive to buy and use, will ensure uniform, reliable cropping throughout the winter.

Before installing supplementary lighting it is important to know some of the established facts regarding chrysanthemums and light and to be familiar with the terms used in light measurement.

The radiation visible to the human eye and which we call light accounts for about 50 per cent of the energy of solar radiation. The remainder is mainly in the invisible infra-red wavelengths. Fortunately, the visible waveband is roughly coincident with the radiation involved in plant growth, so that horticultural installations can make use of lamps which are mass-produced for non-horticultural purposes. Light meters (which must be cosine-corrected) are used to measure light intensity or illuminance which is now expressed in lux rather than the older term 'foot candles'. Because lux is a measure of the brightness of light as seen by the human eye, it is necessary to convert measurements of illuminance to units which give some indication of the value of the light for plant growth. Research workers use units of energy (Joules) for this and measure the intensity or irradiance as Joules per square metre per second ($J/m^2/s$) (or W/m^2 if one uses the Watt unit of energy) and the daily total of radiation as $MJ/m^2/day$. Conversion factors for light measurements may be found in Appendix 8.

Visible radiation figures given as being adequate for normal growth and development in chrysanthemums vary from 1·2 to 1·6 MJ/m/day. Data from Efford EHS indicate that the average levels of visible radiation ($MJ/m^2/day$) received in greenhouses on the south coast of England from 1962 to 1972 were as follows:

November 0·92   December 0·59
January   0·75   February 1·21

Radiation figures considerably lower than these values can be expected in more northern areas of Britain.

A number of workers have demonstrated the benefits of using supplementary light during the winter period to raise the level of visible radiation to at least the minimum considered necessary for good growth both with pot plant (Canham, 1970a; Cockshull and Hughes, 1972) and cut flower crops (Canham, 1972; Machin, 1973). This work is considered in detail in Chapters 8, 9 and 11.

Both low- and high-pressure mercury lamps and low- and high-pressure sodium lamps have been used successfully in year-round pot and cut flower chrysanthemum programmes. Lamps arranged to provide about 7000 lx of illuminance for eight to 12 hours each day are normally recommended. Full details of type of lamp for various uses, layout of installation and the economics of supplementary lighting in Britain are given in The Electricity Council Handbook No. 2 (1973).

Quality of Light

Any radiating body whether it be the sun or a man-made lamp produces a broad spectrum of radiation. Within this spectrum there is a relatively narrow waveband comprising radiation of wavelengths between 380 and 780 nanometer (nm) which, as well as being visible to the human eye, also produces important responses in plants.

WAVELENGTH

Wavelength determines the colour of light. The shortest visible wavelengths appear violet (400 to 440 nm) and with increasing wavelength different colour sensations are produced through blue (around 460 nm), green (around 510 nm), yellow (570 nm), orange (610 nm), red (650 nm) to far-red (700 to 750 nm).

Ultra-violet light, with wavelengths shorter than 400 nm, can be harmful to plant life and may cause cell damage and mutations. Non-visible light at the infra-red end of the spectrum transmits a great deal of radiant heat into greenhouses during the summer period. The harmful effects of this have been controlled by the use of water sprayed down the outside of the glass where necessary equipment is available. The infra-red light cannot penetrate the water and this results in lower greenhouse temperatures.

PLANT RESPONSE

Chrysanthemums respond to light of different wavelengths in different ways. In comparison with plants grown in natural light, plants grown entirely in blue light or in light with a high percentage of blue have short internodes, small leaves and flowers and foliage appears hard and dark green

Plants grown in red light, a higher proportion of which occurs in natural light at dawn and dusk, are relatively soft in appearance, and compared with plants in natural light, tend to have extended internodes. Red light is also capable of suppressing the etiolation which occurs in darkness. Cathey (1974) has used lamps combining red and far-red light for inducing extra stem length in plants without affecting flowering response (page 109).

However, because at the moment artificial light is generally used to supplement daylength rather than to replace it entirely, the morphological differences caused by artificial light of different wavelengths are not sufficient to preclude the use of even virtually monochromatic light sources, such as low-pressure sodium lamps (SOX) on chrysanthemums.

While light of different wavelengths affects the morphology of chrysanthemum plants as outlined above, it appears that the actual wavelength of light within the 400 to 700 nm range does not affect the photosynthetic rate. Plants grown in similar levels of blue and red light have similar dry weights at flowering, despite their different morphological development.

Daylength

Since the classical experiments of Garner and Allard (1920), which resulted in the discovery that the flowering of chrysanthemums could be regulated by the length of the light and dark periods in each daily cycle, a great deal of work has been done (Chapter 11) to perfect the techniques used to modify the natural daylength within the greenhouse.

The varieties of *Chrysanthemum morifolium* which are used in year-round programmes will initiate flower buds when dark periods exceed 9½ hours in length, and will develop these buds following dark periods exceeding 10½ hours. Thus, daylength (or nightlength to be more precise) requires to be under strict control according to the time of year and the stage of development of the crop.

NIGHT-BREAK LIGHTING

Artificial light is used during naturally long dark periods to prevent flower initiation and hence to keep the plants in a vegetative condition for leaf and stem growth. If artificial light is given in the middle of a long winter night, the chrysanthemum responds as if it were growing in the long days and shortnight conditions of summer.

The approximate period during which artificial long days must be given to delay flowering in any place between latitude 50° and 60° extends from early August to the middle of May (Fig. 6). For stock plants (page 50) it is usual for propagators to continue with a two-hourly lighting period throughout the summer months.

Night-break lighting which is normally controlled by time-switch, is most effective when given in the middle of the night to interrupt the dark period. Light given in the evening and early morning may be only partially inhibitory to flowering, and as a general guide for most varieties night-break lighting should be con-

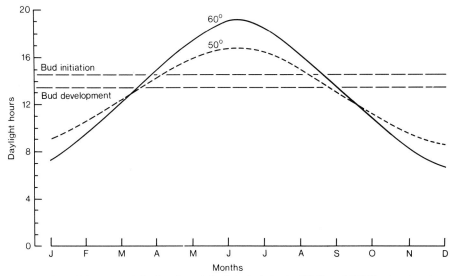

Fig. 6 Annual variation of the mean daily duration of daylight in latitude 50° N and 60° N, showing the normal dates of bud initiation and of the commencement of bud development.

fined to the period between 10 pm and 3 am.

Where the lighting installation provides illumination of not less than 110 lx over the whole bed, the normal lighting periods for flowering crops in southern England in the middle of the night are:

March, April, May, August, September and October	3 hours
November, December, January and February	4 hours

If the illumination reaching the plants farthest from the lamps is between 55 and 110 lx these hours would have to be increased by 1 hour during the lighting period.

To ensure that the plants are not exposed to consecutive dark periods of sufficient length to cause flower bud initiation and development, the lighting times should be so planned that the dark periods do not exceed seven hours.

The light is usually provided by normal domestic type tungsten-filament or incandescent coiled coil pearl lamps and separate bright aluminium reflectors. Pearl lamps give a slightly more even distribution of light and are used in preference to clear lamps. For beds up to 1·5 m wide, a single line of 100-watt lamps spaced 1·8 m apart and 1·2 to 1·4 m above the plants, or 150-watt lamps spaced 3·1 m apart and 1·5 to 1·8 m above the plants, is found to be satisfactory. It is normal in the year-round programme to have several beds together under lights, and under this arrangement the light intensity at the plants farthest from the lamps will not normally be below 110 lx.

CYCLIC LIGHTING

Work published in the United States by Cathey, Bailey and Borthwick, by Cathey and Borthwick and by Waxman, dating from 1961, shows that it is unnecessary to give continuous illumination during the lighting period, because the inhibitory effect of night-break light continues after the light has gone out. It was found, however, that plants being controlled by the methods described above must be illuminated at least every 30 minutes. This is because the blue pigment in the plants called phytochrome is changed by lighting into the active form which

delays flowering, and with a dark interval of more than 30 minutes the active form is not maintained. Cathey and Borthwick have found cycles of six minutes' light during every 30 minutes to be satisfactory, but recommend that cyclic lighting be used over a period four hours per night throughout the lighting season. These recommendations are for the USA, in latitudes lower than those of Britain, and must be considered in relation to the intensity of the light being given. For flowering crops in Britain, where winter nights are longer, a cycle of not less than 10 minutes' light in 30 minutes is recommended, provided the light intensity is not less than 110 lx.

A light cycle must commence and end the normal lighting period shown on this page. Where the illumination reaching the plants is between 55 and 110 lx, cycles of 50 per cent are recommended, that is 15 minutes light on and 15 minutes off, in each 30-minute cycle. With a sequence timer in circuit the grower can run the lighting of a year-round chrysanthemum flowering programme at one-third or one-half the load previously required. Alternatively one can considerably increase the size of the growing area for the same electrical loading.

LIGHT SPILL

When a part of a chrysanthemum crop is being illuminated while other plants in the same or adjacent houses are in natural short days, great care must be taken to ensure that the artificial light is completely screened from the other plants. Where this is not done, serious delay can be caused to crops in short days, both in the same and nearby houses, light reflected from glazing bars and other surfaces being quite sufficient to have this effect. With year-round crops it is usual to entirely cover the beds being illuminated, so that no direct or reflected light can delay the flowering of crops in adjacent beds in short days. Plants are highly susceptible to delay during the first two weeks of shortday treatment.

LIGHTING INSTALLATION

In the normal year-round chrysanthemum cut flower programme approximately one-third of the planted area will require lighting at any one time. It is usual to have all beds permanently equipped with lights, rather than to effect an economy in material, by moving the electric cables with their lamps from bed to bed as the season progresses. An economy can be achieved by having the time-switch and plug sockets mounted on a board centrally placed to serve any number of beds up to about fifteen. The cables above each bed are given sufficient length to reach this distribution board from any position.

With a total greenhouse area of 0·4 ha planted to year-round chrysanthemums, up to 730 m of cable with 400 lamps of 100 watts each will be in use on the beds at any one time representing a current loading of 100/kW per hectare.

The lighting equipment should be installed by a qualified electrical engineer to ensure complete safety (especially in metal-framed houses) and, in large installations, to guard against a voltage drop in the cable which may reduce the illumination below the required level.

The lamps are fixed to the cable* at the appropriate distance with festoon-type holders.

The fitting of the socket of the holders is a simple and speedy matter, two prongs penetrating the rubber sheath of the cable and making contact with the twin wire as the socket is clamped into position. The holder cannot be considered as completely weatherproof, and no part of the installation should be handled while the current is on.

PCP cable with moulded holders spaced at the requisite distances is a satisfactory alternative, is quite waterproof and safer but is more expensive. In addition, the contact with the cable is positive, which is not always the case with the less expensive festoon-type holders.

Although tungsten-filament lamps, which are cheap to install, are normally used for the night-break lighting of chrysanthemum crops, they are relatively inefficient as sources of light, and the spectral composition of the radiation emitted, since it contains far-red radiation as well as red light, is by no means optimal for the purpose.

* Either 7/·067 VR flat twin or 7/·067 PCP sheathed flat twin.

Cathey and Borthwick (1964) and Canham (1966b) have reported upon the effectiveness of fluorescent tubes, the radiation from which contains an appreciable amount of red light with very little far-red. These tubes appear to be more effective and use less current but are more expensive to install than tungsten-filament lamps.

The life of the fluorescent tube, which is estimated at 7500 hours for normal use, is greatly reduced if the tubes are subjected to frequent switching. For this reason, fluorescent tubular lamps are not at present suitable for cyclic lighting.

The high-pressure mercury fluorescent lamp (type MBFR/U) is also effective as a source of night-break light (Canham, 1962), but can only be used efficiently on relatively large areas. Where it can be used efficiently a load reduction similar to that obtained with fluorescent tubes appears to be possible. This lamp too is unsuitable for cyclic lighting as it takes about five minutes to attain full brightness.

Low-pressure sodium (SOX) lamps will provide completely effective night-break lighting, but the critical level of illuminance varies from 10 to 40 lx depending on variety (Canham, Cockshull and Hand, 1977). This could become an important lamp in non-cyclic installations because its efficiency is 32 per cent compared with only 7 per cent for incandescent lamps.

BLACKING-OUT

During the period from March to September, when daylength in Britain is too long for normal bud development, chrysanthemums must be induced to flower by giving artificial short days. This is done by covering the plants with black cloth, black polythene sheeting or other opaque material to extend the normal night period. The material used must be such as to exclude all light from the plants.

Dense black polythene sheeting, usually 150 gauge, specially manufactured for the purpose, is satisfactory as a light excluder and is widely used. It must be handled carefully, however, as it tears readily. Since polythene does not pass water vapour, the condensation water which collects on its underside during the night can lead to leaf diseases under certain conditions, and its wet state in the mornings makes it difficult to handle. To counteract the conditions of very high humidity under the polythene sheeting, growers find it beneficial at times to ventilate the beds in artificial short days by some means, such as opening the end curtains after dark,

For covering beds 1·5 m wide, the material used must have a total width of at least 4·3 m.

For various reasons it is found that results are best where the night period is lengthened both in the evening and in the morning, and the plants are usually covered for the period 6 pm to 7 am; covering before 6 pm can lead to a serious loss of quality. The shade curtains are drawn from the ends of the beds along wires on inverted 'U' frames, and must extend right over the beds to the ground.

If purlin posts or other obstructions prevent this arrangement, the curtains can be rolled up from the sides over the centre of the beds on to the wires, where they are secured until needed in the evening. This laborious arrangement has the disadvantage of partially shading the crop during the daytime, and results may thereby be adversely affected, especially during periods of dull weather.

In the standard year-round programme (page 90) approximately two-thirds of the beds will need blackout material at any one time. This means that with a total house area of 0·4 ha planted to year-round chrysanthemums, approximately 1280 m length of 1·5 m bed will need blackout at the same time. In fast programmes (page 92) the area to be covered will extend to about three-quarters of the total number of beds.

During the period March to September, artificial short days must be continued until the commencement of daylengths short enough for flower bud development, or until one week after disbudding, otherwise they may fail to open and vegetative laterals will appear.

To save labour, some growers omit to draw the blackout on one night a week, usually Saturday. The loss of quality and delay in flowering is generally considered to be negligible.

Maatsch and Bachthaler (1965) found that the best quality plants of several varieties were obtained by uninterrupted shortday treatment. However, the effects on growth of one day of normal length every weekend were slight and the labour saving was justified.

Work at Efford EHS (Anon, 1972) showed that blackout used for five nights a week gave both poorer yield and quality and an increase in flowering time of up to seven days in comparison with blackout used for six nights a week. Ending the blacking-out at disbudding time (compared with the bud-colour stage), following six nights of blackout, produced larger flowers but caused four to five days delay in flowering. It was, however, found to be possible to cease blacking-out one week after disbudding with no delay in flowering.

AUTOMATIC BLACKOUT

To facilitate the covering of out-of-season crops, a number of automated systems have been devised.

With the Maurer method the shading works on the principle of the roller blind, with a 50 or 75 mm aluminium shaft running down the bed. Simply by revolving the shaft, either mechanically or by hand, the shading material is lowered or raised into position. Where mechanically operated, an electric motor with reduction gear is fitted, controlled by a time-switch. Limit-switches are provided to ensure against over-running.

Such an arrangement can be used to shade single beds, but since many layouts consist of four beds in a house 9·1 m wide, the purlin posts can be utilized as a fixing for the shaft. By the provision of suitable framework a bed each side of the purlin posts can be shaded from the one shaft, the equipment being operated by a single motor. More than one such two-bed unit can be controlled by a single motor and beds up to 61 m in length are permissible.

A second automated method has been devised whereby the whole greenhouse is blacked-out by one curtain pulled mechanically from one side to the other, either over a section or over the complete length of the house. This system cannot, of course, be used in houses with purlin posts or other obstructions.

With both methods, end curtains drop into position when the beds are covered, and thus, with time-switch operation, complete automation is achieved.

Although these automated systems are expensive to install, there are a number of advantages in addition to the obvious saving in labour. All beds can be covered and uncovered at the correct time, which is often not the case with hand operation, where an early start has sometimes to be made to complete the operation within the time available. Also, by means of the time-switch, the plants can be uncovered automatically after dark in summer to allow the temperature and humidity around the plants to drop, thus improving the quality of the crop.

TEMPERATURE

Chrysanthemum plants are profoundly affected by the temperature of their aerial environment. A number of authorities including Cathey in the USA and Butters working at Efford EHS (page 98) have investigated the effect of temperature on a number of varieties. Both found that night temperature affected bud initiation and development in flower crops more than day temperature but Butters' work also emphasized the importance of the latter.

Night Temperature

Night air temperature is one of the main factors controlling stem growth rate. The rate of stem elongation is a sensitive indicator of the effects of different temperatures on the plant, and varies immediately with changes of temperature. Plant growth (elongation) virtually ceases by day, the growth rate slowing down as the light intensity increases, the slowest growth rate each day being around noon. During this day period of slow growth, the plant is assimilating carbon from the air around it, the assimilation rate (photosynthesis) depending primarily on the light intensity and air temperature.

At night, or during periods of low light, the translocation of sugar assimilated by the leaves during the day takes place, and thus the 'balance' of the plant is largely controlled by the night air temperature and its relation to the day conditions. With a comparatively high night temperature, the emphasis is on vegetative growth, so that it is important to avoid heat build-up under the blackout material used to promote flowering in spring and summer.

For many years, because of the varieties available, growers have had to maintain a night temperature of at least 15·6° for rapid and uniform bud formation in cut flower crops during the winter months. Recent work at Efford EHS (page 98) has shown that most varieties require a minimum of 16·7° for optimum response in December and January in southern England. However, there are now more tolerant varieties available for which night temperatures of 13·3° are adequate during the winter.

The effect of temperature on the plants is usually influenced by the amount of light available. In general, if the light is good, then the effect of both low and high temperature is minimized. If the light is poor and the night temperature is controlled at 15·6°, small changes in the amount of light available can markedly change the response of the plants and rosetting may occur in temperatures too high or too low according to variety. In southern England it has been found that night temperatures can be controlled during the winter months to ensure good flowering response with the majority of varieties used (Anon., 1977) (Table 4).

Although emphasis has been laid on the need for minimum night temperatures near 15·6° for

TABLE 4   Night Temperature Control According to Natural Light Received During the Winter Months in Southern England

Month	Temperature	Approximate light levels (MJ/m²/day)
October	13·3°	1·25
November	15·6°	0·92
December	16·7°	0·59
January	16·7°	0·75
February to mid-March	15·6°	1·21
mid-March on	13·3°	1·75

fast and continuous bud development in most varieties, bud development in a few varieties is more adversely affected by high night temperature than by night temperatures below 15·6°.

In the 12- to 15-week groups, although a night temperature of 15·6° is required for rapid bud initiation, delay occurs in many of the thermo-negative varieties (page 175) unless the temperature is lowered to 12·8° after the bud becomes visible. With the 9-, 10- and 11-week response groups, night temperatures above 21° will cause delay with a few varieties.

It is important to realize the effect of conditions of low temperature which may be beyond the control of the grower. If, owing to exceptionally cold weather or the temporary failure of the heating system the temperature falls from 15·6° to 10°, or even a little below for up to three nights, the effect of this on the crop will be slight. Indeed, trials (Anon., 1977) have shown that giving one cold night (4·4°) each week in winter has a negligible effect on the crop and a fuel saving of 10 per cent can be expected. If the low temperature period extends for a week or more, the effect may be serious and plants will be affected in different ways, according to the stage of growth they have reached. When temperatures are controlled at 15·6° for the eight hours before dawn and allowed to fall to 10° earlier in the night, some flowering delay and loss of quality will occur. However, these disadvantages are more than compensated for by the fuel economy achieved and is a more satisfactory way of reducing heating costs than by controlling temperatures continuously at ·13·3°. With plants undergoing longday treatment for vegetative growth, the effect of low night temperature (10°) will be to delay the crop for a few days.

Day Temperature

In view of the importance of night temperature, which was apparent very early in the research work leading to the development of year-round growing of chrysanthemums (page 173), the effect of day temperature had not been investigated to any extent until comparatively recently.

In a series of experiments conducted at Efford EHS (Anon., 1974 to 1977) it has been shown that for cut flower crops low day temperatures (15·6°) with ventilation at 17·8° gave better results than higher day temperatures (17·8° ventilating at 21·1°) at any time of the year. Flowering was not delayed by the lower temperature and vegetative growth and flower bud initiation were more even. Also, flowers were larger, pedicels were shorter and the general habit of the spray was better than with plants grown in higher day temperatures.

Heating

The largest item of expenditure in year-round cropping is the cost of cuttings which accounts for about 27 per cent of direct costs. This is closely followed by labour and fuel, each accounting for about 20 per cent in 1977. As fuel is such a high proportion of the total direct costs, it is essential that any heating system should be correctly designed and efficiently operated. The system should give accurate control and maximum uniformity in space and with time at crop level, and be flexible, responsive and reliable. Provision should be made for adequate heat input, it being essential to maintain a minimum temperature of 14° against the average worst conditions if programmes are to be operated with the required precision. Low temperatures will delay the programme and have repercussions on flower production over the subsequent six months.

In a well-constructed greenhouse, under normal conditions with light winds, the heat input to maintain a given temperature is lost partly by radiation and convection to the outside (80 per cent), partly by air leakage (12 per cent) and partly by conduction through the soil (8 per cent). The rate of heat loss is a function of temperature difference and external windspeed. As windspeed increases the rate of heat loss increases, partly due to an increase in the temperature gradient across the glass by the scouring action of the wind on the outer surface and partly to increased air leakage. For a given outside temperature the heat loss doubles as windspeed increases from calm to 6·7 m/s (15 knots). The maximum rates of heat loss occur

TABLE 5   Estimated Fuel Consumption in litres 35 sec oil for Venlo Square Block 2000 m² area maintained at 15·6° in Britain

	South-west	South Coast	South Wales	Humber-side	West Lanca-shire	West Midlands	Lee Valley	South-east Midlands	Clyde Valley
January	15025	16648	17084	18398	18839	18575	18543	18984	19011
February	14020	15480	15475	16207	15479	16357	16357	17084	16766
March	13875	14457	14457	15334	15770	15393	15334	16207	16298
April	10074	10370	10661	11683	12265	10951	11386	11824	12265
May	5842	5551	5987	7301	7737	7011	6133	6424	8147
June	2187	2191	2337	3069	3650	2859	3214	3214	3941
July	1168	1168	1168	1750	1314	1577	1605	1900	2278
August	1168	1168	1459	1750	2046	1809	1896	1900	2482
September	2046	1750	2773	3360	4382	4000	3505	3941	4614
October	6133	6133	7592	8178	8906	9056	8615	9056	9956
November	11243	12120	12997	14020	14747	14457	14311	14893	14893
December	14020	15916	15770	17525	17671	17671	18107	18107	18107
Total	96801	102952	107760	118575	122806	119717	119008	123534	128758

For other grades of oil
200 sec multiply by 0·9314
950 sec multiply by 0·9209
3000 sec multiply by 0·9183

For other areas
4000 m² multiply by 1·8954
8000 m² multiply by 3·6393
10000 m² multiply by 4·5489

For other types of house
7 m spans multiply by 1·0038
10 m spans multiply by 1·0104
12 to 15 m spans multiply by 1·0116
long widespans multiply by 1·0691

in strong winds and not at the lowest outside temperatures so that it is worthwhile considering the provision of shelter in the form of artificial or natural windbreaks. Air leakage rate can be kept to a minimum by good maintenance and by selecting a house design which has a well-sealed glazing system.

Heat loss is also affected by the design, shape and size of a greenhouse unit. This is mainly due to the increasing height of the ridge and to the increase in windspeed with height. Differences are small on spans up to 12 m, but widespan houses have a 7 per cent greater loss than Venlo units covering the same area. The larger the size of a greenhouse block, the smaller is the heat loss per unit area covered. Comparing 1 ha of greenhouses in a single block with 2 by 0·5 ha units, 4 by 0·25 ha units and 8 by 0·125 ha units, the heat loss is greater by 4, 10 and 18 per cent respectively. The shape of a unit is also important. Heat loss is least in blocks which are near square in plan as this shape has the smallest perimeter in relation to the ground area covered. Where the ratio of length to width is 4 : 1, heat loss is increased by 3 per cent and at 16 : 1 by

14 per cent compared with a square block of the same area. In this respect long single wide-spans are at considerable disadvantage.

On a particular site heat loss and therefore oil consumption is affected by latitude, elevation, exposure and proximity to the coast. Table 5 shows for a number of localities in Britain, the estimated oil consumption required to maintain a constant temperature of 15·6° based on long-term meteorological records.

The heat loss coefficient U is given by the relationships

$$U = 4·04 + 0·65V$$

where $U = W/m^2$ °C and V = windspeed in m/s.

For design purposes, it is normal to use a heat loss coefficient of 8 W/m^2 °C. This value includes a fair wind component and ensures the provision of an adequate heat input. In calculating the maximum heat load, it is common practice to use the median winter minimum temperature as representing the average worst conditions. The median winter minimum for the areas covered in Table 5 are:

South West	$-2\cdot8°$
South Wales	$-3\cdot9°$
South Coast	$-5\cdot0°$
Humberside	$-5\cdot6°$
West Lancashire	$-6\cdot1°$
West Midlands	$-6\cdot7°$
South-east Midlands	$-7\cdot8°$
Lee Valley	$-7\cdot8°$
Clyde Valley	$-7\cdot8°$

As a rough guide, a boiler output of about 2600 kW/ha is required in Britain for year-round chrysanthemum cropping.

Detailed information on greenhouse heating systems and associated equipment is provided in Britain by Ministry of Agriculture Fisheries and Food Publications (Appendix 2). Advice on specific problems of design or operation is available from the Mechanisation Advisers of the MAFF, Agricultural Development and Advisory Service.

The grower has the choice of hot water or steam boilers, but as there is a requirement for steam for sterilizing beds, steam boilers would be the normal choice for year-round chrysanthemum production. For heat dispersal in greenhouses, the choice is between warm air, low-pressure steam, low-pressure hot water and medium-pressure hot water. Warm-air systems only give a satisfactory uniformity of temperature distribution if the air is distributed in perforated film plastic ducting. This seriously restricts the narrow pathways between beds, and though attractive in capital cost, this system is not generally practicable for year-round production. Until the 1973 energy crisis, low-pressure steam heating in high-level pipework was popular with many growers. Such systems give a clear, unobstructed floor area but produce large vertical temperature gradients, resulting in poor fuel economy and which now makes them unacceptable. Currently, the choice is between low- and medium-pressure hot water. The latter has the advantages of smaller diameter pipes and a shorter total length of pipework. Hot water systems generally give more uniform temperature distribution, compared with warm air or steam. The best spatial uniformity is ob-tained when pipework is installed at low level and where the major part of the heat input is in perimeter loops.

At times, and particularly during the nights of summer and autumn, humidity may rise to saturation point. This then leads to disease problems and it has been the practice to lower humidity by applying ventilation and heat. Under present conditions, this is wasteful and expensive in energy and should be kept to a minimum.

Economy can be effected by linking the control of ventilator opening to a humidistat which overrides the normal temperature control. Heat is then only applied when the humidity becomes critical.

THERMAL SCREENS

The daylength control blackout systems provide the year-round grower with the foundations of a ready-made thermal screen, where such blackouts operate over a complete bay or span. With the blackout closed there is a potential saving in heat loss of about 40 per cent, with a saving of about 15 per cent of the total fuel usage. There are some practical problems associated with thermal screens. All the heating pipes must be contained within the screen, humidity can rise to high levels under blackouts and care is needed to avoid thermal shock to plants when the screen is drawn back after a cold night. This method of fuel economy has been described by Winspear (1977).

Ventilation and Cooling

Ventilation is necessary to limit the temperature rise from solar gain, to prevent the depletion of carbon dioxide below ambient level, and to control the rise of humidity. Greenhouses may be ventilated by hinged ventilators mounted on the ridge or by fans. Two references in which the subject is comprehensively discussed are given in Appendix 2. Inadequate ventilation results in excessive day temperatures in summer which in turn give poor flower quality and higher pest and disease incidence.

Ridge ventilators and fans are equally effective if correctly designed and installed, but ridge ventilators give more uniform temperatures and

Fig. 7 Adequate ridge ventilation gives good air movement. Note the poor ventilation of the wooden structure in the foreground.

require little energy (Fig. 7). Fans use considerable quantities of power, are expensive to run and give a marked gradient from inlet to outlet, but under still conditions give positive air movement. Whatever system is used, it should comply with the code of practice laid down in Mechanisation Leaflet No. 5 (Appendix 2) that is ridge ventilators should provide an opening equal to at least 17 per cent of the floor area and fans should provide a ventilation rate of 35 l/s/m² floor area. In some countries, notably the USA, additional evaporative cooling is provided by fan and wet pad ventilating systems. These precool the incoming air by drawing it over wet pads of aspen shavings or cellular plastic. The depression of the dry bulb temperature is not, however, generally large enough to warrant their use in Britain.

Automatic Control of Greenhouse Environment

The greenhouse is a structure of small mass and it is therefore sensitive to changes in outside conditions, such as temperature and solar gain. Good automatic control of temperature can only be achieved if the heating and cooling systems have a rapid response and are controlled by a sensitive detector linked to a suitable control system.

The control action initiated by an automatic controller may be continuous or discontinuous. The latter is more commonly found in simple systems such as 'on/off' thermostatic controls. In continuous control action the regulator position varies with the signal from the controller and the output of the system is closely matched to demand. Control systems may be electric, electronic or pneumatic.

Most of the modern systems used in Britain are electronic but in some countries, notably the USA, pneumatic controllers are widely used. There are four basic types of control system and these are described below.

'ON/OFF' CONTROL

In 'on/off' control systems there are only two positions of the regulator and normally it is fully closed or fully open. The value of the controlled condition oscillates above and below the desired value depending on the switching differential and the response time of the system. 'On/off' control is found in some of the older hot water heating systems, but in current practice it is only used on low-pressure steam heating systems and on ventilating fans.

FLOATING CONTROL

In floating action, the regulating unit changes its position at a predetermined rate when the detector signals a change exceeding a threshold value in either direction. If the level of the controlled condition is within the dead zone, no action occurs and the regulator stays in its previous position. This form of control is used in the simple PFC ventilation controllers. Here the thermostat has a centre 'off' position and the rate of change of position is controlled by an adjustable pulse emitter. To give good stability and avoid hunting the pulse rate should be short. However, sudden changes cannot be corrected rapidly.

PROPORTIONAL CONTROL

In proportional action, the regulator position is varied directly with the deviation from the desired value. There is always a difference between the desired level and the actual level known as the offset. This is inherent in all proportional or modulating systems. Proportional control is widely used for the control of heating systems through modulating valves on the steam supply to heat exchangers, on mixing valves controlling hot water flow, and for automatic ventilator control. Controllers normally have an adjustable proportional band, that is the range over which the regulator moves from fully closed to fully open. A large change in temperature causes a correspondingly large movement of the regulating unit, in contrast to the floating controller which can only move step-wise.

INTEGRAL CONTROL

With integral control the regulator position is changed at a rate directly related to the deviation from the desired value. Thus, the larger the deviation the quicker the regulator responds. Corrective action continues until the desired value is achieved. Only when there is a deviation in the opposite direction is the corrective action removed. There is no offset as in the proportional controller but large oscillations can occur about the desired value which die out only slowly.

Integral controllers are rarely used on their own but combined with proportional action. This gives improved quality of control but results in more complicated and expensive equipment.

Over the last few years, multistage controllers have been developed which enable heating and ventilating to be controlled from a single detector at one desired level of temperature or with an adjustable dead band between heating and ventilating. Controllers have also been offered in which day temperature is modulated against incoming solar radiation, temperature being increased with increasing radiation. Most controllers are fitted with the facility to operate different day and night temperatures, the change being effected by a time clock. It is also possible to fit an overriding humidity sensor which will reduce humidity by the application of ventilation and heat. This gives control of some fungal diseases but at the expense of energy use.

More recently, computers have been applied to optimize and control environmental conditions in glasshouses in the Netherlands. The ability to control environmental conditions in greenhouses is, however, not yet matched by biological data to programme such sophisticated control systems. The grower is now faced with a range of controllers ranging from simple 'on/off' types to sophisticated multistage computer types. Before installing any control system he should clearly decide what factors he wishes to control and with what accuracy, and in selecting a system seek advice from the ADAS Mechanisation Advisers. From cost, reliability and ease of maintenance he is well advised to install a system no more complex than is necessary to achieve his objective.

DETECTORS

Accuracy of temperature control is influenced by the sensor as well as the controller. Accuracy of control can only be achieved with sensitive low mass detectors correctly screened from radiation and aspirated. Detectors can produce errors up to 7° during the day from absorbing solar radiation and smaller errors at night by radiant loss. Screening alone will reduce the error to about 2° during the day but the errors can be completely eliminated by screening and aspiration. In addition, aspiration reduces the response time of the detector. All detectors should be mounted in an aspirated screen of the type and to the standard developed by the NIAE. Controllers and sensors do not indefinitely maintain their calibration. Though reliable, they are not infallible and their stability and calibration need to be regularly checked and monitored. Small errors maintained over a long period have large effects on crop performance and timing and on fuel consumption. A thermograph placed in the aspirated screen will give a rapid visual check but thermographs themselves need regular calibration against a certificated whirling thermometer or an Assman psychrometer.

AIR COMPOSITION

The composition of the earth's atmosphere comprises nitrogen (78·03 per cent), oxygen (20·99 per cent), argon (0·94 per cent) and carbon dioxide (0·03 per cent). Of these gases, oxygen and carbon dioxide are the most important constituents of the air in a greenhouse in view of their major role in respiration and photosynthesis respectively.

Oxygen

Respiration, the process by which the plant uses oxygen in combination with the sugars formed in photosynthesis to produce energy for growth, occurs throughout the 24-hour cycle provided that temperature is adequate.

During the day, when oxygen is a by-product of photosynthesis, routine ventilation to reduce heat will normally ensure an adequate supply of oxygen for respiration. It is at night, particularly during periods of natural high temperatures, that oxygen may become limiting and special care will need to be taken by ventilating to avoid oxygen deficiency.

Carbon Dioxide

About 95 per cent of the dry weight of any crop is made up of carbon taken mainly from the carbon dioxide in the air during the photosynthetic process. Because carbon dioxide forms such a small percentage of natural air (0·03 per cent) extremely efficient ventilation must be provided by the grower at all times to try to prevent a lack of carbon dioxide becoming limiting to growth.

Carbon dioxide is produced in the soil by respiration of the plant roots and by organic matter, and so, in a well-aerated fertile soil, an important contribution to the plant's supply of carbon dioxide in the air can be made from this source. There is some evidence that a small amount of the plant's carbon may also be taken up by the roots from the carbon dioxide in the soil air. This is generally found to be at its lowest in winter, rising to a maximum in spring or early summer when biological activity reaches its peak.

The breaking down of organic matter in fertile, well-aerated soils thus produces a ready supply of carbon dioxide for the growing plant, and is no doubt an important factor with well-manured soils. This carbon dioxide, as carbonic acid, also acts upon the soil minerals to bring them into solution.

However, during the winter months carbon dioxide is almost certain to become the limiting factor to plant growth in view of the need to keep the ventilators closed for long periods during the day to prevent temperatures falling below 15·6°.

ADVANTAGES OF CARBON DIOXIDE ENRICHMENT

By artificially supplementing the carbon dioxide content of the greenhouse atmosphere during bright days in the winter months, some beneficial effects on plant growth and ultimately on the flower quality can be achieved. In addition, the rate of plant development is increased, so that in some cases the cropping time can be reduced.

The main benefit from additional carbon dioxide is, therefore, gained by year-round growers who have young plants growing during the winter months, and who have the opportunity to supplement the carbon dioxide content of the greenhouse atmosphere through most of the life of the crop.

A number of experiments have been carried out at Efford EHS to assess the value of carbon dioxide enrichment relative to various day and night temperature regimes, mainly in winter conditions. Extra carbon dioxide cannot compensate for low (13·3°) compared with medium (15·6°) or high (16·7°) night temperatures either for flowering response or quality of flowering stem, although plants flowered slightly earlier and slightly better in comparison with the control. However, day temperatures higher than 17·8°, which depress quality, do not do so in the presence of extra carbon dioxide. Also, when night temperatures are adequate for the variety and the time of year, carbon dioxide enrichment from January to March has given increases in yield of up to 13·6 per cent (boxes per 1000 plants planted) (Anon., 1975).

It is recommended that carbon dioxide enrichment should be given daily from November to March. Day temperatures should be controlled at 15·6°, ventilating at 21·1° (Anon., 1977). The number of boxes marketed per 1000 plants planted increased by 17 per cent over the December to April flowering period due to carbon dioxide enrichment. A maximum improvement in production of 23 per cent was obtained for March flowering.

METHODS OF CARBON DIOXIDE ENRICHMENT

Enrichment of carbon dioxide in the atmosphere cannot be regarded as a substitute for light, temperature or any of the other basic cultural requirements for plant growth. The treatment will, moreover, have a beneficial effect only if these other factors are in balance and it must be remembered that additional fertilizer, particularly nitrogen, may be needed.

Average intensity of daylight in Britain during the winter months is poor but also variable from day to day, and so the grower must be ready to take advantage of any conditions favourable for carbon dioxide application. Light-sensitive cells have been used for controlling this application, but they have their limitations from a practical point of view. Although the cell may be set to turn on the equipment when the daylight reaches a suitable intensity, there is a long delay before the carbon dioxide builds up in the greenhouse to the required concentration of approximately three times the natural level.

One of the most effective practical methods is to ensure that the equipment is turned on early each morning. The level is then allowed to build up, and should the light intensity be adequate later on in the morning, the carbon dioxide is ready to be used, and the equipment can be left on for as long as the good conditions prevail. If, on the other hand, light is poor the equipment may be switched off to avoid wastage.

The relationship between day temperature, ventilation and the carbon dioxide level is important. If under bright conditions when additional carbon dioxide is being added, the temperature should rise above 21°, ventilation will be needed. As soon as adequate ventilation can be given, the plants obtain all the carbon dioxide they need, and artificial enrichment becomes unnecessary.

Gardner (1966) states that the aim is to enrich the atmosphere from the natural value of 300 volumes per million to approximately 1000 volumes per million (0·1 per cent). This is usually done by adding carbon dioxide at a constant rate of 56 kg/ha/h, in temperatures of not less than 15·6°.

Carbon dioxide can be applied in the plant rows, either by the evaporation of dry ice or piped from a distant source and distributed through plastic tubes or low-level irrigation lines. Carbon dioxide produced by burning propane outside the house can also be distributed in this way.

A cheaper method of applying additional carbon dioxide directly in the house is by burning propane, piped from storage tanks or cylinders, in burners suspended over the crop (Fig. 8). The disadvantage of this method is that the heat given out by the burners is uneven and may be unwanted, and the carbon dioxide concentration

Fig. 8   A propane burner for carbon dioxide enrichment.

is heaviest above the crop and not among the plants where it is needed. Also, propane contains up to 35 per cent propylene and if this escapes into the house prior to burning, from leaking pipes or malfunctioning burners, considerable crop damage will result (Hand *et al.*, 1977). Kerosene (paraffin), which is cheaper still, is also used in this way in some countries, but paraffin in Britain is unsuitable for this purpose owing to its sulphur content.

The larger the greenhouse, the larger will be the reserve of carbon dioxide within it, and under still conditions the use of heating pipes, by promoting air circulation, will enable the plants to make some use of this reserve.

Experience gained during winter cropping suggests that where light conditions are relatively poor for growth (in the range 4000 to 8000 lx) there is no advantage to be gained by raising the carbon dioxide concentration above 600 ppm. Under better light conditions concentrations of up to 1500 ppm have given good results.

HUMIDITY

Relative humidity refers to the degree of saturation of air with water vapour and is extremely important to plant growth within a confined space.

Although chrysanthemums grow well within fairly broad limits of relative humidity (from approximatley 70 to 90 per cent), extremes of humidity within the greenhouse should be avoided. Low humidities put a strain on the transpiration and respiration processes occurring in the plants, leading to hard dark growth particularly in high light conditions. Relative humidities in excess of 90 per cent result in soft growth vulnerable to attack by fungal diseases, which are especially virulent in very humid air.

Continuous measurements of humidity in

greenhouses have shown that relative humidity is lower, that is, the air is drier, at the end of the house upon which the wind is blowing. This is very marked under conditions of low humidity of the outside air.

In bright sunshine, the relative humidity at the south end of a house is invariably lower than at the north end, owing to the higher air temperature at the south end. With blocks of houses, the inside houses normally have higher relative humidity values than the outside houses.

Temporary raising of the humidity in the greenhouse is normally achieved by spraying water from mist spray lines or hoses over the plants and ground. The raising of the relative humidity in the house usually presents less difficulty than its lowering.

The lowering of the humidity of the air, especially at night, is often of great importance for the control of fungal diseases, and in the heated houses is achieved by the use of the heating system, or by heat and ventilation together. Heat must often be used, particularly in the autumn in Britain, to maintain the air temperature above the dew point, and thus prevent condensation on the flowers and foliage even though the outside air temperature may be adequate for plant growth and development.

Compared with the hose or spray line method of watering, the drip systems of irrigation generally lead to lower humidities, and this fact can be of importance in cold houses during dull, humid weather, especially during the autumn.

Direct measurements of relative humidity are made by hair and whirling hygrometers, or, where a continuous record is required, by hygrographs. The use of unventilated wet and dry bulb hygrometers, which are unreliable in still air, cannot be recommended under greenhouse conditions. The violent fluctuations in the relative humidity of the macroclimate of the greenhouse present a difficult measuring problem, but reasonable accuracy with hair instruments is possible if the hygrometers are standardized frequently. A particularly useful instrument in this connection is the thermo-hygrograph which, by combining a continuous record of both temperature and relative humidity, enables the water vapour pressure to be read from simple tables.

PART TWO

Raising The Plants

3 Breeding and Selection

A modern developing flower industry is to a large extent dependent for its progress on the quality and quantity of its raw material, the range of varieties available.

Year-round chrysanthemum production is progressing rapidly and techniques such as carbon dioxide enrichment and growth control by chemicals constantly expose the need for varieties suited to these new developments. Inevitably, breeding must lag behind to some extent, because, although a breeder may make his crosses with a particular objective in mind, it is at least five years before the results of this work can be used on a commercial scale, and several years more before the new variety will have been evaluated over a wide range of environmental conditions.

However, new developments in chrysanthemum growing continue to be introduced and there is a demand more than ever before for new plant material.

History

There is no lack of raw material from which to produce modern chrysanthemum varieties. Chrysanthemums were first cultivated more than 3000 years ago in China, but it was not until the seventeenth century that they reached Britain and a further 150 years before they were introduced to North America.

Although the modern florists' chrysanthemum is classified as *Chrysanthemum morifolium* Ramat., there has been much intercrossing between species during the long history of the plant, some during the last 10 years. *C. sinense*, *C. indicum* and *C. ornatum* are all represented in the range of varieties now grown.

The development of the chrysanthemum has followed different lines in the various countries into which the plants have been introduced. At the turn of the century the main type of chrysanthemum bred in Britain was the 'Japanese', or Large Exhibition type to use its modern name. It was not until 1920 that incurve and decorative varieties started to emerge to form the basis from which most of the present market standards have been derived.

In North America, more emphasis was placed on the spray type of chrysanthemum representing a wide range of form, such as pompon, spider, decorative and anemone. They have been steadily developed since the late nineteenth century into the varieties used in year-round programmes and are now extremely popular in Europe.

Objectives

It is interesting to consider the objectives of several international breeders. Although all his breeding and selection work was done in Australia, the late T. W. Pockett bred many famous varieties for use in Britain and North America. H. Shoesmith during his 45 active years as a breeder produced many outstanding varieties. Both those men were influenced to a large extent by the demand of amateurs for exhibition varieties.

The dominant requirement, therefore, was that the flower should surpass, either in form, size or colour, similar varieties which had been produced earlier. Even small differences, perhaps unnoticeable to the layman, would be sufficient for the keen amateurs. This is one of the main reasons why so many excellent standard varieties, many of which are almost identical, have been produced in and for Britain. The British National Register of Chrysanthemums issued by the National Chrysanthemum Society lists over 6000 varieties which have been introduced and cultivated since 1935.

It did not matter that with many of these varieties, cuttings production, propagation and other aspects of cultivation left much to be desired. Keen amateurs are skilled growers and provided that the qualities of the flower were adequate, the end usually justified the means. New commercial varieties were developed either from successful show varieties which had the added qualities of durability of flower and the ability to produce large numbers of flowers per plant, or they were bought outright as promising seedlings on the breeder's nursery by leading growers. Development of new varieties was, therefore, the responsibility of the flower grower and the success of a variety depended on its performance on one nursery in one type of environment and the degree of skill of the grower in being able to select an outstanding variety at sight. Inevitably many varieties were short-lived, but nevertheless many very successful commercial standard varieties for the traditional methods of long-season production emerged in this way. The Balcombe family, the Shoesmith Salmons and the Mayford Perfections are cases in point.

It is not surprising that very few varieties of this type are suitable for the most modern year-round programmes. One exception is Fred Shoesmith which is accepted mainly for its fine flower characteristics, without which it would have been discarded long ago because of its susceptibility to disease and blind growth.

The demands on chrysanthemum breeders in North America have been somewhat different from those outlined above and their varieties have consequently developed along different lines. Although there are active amateur societies, there has never been the same emphasis on exhibiting as in Britain. Chrysanthemum growing became commercialized more rapidly and, due possibly to a more cosmopolitan population, there has always been more interest in wider variations of type and form than in Britain, with slightly less emphasis placed on colour and size of flower. Apart from a few successful individual breeders, the influence of commercial chrysanthemum growers, such as Yoder Bros Inc., and of other bodies such as the University of Illinois, has been substantial.

Spray varieties have been introduced by the University of Illinois since 1908, when first the accent was on anemone and small button pompon types; but, since 1948, J. R. Culbert has been responsible for the introduction of a wider range of spray varieties covering all types and forms.

As Culbert (1957) has stated, the plant breeder should be conscious of the demand and interest expressed by the commercial grower, retailer and ultimate consumer as well as by the home gardener. This should not be the whole concept of breeding, however, and the chrysanthemum breeder should be constantly interested in creating new colours and forms that will in turn create new demands and increase the overall use of chrysanthemums. Culbert gave as an example of this, the introduction of Illini Snowdift (a spider form), which re-awakened interest in the use of chyrsanthemums in corsages and wedding bouquets.

Since the mid-1940s, when year-round growing became established, there has been an urgent need for varieties with the characteristics necessary for this completely new method of production. Many of the varieties in use today have been bred and developed by W. E. Duffet and his staff at Yoder Bros Inc. in Barberton, Ohio. The need for varieties for use over longer periods than their own natural season, and the importance of good cuttings production, ease of propagation and uniformity of bud formation, quickly became apparent.

The florists' chrysanthemum is an international crop, yet, because of widely different climates found in chrysanthemum growing areas, it is unusual, although there are some notable exceptions, for any one variety to be popular in several countries. For this reason the breeding of year-round varieties for production in Britain and the rest of Europe was started by B. J. Machin at Framptons Nurseries Ltd in Sussex in 1964. The success of this policy of breeding and selection with the particular growing areas and markets in mind can be judged from the fact that over 75 million plants derived from this breeding programme were grown in Europe in 1976.

New varieties should not be released simply because they are new or have a novelty value for one section of the chrysanthemum world, but because they meet an urgent requirement or improve an existing variety. They must be acceptable to all sections of the industry, the propagator, the flower grower, the wholesaler and retailer, and not least of course, the consumer. A seedling which is known to have a defect affecting any one of these sections should not be released. Strict application by a breeder to these principles will naturally reduce his output, but it also follows that new varieties produced from a modern breeding programme can be used with confidence during the first years after introduction.

IDEOTYPE

Langton and Cockshull (1976) have, following trials using a wide range of varieties, developed an ideotype, a model of a plant expected to react in a predictable manner in a defined environment (Donald, 1968), for summer flowering in year-round programmes. They considered that breeding material should be as close to the following ideotype as possible:

1 Strong apical dominance during vegetative growth;
2 Immediate and rapid flower bud initiation in short days in both apical and axillary meristems;
3 A very high maximum leaf number giving marked delay of bud initiation in long days (this helps to prevent budding on stock plants);
4 A very high leaf initiation rate in long days;
5 Long internodes and rapid internode extension in short days;
6 Extremely rapid flower development in short days;
7 Moderate peduncle extension in short days;
8 A 'thermozero' temperature response showing little or no delay in flowering at temperatures above and below $15 \cdot 6°$;
9 Easily rooted cuttings which can withstand at least 10 day's cold storage;
10 Strong peduncles and stems which take up water adequately.
11 Large, horizontally displayed leaves;
12 Pink flowers (which can give rise to all other colours by mutation);
13 Low competitive ability in the flowering area.

A winter flowering ideotype would have similar characteristics except that it should form buds uniformly and rapidly in night temperatures between $10°$ and $13°$ and that leaves should be small to medium-sized to induce a low competitive ability.

To the ideotype must be added the flower characteristics of colour, form and size required by the consumer.

Hybridization

The cultivated chrysanthemum basically belongs to the species known as *morifolium* but so many species have been hybridized into it that our modern varieties have very complex origins.

Hybridization describes sexual reproduction, in which process genes are derived from both parents giving rise to new genotypes. These new genotypes will sometimes have characters which have been 'hidden' for some time due to their recessive nature and can only be recovered by making crosses of widely different varieties.

For instance, in 1965 A. A. Jackson at Wye College, of London University, crossed a primitive Chinese seedling with the American spray variety Long Island Beauty, with the object of combining the desirable much-branching habit and delicate flower of the former with a modern year-round variety. The progress of this programme, which revealed some hidden forms of flower, and has been described by Jackson (1971), culminated in the introduction of five Wye chrysanthemums to commerce (Plate 9). Since then Machin has used these varieties to improve pot plant habit while improving flower size and colour and winter response with genetic material from other sources (Plates 7, 10, 11 and 12).

During hybridization, the nuclei of the sex cells (gametes) of the two parents, which contain only half the number of chromosomes of the nuclei of normal cells, combine to form a new individual in which the cells contain the full chromosome complement.

Many varieties have a chromosome number of approximately 54, but the number varies widely with variety from less than 45 to more than 100. The basic number of chromosomes for the genus is 9, but if the chrysanthemum were a diploid, the figure would be 18. The simple Mendelian ratios for inheritance apply only to diploids, so that it is not surprising to find there is no simple scientific formula for character inheritance in chrysanthemums.

There are probably several duplicate genes controlling each of the main characters, so that the appearance of the seedlings cannot be predicted accurately. For example, pink crossed with pink, although producing a majority of pink seedlings, also gives rise to white, yellow, bronze and red types. Two 10-week response group (page 94) parents will give rise to seedlings of all response groups although the average response will be near to 10 weeks.

However, recent advances in knowledge have helped the breeder to some extent. Since the sex cells are formed from the cortex (L2 layer) of the parent plant (page 35 and Fig. 9) a know-

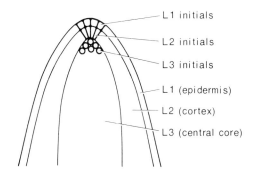

Fig. 9   Diagrammatic illustration of the chimerical layers at the tip of a chrysanthemum stem.

ledge of any chimerical character of the parent is essential if certain breeding objectives are to be fulfilled. For example, it has now been established that Yellow Snowdon (a mutation from the white Snowdon) is a periclinal chimera (page 35) with a yellow L1 (epidermal) layer and a white L2 layer. The breeder will therefore use Yellow Snowdon as a 'white' parent.

Success in chrysanthemum breeding demands a systematic approach, close attention to detail and adequate resources to house the great

quantity of seedlings produced. It involves at least five years of testing the seedlings for new varieties. The breeder must be aware of the trends of fashions and the changing production techniques in the crop. He must look ahead to requirements five to ten years hence. Somewhere in his parent lines he will require all the characters necessary to produce chrysanthemums which will be good enough to meet the future demands of growers and consumers. At the same time he must discard as parents those varieties which have characters which cannot be tolerated in modern varieties, such as lack of vigour, unreliable response to controlled environments and susceptibility to pests and diseases.

There are many incompatibilities in chrysanthemum breeding due to the plant's very complex nature and the wide variations between chromosome numbers and other important factors. After many years of trial and error, breeding lines are established which can be relied upon to give large numbers of seedlings and a fair number of new varieties.

Many hundreds of crosses have to be made and many thousands of seedlings tested before it is possible to introduce a variety good enough to improve on existing varieties.

EVALUATING THE SEEDLINGS

Seedlings can be flowered round the year with control of daylength so there is a minimum of delay between sowing seed and the first trial. If the objective had been to produce summer flowering varieties, then a January sowing resulting in young plants in March for June or July flowering will be the best programme. If the cross has been made to produce winter varieties or to improve production in poor light conditions, then the sowing date will be delayed to provide young plants for September.

Flowering the seedlings on single stems at a spacing of 15 by 15 cm will allow plants of different vigour to develop alongside each other reasonably well.

The first trial is extremely important in that all but the most promising material must be discarded ruthlessly to avoid subsequent waste of time and money. A wrong judgement at this stage will mean the loss of the seedling for good. It is usual to flower a few established varieties alongside the seedlings for comparison. There is frequently an excessive amount of hybrid vigour in new seedlings which is lost in subsequent years, and this, together with the wider than normal commercial spacing, must be taken into account when saving seedlings for further trials.

Normally about 5 per cent of the seedlings are retained for second year trials. The stools are lifted and a small number of vegetative stock plants built up. During the second year, flower trials are conducted on a regular basis and a complete analysis of the response and characteristics of the flowers, stems and foliage is made. After this a decision must be made regarding the future of each seedling. A few, perhaps one in every thousand of the original number, may be considered worthy of introduction pending the result of the more extensive third year trials which include marketing. To save time later, cuttings from a selected flowering plant are subjected to rigorous testing for fungal and virus diseases. If these cuttings prove to be free from disease, the initial stock can be multiplied to production proportions for release. This takes two years from the single stool selection stage, that is up to four years from the date of the original cross.

From the time of planning the cross, a period of at least five years will elapse before the results can influence the chrysanthemum industry. It is not surprising, therefore, to find that modern breeding programmes are no longer small family affairs but require the resources of specialized departments of leading firms in the chrysanthemum industry.

Mutation Breeding

The basic characters of any variety are determined by the genetic blueprint laid down during sexual reproduction. This genetic blueprint of a variety is called its genotype.

The genotype, although identical in all plants in a single clone, can give different results according to the environment in which the plants are grown. Bluechip flowered in January, for example, will have poor colour, thin open-centred flowers, weak stems and small pale leaves. The same genotype flowered in May will have large full flowers of good colour borne on strong stems with luxuriant foliage. These are two phenotypes of the same genotype.

While new genotypes are produced by sexual reproduction, mutation resulting in a different genotype can occur either naturally or by induction. These 'sports', as they are called, are perpetuated by vegetative reproduction provided that the change has taken place in a position on the plant from which vegetative shoots can be derived.

It has been demonstrated that the rate of mutation can be substantially increased by subjecting chrysanthemum plant material to gamma-rays or X-rays. Jank (1957) found that X-rays induced more mutations in pink varieties than in other colours. Sheehan and Sagawa (1955) reported that 7500 rad (r) of gamma radiation were lethal to Bluechip, but that mutations in flower colour occurred after exposure to between 2040 and 3996 r. Bowen, Cawse and Dick (1962) showed that the most effective treatment for chrysanthemums lay in the range 3000 to 4300 r. About 40 per cent of their irradiated plants were colour mutations and the frequency varied markedly with variety.

Chan (1966) induced mutation by X-rays in a number of popular commercial varieties with single doses of 1200 to 4000 r. After treatment the plants were pinched and the tips rooted and grown on alongside the parent plants. After treatment with 1500 r, 28 per cent of the shoots of Delmar produced mutations. Fred Shoesmith had 16 per cent of its shoots showing mutations but Shane and Icecap only 3 per cent. More than 90 per cent of the total mutations were obtained from the lateral shoots of the treated parent plants. Again pink varieties were found to be more prone to mutation than white or yellow varieties.

It has been found in research work (Broertjes, 1966) and in practice that mutations for colour follow a distinct pattern (Fig. 10). Pink varieties can be made to produce bronze, yellow or white

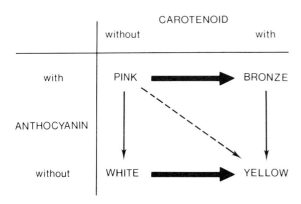

Fig. 10   The directions and relative frequency of flower colour mutations.

mutations, but neither bronze, yellow nor white varieties will mutate in the reverse direction to pink. Bronze varieties will produce red and yellow sports while white varieties generally yield a yellow mutation quite easily. Since this directional pattern of mutations seems to be based on either the loss of a whole chromosome, part of a chromosome or a single gene (Dowrick and El-Bayoumi, 1966), it is wise for a chrysanthemum breeder to make the initial cross with the intention of producing pink seedlings (Plate 25) from which all other colours are possible either by natural or induced mutations.

Apart from colour changes, other important characters of the plant can be improved by selection after gamma or X-ray radiation. Vigour and quality of growth, flowering time in short days and uniformity of production are three of the factors affected and generally result from changes in the vegetative characteristics of the plant. These changes can, therefore, be extremely difficult to detect at first and a great deal of skill is required in the assessment of the results of radiation on vegetative growth.

CHIMERAS

A thorough knowledge of the chimerical structures in chrysanthemums is necessary to understand the complexities of colour and other mutations occurring naturally or by induction.

It has been shown by Bowen, Cawse and Dick (1962) that the mutations which occur following radiation result in sectoral or peri-

clinal chimeras. Sectoral chimeras involve changes in all tissues in one section of a plant, and are uncommon but easily fixed. Periclinal chimeras, however, where one of several layers of tissue are changed, are more common and have given rise to some valuable sports following radiation.

Fig. 9 illustrates the chimerical nature of the meristem tip of a chrysanthemum stem and how the different layers, L_1, L_2 and L_3, are formed in a periclinal chimera.

Analyses of mutations in the Indianapolis family have led to a greater understanding of directional mutations and of the exact nature, layer by layer, of periclinal chimeras within a family developed from an original seedling (Stewart and Dermen, 1970). Pigmentation of the flowers in the Indianapolis family consists of a pink anthocyanin in the vacuole of cells and yellow chromoplasts (containing carotenoid pigment) in the cytoplasm lining the cell walls.

Pink flowers (Indianapolis Pink) have anthocyanin in the upper epidermis only and no carotenoid, while white flowers (Indianapolis White) have neither anthocyanin nor carotenoid in the mature petals.

Fig. 10 shows how, by gene mutation, pink flowers will occasionally sport to white. By the loss of a chromosome, which contains genes which inhibit the formation of yellow chromoplasts, pink flowers frequently sport to bronze while white flowers have a similar tendency to sport to yellow (Plate 2). The sporting of pink chrysanthemums directly to yellow is extremely rare naturally because it involves two simultaneous mutations, but is more frequent following radiation techniques.

Petals contain only the L_1 and L_2 layers but the situation is confused in that in those chrysanthemums which are genetically pink in the L_2 layer, and will therefore breed as pink parents, no anthocyanin is produced in the L_2 layer in the petals. Thus a variety which is white in L_1 and pink in L_2 will have a white flower but will breed as a pink. A variety which is pink in L_1 and white in L_2 will have a pink flower yet breed as a white. Pale yellow varieties are yellow in L_1 and white in L_2 (Lemon

Polaris) (Plate 3) so will produce yellow flowers yet breed as a white. Deeper yellows (Yellow Polaris) (Plate 4) have a white L1 and yellow L2, thus breeding as yellow, while golden types (Golden Polaris) (Plate 18) will have yellow chromoplasts in both L1 and L2 layers.

Since pink anthocyanin is produced in the upper epidermis only, the lower surface of the petals of pink varieties appear very pale by comparison with the upper or inner surface. Bronze varieties also contain anthocyanin in the upper epidermis only and vary to golden bronze according to the amount of yellow pigment present in each layer.

Sports may occur, not only from a genetic change in a layer but also from chimerical instability. In the latter, abnormal cell division may have the effect of either replacing one layer by another so that a solid mutant, consisting of cells from either the L1 or the L2 layer, is formed. These and other aspects of mutation in chrysanthemums have been discussed in more detail by Langton (1976).

In vitro MULTIPLICATION TECHNIQUES

For a number of years, *Chrysanthemum morifolium* has been multiplied *in vitro* for plant health and other purposes from various parts of the parent plant (Ben-Jaacov and Langhans, 1972; Earle and Langhans, 1974a, 1974b). Rapid multiplication of chrysanthemums which are periclinal chimeras can lead to some variability of plant material. For instance in a system in which it was possible to produce 100,000 new shoots from a single 'meristem-tip' within six months, Ben-Jaacov and Langhans found that in one batch 28 per cent of the plants had sported from white to yellow. However, except for a few isolated plants, the rapid multiplication technique of Earle and Langhans did result in progeny uniform for colour in the variety Indianapolis White. This is important because if the desirable variety happens to be a periclinal chimera (as in this case), the object of multiplication is to preserve the chimerical state in the progeny.

Investigations into the problems involved when radiation results in the production of sectoral and periclinal chimeras has been a major part of the work of Broertjes and his colleagues at the Association Euratom-Ital, Wageningen, Netherlands for many years. Recently they have been attempting to reproduce chrysanthemums from single cells so that solid mutants, rather than chimeras, may be saved after radiation. They have found that plantlets can be raised *in vitro* extremely

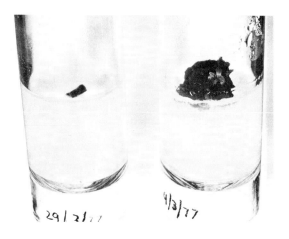

Fig. 11   Plantlets raised *in vitro* from section of pedicel.

rapidly from sections of pedicel and other parts of the flower head (Roest and Bokelmann, 1975) (Figs 11 and 12). Because these plantlets arise from single cells in the epidermis, solid mutants, from which genetically stable stock may be built up, are produced if the multiplication technique follows X-ray radiation. One or two important aspects arise from this work. As they point out (Broertjes, Roest and Bokelmann, 1976), although it is now easy to produce solid mutants following radiation procedures, these mutants may not be the most desirable commercially. Mutations in the L1 layer, from which these solid mutants are derived, are those which mainly concern colour. Mutations for plant height, vigour and flower size are generally located in the L2 layer and these would be lost following the Dutch technique. However, if solid mutants derived from periclinal chimeras are commercially acceptable

Fig. 12   Plantlets raised *in vitro* from section of pedicel.

then there is the important advantage of more uniform plant material for both propagators and growers.

Maintenance of Good Clones

Compared with hybridization and radiation techniques, this third aspect of breeding and selection is, although less spectacular in its results, no less important. Many new varieties are short-lived because they fail to maintain their early promise and 'degenerate' rapidly. Sometimes this is simply due to disease, particularly where unhygienic propagation methods are used. Often an undesirable genetic mutation will occur, which, if undetected, can be multiplied and spread very quickly. Single plant selections of good or improved genotypes will help to counteract this. The deterioration of varieties by these two factors, which is often referred to loosely as 'over-propagation', can only be prevented by the careful selection and handling of plants for stock production.

SELECTION

The random selection of plants from the flowering houses for stock purposes, their subsequent culture in unsuitable surroundings and the age of many of the varieties were probably the main reasons for the prevalence of disease in many British chrysanthemum stocks in the past. In many varieties fungal organisms were present, but more serious than this, viruses, either individually or in combination, were found in almost all varieties. Although, in many cases, the symptoms are slight or even absent, the disease has a weakening effect on growth and is an ever-present threat to other varieties.

The aim of the grower should be to secure clean stocks of the best varieties and at the same time to adopt methods which will keep these stocks free from disease. The concept of disease-free stocks of all the important commercial varieties has been realized through the work of the specialist propagators, and by the establishment of such organizations as the Nuclear Stock Association in Britain.

Stock selection may be divided into two main operations: first, the visual selection of apparently healthy stocks, which is almost always carried out by the grower rather than the scientist, and second, the culturing and indexing of stocks for diseases in their various forms (pages 40 and 45), which is almost exclusively carried out by plant pathologists and specialist propagators. This work is often lengthy and difficult, involving scientific knowledge and processes not normally available to the average chrysanthemum grower.

The visual selection of the best stocks should always be made at flowering, because chrysanthemums are grown for their flowers. There are several considerations involved. The plant must be true to type and must retain all the best characteristics of the variety. The colour, shape and size of the flowers should be as uniform as possible.

Plants in the centre of the bed producing high-quality flowers are to be preferred to plants carrying flowers of similar quality near the side or ends of a bed where light conditions are normally better. Selection is best carried out immediately before the first flowers are cut. If the flowers are then cut and the selected plants removed, the risk of possible spread of disease from unselected material on the cutting knife is minimized. Alternatively, the whole plant may be pulled up, and the flower removed in the laboratory.

The most important aspect of selection is the avoidance of diseased material. Unfortunately, several diseases, including some viruses, cannot be detected by eye. Others are difficult to detect, because the symptoms are not markedly noticeable, especially with those diseases which principally affect the foliage. Some

varieties which do not themselves show the disease may be disease carriers, and they were often selected as clean but could transmit the disease to susceptible varieties the following season.

Although plants completely free from disease can be produced only by culturing and indexing techniques, much can be achieved by visual selection. Several fungal diseases, such as Verticillium and Fusarium wilt, produce the obvious symtoms of wilting and necrosis of tissues and are easily recognizable. Especially important are the viruses which affect the flower and result in colour break and twisting of petals. In more than one instance, virus-infected material has been selected for stock as a colour variation of the parent type, a case where selection has completely defeated its own purpose.

Rigorous selection must be carried out every year, because not only are clean stocks liable to reinfection, but in some diseases symptoms become apparent only in the second year after infection. The aphid-transmitted Aspermy virus (causing flower colour break) may not be apparent the first year if infection occurs late in the season, but the severity of symptoms increases in the following season.

The policy of stock selection must therefore be to choose only the best and not merely to discard the worst. Indeed, it has been the practice of some propagators to make single plant selections from large plant populations and multiply rapidly from these 'superior' specimens.

CLONAL DIFFERENCES

Investigations reported by Machin (1973) have shown that there are less obvious reasons for deterioration of stocks than those of disease and undesirable mutation. Special procedures of selection and propagation are necessary to prevent this deterioration.

Machin had noted that, after some years of experience with single plant selections, in many cases the mean characteristics of the populations of plants derived from the selected plant did not closely resemble the parent and that the plants within each population varied more than variations which could be expected from differences in microclimate within the greenhouse.

In order to study this apparent clonal instability more closely, clones of two varieties, Heyday and Polaris, were built up as quickly as possible. The clones were derived from meristem-tips dissected from axillary buds on a single shoot and from apical buds from shoots on the same stock plants.

In the first flowering trial of the different clones, particularly with Heyday, significant differences in growth were recorded. For instance, there was a difference of seven days in flowering time between two clones which were derived from two vegetative buds on the same shoot of the stock plant. A reduction of 18 per cent in quality was found (stems per box) in the later flowering clone. Differences in flowering performance due to the origin of a clone continued in these trials for two years.

The above results appear to challenge one of the basic laws of plant propagation. It has been assumed in horticultural practice that, with vegetatively propagated plants, individual members of a clone will behave similarly provided they have been raised and flowered in uniform environmental conditions. Machins' results are at variance with this accepted view of clonal stability but they do explain why many single plant selections in the past have been unsuccessful in improving the variety.

It seems that, in chrysanthemums, each vegetative bud when used for propagation, gives rise to individuals which, although apparently genetically identical, are very slightly different from each other. The reasons for these differences have not been studied but it seems clear that the differences can be transmitted through vegetative propagation. Each flowering stem results from the interaction of the character of the apical bud with the environment. Single plant selection does not result in the saving of this bud since it has been lost in the flowering head. What has been saved at the base of the plant is a collection of vegetative buds of unknown character but which are closely related to the selected bud.

Machin's work has clearly shown how widely the characteristics of flowering plants raised from related buds can differ and that single plant selections made from the best clones at flowering time and used indiscriminately to produce new stock may perpetuate only the average (or below-average) plants.

Single plant selection should still be carried out, because this is the only way to recognize and save improvements due to genetic change. However, all vegetative growing points on the selected plant should be isolated and treated as individual clones, the best being found by subsequent flower trials. Production stock should then be multiplied from the still vegetative mother stock.

4 Plant Health

Having bred a new variety or selected a new mutation or clone, the next step is to produce by visual inspection and other means a nucleus entirely free from disease. From this nucleus will be built the stocks from which the production cuttings will be taken.

CULTURING FOR FUNGI AND BACTERIA

The purpose of culturing is to obtain chrysanthemum cuttings free from the systemic fungal and bacterial wilt diseases such as Fusarium and Verticillium. The rogueing and selection of stock plants undoubtedly reduces the incidence of these diseases, and some authorities maintain that a bacterial wilt infection will cause such severe symptoms on the plant that the plant will be removed during rogueing operations; but this view is not universally held. These visual methods of selection may be unreliable, however, owing to the presence of symptomless carriers and the fact that under certain environmental conditions, disease symptoms may be difficult to detect.

Cuttings for culturing are selected from the best plants of the variety to be tested, and thin transverse sections are taken from the base of the stem. These are then placed in broth or on agar in a test-tube and incubated for 18 days. The cuttings are discarded if fungal or bacterial growth of any sort becomes apparent by the end of the incubation period.

Handling the Cuttings

Cuttings suitable for culturing should be 37 to 50 mm longer than those normally used for propagation. They should be in a vegetative condition and taken from previously selected stock plants.

All cuttings required for mother stock must be tested. It is not sufficient to test one cutting of a batch taken from one stock plant and to assume that if one is clean the whole batch will be clean, because it is possible for fungal diseases to be present in only a small proportion of the plant. Once the cuttings have been collected the subsequent processes must follow in clean draught-proof conditions. The cuttings must not be placed in water at any stage of the test.

The lower leaves are removed from the cuttings which are placed in a sterilant consisting of 20 per cent hypochlorite solution so that the bottom 25 to 37 mm of the cutting is immersed. This will destroy any disease organisms present on the surface of the cutting. After five minutes the cuttings are removed and placed between layers of filter paper.

Working quickly at this stage, one cutting at a time is taken and 6 mm of the base is cut off with a pair of sterilized scissors and discarded. Next, four sections 1·5 mm thick are cut into a tube containing the agar and a further four sections into a tube containing nutrient broth if tests on both media are required. Then, the remaining portion of the cutting which was immersed in the sterilizing solution is cut off and discarded.

An alternative sterilizing technique (Hellmers, 1958) is to wash the base of the cutting with a sterilized rag soaked in a mixture of 70 per cent ethanol plus 5 per cent 8-hydroxyquinoline sulphate. Next, one cutting at a time is placed in a 5 per cent aqueous solution of mercuric chloride for 20 to 30 seconds and then taken out and rinsed with the ethanol plus 8-hydroxy quinoline sulphate solution. The lowermost portion of the cutting is then wiped with this same mixture, which is burned off over a spirit flame. Sections are then cut off as described above.

After taking sections from one cutting and before passing to the next the scissors must be sterilized by dipping into alcohol and igniting. The test-tube containing the medium must be kept open for the minimum possible time to prevent contamination by airborne spores.

The test-tube is labelled to correspond with the cutting from which the segments were taken and then, in the case of broth, the test-tubes are placed in an incubator at 22° to 24°. In the agar test the tubes can be kept at room temperature.

The cuttings can be cold stored at − 0·6° for the period of the test, but must be kept isolated from each other by wrapping in polythene, or they can be rooted, each in a separate container. All contact between plants, either by leaves or through water which drains from the containers, must be avoided.

After 18 days the test-tubes are inspected for bacterial or fungal growth and any tubes show-ing such growth are discarded. This growth may occur on the sections of the cutting, or from contamination by air-borne spores on the medium away from the sections. As it is often difficult to differentiate between growth from diseased cuttings and growth from secondary contamination, all tubes showing any growth must be discarded.

Cuttings corresponding to the sections on which no disease growth is visible are rooted in a sterile medium in isolation.

It should be understood that cultured stock is not immune from systemic fungal and bacterial organisms, and reinfection will occur unless the plants are grown on in isolation. Routine spraying or fumigation must be carried out to keep pests to a minimum.

The newly cultured clean stock should be potted on into sterilized pots and compost

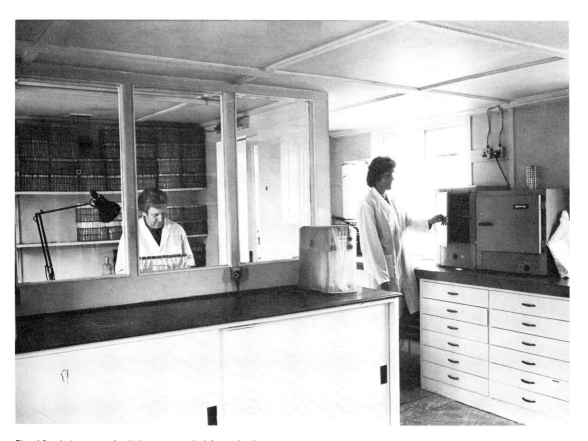

Fig. 13   Laboratory facilities are needed for culturing.

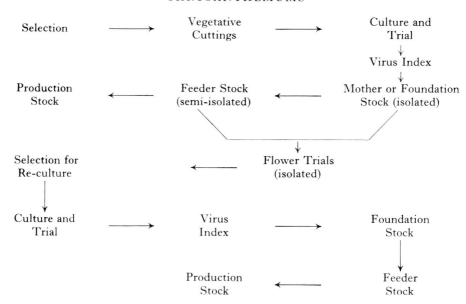

Fig. 14   Programme showing the various stages in the production of disease free stock is shown below. The total time needed for this work is three to four years.

and be regarded as mother or foundation stock. Before using this stock for the supply of feeder and production stocks (Fig. 14) it is advisable to re-culture the apical shoots as a further safeguard against disease. It must be stressed that a diseased plant in the mother stock from which all the ultimate crop plants will be derived is far more dangerous than a diseased plant in the production stock.

Preparation of Material

The agar medium is prepared as follows: 17.7 g of dehydrated potato dextrose agar is weighed out and heated with 483 ml of distilled water until completely dissolved. While still warm the agar solution is poured into 4 by 12 mm test-tubes to a depth of 12 to 20 mm and the tubes are sealed.

The broth is best made from nutrient broth tablets (Oxoid or Difco) prepared according to the maker's instructions and adding 1.5 per cent glucose. The tubes are filled to a depth of 12 to 24 mm and closed with aluminium caps or cotton-wool.

The tubes and their contents are sterilized in an autoclave or pressure cooker at a pressure of 0.7 Kg/cm² for 20 minutes.

As a preliminary step, it is advisable to experiment with cuttings known to contain fungal or bacterial organisms. This will show whether the techniques used are resulting in the growth of these organisms in the test-tubes and will help to make familiar the appearance and growth habit of each disease. It is, however, unnecessary to identify the actual disease organism in the test-tube, because the cuttings should be destroyed if growth of any kind is noticed. A further test is to culture diseased and apparently healthy cuttings alternately. This will show whether the sterilization of equipment between each culture is sufficient to prevent contamination from diseased to healthy material.

THE CONTROL OF VIRUS DISEASES

At least 20 virus diseases of chrysanthemums have so far been identified by research workers. Some of these viruses were present to a greater or lesser extent in the chrysanthemum stocks of most of the British varieties, and in some cases total infection has been found.

Tomato Aspermy virus is responsible for severe flower distortion in many varieties. The disease which it causes should be known as Aspermy Flower Distortion, although it is sometimes referred to by the misleading name of Chrysanthemum Mosaic.

The flowers of infected plants are usually reduced in size and show varying amounts of distortion and loss of colour. Colour bleaching occurs in red, bronze and pink varieties, producing streaks or flecks of white or yellow on the ray florets. Plants infected late in the season may show only one or two affected flowers and are liable to be overlooked during rogueing. The virus is transmitted by aphids and can infect many other plants, including tomato. This disease has been discovered in many varieties including Princess Anne and sports. The symptoms vary greatly between varieties, between plants in the same variety and even between flowers on the same plant. The flecks of paler colour on the ray florets are pale grey on Purple Prince, bright yellow on Shirley Late Red, whitish on August Pink and so on. White and yellow varieties normally show no colour changes. The amount of flower distortion ranges from severe twisting, tubing and irregularity of the florets to a slightly untidy appearance. Some varieties, such as Princess Anne, show symptoms more severely in poor light and low-temperature conditions. Others, such as Yellow Wallace, show no symptoms when infected. Market Gold, however, responds to extra applications of nitrogen by producing only slightly affected flowers compared with the tightly packed curled florets seen in infected plants grown with normal feeding.

Cucumber Mosaic virus is indistinguishable from Aspermy virus in the symptoms it produces in chrysanthemums, but is often less severe. It is not common in chrysanthemums in Britain, although it has been isolated from the varieties Silver Lustre, May Wallace and Shirley White.

Virus B (Mild Mosaic) was extremely widespread and most stocks of several varieties, including American Beauty, Balcombe Perfection, Mayford Crimson and Shirley Late Red, were probably totally infected. In most varieties this virus causes little or no damage to the flowers but can increase the severity of certain other viruses where it is present in combination with them. Some varieties react by producing faint leaf mottling or pallor of the main veins in the cutting stage, but the plants grow out of these symptoms and many varieties show no symptoms.

English Stunt virus has over a long period of time, but only infrequently, appeared in English stocks. American Stunt virus was introduced into English stocks with the influx of varieties from the USA in the last two decades. The symptoms which these two viruses produce are very similar; plants are stunted, and while in many of the varieties the leaves are smaller than normal, in some varieties small yellow-green dots or flecks appear on the leaves in summer. In many varieties the flowers are often dwarfed, lose colour, and are of generally poor quality. Infected plants flower up to 10 days earlier than healthy plants. No insect has been found that can transmit Stunt virus, and it is possible that most of the spread takes place when the plants are handled. Two important features of American Stunt virus are that it is much more readily spread by handling than is English Stunt virus, and, unlike the English virus, it cannot be eliminated from the plant by heat therapy (page 44). British-grown varieties in which the virus has been found include Princess Anne and sports.

Fortunately, American Stunt virus has now been almost entirely eliminated by intensive rogueing and indexing.

Tomato Spotted Wilt virus which is now extremely rare in Britain, causes necrotic areas or rings on the leaves of plants of some varieties. The leaves may later develop a rusty appearance and necrotic areas develop on the stems or leaves. Sometimes the lower leaves are killed. Older plants often appear almost normal, and a number of varieties exhibit no symptoms at all. The chief danger with this disease is that infected chrysanthemums serve as a source of infection for many other plants, especially tomatoes, in which the virus causes much more serious symptoms. Thrips spread the virus from plant to plant, and it is inadvisable to grow chrysanthemums and tomatoes in the same house.

Virus D is rare, but some varieties are infected without showing symptoms. Flower distortion, bleaching and colour breaking, sometimes with reduced flower size, develop on infected plants of susceptible varieties, the symptoms overlapping those produced by Aspermy virus, but the colour breaking tends to be in dots and lines.

Virus E causes a reduction in flower size, with short, fused and tangled florets, and characteristically with tight packing of the central florets. Flowers may be bleached and may fail to open. This virus is most commonly found in Balcombe Perfection and its sports.

A group of viruses, known as the Mosaic viruses, are carried in a range of varieties without any symptoms being expressed. The existence of a number of distinct Mosiac viruses has been established through the use of special indicator varieties of chrysanthemum (page 46) which develop symptoms including leaf mottling, distortion and dwarfing, and brown streaking of the florets.

One Mosiac virus, Vein Mottle, has been found, through the use of indicators, in several British varieties. It is usually carried without symptoms developing in the plant, but if other viruses are present it may exaggerate their effect.

Rosette viruses are expressed through the same type of symptom as is caused by the Mosaic group. Their identity is also established through the use of a range of indicator varieties.

Ring Pattern virus has been found in the variety Roseverne, causing ring and line patterns on the leaves in winter and spring, but is generally insignificant.

Chrysanthemum Latent virus is apparently very rare in British stocks. It has been found in the variety Shirley Late Red, but has no visible effect on many other varieties when they are artificially infected.

Another disease which has been found in Balcombe Perfection and its sports is Chrysanthemum Green Flower, which is one of the Aster-yellows type of pathogen. Affected plants have spindly growth and small green flowers. Roots die back leading eventually to the death of the plant. Diseases of this type are associated with mycoplasma tube organisms.

Much still remains to be established on the distribution and prevalence of these and other viruses in the range of chrysanthemums grown, as they are carried in many varieties without symptoms being expressed.

Control Measures

Plants infected with any virus should be destroyed as soon as the symtoms are detected, because cuttings from infected plants are themselves infected.

Flower-distorting viruses rarely produce obvious symptoms on leaves, and so rogueing must be done at flowering time. Conversely leaf-mottling viruses often do not produce flower symptoms and should be rouged in the cutting stage in the spring. Plants are often infected with more than one virus, and when this occurs the symptoms can be much more severe even though one of the viruses present may be symptomless by itself.

Control of these diseases by rogueing will be much more effective if it is combined with selection in raising and maintaining the quality of stocks. It should be a rule to propagate only from the very best plants selected at flowering time and not merely to discard the worst-affected plants. Efficient control of aphids and thrips will help to reduce the spread of infection from plant to plant.

The establishment of completely virus-free stocks by heat therapy and indexing is undoubtedly a progressive approach to the virus problem which deserves special attention.

Heat Therapy

It has been found that the heat treatment of chrysanthemums at 36° can remove infection by Aspermy, English Stunt, Ring Pattern and most Mosaic viruses. It will not, however, remove viruses B, D, E, Vein Mottle, American Stunt, the Rosette types and a minority of the Mosaics. One technique is to grow the plants in containers or on raised benches in a house in which a temperature of 36° can be maintained. The plants are grown at normal temperature and pinched, and when the side shoots appear the heat is slowly raised to 36° and held there for four weeks. Very short cuttings (approximately 10 mm long) are then taken and rooted prior to testing for virus.

It is also possible to grow plants in a small completely closed 'box' constructed of asbestos sheet, electrically heated and ventilated, and lit by mercury vapour lamps. This greatly simplifies temperature control in the box, as it is independent of variable weather conditions.

Another technique which is used is to grow the plants in a 'miniature greenhouse'. This is similar to the closed asbestos box. but the sides are constructed of glass, thus removing the need for the mercury vapour lamps. The miniature house is stood on a bench within a normal greenhouse.

During the heat treatment some plants may be lost, but tip cuttings from the remainder should be free from Aspermy and English Stunt. This is not always the case, however, and it is essential that a test be carried out to ensure that these viruses have been removed.

Indexing

INOCULATION

In the inoculation technique use is made of plants which readily show leaf symptoms of the virus to be indexed. These test plants are grown in pots and kept in an insect-proof greenhouse at a temperature of 18° to 21° (Fig. 15). Leaf or

Fig. 15   Insect-proof greenhouse showing tobacco plants used in the inoculation technique for showing Aspermy virus.

flower tissue of the chrysanthemum plant to be tested is removed and macerated in a little M/15 phosphate buffer solution at pH 7. Celite, a diatomaceous earth, is dusted lightly on to the leaves of the test plants, which are then wiped gently with the forefinger dipped in the inoculum. The sharp crystals of the celite puncture the cells of the leaves and inoculate the cells of the test plant with the macerated tissue of the plant to be indexed. After a few moments the inoculum is rinsed off the leaves with water.

In virus-infected plants the flower petals contain a higher concentration of infective virus than do other parts of the plant. If the plants to be tested are not in flower the young leaves should be used to provide the inoculating material.

Symptoms developing on inoculated leaves are termed local lesions, while those on the uninoculated younger leaves of the test plant are known as systemic symptoms. Thus, with Aspermy virus, the local lesions are pale green spots visible on tobacco leaves after three to seven days, and are followed by severe systemic mottling and distortion of the younger leaves after two to five weeks. Virus B, however, causes local yellow lesions on petunia after two to five weeks, and does not become systemic. Symptoms of Cucumber Mosaic on tobacco are similar to those of Aspermy but much less severe. Tomato Spotted Wilt virus causes brown local lesions on tobacco, sometimes followed by systemic brown spots, flecks and streaks on the younger leaves and stems.

GRAFTING

Graft indexing is used to detect several viruses which cannot be identified by the inoculation technique. Use is made of the fact that the viruses Stunt, the Mosaic group including Vein Mottle, and the Rosette group will cause distinctive symptoms on some varieties of chrysanthemum.

The test consists of inarch grafting a cutting from the stock plant to be tested on to an indicator plant, usually the variety Mistletoe in Britain as it is found to be reliable in its development of clearly visible symptoms; but other varieties, Blanche Poitevene, Blazing Gold and Good News, are also used. Until the graft union has taken the cutting base is stood in a small tube of water to prevent flagging.

As an alternative to the use of a tube of water, the cutting to be tested may be rooted prior to grafting. The roots of the test cutting are cut away when the graft union has taken.

At least two grafts to Mistletoe should be made for each stock plant tested, and all grafted plants must be grown in isolation to prevent the spread of virus among them.

The grafted plant must be grown for at least six months before the stock plant can be declared free from Stunt or the various Mosaic viruses. During this time cuttings from the stock plants can be taken and rooted, provided each one is kept in isolation, so that at the end of the test period a reasonable number of cuttings are available (Fig. 16).

It is sometimes advantageous to cut back the grafted plants during the test, as this seems to reduce the time required for symptoms to develop and it also keeps the plants to a manageable height. At no time during the test should a plant be handled before sterilizing hands and instruments used on the previous plant.

This grafting programme is best carried out in early summer, as Stunt is a virus whose symptoms on the Mistletoe plants show only at high temperatures and, they can be completely masked during the winter. However, where an extensive grafting programme is to be carried out grafting throughout the whole year may be necessary. Artificial long days must be given to the plants during natural short-day conditions.

Virus symptoms on Mistletoe are a mottling as shown by the various Mosaic and Rosette viruses, and a yellow spotting shown by Stunt virus.

Care of Clean Stock

Owing to the length of time involved in virus indexing and the relatively small number of virus-free plants which will be obtained, the indexing should be done after productivity selection from cultured plants in the stock production time-table.

46

Fig. 16 Initial stock multiplication from grafted plants, kept in isolation in the greenhouse.

When a variety has been declared free of all disease the initial number of plants is rapidly built up. This mother stock (Fig. 17) is grown in isolated conditions and is recognized by a distinctive label.

Working on the principle that the first cuttings taken from the stock plant are as good in every way as the stock plant itself, these progeny are also given the same label. They will be used to replace the mother stock, and this process is continuous until after six months or a year a further selected, cultured and virus-indexed batch of the same variety is introduced.

The remainder of the first batch and all the second batch of cuttings taken from the mother stock are given a different label and are used as feeder stock. Again the first progeny of this stock retains this same label and the second crop would have a third label. Similarly, the third batch of cuttings from the mother stock would have the same third label. In this way the quality of each batch of stock relative to the initial mother stock is known, and whenever further batches of stock are required only the best stock plants are used.

Having obtained virus-free stock, it is of great importance to prevent reinfection. Clean stock should be kept in a strictly isolated insect-proof house and routine precautions taken against aphids, the principal vectors of these diseases.

Where clean stock is used in the flowering houses, good control measures may restrict

47

Fig. 17 Multiplication of mother stock in raised benches.

reinfection by virus to about 5 per cent of the stock per annum. As clean stocks are built up, however, and diseased stocks reduced, the percentage of reinfection each year should steadily decline.

MERISTEM CULTURE

Meristem culture is a technique which may be used alone, or more often in combination with heat therapy, to obtain virus-free stocks. It is particularly useful in eliminating those viruses which are not removed by heat therapy.

In essence the technique consists of removing under a microscope the extreme apex, or meristem-tip, of the cutting, usually together with one pair of leaf rudiments, or primordia, the fragment removed usually being about 1 mm in length (Fig. 18). This fragment is placed in a sterilized test-tube on a medium containing a range of plant nutrients, including a rooting hormone. When this has occurred the meristem-tip is transferred to another medium containing

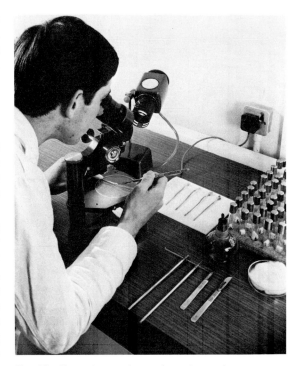

Fig. 18 Removing meristem-tip under a microscope.

48

a rooting hormone, and when sufficiently large the young plantlet is potted up.

As with plants obtained after heat treatment, those resulting from meristem culture must be tested for the presence of viruses, as not all meristems taken will in fact be free from virus. It is advisable to carry out these tests both immediately and after several months have elapsed, as a plant may initially appear virus-free but in fact contain a concentration of virus too low to induce symptoms at first, but which after a period of time will build up to a detectable level.

5 Stock Production

It has been the general practice in the past to make use of the stool of the parent plant for propagation. A stool consists of a short portion of the old flowering stem, its roots and the rhizomes or underground stems. Shoots for cuttings may develop either on the main stem (stem cuttings) or from the axils of scale leaves on the rhizomes (stool cuttings).

A much better type of stock, essential for the modern methods of chrysanthemum production, is the stock plant. This is a young vegetative plant grown from a cutting and pinched to induce the growth of lateral shoots. These short, vegetative laterals, which from the standpoint of origin may be classified as stem cuttings, are used for the production of flowering plants. Stem cuttings have often been considered to be inferior to cuttings from the base of stools, but there is no scientific evidence to support this view, provided that both are in a vegetative condition. Preference for base cuttings may be due to the fact that stem cuttings taken from stools are more prone to produce a flower bud soon after rooting, giving a check to early growth and thus a loss of uniformity in the batch of young plants.

The results of scientific work suggest that the flowering stimulus, which is initiated in the leaves under shortday conditions, travels first up to the tip of the stem, where it induces bud formation, and then passes progressively down the stem, causing bud formation in the lateral growths. This flowering stimulus may or may not pass into the rhizomes, depending on the number of shortday inductions and the variety. Thus, bud formation is more likely in stem cuttings than in stool cuttings. Nevertheless it often occurs in both.

Stock and the Environment

Environmental conditions profoundly affect the growth of stock plants and thus influence the production of cuttings. The effect of short days in the autumn on the parent plant will probably be to induce bud formation in the lowest portion of the main stem and perhaps in some axils on the rhizomes. However, if night temperatures are constantly below 10°, bud initiation in short days is very unusual, especially where stools are concerned. Therefore, where stock houses containing stools are kept cool in winter, further bud initiation does not usually occur, but temperatures of between 7° and 10°, normal in such houses do not encourage growth and the production of cuttings is slow.

Winkler (1967), using the varieties Luyona and Mefo, showed that the production of cuttings from stock plants rose by 36 per cent as the night temperature was raised from 10° to 16°. However, temperatures should vary to some extent with the time of year. A minimum temperature of 16° should be maintained from November to February in Britain. But, because good light conditions are known to compensate to some extent for a slight lowering of night temperature in autumn and spring, temperatures of 14° or 15° can be recommended especially in conjunction with carbon dioxide enrichment.

In order to prevent flower bud formation in the stock plants at the higher temperatures, artificial longday treatment must be given from early August until mid-May. The lighting periods recommended on page 15 for flowering crops may also be applied to stock plants, with the addition that as a precautionary measure it is usual for propagators to continue with a two-hourly lighting period throughout the summer months.

The treatment of the stock plants depends to some extent on the dates on which the cuttings are required and on the cultivation programme to be adopted. The relatively soft cuttings produced by growing stock plants in artificial long days and a temperature of 14° to 16° during the winter months would be severely checked if subsequently used for the traditional pot cultivation technique. The young plants would require careful hardening off before placing in cold frames or being put out-of-doors, practices which defeat the modern approach of rapid growth with few checks. Indeed, if cuttings are raised under longday conditions in a temperature of 16° and subsequently allowed to grow in shortday conditions, budding will immediately occur in many varieties whatever the temperature. This budding will continue until the natural longday and higher temperature conditions of late spring begin to take effect.

In the past several hundred stools of each variety were often selected and planted in low-temperature and shortday conditions for stock purposes. High temperatures and artificial long days can be used profitably by all growers, irrespective of their methods of cultivation, for the rapid build up of specially selected stock. The all-round quality of crops is considerably increased if only a few of the very best parent plants are selected and grown in conditions more conducive to rapid and vigorous growth.

Comparison of Methods

In deciding the method of stock production the grower must compare the disadvantages of the older method, which involves the handling of many stools, tending to lead to lack of uniformity and inferior quality in subsequent crops, with the cost of maintaining higher temperatures and of installing and operating the lighting equipment necessary for the modern techniques.

There are several advantages of stock plants over stools for the production of cuttings. A stool is a product of a plant which has flowered in shortday conditions and as mentioned already many of the shoots may contain unwanted buds. A stock plant, if grown in a controlled environment, can be kept in a completely vegetative condition.

Another important consideration is the position of cutting material in relation to the soil level. Stool shoots borne on the rhizomes are in very close contact with the soil and this, from the standpoint of pest and disease control, is undesirable. The microclimate at soil level is invariably more humid than at 15 cm above the soil. Similarly, with leaf cover, the temperature is usually lower at soil level and this, combined with the damp conditions, is conductive to the growth of fungi around the stool shoots.

The question of the control of chrysanthemum eelworm arises in this respect. The only known means of spread of this organism is in water, either in a continuous film on the leaves under very humid conditions or in droplets of water splashed up from the soil. The use of stock plants with their cuttings borne well above ground level, and with careful application of water to the soil, preferably by means of a trickle irrigation system (page 72), has undoubtedly helped to control this pest.

Another advantage in having stock plants in an environment conducive to rapid growth is that in vigorously growing shoots certain diseases, such as Verticillium and Fusarium wilts, are not immediately present in the apex of the stems even though the lower regions of the plants may be infected. This is also true of eelworm infection because the pest does not normally spread in the plant tissues as rapidly as the plants themselves elongate. Thus, cuttings taken from the tips of stock plants are much more likely to be free from diseases and pests than shoots borne on stools.

Uniformity of cutting material is more easily obtained from stock plants than from stools. The vigour of a shoot arising from a rhizome depends on the amount of stored food material in the latter. This is extremely variable and depends upon the age of the rhizome and its position on the stool. The aerial shoots of stock plants, having been formed as the result of a pinch, are all of a similar age and in a similar position on the plant and are therefore much more uniform in both vigour and size.

Stock for Year-Round Programmes

Stock plants producing cuttings for year-round programmes must be grown in a completely controlled environment to ensure a steady supply of vigorous vegetative shoots (Fig. 19). It can be said that the correct environmental control of stock plants conditions their progeny

Fig. 19 Snapping cuttings from stock plants in a widespan greenhouse.

for year-round growing. The cuttings taken are extremely sensitive to daylength and temperature and will readily remain vegetative in long-day conditions and will form and develop flower buds quickly and evenly when shortday treatment is commenced.

Indeed, for the fastest growth and flowering, light and temperature conditions in the stock plant house should be similar to those used for the first few weeks of growth in the flowering house. When, during February, Machin (unpub.) compared the rate of growth of young plants raised from cuttings imported from the Canary Islands with that of plants produced from stock plants grown in Sussex in December and January, the latter were found to have a growth rate 100 per cent greater than the former. Even though the plants derived from the

Canary Islands were larger, in terms of height, leaf number and dry weight, at the start of short days, because they were approximately three times heavier as unrooted cuttings, the cuttings from Sussex produced earlier flowers of equal quality. These facts apply to all cuttings imported from southern production areas in winter.

However, unless the year-round propagator is able to produce cuttings from stock plants grown in Britain economically by the use of supplementary light and growth retardants (page 88) he has to grow stock plants in more southerly latitudes during the winter, or face a serious shortage of cuttings. This problem occurs because the demand for cuttings, which includes plants for stock, decreases only slightly during the autumn, and the demand in winter

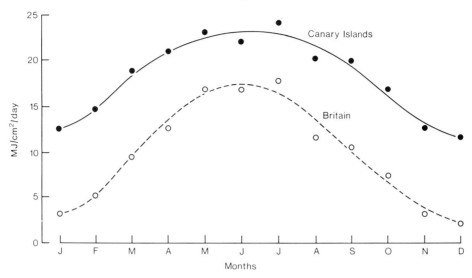

Fig. 20 A comparison of the light levels in Britain and the Canary Islands. Worst light in Canary Islands is equal to late March and late September in Britain (MJ/m²/day).

is as great as at any time of the year. However, in Britain, the production of cuttings in winter is about one-third that of the summer months. When the additional growing time is taken into account, at least four times the stock area is needed in the winter compared with the summer to produce the same number of cuttings.

Because of this most of the leading propagators in Europe have developed stock areas in lower latitudes for winter production. Owing to the higher light levels both the quality of the cuttings and the rate of growth of the stock plants is improved, compared with stock plants grown in northern areas during the winter (Fig. 20).

Mother plants are reared at the home nurseries to produce the stocks for the southern areas. In order to improve the quality of the mother stock, carbon dioxide enrichment is given under suitable weather conditions during the winter months.

CALCULATING STOCK REQUIREMENTS

In Britain, stock planted in late spring or early summer takes an average of seven weeks to produce its first flush of rooted cuttings. The stock plants are pinched approximately 10 days after planting, and the first cuttings may be taken three weeks later and rooted in another

$2\frac{1}{2}$ weeks. Some of the slow-growing varieties such as Bonnie Jean and Tuneful require an extra few days for all stages, and this has to be allowed in planning the stock.

Production is much slower at other times of the year, the extreme being for stock planted in October and November, when the average period from planting to the first rooted cuttings is 10 weeks, that is, two weeks from planting to pinching, five weeks for cutting production and three weeks for rooting. It is of vital importance for the propagator to know the variation in the number of cuttings produced by stock plants round the year in his area. For stock planted 12·5 by 12·5 cm and maintained at 16° night temperature, the summer average in England is about 1·2 cuttings per plant per week. This number varies widely with variety and, with some of the slower-growing varieties the number is reduced to less than one cutting per week. With certain fast-growing varieties such as Altis and Polaris, however, summer production exceeds two cuttings per plant per week. In mid-winter the average drops to 0·5 cutting, again with a varietal variation from 0·3 to 0·7 cutting per plant per week.

Numerous trials involving details of pinching date, the interval from pinching to taking the cuttings, the rooting period and the number of cuttings produced has enabled charts to be compiled for each production area giving the stock production details for every variety for each season of the year.

One advantage of propagating for year-round growing is that the flowering programmes can be compiled well in advance, and thus the numbers of stock plants needed at each stage are known in good time. In this way year-round stock planning can be extremely accurate.

Production stocks of each variety need not be carried all the year round. Stock plants of the varieties needed for flowering from December to February are substantially reduced from late October until March or April. After this period, the numbers are increased again for planting from mid-June onwards to produce cuttings for August to October. Because most of the 9-, 10- and 11-week varieties are not at present used in any quantity for flowering from December to February, cuttings are not required from late August to late October; but stocks have to be increased towards the end of this period to supply cuttings from November onwards for spring flowering.

Successive plantings of stock plants of each variety should be made by the propagator to ensure a continuous supply of young vegetative material. The life of a stock plant is limited to three or four flushes of cuttings, partly because as the stock plants age, the cuttings are more difficult to snap and also extra rooting time must be allowed. Other important reasons are that the tendency towards crown bud formation in the shoots increases, and the uniformity of growth decreases, with the age of the stock plant. Consequently in the summer, from the date the first cuttings are taken, the stock plants are allowed only a further 13 weeks of production before they are pulled out and replaced. In the winter, when growth is slower, the stock is discarded approximately 15 weeks after the date the first cuttings are taken. For these reasons the propagator has to reserve one-seventh of his total production for stock purposes.

The number of cuttings involved in year-round growing is of interest both to the propagator and to the grower. For 0·4 ha of year-round chrysanthemums grown on single stems at least 520,000 rooted cuttings are needed in the year, assuming that two-thirds of the ground area is planted. For the 'direct shortday planting system' (page 102) approximately 870,000 plants are required per annum in a two-thirds planted flowering area. The full development of this system could produce at least six crops a year with a 90 per cent or more utilization of flowering area involving up to 1,400,000 plants.

Stock Nutrition

The principles underlying the watering and feeding of stock plants are similar to those which apply to the growing crop (page 71), except that a higher nitrogen level may be desirable. One reason for this is that cuttings containing a relatively high percentage of nitrogen are found to root more readily than those deficient in this element.

The effect of stock plant nutrition on the growth and flowering of year-round chrysanthemums has been investigated by Machin (1973). Using five different treatments in a number of experiments at various times of the year he showed that low nitrogen nutrition of stock plants significantly reduced the number of flowers per stem and total flower and plant dry weight in the subsequent cut flower crop. In one experiment even the length of the pedicels in the flowering plants was reduced by low nitrogen nutrition of the stock plant. Flowering time was also reduced when high nitrogen compared with low nitrogen was given to stock plants. Machin concluded that stock plant nutrition should be in the approximate ratio of 3 parts nitrogen (N), to 1 part potassium (as K_2O), with a substrate analysis of 80 to 100 ppm nitrogen.

Other Aspects of Stock Production

COMPOST

The use of a sterilized compost for stock plant growth is essential for disease control and to avoid the risk of eelworm. If stools are employed the soil in which they were flowered may have contained a high soluble salt content at the end of the growing period from previous fertilizer applications. This may cause yellowing of the foliage and death of the stock, especially if the soil dries out. Stools are best lifted and planted in fresh compost, John Innes potting compost being ideal for this purpose (Appendix 5). As a further measure against eelworm the stools should be washed and either given hot water treatment (46° for 5·5 minutes) or drenched with a thionazin solution (page 55).

VERNALIZATION REQUIREMENT

In view of the results reported by Schwabe (1953) the vernalization requirements of chrysanthemums (the requirement of a period of low temperature after flowering), it is necessary to discuss the effect of temperature on the stools, and the subsequent behaviour of the cuttings taken from them.

The failure to subject stools or their cuttings to low-temperature treatment has, in certain varieties, resulted in rosetted or otherwise abnormal growth and failure to flower. Base cuttings from stools of varieties requiring vernalization, but grown at 16°, exhibit rosetted growth at some time during their development if kept at this temperature. If the young plants are given shortday treatment or are grown in natural short days (with a temperature of 16°) rosetting occurs immediately. Normal elongation takes place if longday conditions are given at once, but a terminal rosette may form when short days return and the characteristic delay in flowering will be evident.

These symptoms have not generally been noticed in the past in countries where it has been the standard practice to grow the stools in winter in night temperatures below 10°, and a period of one month at this temperature has satisfied their vernalization requirement.

Workers in the USA have also seldom recorded rosetting or other delays in flowering even though temperatures of 16° are maintained throughout the period of stock production and subsequent growth of the young plants. There are several explanations for this. The first is that after selection, the stock plants are not flowered, and stem cuttings produced in artificial long days are used. These cuttings may not require vernalization as do those produced by underground rhizomes. Second, in view of the demand for chrysanthemums that grow vigorously and respond to shortday treatment in a constant temperature of 16°, new varieties are tested in this temperature regime. Any vernalization requirement shown by a variety, manifested by rosetting or failure to flower, would lead automatically to its elimination as a suitable type.

Thus, growers interested in the production of year-round varieties should either use the stock plant method of production or, if stool cuttings are to be used, test each variety for vernalization requirement by placing it in short days with a temperature of 16°, after the parent plant has been grown and flowered. It should be emphasized, however, that vernalization is not necessary in all British varieties. Vince (1956) showed that some varieties such as The Favourite, have no low-temperature requirement and others like Magnet, show only a short delay in flowering where no low-temperature period is given. However, with Mayford Crimson, President and Rose Princess, rosetting occurred in sustained high temperatures, and similar results were found in trials in southern England with Mayford Supreme and Mason's Bronze.

To ensure that the vernalization requirement is met, selected stools should be subjected to a night temperature range of 7° to 10° for at least four weeks. Subsequently, stock plants may be safely grown in constantly high night temperatures (16°) provided they remain in a vegetative condition and stem cuttings are used.

NATURE OF SHOOTS

It is especially important that shoots of a similar age (with the same number of leaves) be used as a source of cuttings. Furuta and Kiplinger (1955) have shown that crown buds are formed on the variety Soprano under longday conditions provided sufficient time is allowed for growth. When tip cuttings from shoots of different ages were rooted and the resultant plants were not pinched the height of the crown bud varied, depending on the age of the shoot. This led to great variations in the flower spray formation.

Indeed, a number of workers (Schwabe, 1950; Furuta, 1954; Vince, 1955a; Kofranek and Halevy, 1974) have reported that bud initiation can occur in chrysanthemums grown only in long days. Machin (1955) found that, despite applying shortday treatment after a period of 35, 45, 55 and 65 long days respectively, all plants of the variety Loveliness formed buds after approximately 30 leaves had been formed. He assumed that with this and other varieties grown (Primrose Poitou 21 leaves, Rose Chocod 22 leaves and Apricot May Wallace 29 leaves) a certain amount of vegetative growth must be made before bud initiation is possible. However, when this growth stage is reached after a further amount of vegetative growth, depending on variety, bud initiation will occur. Machin concluded that the most accurate criterion for flower bud initiation was the total number of leaves formed below the apical flower bud.

Cockshull (1975) has demonstrated that chrysanthemum stock plants of nine year-round varieties eventually formed buds in longday conditions after a certain number of leaves had been formed. Varieties such as Bright Golden Anne and Bluechip, notorious for premature budding on stock plants, on average produced 24·3 and 33·8 leaves, respectively, prior to bud formation. Other varieties (Polaris 43·5 leaves, Golden Crystal 54·2 leaves and Tuneful 64·2 leaves) needed a longer period of vegetative growth before budding.

The work of Cockshull emphasizes the need for quality control in stock plants. Prior to taking the cutting it is essential to minimize the number of leaves initiated in its growing point so as to maximize the potential for further vegetative growth. This particularly applies to stock grown in high light areas (southern Europe and the Middle East) because bud initiation in long days occurs earlier in high than in low light conditions for a given variety. It is, therefore, especially important to keep stock plants snapped back and to take cuttings as soon as possible.

USE OF SUPPLEMENTARY LIGHT

The use of supplementary light has been found to improve the performance of stock plants during seasons of low natural light. Anderson and Carpenter (1974) showed that when stock of the variety Bright Golden Anne was given 100 W/m^2 supplementary light, using sodium or mercury vapour lamps, it produced 43 per cent more cuttings in November and December, 102 per cent more in January and February and 33 per cent more in March and April compared with unlit plants. Cutting quality was improved by up to 100 per cent. Machin (unpubl.) has confirmed these results for other varieties in winter conditions in Britain. Using sodium lamps giving a supplementary light level of 0·68 MJ/m^2/day from January to March he increased production and quality of cuttings in five varieties (Table 6).

TABLE 6 Use of Supplementary Light to Improve Cutting Production on Stock Plants from January to March 1974 (from Machin, unpublished work for Perifleur Ltd)

Variety	Percentage increase in production over control	Percentage increase in quality over control (mean wet weight)
Pollyanne	88	10
Hurricane	21	27
Polaris	89	30
Southdown Chip	39	21
Snowdon	10	41

It is interesting to note that with some varieties the effect of light tends to increase the number of cuttings per stock plant rather than to improve their quality; with others the reverse is true.

USE OF GROWTH RETARDANTS

Stock plants of some varieties grown in environments causing rapid stem elongation, such as high temperatures or poor light, have been treated with the growth retardant Alar to improve the quality of the cuttings. Where this has been done it has been found that, by improving the quality of all shoots on the stock plant, the production of cuttings has also increased. However, Alar needs to be applied regularly for this purpose and after several applications shoots in various stages of development will have taken up different amounts of the retardant. This has the effect of inhibiting growth after planting and leads to uneven plant elongation and flowering.

Machin (unpubl.) has found that these problems are overcome by using the growth retardant Phosfon 1·5 in granulet form. Because Phosfon is incorporated into the substrate all shoots on the stock plant are affected equally. Also, once the shoots are removed as cuttings they are removed from the direct influence of Phosfon through the roots. The shortening effect then ceases and elongation of growth returns to normal.

In large-scale experiments in Sussex, Machin was able to improve cutting production in the variety Hurricane by 26 per cent and quality (mean wet weight) by 20 per cent during January and February by mixing 600 g/m³ Phosfon 1·5 granulet in the substrate. These figures were remarkably similar to the improvement induced on stock plants of the same variety using supplementary light of 0·68 MJ/m²/day from sodium lamps as a comparison (Table 6). When Phosfon and supplementary light treatments were combined, greater benefits were obtained

TABLE 7 Use of Supplementary Light and Phosfon 1·5 Granulet to Improve Cutting Production on Stock Plants from January to March 1974 (from Machin, unpublished work for Perifleur Ltd)

Variety	Percentage increase in production over control	Percentage increase in quality over control (mean wet weight)
Pollyanne	133	44
Hurricane	49	19
Polaris	100	76
Southdown Chip	42	26
Snowdon	14	36

with some varieties (Pollyanne and Polaris) but not with others (Southdown Chip and Snowdon) compared with the use of either supplementary light or Phosfon (Table 7). Clearly there was some interaction between genotype, amount of light and Phosfon.

In view of some of the problems involved in importing large quantities of cuttings from lower latitudes during the winter, and their relatively poor performance compared with cuttings grown in the environment in which they will flower, the use of growth retardants and supplementary light on stock during the winter could become more important.

6 Rooting Cuttings

There are two important factors in the production of rooted cuttings for year-round programmes. These are the physical nature of the unrooted cutting and the rooting environment, because both affect the flowering response and quality of flowers.

THE UNROOTED CUTTING

Vigorous, rapidly growing vegetative shoots provide the best type of cuttings (Fig. 21). Root initiation and development is rapid in the op-

timum rooting environment, and the check to growth, unavoidable during rooting, is therefore reduced to the minimum. This vigorous type of shoot is produced only on stock plants grown in high temperatures and good light conditions. Experience has shown that thick, short-jointed shoots from stools grown in low temperatures and short days are not the best to propagate from. It is true, of course, that the latter will stand up to unfavourable conditions and rough handling rather better than the former.

The practice of making cuttings with a knife-

Fig. 21   A cutting taken from a rapidly growing vegetative shoot will produce roots quickly.

cut immediately below a node, and the subsequent removal of base leaves, is unnecessarily laborious and was probably one of the main reasons for the prevalence of disease in many chrysanthemum stocks in the past. Bacterial and fungal organisms initially present in a few cuttings can be spread rapidly by means of the propagator's knife. The snapping of cuttings from stock plants and their insertion directly into the bench is an important advance in disease prevention.

A further advantage of this method is that the time taken for the collection and insertion of cuttings may be decreased substantially, and there are no differences in the rooting performance of nodal or internodal cuttings where the optimum conditions are provided. Indeed, if the bases of the shoots are relatively hard, an internodal cutting roots more quickly because the developing root primordia meet less resistance from cell fibres in the cortex of the stem.

The shoots of stock plants grown in long days at a night temperature of $16°$ snap cleanly, especially if a weak liquid fertilizer containing a high proportion of nitrogen is applied with each watering.

The removal or trimming of leaves of cuttings is undesirable because any reduction in leaf area results in a corresponding decrease in the amount of food material available for rooting. However, the potentially higher rate of transpiration with more leaves has to be met by providing conditions of high humidity in the rooting house.

Length

Usually the length of cutting is standardized according to the season or the use to which the cutting will be put because any discrepancy from the set standard leads to difficulties in grading after rooting, and in planting in the flowering house.

During the summer the standard length is set at 50 mm. This is measured from the base of the cutting to the growing point. The cuttings of pot plant varieties and of some of the most vigorous cut flower varieties are taken at 40 mm and some of the slow-growing types at 60 mm during this period.

In the winter, a larger plant is required to offset the decrease in leaf area due to poor light conditions. At this time, the cuttings of the majority of varieties are taken at 60 mm in length, the length being varied by up to 15 mm, if necessary, according to the vigour of the variety.

Other Physical Measurements

Microscopic examination of a vegetative unrooted cutting, 50 mm in length, shows that it contains approximately 15 leaves. This is roughly 50 per cent of the leaf number of the flowering plant. The final size and quality of these longday leaves present in the unrooted cuttings have been shown to affect the subsequent response and quality of the flowering plant. All the physical measurements of the unrooted cutting, that is its length, number of leaves, diameter of stem, dry weight of stem and leaves and leaf area are important in this respect.

Physical 'grades' of unrooted cuttings have been compared (Anon., 1971) in the direct longday planting system (page 89). Cuttings with a basal stem diameter between 3·2 and 4·8 mm gave consistently better results than thinner cuttings (less than 3·2 mms stem diameter) whereas long cuttings (70 mm), although leading to slightly taller flowering plants compared with short (30 mm) cuttings, did not improve flowering response or quality. However, in one experiment the combined effect of thick and long cuttings was towards earlier flowering and improved quality compared with thin and short cuttings. In later work (Anon., 1972) it was shown that even when a uniform grade of unrooted cutting was used, rooted cuttings could usually be divided into three size grades at planting time. When rooted cuttings were planted at random without grading the stronger plants grew well at the expense of the weaker ones, but the overall difference in production was small in comparison with a crop where tall rooted cuttings were planted in the centre of the beds with small plants along the edges. This latter method, however, resulted in a more uniform crop with less waste.

Machin (1973) experimented with three grades

of unrooted cuttings of two varieties, Polaris and Heyday. Cuttings were weighed individually on taking and graded as follows into mean wet weights (g):

	Heavy	*Medium*	*Light*
Polaris	0·85	0·66	0·45
Heyday	0·76	0·59	0·48

Cuttings were inserted into peat blocks (direct shortday planting system, page 102) in January and allowed 19 long days prior to direct planting into the shortday flowering area. Flowering commenced on 26 April and the results are given in Table 8.

With Polaris, lighter unrooted cuttings led to shorter stems, fewer leaves, fewer flowers, lower total flowering plant dry weight and later flowering (Table 8). With Heyday the lighter grade of unrooted cutting led to an even greater (five days) flowering delay compared with Polaris but the delay had the effect of increasing the quality of flowers compared with that achieved by the heaviest unrooted cuttings.

A further experiment using the length of an unrooted cutting as the factor of comparison led Machin to believe that weight rather than length of an unrooted cutting was the better measurement of physical quality.

The weight grading of cuttings taken from individual boxes of unrooted cuttings, which would commercially be regarded as uniformly high quality, can result in weight grades in which the heaviest cuttings (100 per cent heavier)

produce flower crops seven to 10 days earlier than the lightest cuttings (Machin, unpubl.). If weight grading cannot be done it is far better to select cuttings by eye for uniformly high leaf area measurement and thickness of stem rather than rely on strict control of length of stem.

Type

There are a number of references concerning what may best be described as the 'qualitative' aspect of the physical nature of the unrooted cutting. Furuta and Kiplinger (1955) reported that shoots of a similar age on the stock plant should be used as the source of unrooted cuttings. Probably they should have stated that shoots at a similar 'stage of development', in terms of number of leaves, should be used. When tip cuttings taken from shoots of different ages (stages of development) were used for single-stem crops there were wide variations in the type of spray produced, due to differences in 'crown' bud formation. In some cases the crown buds, which can occur in longday conditions after a certain amount of growth has been made, must have been present in the shoots on the stock plants.

Work at Efford EHS (Anon., 1973) has confirmed these results and shown that premature budding and 'compound' spray formation in the varieties Polaris and Rosechip can be related to the stage of development of the shoot on the stock plant from which the cuttings are derived. For instance, the length of the pedicels of the

TABLE 8   Flowering Plant Characteristics in Two Varieties from Three Weight Grades of Cutting (from Machin, 1973)

	Heyday				Polaris			
	Heavy	Medium	Light	LSD at P = 0·05	Heavy	Medium	Light	LSD at P = 0·05
Shortdays to flowering	85·9	89·8	91·2	0·9	83·5	84·6	85·8	0·9
Flower number	7·3	7·0	7·1	n.s.d.	9·0	8·0	7·0	0·3
Stem length, cm	85·0	88·0	91·0	3·0	82·0	81·0	78·0	2·0
Dry weight flower, g	3·7	4·0	4·4	0·3	3·9	3·3	2·9	0·2
Dry weight total plant, g	11·3	11·7	11·9	n.s.d.	10·9	10·0	9·0	0·8
Leaf number	24·7	24·6	24·5	n.s.d.	21·1	20·0	19·3	0·8

flowering plants in Polaris were 19·0 cm when cuttings were removed leaving two leaves on the shoot of the stock plant, 23·1 cm leaving four leaves and 32·6 cm leaving six leaves. In this experiment the leaves produced prior to crown bud formation were not counted so that it is not known whether premature budding occurred in the shoots of the stock plants or subsequently during the longday period of the crop.

Thus it is important to remove the cuttings from the stock plants as soon as they can be taken, leaving two leaves on the shoots for further production. As already mentioned, crown buds can form in stock plants even under longday conditions, and if the shoots are allowed to grow too long before the removal of their tips as cuttings, unwanted buds may be present. Shoots which contain premature flower buds are especially undesirable for use in the year-round programme, because the buds check vegetative growth, and, although subsequent thinning to one lateral shoot may be carried out, the quality of the stem and uniformity of flowering are reduced throughout the bed.

Chan (1955) found that 'hard' cuttings, presumably with a woody type of growth, produced flowering plants with fewer flowers than 'soft' cuttings.

THE ROOTING ENVIRONMENT
Temperature

The optimum air temperature at night for the rooting of chrysanthemums is 18° (Post, 1949a). However, the slight differences between the rooting performances of cuttings rooted at 18° and 16° do not appear to warrant the cost of extra heating. Below 16° root development rapidly decreases and marked differences have been noticed between cuttings rooted at 16° and 10°.

For the most rapid rooting of cuttings and subsequent well-balanced growth, a night temperature of 16° is probably best throughout the year. With this temperature, artificial longday conditions have to be given from early August to mid-May, to prevent flower bud initiation in the cuttings.

To maintain a good balance between root and shoot growth in the cuttings it is essential to co-ordinate an aerial temperature of 16° with a bottom heat of 18° to 21°. A simple arrangement of thermostatically controlled electric soil warming wires or of steam or hot water pipes enclosed under the bench serves the purpose admirably.

It is important to realize that the best root and shoot development does not depend on temperature control alone. High temperatures must be combined with good light conditions so that a maximum photosynthetic rate is possible in the leaves and the translocation of the resulting supply of food material to the base of the cuttings is rapid.

Light

In view of the importance of good light for rooting there has been some recent research on the effects of artificial lighting during the rooting process. Canham (1974) using white fluorescent lamps as the total light source found that satisfactory rooting in 14 days was obtained in relatively low light levels of illuminance, 8 W/m², but increasing it to 32 W/m² improved rooting performance, especially during the second week of treatment.

However, conditions favourable to photosynthesis are also favourable to transpiration and unless water is supplied frequently to the rooting medium and a high humidity is maintained, wilting of foliage will occur. This leads to a marked decrease in the rate of photosynthesis and a corresponding increase in the time taken for root development. Good natural conditions for rooting occur during the long days and high light intensities of late spring and summer in Britain.

Nutrition

Nutrition of the rooting cuttings is not the normal practice of commercial propagators but there is evidence to suggest that inadequate nutrition during rooting can have adverse effects on the growth and flowering of year-round crops. The increase in dry weight in the rooting cutting occurs mainly in the leaves and root, the required nitrogen being utilized from the lower more mature leaves (Good and Tukey, 1967).

Nitrogen is easily leached from these lower leaves during mist propagation but is less readily leached from the young tips of the cuttings after translocation. They had previously shown (1966) that mist propagation led to an appreciable amount of leaching of mineral nutrients from the foliage and that nutrients in the young plant were rapidly reduced still further by the demands of the growing plant itself. These writers and others (Morton and Boodley, 1969; Wott and Tukey, 1969; Wille, 1974) have demonstrated the value of using fertilizers applied in the mist for improving the rate and quality of growth. The plants responded to nutrient mist propagation by improved flowering response and increased size and number of flowers.

The optimum and toxic levels of certain minerals such as calcium (Paul and Smith, 1966), sodium (Paul and Leiser, 1968) and magnesium (Paul and Thornhill, 1969) have also been investigated.

Rooting Medium

In view of the abundant water requirements of cuttings in high temperature and good light conditions, a very well-drained rooting medium should always be used.

The ideal medium is one which permits good drainage and does not pack down, but at the same time remains in close enough contact with the plant to permit the development of a compact root system. A mixture of three parts by volume of coarse (3 mm) sand and two parts granulated peat provides a very porous medium which is also retentive of moisture while remaining well aerated. A lighter medium may be employed, made up of 60 per cent perlite and 40 per cent granulated peat. This, and other light mixtures, promote the formation of a compact, well-developed root system.

Insertion and Spacing

The technique of inserting cuttings has greatly improved over the past few years, especially where benches are used. The holes in the rooting medium are punched with dibber boards, and cuttings are inserted without firming, because watering-in moves the medium into close contact with the base of the cuttings.

Correct spacing of cuttings in the rooting benches is important, especially during the winter months when light is limiting. A spacing of 50 by 45 mm should be allowed in the winter, 45 mm square in spring and autumn and from 35 by 30 to 35 mm square in the summer.

For pot plant cuttings the spacing is normally wider than for cut flower cuttings to restrict the rate of elongation in the benches to the minimum.

Roots appear within five to 10 days and plants are well rooted within 12 to 18 days depending on the season of the year.

Rooting Hormones

While chrysanthemum cuttings root well without the aid of root-promoting substances, there are several instances where the use of hormones is advantageous. In most varieties rooting hormones reduce the time of rooting by two or three days, an important point when large quantities of young plants are required in a short time. As some varieties require more time to root than others, the application of hormones to the former may be desirable to produce a uniform batch of cuttings ready for planting at the same time. The dipping in hormones in liquid form is not recommended owing to the rapid spread of disease organisms in a liquid medium. Likewise the standing of cuttings in water before insertion in the bench is a practice to be avoided.

Watering

Immediately after insertion thorough watering-in by rose is necessary to firm the cuttings. Thereafter, the amount of water needed daily during rooting depends to a large extent on the season of the year. Even during December, January and February at least one thorough watering, sufficient to bring the water content of the medium to its maximum capacity, and several light overhead mistings are necessary daily to keep the cuttings turgid.

For ease and efficiency of management, rooting should be considered as having three stages. During the first week, after watering-in, much moisture is usually required, both as a heavy spray or rose watering at least once a day, in conjunction with several light over-head mistings. Early in the second week, after the first roots have formed, less water is necessary and rose watering can generally be dispensed with. During the third period the rooted cuttings are allowed to dry off somewhat to facilitate lifting.

For spraying the cuttings in the rooting benches, hand-lances or mist spray lines are sometimes used. Automated systems of misting, either with time-switch or artificial 'leaf' or photo-electric cell control are more common and have the advantage of saving labour. Care must be taken however, to avoid excessive wetting with automatic systems, which may lead to soft plants and to the spread of fungal diseases. For this reason mist spray lines are sometimes manually controlled, one valve operating a number of spray lines depending on the water supply and the pressure.

Organization

Cuttings may be rooted in pots, boxes or benches, depending on the numbers required. On large nurseries benches are found to be the most economical of material and labour (Fig. 22). For ease of access centre benches should measure no more than about 1·5 m in width and side benches up to 1·3 m, with a depth of 13 to 15 cm.

Normally, planting in the year-round programme is planned for the same day of each week, and the propagator has to ensure that all varieties are well rooted for this date. This means that the exact length of time required for the rooting of each variety must be known.

Varieties have been classified into three groups for rooting; fast, medium and slow, and are allowed approximately 2, 2½ and 3 weeks respectively for rooting in the summer. In the winter the rooting time is increased to 2½, 3

Fig. 22   Large-scale rooting unit on a commercial propagator's nursery.

and $3\frac{1}{2}$ weeks, respectively.

When the rooted cuttings are lifted from the rooting benches special attention must be paid to grading. Normally, a surplus of up to 20 per cent is planned so that both the largest and the smallest cuttings can be discarded and a uniform batch of plants be sent out to the planting areas.

Growth Retardants

During recent years it has been occasionally found necessary to use growth retardants in the rooting bench to prevent undue stretch of pot plant varieties such as the Princess Anne family. One application of Alar (66 g/100 l)* has been used successfully when applied as soon as cuttings have regained turgidity following insertion.

Read and Hoysler (1969) found that dipping the unrooted cutting momentarily in certain concentrations of Alar (66 to 264 g/100 l) significantly increased both the weight and number of adventitious roots compared with control cuttings.

Disease Control

Unfortunately, conditions which favour good rooting also favour the growth and rapid spread of many of the pathogenic bacteria and fungi.

It is laborious to change the rooting medium between each batch of cuttings and even where this is done, sand and peat cannot be regarded as being completely sterile, especially after having been stored on a nursery for any length of time. An efficient, successful and very economic

* This is 66 g/100 l of active ingredient. Alar contains 85 per cent of its active ingredient N-dimethylamino-succinamic acid (daminozide), so the actual weight of Alar used is 78 g.

Fig. 23   A method of steam sterilizing, with header pipe injecting steam under the polythene sheet.

method of steam sterilizing the rooting medium *in situ* has been described by Post (1949a), from work by Dimock and Post (1944), and is used extensively (Fig. 23). A low-pressure steam pipe down the length of the house is tapped at intervals of about 15 m so that the bench may be steamed in sections. A thick rubber hose leads from the nearest tap on the steam pipe to the top of the bench to be steamed, where it is connected to a 10 cm canvas or nylon hose, or aluminium pipe, laid down the centre of the bench and which has been punctured on either side by holes of about 5 mm diameter at 23 cm intervals. A steam-proof 8 mil natural PVC sheet is then drawn over the whole bench and hose, and is held down, if necessary, by chains or other weights laid along the sides of the bench. If the sides of the bench are of regular shape, it is usual when the steam is turned on, for a water seal against escaping steam to form between the cover and the bench sides, and weighting of the sheet is not then necessary.

This method of steaming leads to a very uniform rise in temperature throughout the medium because the pressure initially built up under the PVC cover distributes the steam and forces it uniformly through the rooting medium in the bench. The temperature should be raised to 68° in all parts of the bench and then the steaming sheet left in position for at least 20 minutes after the temperature is reached to kill disease-producing organisms. The required temperature is normally reached very rapidly, the time taken varying with the pressure and volume of the steam, the area of the bench and the initial temperature and water content of the medium.

Rooted Cuttings

The treatment of the young plants after rooting depends on the cultivation programme to be followed, but in all cases removal of the rooted cuttings from the rooting benches within three weeks of insertion is desirable. This is because of the possible lack of nutrients in the medium and the need for spacing. Cold storage of rooted cuttings should normally be avoided, because this may cause root damage and a slow deterioration in quality. However, unrooted cuttings may be safely stored for a limited period.

COLD STORAGE

An invaluable aid to the propagator is the cold store. Unrooted chrysanthemum cuttings from stock plants may be stored with no ill effects at a constant temperature of $-0.6°$ to $0.6°$ provided they are cooled quickly after taking and are placed in sealed containers to prevent the loss of water vapour. The normal safe period of cold storage varies from three to eight weeks depending on variety and time of year. Cuttings grown in good light and high temperatures are best suited for cold storage, since they contain a high percentage of carbohydrates. Certain varieties, such as Hurricane, do not store well, especially during winter months, and temperatures up to $3.3°$ have to be used.

Lockhart and Swain (1966) stored stool cuttings from November to May at $-2.2°$ to $1.1°$, which subsequently produced normal flowering plants in the field. It was found, however, that temperatures below $-2.2°$ injured the stool cuttings.

The great value of the cold store is that it enables cuttings of any particular variety to be gathered and stored over a period of one or two weeks and then rooted on the same date to produce a uniform batch of plants.

PART THREE

Growing the Crop

7 General Cultivation

SOIL, PREPARATION AND PLANTING

Year-round cut flower chrysanthemums are grown in either ground beds or raised benches. All general cultural techniques currently in use are described in this chapter, and possibilities for the future are discussed.

Soil

The ideal soil for chrysanthemum growing is probably a well-drained sandy loam of good texture and aeration, with a neutral or slightly acid pH (6·5 to 7·0) and a high organic content. Such a soil, moulded in the hand, will have neither the silky feeling of silt nor the sticky feeling of clay, while the sand grains will give a feeling of grittiness.

Heavy clay soils, which are moisture-retentive, are difficult to work and the surface layers are slow to warm up, especially in the early season. They may be lightened and made more workable by the addition of grit and peat to the top few centimetres.

Very light sandy soils are not recommended, owing to their poor moisture-holding properties. Such soils, if used, need a heavy dressing of well-rotted manure to act as a reservoir for water and fertilizers during the growing season. If there is much straw in the manure, or if much peat is used, additional fertilizers, particularly nitrogen, will most probably be required.

For raised beds or benches free drainage through the soil and from the base of the bed is of great importance. Benches are usually between 1·1 and 1·5 m wide, constructed of wood board, asbestos cement or concrete, and contain between 10 and 15 cm depth of soil.

Loamy soils used for bench work are lightened by the addition of up to 2 parts coarse sand, 1 part peat and 1 part well rotted manure to 3 parts of soil. The composition for best results will vary with the soil type and with the method of watering to be adopted. Because very frequent watering during the growing season will be needed, the main consideration is a soil that will remain open and well aerated. If trickle type irrigation is used, very little sand need be added to fibrous loam, while for hose watering comparatively large quantities of sand or grit will be needed to enable the soil to withstand the impact of the water on the surface without panning. In the USA vermiculite is sometimes added to bench soil.

Following the initial application of manure, peat is preferred as a source of humus. Dressings of up to 50 tonnes/ha are added to the beds before planting each crop to maintain the high level of humus needed for this intensive method of growing. Thorough mixing with the surface layers of the soil is essential, as excessive layers of unmixed peat will depress growth.

As a further addition to the humus content, it is the practice of some growers to chop up and incorporate the haulm of the previous crop prior to steam sterilization.

Preparation

Prior to starting a year-round cut flower programme the soil should be sterilized with methyl bromide* or other chemical means, or pasteurized by steaming. With the surface method of steaming soils or where 75 mm land drains are available for steam injection, beds may be quickly sterilized. Land drains are usually laid permanently in position in continuous lines 60 cm apart on the base of the raised bed or bench, or at a depth of 30 cm (measured from the soil surface to the upper side of the pipe) in ground beds, and can thus be used for steaming by coupling up to a steam pipe.

Frequent steaming is the rule in the produc-

---

* The use of methyl bromide as a soil fumigant has been discussed fully by Maw and Kempton (1973).

Fig. 24   With the surface method of steaming, vacant beds may be safely steamed next to cropped beds.

tion of cuttings and stock plants, and for year-round growing the beds are often steamed between each crop. However, results at Efford EHS, (Anon., 1976) suggest that three successive flower crops may be grown without steam sterilization with very little reduction in yield compared with sterilization between each crop.

With the surface method of steaming, it is found that vacant beds may be safely steamed next to cropped beds (Fig. 24). With adequate sterilization or pasteurization, as many roots as possible should be left in the soil when a flowering crop is removed, because a valuable addition to the fibre in the soil may be made in this way.

A disadvantage of the surface method of sterilizing ground beds, where steam is blown in under a weighted PVC sheet, is that unless the air in the soil can escape downwards (as in a raised bed), the depth to which the steam can penetrate is very limited. A further disadvantage

is that whereas the soil 15 cm down is barely heated for the correct time, the surface is subjected to prolonged heating.

This overheating could have unwanted effects on the soil in releasing chemicals, such as manganese, to toxic levels or in disrupting the nitrogen cycle. Steaming for 20 minutes after a temperature of 82° has been reached at 80 mm rather than 15 cm might counteract this problem (Anon., 1976).

Following steaming, the concentration of fertilizer and other residues in ground beds can be effectively reduced by leaching with substantial amounts of water. This soaking is best carried out in stages by applying 25 to 50 mm of water at a time from mist spray lines, followed at daily intervals, if time permits, by further applications up to a total of 20 to 30 cm of water. One leaching a year is usually found to be sufficient, but some growers 'flood' for each crop. To facilitate the planting of the subsequent crop, the water may be applied in summer on well-drained soils just prior to harvesting the preceding crop. The leaching of residues out of benches may present a problem unless open composts are used, since capillary conduction through the soil is intercepted by the base of concrete or other material. The use of liquid fertilizers represents some safeguard against the accumulation of salts in the soil. Where the soil structure in benches becomes badly impaired under the impact of hose watering and intensive cropping, the practice is to replace this soil from outside land. Ideally the top 15 cm of grassland should be brought in and sterilized in the benches. The old soil is taken outside, spread and grassed down for further use. Land intended to supply greenhouse soils should always carry a cover crop to produce fibre in the soil.

Where the soil is considered unsuitable for chrysanthemum growing a method of cultivation reported by Allen (1965) could be considered. It was found that rooted cuttings of eight chrysanthemum varieties made uniform and vigorous growth on a layer of compost 40 to 75 mm deep placed on beds composed of straw bales or wads, isolated by polythene from the soil. The chrysanthemums, planted on two different dates and at two different spacings, established themselves quickly irrespective of the thickness of the compost. Liquid feeds containing potash and a high level of nitrogen were applied during the vegetative period.

The use of loamless media in sunken polythene beds has been investigated (Wadsworth and Butters, 1972; Butters and Wadsworth, 1974). Using various proportions of peat and sand good crops were obtained throughout the year, although minor problems of phosphorous deficiency and boron toxicity had to be overcome by variations in the compost formulation. In these media it was found that the nitrogen and water requirements were closely correlated and potassium requirement was highest during the winter months.

Planting

A special feature of year-round growing is the use of cuttings at all times of the season, taken directly from the rooting benches to the cropping area and planted the day after the soil is steam sterilized. In this way the plants become established before they can be seriously affected by the build-up of ammonia which sometimes occurs following steaming.

There should be little or no check to growth from the time the cuttings are taken until flowering. Consequently it is extremely important to plant the cuttings immediately they are rooted. If during very hot weather the cuttings are slightly dry at the roots, it is advisable to place them upright in trays of water for a few hours before planting.

Before planting, care should be taken to grade the cuttings. The largest plants should be planted at the north end of the beds and the smallest plants at the south end, where they will have the benefit of extra light. This is particularly important for winter crops.

The importance of planting all the larger plants together and all the smaller plants together, even if the difference in vigour is slight, cannot be emphasized too strongly. If this is done a crop of uniform quality can be expected. Small plants surrounded by larger plants will always remain smaller and weaker than the remainder and will produce an indifferent crop. This cannot be tolerated in a crop where high-quality production is necessary.

The benefits resulting from grading cuttings will be lost if the plants are inserted at varying depths. Rapid growth during the first four weeks is essential, and to ensure this the roots must not be buried more than 12 mm below soil level. The plants should not be firmed. Immediate ball-watering to settle the soil closely around the roots, followed by frequent overhead damping to prevent wilting allows the plants to grow away rapidly.

Before planting, a marker rake made to the same width as the cropping benches or ground beds, and with tines spaced the same distance apart as the rows, is drawn down the length of the bed, a line being used as a guide for the first row. The marker rake thus indicates the rows and the position of the plant in the rows is marked by another rake. Where, as is often the case, the planting distances are square, the same marker rake is drawn across the bed. Having thus indicated each planting station, the planting hole is made by inserting the middle and forefinger to the appropriate depth and pulling the soil forward until the hole is just large enough to accommodate the plant roots. The plant is then dropped into its position. As the fingers are withdrawn the soil drops back into place, unless the soil is too wet. With experienced planters, the marker rake is used across the bed only. The number of plants and their distance apart across the bed are known, and this distance is estimated by eye as the plants go in.

Sometimes, when the wire or string netting support exactly corresponds with plant spacing, the netting is lowered on to the soil surface and each square is planted.

Shallow planting is essential because the young roots need the maximum amount of oxygen in the early stages. After the bed is planted, it is thoroughly watered with a fine rose or sprinkler, and this has the effect of settling the soil so that no other firming is necessary or desirable. Planting into wet soil, which cannot be recommended under any circumstances, would be quite impossible with the method described.

The fact that the planted bed may not immediately present an appearance of mathematical precision need be no cause for concern, for the young shoots will soon space themselves in accordance with the available light and any slight irregularities will quickly disappear.

Planting distances for single stem production, which is normal with year-round crops, vary according to variety and time of planting.

In southern England distances of 12·5 by 10·0 or 12·5 cm in summer and 15·0 by 12·5 or 15·0 cm in winter have given good results.

WATERING

Watering is an important aspect of husbandry with any crop. With year-round chrysanthemums it is essential that water be properly applied in the correct quantity according to the time of year.

Water Requirement

To enable the water need of crops to be readily assessed, the average potential transpiration figures for all areas of Britain, taken from Meteorological Office figures, have been published by the Ministry of Agriculture (1965). The published figures of potential transpiration are based on the average weather conditions in the areas concerned, but since sunshine plays the dominant role, a correction factor depending on the prevailing sunshine hours is used to give a closer assessment of actual water need. The current figures of the actual transpiration losses calculated monthly by the Meteorological Office for most areas of Britain are available to growers from the Agricultural Development and Advisory Service.

Searle (1973) has shown how, by the use of tables prepared for all areas of Britain, the amount of water needed by plants for maximum growth can be assessed throughout the growing season. The calculations have been based on the broad principles of the Penman transpiration formula (Penman, 1949).

Apart from the regular watering of established crops, large quantities of water may be required between crops to leach excess salts which might otherwise adversely affect uptake of water and nutrient by osmosis in plants of subsequent crops.

Osmotic pressure directly influences the rate of entry of water into the roots and thus the rate of growth of the plant. In extreme cases, the resultant hard, grey plants may stop growing, their growth depending apparently on their ability to build up their own osmotic pressure as a counter-measure.

The best results with leaching are achieved with slow periodical applications of water in the form of mist spray. Applications of up to 23 to 30 cm of water given in extreme cases by this means are to be found effective, especially where the water is applied in stages over several days to allow for the salts to go into solution before the next application. Coarse textured soils permit a greater proportional leaching of salts than fine textured soils.

In some locations the water itself is found to contain harmful salts, and its leaching effect is thereby reduced, while in other areas the water steadily raises the pH of the soil. Soil analysis and the measurement of pC (or cF)* values by soil conductivity meter will indicate the salt status of the soil and are necessary precautions. The use of liquid fertilizer (page 76) is found to reduce the danger of a high salt concentration for fertilizer residues, and provides a safer level for balanced growth.

The maintenance of adequate moisture in the soil will reduce the effect of the osmotic pressure of the salt solution, and in some greenhouse soils this fact alone may account for the increased growth observed with more frequent watering.

Water Application

The rooted cutting should be planted into soil which is fairly moist and has a moisture level equivalent to that of a potting compost.

During the establishment period frequent and even misting is necessary to keep the plants turgid until the roots become established and begin to function properly. It is most important to get the plants off to a good start, as this will reduce the number of long days needed to attain the required stem length. A stagnant atmosphere should be avoided, as this may encourage disease.

Foliage and flower quality can only be maintained by frequent watering during periods of maximum growth. Spomer and Langhans (1975) have shown that growth in chrysanthemums grown in benches of peat, sand and leaf mould increased as the pore saturation was increased to 90 per cent. The degree of pore saturation for optimum growth depends, of course, on the nature of the growing medium and in greenhouse soils a lower figure than this would be necessary for optimum growth.

There is one school of thought which advises severe restriction of water, commencing prior to the start of short days and continuing for three to four weeks afterwards, to best pro-

* cF is the conductivity factor of the soil solution and pC is the negative logarithm of the specific conductivity of the soil solution.

mote the change from vegetative to reproductive growth. This is thought to be especially important during the winter because it prevents the plants becoming excessively vegetative. However, water application should be adjusted carefully according to weather and time of year so that the plants receive sufficient for each stage of growth. Only if the plants are over-watered, or under-watered, will the rate of budding be affected. If plants are kept too dry leaf area will be reduced resulting in a lower rate of photosynthesis and ultimately poor quality flowers.

IRRIGATION SYSTEMS

A number of methods of irrigation have been devised to replace the hand-held hose, the use of which leads to soil capping and poor aeration. These include overhead mist spray lines (Fig. 25) and other types of sprinkler irrigators, and self-travelling sprayers. The disadvantage of these methods is that both foilage and flowers are wetted on each application. With a tall, closely planted crop watering tends to become uneven and the plants remain wet for long periods after each irrigation. Work among the wet plants is difficult and during much of the season there is a serious danger of spreading fungal diseases.

With sub-irrigation methods, the disadvantage of wetting the foliage is avoided, but other difficulties arise. Costly watertight beds have to be built, and with the constant-level method, anaerobic conditions and high salt concentrations tend to develop in the soil or other growing media used. Disastrous results have been known to occur.

With trickle irrigation and similar systems it is economically possible to maintain adequate moisture with good aeration in the soil under the normal conditions of commercial production. This is especially true for pot plants in any situation at all times of the year.

With the trickle irrigation method the water is applied through small drip nozzles buttoned into rubber tubes (extension lines) at a spacing usually double that of the plant rows.

The extension lines are in turn attached

Fig. 25   Irrigation by overhead mist spray lines.

through a special nozzle to a main hose running the length of the bed and leading from the water main by way of a filter and feeding diluter. Provision can be made for more water to be applied at the edges of the bed, and the hole size of the nozzles in the main hose is adjusted to counteract the loss in pressure along the hose. The application rate can be as high as 1·1 to 1·7 l per drip nozzle per hour, the equivalent of about 20 l/m².

A feature of this and similar systems is that the water oozes out at ground level and soaks into the soil as fast as it appears, leaving the crumb structure and aeration of the soil substantially unimpaired. This is of the greatest practical importance, particularly on soils which tend to 'cap' after watering by hose.

Applied in small quantities the water issuing from the nozzles spreads downwards rather than along the surface, re-moistening the soil under growing plants to a depth of 45 to 60 cm or more as required. Below the surface the moisture

can spread horizontally to a considerable extent giving a cone effect. The pattern of this spread will depend on the texture of the soil, its compaction, its initial moisture content and on the quantity of water and the rate of application.

With trickle irrigation and similar systems soil characteristics play a most important part because the water is applied at one point and depends primarily on capillary conduction for its spread under the surface.

Other similar semi-automated methods of low-level irrigation for ground watering include the drip-watering system, the water being delivered from small tubes without nozzles, and the lay-flat punctured plastic hose, which is laid longitudinally down the bed. The latter method is now commonly used because of its low cost.

With other systems ground pipes are used, either in the beds, fitted at intervals with diffuser-type nozzles dispersing the water over the soil surface at a relatively high rate, or along

73

the sides of the beds, the pipes being drilled with small diameter holes from which the water issues in a fine jet towards the centre of the bed.

Because trickle irrigation (small bore) systems are normally used for applying liquid fertilizer in the irrigation water, the whole installation must be flushed through periodically with plain water to prevent blocking by crystallizing fertilizers (especially phosphate) and bacteria. Some manufacturers recommend rinsing out with a weak solution of nitric acid if blocking becomes a problem.

All the irrigation systems described can be operated either semi-automatically, that is turned on and off by hand, or completely automatically. Complete automation is achieved by a control panel operating solenoid valves in the water mains. Time clocks are set to apply the water for predetermined periods at any time during the day and night. Alternatively, the solenoid valves may be operated by a soil moisture tensiometer, an electronic 'leaf', evaporimeter, a pot plant on a weighing machine or similar device measuring actual water loss from the soil or from the plants, or by direct measurement of incoming radiation.

There is a risk with all the drip-watering systems, when used for applying the fertilizer, of a differential movement of potash and nitrates in the soil. Potash accumulates immediately beneath the watering points, while nitrate tends to accumulate between them. This is unlikely to present a problem with fast-growing chrysanthemums, provided the beds are well cultivated and flooded between crops.

SPREAD AND PENETRATION

Water will spread laterally more quickly into areas of moist soil than into dry soil, the re-entry of water by capillarity into dry soil being extremely slow. Where adequate lateral spread is desired, it is important to ensure that capillarity in the soil is not impaired or lost by drying out. In well-drained, very dry soil, gravity will claim the greater part of the water applied and lateral spread will be limited. The amount of the spread with the drip systems of irrigation will depend also on the type of soil, being greatest in compacted fine textured soils. On some soils a measure of compaction is often needed before these systems are used. Spread is also greatly affected by the nature of the subsoil. A heavy clay subsoil has the effect of spreading the water widely. This assists distribution in the top soil into which a proportion of the water rises by capillarity. With a gravel subsoil drainage is more rapid.

The dry soil surface round the plants, with adequate water at the root, is one of the main features of drip irrigation systems. The fact that a dry area of soil usually bounds each wetted zone, and that part of the soil surface is dry, with the structure unimpaired, appears to lead to good aeration in the soil during the whole life of the crop. A dry soil surface tends to lead to a drier atmosphere and thus humidity in the air above is reduced. This, and the fact that no water flows over the soil surface, can have a beneficial effect in controlling fungal diseases.

QUANTITIES REQUIRED

In greenhouses the maximum demand of a strongly growing crop, where the leaves effectively cover the whole of the soil area will be about 38 mm per week (about 25 l/m²) during periods of very sunny windy weather with dry air. The *average* water need is a little over 25 mm of water per week in average summer weather in southern England. With hose watering this is usually given twice a week in applications of a little more than 12 mm each time. Sheard (1955) gives the following figures as a general guide to the daily water needs of a greenhouse crop where trickle irrigation is used:

Very dull	1100 l/ha
Dull	1850 l/ha
Moderately bright	4600 l/ha
Bright	6400 l/ha
Very bright	9200 l/ha

These quantities are intended to apply to the season of active vegetative growth, when young leaves are continually being formed. As soon as the plant forms buds no further leaves are formed, and a steady reduction in water need from the ageing leaves on the plant must be expected. This reduction will normally more than offset the transpiration demand of the bud and flower, so that somewhat less water than the average amounts will be needed. Where measuring devices are not available as a guide, a reduction of about 10 to 20 per cent on the figures above could safely be made under average conditions as the buds develop.

FEEDING

There are three distinct methods of feeding year-round chrysanthemums: base fertilization, liquid feeding and foliar feeding. Each technique has, in certain circumstances, advantages over the others and must be fully understood by the grower. A carefully integrated feeding programme will produce the most successful crops. The nutrition of chrysanthemums has been summarized by Adams (1976).

Base Fertilization

Soil for any method of production, whether in ground beds or in benches, should be tested periodically by a recognized method for its fertilizer status, and any deficiencies made good before planting. Base fertilizers should never be added to soils of unknown nutrient content. Testing for fertilizer elements is especially important where mineral deficiency symptoms, such as interveinal chlorosis and tinting of the leaves, have been seen. Post (1949a), using the Spurway (1933) soil testing method, recommends a level of 10 to 50 parts per million (ppm) nitrate, 5 to 10 ppm phosphate and 30 to 50 ppm potash for chrysanthemum production. He gives the optimum pH as 6·0, but chrysanthemums can be successfully grown in soils with a reaction considerably higher than this. The pH reading, which indicates the amount of active lime present, is determined by a comparatively simple but valuable test that may be carried out by any chrysanthemum grower.

Base fertilization is useful, not only for restoring a nutrient imbalance but also at certain times of the year when nutrition by other means is difficult. During the winter months, when growth is slow and uneven, and when water requirements are small, neither liquid nor foliar feeding is practical. However, the roots of plants are continuously in contact with the soil salt solution derived from base fertilization, and uniform and continuous nutrition results.

It must be remembered that fertilizers supplied as base dressings will be available throughout the life of the crop. Any nutrient requirement for any particular phase of growth can only be provided by adding fertilizers in the form of liquid or foliar feed to a base of nutrient already in the soil. Another disadvantage of base fertilization is that great skill is required to spread the fertilizers evenly.

Phosphate is best applied in the base dressing before the crop is planted to avoid the problems of application through trickle irrigation systems.

If all the major elements of nutrition are in short supply then a general well-balanced fertilizer such as 10 per cent nitrogen (as N), 10 per cent phosphorus (as water-soluble P_2O_5) and 20 per cent potassium (as K_2O) will suffice.

Where base dressings are normally used, and there are some growers who rely on them entirely, care must be taken that fertilizer residues do not build up from one crop to the next. In some cases, where nitrogen in a relatively long lasting form, such as urea formaldehyde, has been used over a long period, serious scorching of roots has occurred due to ammonia toxicity following steam sterilization. It may be preferable to use fertilizers which are both rapidly available and more readily removed by leaching following the regular watering of the crop. Thus, ammonium nitrate is safer to use as a base dressing compared with urea formaldehyde or hoof and horn.

Soluble salts are estimated by a pC meter. The test is based on the electrical resistance of the soil to the flow of an electrical current. Values of less than 3·0 on the pC scale (Whittles and Schofield-Palmer, 1951) reflect a rather dangerous level of soluble salts in the soil.

In soils with pH values lower than 6·0, correction of acidity is best achieved by the addition of calcium carbonate as a base dressing.

Liquid Feeding

Liquid feeding is the application to the growing

crop of plant nutrients in solution and is generally preferred to dry feeding.

The plant takes up the nutrients it needs from the soil solution. Before the nutrients can become available to enter the soil solution they have to be broken down by the complex chemical and biological processes continually taking place in the soil. The use of fully soluble, simple fertilizer mixtures by-passes these break-down processes. As a result there is a rapid growth response after application and thus the nutrient materials are more efficiently used than when applied in a dry form. The results of liquid feeding are normally seen within 48 hours, so that plant needs may be closely assessed and the growth controlled and the amount of fertilizer lost in drainage reduced to a minimum.

The use of liquid fertilizers has other advantages when compared with the application of dry fertilizers. The labour of applying the fertilizer is greatly reduced, because this may conveniently be applied in the irrigation water, and the risk of damage to the plant stems and foliage is avoided. Indiscriminate applications of dry fertilizer over the years have been found to lead to an immobilization of fertilizer in the soil in non-available forms, and to a build-up of soluble salts. A high level of salts in the soil, usually in the form of sulphates, depresses the growth and quality of the plant. Chrysanthemums appear to be particularly susceptible to this trouble.

Liquid fertilizer may be used with advantage on most soils because the solution can be made up from materials free from sulphates or other undesirable ingredients. This method of feeding is applicable to any system of watering because diluters and pick-up devices can be fitted to the main hoses.

Liquid fertilizers can conveniently be bought in a wide range of mixes, either as a liquid or in solid form ready for mixing, and are suitable for all soil conditions and crop programmes. Generally the proprietary brands contain trace elements, and a number contain a colourant which, in use, acts as a visual guide to the strength of fertilizer being applied.

Where very large quantities of fertilizer are used, feeds can be made up from dry fertilizers by the grower. The fertilizers most commonly used to supply nitrogen and potash are ammonium nitrate and potassium nitrate. Phosphate is rarely used as a liquid feed, with irrigation water high in calcium, as the phosphate precipitates the calcium which may block the irrigation equipment.

MIXING

A method of mixing used by some growers is to buy pure potassium nitrate (not Chilean nitrate of potash, which is intended for use as a dry fertilizer) and to make this up into a near saturated solution of 200 g of fertilizer in 1 l of water. The container used for mixing is best made of wood, plastic or glass, a large cask or water-butt being very suitable. Metal vessels should not be used. When mixed, the solution is kept in a frost-free place, preferably at a temperature near 16°, to prevent crystallization.

To the basic potassium nitrate solution, which has a nitrogen to potash ratio of about 1 to 3·5, is added a proprietary concentrate high in nitrogen and containing the trace elements and a colourant. With this concentrate, a liquid feed with correctly balanced proportions of nitrogen and potash may be prepared for all seasons of the year and for any stage of growth.

Alternatively, by making up a saturated solution of ammonium nitrate and mixing this with the potassium nitrate, high potash or high nitrogen feeds may be made up by the grower entirely from dry fertilizer.

Great care is needed with the mixing of fertilizers to ensure that the correct ingredients are used in the right proportions and are thoroughly dissolved.

Where an overhead tank is used for watering, the appropriate amount of fertilizer solution can be added to the water in the tank, mixed well and applied with the irrigation water.

For other irrigation systems a number of satisfactory diluters and proportioners are available for applying the feed. Venturi pick-up and charge type diluters are used with some installations, but where a high degree of precision is required, the injector type proportioners are used. These can give accurate dilution with any type of irrigation system, including hose watering.

The most direct method of describing a liquid feeding treatment is in terms of the concentration of the nutrients in the diluted feed as applied to the soil. The concentration is expressed in ppm of N and K_2O and, where necessary, of P_2O_5. A knowledge of the methods of calculation involved makes it possible not only to compare different recommendations on one common basis but also to vary the composition of feeds at will (Appendix 7).

To get the full benefit of liquid feeding it is essential that the correct quantity of water be applied at each watering. Saturating the soil to the point of waterlogging has the effect of filling all the pore spaces with water, thus displacing the air. If this condition persists plant roots will be suffocated through lack of oxygen for respiration. If too little is applied, the water and the fertilizer solution may not reach the plant roots. In this case evaporation from the soil surface, especially in the summer, may lead to a concentration of fertilizer near the soil surface, which may become available later when no longer needed.

Foliar Feeding

Foliar feeding describes the introduction of nutrient direct into the plant through the leaves. The advantages of foliar feeding have been described by Machin (1975). It can be used, in some circumstances, when neither base fertilization nor liquid feeding can be successful because the physical nature of the soil or compost is not conducive to adequate root growth. In these cases, or where, for instance, a high pH will prevent iron uptake, foliar feeding is the only method which is likely to be successful. Minerals in chelated form are readily taken into the plant through the leaves and reach the site of usage rapidly. Compared with other methods of feeding, foliar application is more efficient because a much higher percentage of the feed is taken in by the plant. However, foliar feeding does nothing to change any nutrient deficiency

or physical problem occurring in the soil. Until these are corrected, foliar feeding will need to be continued for as long as the plants require nutrition.

Elements of Nutrition

The role of the elements of nutrition and deficiency symptoms in chrysanthemums and appropriate fertilizers were described in some detail by Machin (1976) (see Appendix 3).

Six chemical elements are required by plants in relatively large amounts and are known as macroelements. These are nitrogen, phosphorus, potassium, calcium, magnesium and sulphur. Other chemicals are required in much smaller quantities and are known as micronutrients or, more commonly, trace elements. These include iron, manganese, boron, copper and zinc.

NITROGEN

Nitrogen occurs in plants as part of chlorophyll and is a major constituent of amino acids, alkaloids, proteins and protoplasm. Since these materials are the very basis of plant life, any deficiency of nitrogen will have a profound effect on growth. Lack of nitrogen causes a reduction in the chlorophyll content of the leaf, giving the leaves a yellowish-green colour instead of a darker bluish-green. Since protein and protoplasm are essential for new cell formation, nitrogen deficiency stunts growth considerably. It follows also that nitrogen starvation can result in flowering delay as a direct result of the slowing down of cell formation.

Excessive amounts of nitrogen can also result in flowering delay and poor growth for two reasons. Very high nitrogen may cause vegetative growth to be excessive and the plant finds it difficult to form flower buds at the correct time. Toxic levels of nitrogen in the soil may damage the tender root hairs, leading to stunted growth because the damaged roots cannot take in sufficient plant food.

Nitrogen is often adequate for the early stages of growth, but because of incorrect base dressings or liquid feeding, supplies may become low during the life of the plant. When this occurs, it is difficult to detect the beginning of the deficiency symptoms and they may not be observed until too late for remedial action. The following notes describe the symptoms of slight or moderate nitrogen deficiency. (See also Appendix 3.)

Leaf size and rate of growth are reduced as nitrogen becomes deficient. The intensity of the green colour decreases and leaves become yellowish. In young leaves the margins may be slightly greener than the remainder. Upper leaves tend to remain greener than lower leaves. Petioles are stiff, making the leaves stand out at right angles to the stem. Flowering is only delayed with severe deficiency and the flower colour is usually unimpaired, although the size is reduced. In cases of very severe deficiency, numerous reddish necrotic spots, about 1 mm in diameter, develop near the margins of leaves, beginning with the lower leaves and working up. These are most discernible on the undersides of the leaves. Subsequently, some of the lower leaves become completely necrotic, starting with the margins. Brownish-red lesions develop on the stem, particularly near leaf axils. Roots are longer with less branching. Symptoms are very difficult to distinguish from sulphur deficiency, but the latter is not very common. The height of the plant is not reduced except in severe deficiency.

There is evidence (Crater *et al.*, 1973; Tsujita *et al.*, 1974) that different sources of nitrogen have different effects on the plant. Ammonium sulphate or calcium nitrate appear to accelerate flowering response compared with other nitrogen fertilizers, while ammonium nitrate produces plants with stronger stems.

Application Nitrogen can be applied either as ammonium salts or nitrate salts, both of which can be used by the plants relatively quickly. Slower release forms of nitrogen are available as hoof and horn, and urea formaldehyde.

Nitrate salts are the most rapidly available to plant roots because they can be absorbed directly and the results from feeding can be seen in a few days.

Fertilizers containing nitrogen are listed below, together with the percentage nitrogen content weight for weight.

Inorganic	Percentage N (W/W)
Ammonium nitrate	35·0
Ammonium sulphate	21·0
Nitro chalk (ammonium nitrate and calcium carbonate)	21·0
Sodium nitrate	16·0
Calcium nitrate	15·5
Chilean nitrate of potash	15·0
Potassium nitrate (99 per cent)	13·8
Potassium nitrate (97 per cent)	13·0
Mono-ammonium phosphate	12·0
Magnesium ammonium phosphate	6·5

Organic	
Urea	46·5
Urea formaldehyde	38·0
Dried blood	11·0–13·0
Hoof and horn meal	11·0–13·0
Meat and bonemeal	6·0
Bonemeal	4·0

PHOSPHORUS

Phosphorus (P) in plants is closely associated with the most rapidly growing tissues. These are in the meristem region at the apex of the shoots, in the root hairs and around the cambium layer in the active xylem and phloem cells of the conducting tissue in the stems.

It has the capacity to move around freely in the plant, more so than most of the other fertilizer elements. Much of the phosphorous taken in through the roots remains in a water-soluble form and moves from mature leaves to the younger tissues as necessary.

Phosphorus also forms an important part of nucleic acids, chemicals forming an integral part of all plant cells.

A reduction in the size of new leaves is one of the first symptoms of phosphorus deficiency although the leaf colour remains good. As the deficiency progresses, growth of the main stem slows and finally stops. Foliage takes on a dull, greyish hue although it is still relatively dark green. Yellowing, marginal necrosis and, finally, complete necrosis of older leaves develops at such a rate that there are only a few transitional leaves between those completely green and completely dead. Flower colour is normal and flowering is only slightly delayed, except by severe deficiency.

Application The phosphate fertilizers are usually qualitatively expressed in terms of the amount of soluble phosphoric acid present (P_2O_5). The various formulations are either quick-acting as with superphosphate, or release phosphate slowly over a long period as with bonemeal. The coarser grades of bonemeal or bone flour release P_2O_5 over a longer period than fine grades.

Inorganic	*Percentage* P_2O_5 (W/W)
Mono-ammonium phosphate	60·0
Triple superphosphate	47·0
Magnesium ammonium phosphate	45·0
Superphosphate (powder)	18·5

Organic	
Bone flour	60·0–70·0
Bonemeal	23·0–50·0
Meat and bonemeal	20·0
Basic slag	7·0–16·0

POTASSIUM

Potassium is most prevalent in the rapidly growing tissues of the plant, especially the root tips, the apical buds and the cambium layer. It is necessary for carbohydrate formation and starch in particular. It is closely associated with nitrogen assimilation and is probably necessary for the formation of nucleoproteins. Potassium also acts as a catalyst for cell division. It is therefore an essential plant nutrient and its association with the function of nitrogen is especially important.

A severe reduction in leaf size is one of the first symptoms of potassium deficiency. Height, however, is only slightly reduced although stems become weak and spindly. A marginal chlorosis develops on the lower leaves and is quickly followed by marginal necrosis and the whole leaf soon dies. This sequence progresses up the plant. In severe deficiency only a few leaves exist in the transition zone between a completely necrotic and a green leaf. There is a clear tendency for leaves to curl under when the deficiency is moderate. Under these conditions, a few lower leaves become necrotic while interveinal chlorosis and some marginal necrosis occurs on a number of the middle leaves. Flowering is only slightly delayed and flower colour is normal.

Application Potassium fertilizers are generally quick-acting and are expressed according to the percentage of oxide (K_2O) contained.

Inorganic	*Percentage* K_2O (W/W)
Muriate of potash	60·0
Potassium sulphate	50·0
Potassium nitrate (99 per cent)	46·4
Potassium nitrate (97 per cent)	43·7
Chilean nitrate of potash	10·0
Magnesium potassium phosphate	7·0

CALCIUM

Calcium is necessary for the formation of cell walls in plants and therefore a constant supply is essential for normal growth. Because calcium cannot be translocated from one part of the plant to another, as can phosphorous, any breakdown in the continuity of supply will have immediate effect. Thus, slight deficiency of calcium rapidly results in a complete cessation of top growth and death of the roots, which become dark and adhere together. Plants are unable to maintain turgor. The apex of the shoot soon dies and large areas of the upper leaves, which are small, become necrotic, drying to a bluish-brown shade. Middle leaves remain healthy for some time but gradually develop a spotty chlorosis.

At less severely deficient levels of calcium, plant growth is retarded somewhat, but the plants appear quite normal except that the leaves tend to be blunt and short. When flowering occurs, large areas of upper leaves, usually near the petiole, and either in the interior or near the margins of leaves, suddenly become necrotic and turn dark brown to black. Portions of the stem near the base of the flower also die. Time of flowering and colour are normal but the flowers are very subject to heat injury.

Application Calcium is best applied as a basic dressing of ground limestone or chalk (calcium carbonate).

MAGNESIUM

Magnesium is a constituent of chlorophyll and insufficient quantities cause a chlorosis of the leaves (Plate 22). Most soils contain sufficient magnesium but with some soils and in soilless composts it is necessary to add a magnesium salt in the base dressing.

At very low levels of magnesium, plants rapidly develop a severe chlorosis in the upper leaves, the veins remaining green. Initially, the interveinal area is light yellow, but in time becomes nearly white. Root growth is reduced but roots appear healthy. When magnesium deficiency develops more gradually, margins of lower leaves become chlorotic; this condition soon extends over the entire leaf, leaving the veins green. The symptoms rapidly move up the plant but are less severe in upper leaves. Leaves show a well-defined tendency to curl under. In time, severely deficient leaves tend to develop reddish pigmentation on margins. Flowering dates and flower colour are normal, but size is small with severe deficiency. Where plants become deficient in magnesium at flowering time, symptoms appear on upper or middle leaves, rather than on lower leaves.

Application Magnesium is best applied as Epsom salt (17 per cent MgO) as a base dressing or foliar spray.

SULPHUR

Sulphur is an essential constituent of many plant proteins. The deficiency symptoms are similar to those of nitrogen starvation and need no further description.

Application Any sulphate salt used for the addition of other nutrients (ammonium sulphate or potassium sulphate) can be used to correct sulphur deficiency.

IRON

Iron is not a constituent of chlorophyll, but is necessary for its formation. Thus, a shortage of iron causes a chlorosis very similar to magnesium deficiency.

The symptoms develop very rapidly, producing typical interveinal chlorosis on the younger leaves. Growth proceeds slowly with the chlorosis becoming more severe until the entire leaf looks bleached. Large irregular necrotic areas subsequently develop on the nearly white leaves. Bud formation occurs normally, but the plants will probably not flower.

Application Iron is best applied to the plants in the chelated form as a foliar spray because other forms of iron may be bound in the soil and remain unavailable to the plants.

MANGANESE

Manganese is a constituent of some enzymes which govern the production of proteins in plants.

Deficiency symptoms develop rather quickly when manganese is deficient. Leaves originally on the cuttings at the time of planting retain their normal colour but newly formed leaves develop a uniform light chlorosis, a light, limey-green shade with no veinal pattern. Leaves are small and growth spindly. Height is approximately normal but flowering is considerably delayed. Flower colour is normal. As the deficiency becomes severe, small round white necrotic spots develop anywhere on upper leaves, but are most pronounced near the edges. On the older leaves, bronzed blotches about 5 to 10 mm in diameter develop anywhere on the leaf, and gradually become necrotic. The root system appears to be normal but is small. Necrotic spots frequently develop on the underside of the petioles near the midpoint which results in drooping of the leaves.

Application This and other trace elements are best applied as one of the fritted trace element mixtures. These contain manganese, boron, copper, zinc, iron and other trace elements and can be added to loam-free composts at the rate of 192 g/m^3.

BORON

The primary role of boron in plants appears to be concerned with the uptake of calcium by the roots and with its efficient use within the plant. Thus, a shortage of boron typically affects the meristems of actively dividing tissues.

The first symptom of boron deficiency is a light marginal chlorosis on the leaves on the upper half of the plant. The middle leaves, and later the upper leaves, become mildly chlorotic and develop a smooth leathery texture. Reddish spots develop near the leaf axils and along the stem. Sometimes the leaves near the top of the plant are unable to maintain turgor in longday conditions. The apical meristems die and multiple shoots develop at the top of the plant with many malformed leaves. Little stem elongation occurs after the symptoms become well defined. Flowering time is normal. Petals are rolled and leathery, and flower colour is often paler than normal (Plate 23).

Application Boron can be supplied by adding borax to the liquid feed at a rate of 170 g/100 l of stock solution subsequently diluted at 1 in 200.

COPPER

Copper is a constituent of certain important enzymes in plants. Deficiency symptoms are rarely seen and only in soilless composts.

Mild copper deficiency causes greater internode elongation than normal and the leaves become longer than usual. The plant acquires a light spindly appearance. Ultimately, flower development is delayed about four to five days although colour is normal. Leaf symptoms first appear on middle leaves and take the form of a chlorosis near the margins or at the indentation between lobes. The main and secondary veins remain green, but in the area near the leaf margins where the chlorosis is developing, the fine veins are often seriously chlorotic. Only the area near the main and secondary veins and the very tips of lobes remain green. When this pattern develops, no further growth of the side shoots occurs. Axillary shoots higher on the stem are progressively less chlorotic and, eventually, make excellent growth. The extent of axillary growth in normal plants is just the reverse, long shoots being found near the bottom of the plant due to their greater age. The leaf symptoms which first appear on middle leaves slowly extend to other leaves as the plant matures. As flower bud development occurs, symptoms appear on younger leaves.

The effects of more serious copper deficiency on two varieties of spray chrysanthemums, Hurricane and Pollyanne, have been demonstrated at the GCRI, Littlehampton, Sussex

(Graves and Sutcliffe, 1974; Adams, Graves and Winsor, 1975a).

Chlorosis and later necrosis of leaves was followed by a delay or complete suspension of bud formation and development. There was a complete loss of apical dominance and the plants appeared to be incapable of flowering.

ZINC

Zinc is essential for growth hormone formation. Deficiencies can occur in chrysanthemums, especially in soilless composts when zinc is not added as a trace element.

The deficiency develops as the plant approaches the flowering stage, appearing first as small chlorotic spots which occur at any position on the middle or upper leaves except near the basal portion. Shortly after the symptoms appear, the basal area of the leaf is also affected. The chlorotic spots gradually enlarge and small necrotic spots are found in their centre. As flowering occurs, the deficiency appears in progressively younger leaves.

Feeding in Practice

Liquid feeding should commence when the rooted cuttings are established, usually after four days.

A number of workers have noted the importance of nitrogen during the longday phase of cropping (Lunt and Kofranek, 1958; Winsor and Hart, 1965; Joiner, 1967). For this period a liquid feed containing approximately 150 ppm N and 100 ppm K_2O is recommended. For fertilizer supplied in powder form, a satisfactory analysis would be 30 per cent N and 20 per cent K_2O at a concentration of 100 g/l of water and diluted at 1 : 200.

There is evidence (Anon., 1972) that there is a significantly early flowering response in peat/sand beds to high levels of potash relative to nitrogen for winter crops but this result does not occur consistently in soil beds. It has also been shown that nitrogen must not be allowed to become deficient even in winter, because low nitrogen levels reduce the quality of the flowering plant in both soil and peat/sand substrates (Winsor and Hart, 1966; Adams, Graves and Winsor, 1971).

However, in winter the nitrogen proportion is reduced and the feed should contain about 100 ppm N and 150 ppm K_2O. The nitrogen proportion is gradually increased again as the light improves.

The recommendation of Massey and Winsor (1974) following several years of work on the nitrogen nutrition of the variety Hurricane, is that following a light base dressing of nitrogen (25 to 50 g urea/m²) liquid feeds should contain 200 to 250 ppm N.

Interactions of Nutrients

Apart from achieving the correct balance between nitrogen and potassium, there are several other well-known relationships between elements which have to be borne in mind.

One of the best known examples is the mutually antagonistic reaction between potassium and magnesium. High potassium levels prevent the satisfactory uptake of magnesium and deficiency symptoms result even though sufficient magnesium may be present in the compost.

Where fertilizers with a high magnesium content are used (magnesium ammonium phosphate) deficiency symptoms of potassium can occur.

Excess of manganese in the soil can result in poor growth. Manganese toxicity can occur in some soils (brick earth) after steam sterilization especially where pH and phosphate levels are low. Raising the pH to 7 to 7·2 and adding phosphate will help solve this problem.

Trace element deficiencies are not common but when they do occur they are always worse under alkaline conditions, especially if the level of nitrogen is high and the light is poor at the time. The adverse effects of high nitrogen can be countered by raising the phosphate level. Iron and boron deficiencies often occur under these conditions. The use of fertilizers which will not cause the pH to rise will do much to prevent trace element deficiency problems especially in soilless composts. Table 9 shows how the pH can rise through the life of a pot plant according to the fertilizer used (Bunt, 1976a).

TABLE 9   Effect of Various Fertilizer Combinations on pH

Treatment	Compost pH (water extract)
pH at start of experiment	6·15
pH at finish:	
Plain water	7·35
Ammonium nitrate	
Monoammonium phosphate	
Potassium nitrate with ammonium	
added at:	
Nil ppm of N	6·83
32·5 ppm of N	6·42
65·0 ppm of N	5·89
97·5 ppm of N	5·20
130·0 ppm of N	4·38
Ammonium nitrate ⎫	
Monoammonium phosphate ⎬	6·05
Potassium sulphate ⎭	
Calcium nitrate ⎫	
Monoammonium phosphate ⎬	7·31
Potassium nitrate ⎭	

pH determinations made on a summer crop of chrysanthemums 10 weeks after potting.

All feeds contained 200 N 30 P 150 K ppm and were made with bore hole water containing 250 ppm equivalent calcium carbonate.

In winter, pH changes due to water quality and fertilizer composition are less marked.

SUPPORTING

Traditionally, where beds are blacked-out individually by hand, strong arch supports are needed. For these 13 mm galvanized light barrel is used, the hoops spaced approximately 3 to 3·5 m apart. The supports should have sides approximately 1·8 m long, 1·4 m of which are above ground level. The arch supports at the ends of the beds are 19 mm galvanized light barrel, usually concreted in and supported by stay irons. Where heavier end supports are used it is possible to reduce the weight of the intermediate supports and use 9 mm round black reinforcing rod, although the smaller bearing surface can be a disadvantage.

In modern programmes where some form of automatic or whole house blackout is used, the crop supports have to fulfil this function only, instead of the dual function of also supporting the blackout. In such cases the cross piece may be left out and the support depend on individual posts which may be of metal or 25 by 25 mm timber. Also the supports, particularly at the ends of the beds, should have a sleeve of a suitable diameter pipe fixed into the ground so that the crop supports may be removed for steaming between crops.

However, before designing crop supports without cross-members some thought should be given to the support required for crop lighting and to the method of flower harvesting to be adopted. Traditionally, harvested stems are placed for collection upon the blackout support wires, which are held in place by the cross-members of the hoops. Where these are not provided an alternative method of handling has to be devised. A single layer of wire and string, fish net or nylon net with a mesh equivalent to the plant spacing to be used for the greatest length of time will be required to support the plants. In this way the net may be lowered to the ground to act as marker for planting and

raised by means of supporting rods at each end of the bed on the outside of the support posts.

DISBUDDING

The year-round grower must always aim to produce standards and sprays of the highest quality, especially during the period of competition from natural season crops. The correct technique and timing of the disbudding operation is an important factor in the production of a high-quality spray, disbudded bloom or pot plant.

Methods of disbudding vary according to the type of chrysanthemum grown (Fig. 26). Many of the varieties produced in Britain are disbud or standard types, in which the largest bud (the terminal bud) is reserved and all axillary buds are removed as soon as they are large enough to handle. Using the thumbs of each hand, the small buds are rubbed out with a horizontal action rather than pressing the buds downwards, which may result in tearing the stem. The term in general commercial use for this operation (taking the bud) is an unfortunate

Fig. 26 The disbudding of a standard and a spray variety. The buds to be removed are indicated by the black marks (From Post, *Florist Crop Production and Marketing*, by permission of Orange Judd Publishing Co. Inc., New York.)

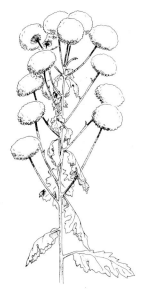

Fig. 27   Terminal spray produced by continued short days from the start.

Fig. 28   Compound spray with short laterals having terminal clusters produced by four short days (to induce the crown bud) followed by five long days (to produce secondary growth).

one since the bud in question is the one left on the plant. The term 'taking the bud' therefore is best interpreted as 'reserving the bud'.

The disbudding of spray varieties is often less complicated and varies with the type of spray produced. It is usually less laborious because in this case only the large apical bud is removed and the axillary buds allowed to develop.

Terminal sprays usually contain buds of equal size which develop at similar rates, and ultimately form flowers of similar size and quality. The terminal spray is therefore regarded as the most desirable.

Fig. 29   Compound spray produced by giving four short days (to crown the stem) followed by 15 long days (to produce the laterals).

Fig. 30   Compound spray with long laterals produced by six short days followed by 15 long days.

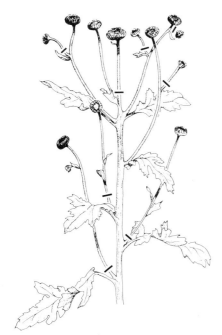

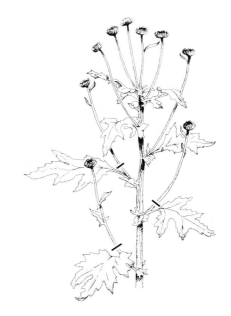

Fig. 31 Compound spray. The quality of this type of spray can be improved by disbudding as indicated by the black marks.

Fig. 32 Terminal spray formed under controlled daylength conditions. The lower buds can be removed as indicated to produce the highest quality spray.

Normally the controlled growing of spray varieties produces a terminal spray (Figs 27 and 32), because artificial shortday treatment causes immediate and rapid bud formation down the stem. With terminal sprays disbudding is simple, because with very few exceptions only the apical bud need be removed. This should be done as soon as the bud is large enough to handle, as its removal allows for the full development of the surrounding lateral buds.

Compound sprays are formed by many varieties (Dramatic and White Sands) and are characterized by the formation of small buds on the stalks or pedicels of the lateral buds surrounding the main apical bud (Figs. 28 and 31). Many factors can cause this compound spray formation (page 195). On some varieties, such as Portrait and Bluechip, extra buds can be formed by exceptionally good light conditions, at the start of shortday treatment. In these varieties the laterals are the same length as in the terminal spray, and the final quality of the spray, especially with the larger decorative varieties, can be improved by removing the small buds on

the laterals although this is not currently considered economic.

In other cases the formation of a premature crown bud low down on the main stem may have caused the lateral shoots to attain a considerable length, each lateral subsequently reacting to shortday treatment by forming a central terminal bud surrounded by a large number of lateral buds. This phenomenon (Figs 29 and 30) is usually caused by interrupted daylength conditions which may be deliberately applied or may occur by accident. Compound sprays can be formed, therefore, if shortday conditions, which initiate a crown bud, are followed by longday conditions, which allow further vegetative growth.

In the summer, sunlight in the evening and morning may be so intense as to penetrate the blackout and arrest the development of the crown bud, and in the winter either low temperatures or light spill from beds in longday treatment can have a similar effect. Other factors adverse to rapid and uniform flower bud initiation include inadequate nutrition and these may also lead to compound spray formation.

Occasionally, a premature bud appears low down on the stem because it was present in the shoot when the cutting was taken.

The disbudding of compound sprays varies with the position of the crown bud. If it is formed from 15 to about 45 cm from the ground, the crown bud and all lateral growths but one are removed. The best lateral shoot (normally the uppermost one) is allowed to grow on and will form a normal terminal spray.

If the crown bud develops at a height of about 60 cm or more above ground level it is removed, but all laterals are usually allowed to develop. In cases where many buds develop around the crown bud on each lateral these crown buds may in turn be removed and the spray allowed to flower as a compound type. To leave these crown buds and remove the surrounding terminal buds is considered uneconomical, except in special cases, even though the disbudding will result in earlier flowering.

Therefore, it is difficult to make any hard-and-fast rule regarding the disbudding of spray varieties, but the main consideration should be to leave at least four and up to twelve buds of uniform size, equally spaced on each spray.

GROWTH REGULATORS

Growth regulators have been defined as organic compounds, other than nutrients, which used in small amounts promote, inhibit or otherwise modify physiological processes in plants.

The control achieved by growth regulation is imposed upon that normally obtained by variations of temperature, light, feeding and watering.

Plant growth regulators or hormones influence the growth of chrysanthemums at all stages from rooting to senescence. Many of them occur naturally and often behave as chemical messengers influencing the plant either near the region of synthesis or in a completely different part of the plant. Five types of natural plant hormone are known. These are auxins, gibberellins, cytokinins, 'growth in-hibitors' (abscisic acid) and ethylene.

There are now, however, an increasing number of synthetic growth regulators which act either chemically (by blocking or enhancing the effectiveness of endogenous growth regulators) or physically (by selectively penetrating and rupturing a restricted part of the plant). They are generally named collectively according to their mode of action.

The classification, chemical composition and action of both natural and synthetic growth regulators have been described by Cathey (1970) and Menhenett (1976b). The effects of growth regulators on chrysanthemums have been reviewed by Dicks (1976).

Pruning Agents

These chemicals kill the apex of the stem, including flowers and some top leaves, and thus allow the development of lateral shoots in the plant. These side shoots develop slightly less quickly than in those plants in which the apex has been removed by hand.

Five types of pruning agent have been identified. They are petroleum products, fatty acid esters, fatty alcohols, organic solvents and alkyl propargyl sulphites. A great deal of development has been done with these chemicals particularly with the fatty acid esters (Joiner and Pickhardt, 1970; Uhring, 1971) but it has proved difficult in practice to apply fine chemical films over the plants. In many cases the results are spoilt by damage to the plant down the stem so that, although potentially labour saving, pruning agents cannot yet be used with confidence.

Disbudding Agents

These are chemicals which selectively kill only partly initiated flower buds without damaging those already fully initiated. Certain fractions of selected heavy aromatic petroleum products have given results of limited promise.

With one important variety, Fred Shoesmith, results have been good (Cathey, Yeomans and Smith, 1966) although the timing of application is critical. However, the responses with different varieties vary considerably and in

TABLE 10 Optimum Treatments Using Substituted Oxathiin as a Chemical Disbudding Agent

	Variety		Optimum percentage	Optimum application (short days)
Cathey	Bright Golden Anne		0·25	21
Parups	Promenade		0·5	20
	Improved Indianapolis White		0·5	20
	Festival		0·5	20
	Wildfire		0·5	20
Zacharioudakis	May Shoesmith	either	0·5	18
		or	1·0	21

many the lateral buds are aborted only partially or not at all. Encouraging results have been reported using a substituted oxathiin (Cathey, 1976; Parups, 1976; Zacharioudakis and Larson, 1976). The results, briefly given in Table 10, emphasize different varietal requirements and the critical timing of the application.

Fig. 33 The effects of gibberellic acid on stem and pedicel elongation. The plant on the left was untreated while the centre plant was sprayed during the third week of short days for maximum stem elongation. The plant on the right was sprayed during the fourth and fifth weeks of short days for pedicel elongation. The gibberellic acid was used at a concentration of 100 ppm.

Clearly much more research is necessary before the use of disbudding agents will replace disbudding by hand. In any case, most year-round varieties are spray types in which the first initiated buds are those which need to be removed.

Growth Stimulants

Chemicals which stimulate many developmental phases of plant growth are known as gibberellins. About 50 natural gibberellins, of which gibberellic acid (GA_3) is the most common, have been isolated and identified.

Growth and flower formation in chrysanthemums can be controlled to some extent with gibberellins. These substances induce elongation of the plants when applied at any time during growth (Fig. 33).

Experimental work (Cathey, 1958; Lert, 1959; Stuart and Cathey, 1959) has shown that the time of application and the concentration used is of great importance. The period of greatest elongation of the main stem for 9- and 10-week varieties results from application of gibberellin during the third week after the start of short days. For elongation of the pedicels the plants are most sensitive during the fourth week after the start of short days. Floret development is accelerated by gibberellin applied in the seventh week of short days.

Concentrations greater than 500 ppm result in extreme lengthening of the plant and in undesirably weak stems.

Growth Retardants

Chemicals which scale down many species of plants are called growth retardants. Treated plants have a more compact habit and darker green foliage compared with untreated plants. 'Retardant' is, perhaps, an unfortunate name since many other aspects of plant growth, apart from height, are affected according to species. These include drought resistance and salt tolerance, decrease in water loss, decrease in sensitivity to air pollution, enhancement of the number and rate of development of roots in cuttings and longevity of flowering plants.

Internode length is decreased without affecting the number of leaves and plants therefore become more compact. Improved leaf colour results either from the development of thicker leaves, or from a closer packing of an increased number of cells within the leaf.

As the apical meristem of a shoot tip develops it produces cells which form another dividing zone just behind it, the sub-apical meristem. It is from this region that the cells which eventually provide the main stem tissue are derived, and it is here that growth retardants exert their main effect on stem growth.

So far as chrysanthemums are concerned two of the most successful growth retardants are Phosfon (chlorphonium chloride) and Alar (N-dimethylaminosuccinamic acid). Details of their use on cut flower and pot plant crops are given on pages 111 and 135, respectively. Both Phosfon and Alar have been shown to inhibit transverse divisions in the cells of the sub-apical meristem, and thus reduce the number of cells in each internode compared with an untreated plant.

Gibberellins are involved in the maintenance of sub-apical meristem activity and there is good evidence (Sachs and Kofranek, 1963) that Phosfon exerts its influence on the meristem by inhibiting the synthesis of these materials. In the case of Alar the evidence is less substantial but it is also thought to block gibberellin synthesis but at a later stage (Ryugo and Sachs, 1969; Wylie, Ryugo and Sachs, 1970).

New growth retardants continue to be developed (ancymidol and Alden (piproctanylium bromide)), but early results appear to show little improvement in their effect on plant growth and no more economy of use over existing products. However, if all lateral shoots are sprayed, single applications of Alden are more effective than those of Alar in summer. Both Phosfon and Alden are superior to Alar in that use of the latter can often lead to bleaching of flower colour.

An important practical point is that retardants which are thoroughly mixed in the compost (Phosfon) tend to be taken up by the plant more uniformly than those sprayed on to the foliage (Alar and Alden) unless the spraying is done extremely carefully.

8 Cut Flower Production

Chrysanthemums were first grown in year-round programmes in Britain in 1955. Since then the year-round crop has spread to many other countries in Europe and elsewhere, despite some production problems, for instance, winter growing in the northern areas of Europe and marketing difficulties due to consumer prejudice against out-of-season chrysanthemums.

THE DIRECT LONGDAY PLANTING SYSTEM

The production system used in the first programmes and which has been developed continuously, makes use of rooted cuttings planted directly into the flowering area into longday conditions. Following a period of long days necessary for adequate leaf and stem development shortday conditions are given until flowering.

Most year-round growers still use this system, but to distinguish it from newer and developing systems it will be called 'The direct longday planting system' for purposes of description.

Planning the crop involves the compiling of a programme tailored to fit the area of cropping and suited to local environmental conditions to give a regular supply of cut flowers round the year.

Programming

A year-round programme is essentially a number of individual flowering units each grown sequentially to form a continuous flowering schedule.

When flowers are timed for a particular market, the cropping programme is invariably calculated back from the flowering date. Plans should be made at least twelve months ahead of the proposed flowering dates, so that arrangements can be made with the propagation unit to have the necessary rooted cuttings available at the programmed dates of planting.

A crop aimed at one particular market may be planned as follows:

1 Enter the date the flowers are required;

2 Make an allowance for shortday treatment from the date of its commencement to the proposed flowering date; the time allowed will vary from eight to 15 weeks depending on the season of the year and on the response group of the variety (Appendix 1);

3 Allow the appropriate number of weeks of longday treatment from the date of planting to the date of commencement of shortday treatment; a guide to the period of longday treatment required at any time of the year in southern England may be found in Table 11 on page 90;

4 Year-round programmes normally consist of single stem crops, but if the plants are to be pinched for two stems allow 10 to 21 days from the date of planting to the date of pinching, depending on the season and the type of crop.

FLOWERING UNITS

The first concern of the year-round crop planner is to decide the best number of flowering units. This is often predetermined by the number and size of the greenhouses available for the crop. Beds should be 1·5 m wide, or as near this width as possible, but not under 1·2 m. In a greenhouse 9·1 m wide a good layout is to have five 1·2 m beds. If there are four houses available, then the number of flowering units will be 20.

When considering any area for year-round growing the main considerations are that the greenhouses should be of good construction, well

TABLE 11   Standard Year-Round Cropping Programme for 10-, 11- and 14-week varieties
16 Units Single Stem Crops

Unit No.	Plant date	Lights On	Lights Off	Blackout On	Blackout Off	Weeks to crop	Response	Flower date
1	3 Nov	3 Nov	15 Dec	No	—	17	11	2 Mar
2	10 Nov	10 Nov	22 Dec	No	—	17	11	9 Mar
3	24 Nov	24 Nov	5 Jan	No	—	16	10	16 Mar
4	1 Dec	1 Dec	12 Jan	No	—	16	10	23 Mar
5	15 Dec	15 Dec	26 Jan	20 Mar	*	16	10	6 Apr
6	22 Dec	22 Dec	2 Feb	20 Mar	*	16	10	13 Apr
7	5 Jan	5 Jan	9 Feb	20 Mar	*	15	10	20 Apr
8	12 Jan	12 Jan	16 Feb	20 Mar	*	15	10	27 Apr
9	19 Jan	19 Jan	23 Feb	20 Mar	*	15	10	4 May
10	2 Feb	2 Feb	2 Mar	20 Mar	*	14	10	11 May
11	9 Feb	9 Feb	9 Mar	20 Mar	*	14	10	18 May
12	16 Feb	16 Feb	16 Mar	20 Mar	*	14	10	25 May
13	23 Feb	23 Feb	16 Mar	20 Mar	*	13	10	25 May
14	2 Mar	2 Mar	23 Mar	23 Mar	*	13	10	1 Jun
15	9 Mar	9 Mar	30 Mar	30 Mar	*	13	10	8 Jun
16	16 Mar	16 Mar	6 Apr	6 Apr	*	13	10	15 Jun
1	23 Mar	23 Mar	13 Apr	13 Apr	*	13	10	22 Jun
2	30 Mar	30 Mar	20 Apr	20 Apr	*	13	10	29 Jun
3	6 Apr	6 Apr	27 Apr	27 Apr	*	13	10	6 Jul
4	13 Apr	13 Apr	4 May	4 May	*	13	10	13 Jul
5	20 Apr	20 Apr	11 May	11 May	*	13	10	20 Jul
6	27 Apr	27 Apr	11 May	18 May	*	13	10	27 Jul
7	4 May	4 May	11 May	25 May	*	13	10	3 Aug
8	4 May	4 May	11 May	25 May	*	13	10	3 Aug
9	11 May	No	—	1 Jun	*	13	10	10 Aug
10	18 May	No	—	8 Jun	*	13	10	17 Aug
11	25 May	No	—	15 Jun	*	13	10	24 Aug
12	1 Jun	No	—	22 Jun	*	13	10	31 Aug
13	1 Jun	No	—	22 Jun	*	13	10	31 Aug
14	8 Jun	No	—	29 Jun	*	13	10	7 Sep
15	15 Jun	No	—	6 Jul	*	13	10	14 Sep
16	22 Jun	No	—	13 Jul	*	13	10	21 Sep
1	29 Jun	No	—	20 Jul	*	13	10	28 Sep
2	6 Jul	No	—	20 Jul	*	13	11	5 Oct
3	13 Jul	No	—	3 Aug	30 Sep	14	11	19 Oct
4	20 Jul	3 Aug	10 Aug	10 Aug	30 Sep	14	11	26 Oct
5	27 Jul	3 Aug	17 Aug	17 Aug	30 Sep	14	11	2 Nov
6	3 Aug	3 Aug	31 Aug	31 Aug	30 Sep	15	11	16 Nov
7	10 Aug	10 Aug	7 Sep	7 Sep	30 Sep	15	11	23 Nov
8	10 Aug	10 Aug	14 Sep	14 Sep	30 Sep	16	11	30 Nov
9	17 Aug	17 Aug	21 Sep	21 Sep	30 Sep	16	11	7 Dec
10	24 Aug	24 Aug	28 Sep	28 Sep	30 Sep	16	11	14 Dec
11	31 Aug	31 Aug	28 Sep	28 Sep	30 Sep	18	14	4 Jan
12	7 Sep	7 Sep	5 Oct	No	—	18	14	11 Jan
13	7 Sep	7 Sep	12 Oct	No	—	19	14	18 Jan
14	14 Sep	14 Sep	19 Oct	No	—	19	14	25 Jan
15	21 Sep	21 Sep	26 Oct	No	—	19	14	1 Feb
16	28 Sep	28 Sep	2 Nov	No	—	19	14	8 Feb
1	5 Oct	5 Oct	9 Nov	No	—	19	14	15 Feb
2	12 Oct	12 Oct	16 Nov	No	—	19	14	22 Feb
3	2 Nov	2 Nov	14 Dec	No	—	17	11	1 Mar
4	9 Nov	9 Nov	21 Dec	No	—	17	11	8 Mar
5	23 Nov	23 Nov	4 Jan	No	—	16	10	15 Mar
6	30 Nov	30 Nov	11 Jan	No	—	16	10	22 Mar
7	7 Dec	7 Dec	18 Jan	20 Mar	*	16	10	29 Mar
8	14 Dec	14 Dec	25 Jan	20 Mar	*	16	10	5 Apr
9	21 Dec	21 Dec	1 Feb	20 Mar	*	16	10	12 Apr
10	28 Dec	28 Dec	8 Feb	20 Mar	*	15	10	19 Apr
11	18 Jan	18 Jan	15 Feb	20 Mar	*	14	10	26 Apr
12	25 Jan	25 Jan	22 Feb	20 Mar	*	14	10	3 May
13	1 Feb	1 Feb	1 Mar	20 Mar	*	14	10	10 May
14	8 Feb	8 Feb	8 Mar	20 Mar	*	14	10	17 May
15	15 Feb	15 Feb	15 Mar	20 Mar	*	14	10	24 May
16	22 Feb	22 Feb	15 Mar	20 Mar	*	13	10	24 May

* Cease blackout one week after disbudding.

sited with good aspect and orientation. They must have full headroom and must be capable of providing at least a two-thirds planting area, and the beds must be clear of purlin posts and all other obstructions. For economy in heating it is an advantage with some layouts to have a heating pipe, running along the side of each bed near ground level. With small-bore pipes, it is usual to have up to two-thirds of the pipes overhead.

The optimum number of units, in a normal programme, is 16 which gives a flowering interval of not more than seven days between units for most of the year. However, because the bed and path dimensions and thus the percentage of the flowering area cropped is the most important economic consideration, it is usually not worth sacrificing production in favour of the 16-unit system. Successful year-round programmes have been planned using from eight to 23 units according to the particular situation.

It should be stated, however, that eight units is the smallest practical number, because with fewer units than this the programme ceases to be year-round and merely becomes a number of spot crops maturing every three weeks.

If 24 or more beds are involved it is better to increase the number of beds per unit to two, so that 24 beds give a 12-unit programme, and 32 beds would be used as a 16-unit programme, each with two beds to the unit. The ideal is to have a separate house for each unit, which simplifies heating and daylength control as well as cultural operations.

Year-round programmes are in operation in widely different areas of Britain from Scotland to the Channel Isles. Owing to the wide environmental differences it is necessary to plan each programme to suit the area of production. Type and orientation of greenhouse, quality of soil and other factors profoundly influence the details of the cropping programme.

In northern areas of the British Isles especially, it is wise to plan a conservative (standard) programme.

THE STANDARD PROGRAMME

Having decided upon the number of units, the first cycle of the programme can be planned using the known flowering interval between units for this number of units.

As mentioned previously for a 16-unit programme the flowering interval for most of the year is seven days (Table 11). With 20 units a seven-day interval round the year is easily achieved and at certain times two units are planted together, so the weekly output is doubled. Whenever possible this increase in production is aimed at the best markets. Ten- and 12-unit programmes have average flowering intervals of 12 and 10 days, respectively.

The planting date of the first unit is, of course, the starting-point. Entering this, and allowing the number of weeks necessary for adequate growth and quality of crop for the time of year, the programme for the first unit is worked out. The flowering dates are then entered for the first cycle according to the flowering interval. Normally, one week of double output is possible during May with a 16-unit programme. From the flowering dates the planting date for each unit is found by counting back the total number of weeks necessary for each crop.

The first cycle completed, the next step is to plan the replanting dates of each unit leaving the smallest safe margin between flowering and replanting. In many programmes there is a two-week interval between flowering and replanting round the year. In summer the majority of growers do not now blackout the beds on Saturday nights, and this practice can delay flowering by up to one week. However, where automated blackout systems are installed it is necessary to allow only one week between flowering and replanting during the May to November period.

From December to March two weeks are usually allowed between flowering and replanting, because during this period there is more danger of slight delay in flowering due to factors beyond the control of the grower. In exceptionally cold weather, for example, it may prove physically impossible to maintain the 15·6° minimum night temperature for several days. Prolonged periods of very low light conditions also tend to delay flowering to some extent and as

TABLE 12   First Year-round Cropping Programme for 10-Week varieties (16 Units Single Stem Crops)

Unit No.	Plant date	Lights On	Lights Off	Blackout On	Blackout Off	Weeks to crop	Response	Flower date
1	3 Nov	3 Nov	8 Dec	No	—	16	11	23 Feb
2	10 Nov	10 Nov	15 Dec	No	—	16	11	2 Mar
3	10 Nov	10 Nov	15 Dec	No	—	16	11	2 Mar
4	17 Nov	17 Nov	22 Dec	No	—	16	11	9 Mar
5	1 Dec	1 Dec	5 Jan	No	—	15	10	16 Mar
6	8 Dec	8 Dec	12 Jan	No	—	15	10	23 Mar
7	8 Dec	8 Dec	12 Jan	No	—	15	10	23 Mar
8	22 Dec	22 Dec	19 Jan	20 Mar	*	14	10	30 Mar
9	5 Jan	5 Jan	26 Jan	20 Mar	*	13	10	6 Apr
10	12 Jan	12 Jan	2 Feb	20 Mar	*	13	10	13 Apr
11	19 Jan	19 Jan	9 Feb	20 Mar	*	13	10	20 Apr
12	26 Jan	26 Jan	16 Feb	20 Mar	*	13	10	27 Apr
13	2 Feb	2 Feb	23 Feb	20 Mar	*	13	10	4 May
14	9 Feb	9 Feb	2 Mar	20 Mar	*	13	10	11 May
15	23 Feb	23 Feb	9 Mar	20 Mar	*	12	10	18 May
16	2 Mar	2 Mar	16 Mar	20 Mar	*	12	10	25 May
1	9 Mar	9 Mar	23 Mar	23 Mar	*	12	10	1 Jun
2	16 Mar	16 Mar	30 Mar	30 Mar	*	12	10	8 Jun
3	16 Mar	16 Mar	30 Mar	30 Mar	*	12	10	8 Jun
4	23 Mar	23 Mar	6 Apr	6 Apr	*	12	10	15 Jun
5	30 Mar	30 Mar	13 Apr	13 Apr	*	12	10	22 Jun
6	6 Apr	6 Apr	20 Apr	20 Apr	*	12	10	29 Jun
7	6 Apr	6 Apr	20 Apr	20 Apr	*	12	10	29 Jun
8	13 Apr	13 Apr	27 Apr	27 Apr	*	12	10	6 Jul
9	20 Apr	20 Apr	4 May	4 May	*	12	10	13 Jul
10	20 Apr	20 Apr	4 May	4 May	*	12	10	13 Jul
11	27 Apr	27 Apr	11 May	11 May	*	12	10	20 Jul
12	4 May	4 May	11 May	18 May	*	12	10	27 Jul
13	11 May	No	—	25 May	*	12	10	3 Aug
14	18 May	No	—	1 Jun	*	12	10	10 Aug
15	25 May	No	—	8 Jun	*	12	10	17 Aug
16	1 Jun	No	—	15 Jun	*	12	10	24 Aug
1	8 Jun	No	—	22 Jun	*	12	10	31 Aug
2	15 Jun	No	—	29 Jun	*	12	10	7 Sep
3	15 Jun	No	—	29 Jun	*	12	10	7 Sep
4	22 Jun	No	—	6 Jul	*	12	10	14 Sep
5	29 Jun	No	—	13 Jul	*	12	10	21 Sep
6	6 Jul	No	—	20 Jul	*	12	10	28 Sep
7	6 Jul	No	—	20 Jul	*	12	10	28 Sep
8	13 Jul	No	—	27 Jul	*	12	10	5 Oct
9	20 Jul	No	—	3 Aug	30 Sep	12	10	12 Oct
10	20 Jul	3 Aug	10 Aug	3 Aug	30 Sep	13	10	19 Oct
11	27 Jul	3 Aug	17 Aug	10 Aug	30 Sep	13	10	26 Oct
12	3 Aug	3 Aug	24 Aug	17 Aug	30 Sep	13	10	2 Nov
13	10 Aug	10 Aug	7 Sep	31 Aug	30 Sep	14	10	16 Nov
14	24 Aug	24 Aug	21 Sep	14 Sep	30 Sep	14	10	30 Nov
15	31 Aug	31 Aug	28 Sep	21 Sep	30 Sep	14	10	7 Dec
16	7 Sep	7 Sep	12 Oct	No	—	15	10	21 Dec
1	14 Sep	14 Sep	19 Oct	No	—	15	10	28 Dec
2	21 Sep	21 Sep	26 Oct	No	—	15	10	4 Jan
3	21 Sep	21 Sep	26 Oct	No	—	15	10	4 Jan
4	21 Sep	21 Sep	26 Oct	No	—	16	11	11 Jan
5	28 Sep	28 Sep	2 Nov	No	—	16	11	18 Jan
6	5 Oct	5 Oct	9 Nov	No	—	16	11	25 Jan
7	12 Oct	12 Oct	16 Nov	No	—	16	11	1 Feb
8	19 Oct	19 Oct	23 Nov	No	—	16	11	8 Feb
9	26 Oct	26 Oct	30 Nov	No	—	16	11	15 Feb
10	2 Nov	2 Nov	7 Dec	No	—	16	11	22 Feb
11	9 Nov	9 Nov	14 Dec	No	—	16	11	1 Mar
12	16 Nov	16 Nov	21 Dec	No	—	16	11	8 Mar
13	30 Nov	30 Nov	4 Jan	No	—	15	10	15 Mar
14	7 Dec	7 Dec	11 Jan	No	—	15	10	22 Mar
15	21 Dec	21 Dec	18 Jan	20 Mar	*	14	10	29 Mar
16	4 Jan	4 Jan	25 Jan	20 Mar	*	13	10	5 Apr

* Cease blackout one week after disbudding.

shown in the programme in Table 12, the 10-week varieties will require 11 weeks to flower from January to March.

From the replanting dates the total number of weeks for each crop is again calculated and the corresponding flowering dates are entered.

It will be seen from Table 11 that the period from planting to cutting for each bed varies from 13 weeks in the summer to 19 weeks in the winter. This is entirely due to the amount of light available at each season. During the winter in the latitude of southern England, 19 weeks of growth are necessary to ensure a crop of good quality on the average nursery using 14-week varieties.

If this were the only criterion, then the summer crop could be produced in fewer than 13 weeks, but this would lead to a reduction in stem length in many varieties which would be unacceptable to the markets. Thus, for planting dates from early August until late September the total number of weeks for the crop rises steadily from 13 to 19. This means that in the 16-unit programme two weeks may sometimes elapse between flowering dates in November, December and January, and the even flow of flowers is reduced during these months. This is usually acceptable to the year-round grower in view of the competition from natural season chrysanthemums.

For planting dates from mid-November to mid-February, the situation is reversed in that total cropping time is steadily reduced from 19 to 13 weeks. This means not only a return to the seven-day cropping interval for the period from the end of March to the end of May when flowers are normally scarce, but occasionally a double quantity of flowers where two units are planted simultaneously. By replanting with the least delay the period during which extra production is possible may be extended until the end of the 13-week cropping period in late October.

THE FAST PROGRAMME

In a fast programme longday treatments for vegetative growth are reduced by seven days for summer and autumn crops. Also, 10-week varieties are used throughout the winter. A comparison of a typical fast programme (Table 12) with the standard programme (Table 11) will illustrate the saving of time during a year by the use of the former. It is possible, therefore, using selected vigorous varieties grown in modern greenhouses, to increase from $3\frac{1}{4}$ crops with the standard programme to $3\frac{1}{2}$ crops or more per year with the fast programme.

Where sufficient area is available for two programmes, both a standard and a fast programme can be used. The standard programme caters for the slower-growing, short-jointed varieties such as Elegance, Bonnie Jean and Tuneful which require additional long days in summer, while the fast programme is ideal for vigorous varieties such as Polaris, Fandango and Snowdon.

PINCHED CROPS

At certain times of the year pinched crops may be used in the programme, each plant being normally allowed two flowering stems. This, of course, halves the number of plants required and considerably reduces the costs of stock plant production and propagation.

In some cases, pinched crops are useful in the winter or spring at the commencement of a programme, when several beds can be planted together using pinched and single stem crops to fill the first house quickly to avoid heating an empty area. Suitable planting and pinching dates, and an adjustment of daylength control ensures that the beds flower in the desired rotation.

Some growers feel that since the cost of plant material is halved, pinched crops would be more economic to grow. However, when allowance is made for the extra production time needed, up to three weeks in winter, and the better quality of the single stem crop, opinion is in favour of the latter and pinched crops are rarely used in established year-round programmes.

Varietal Response

Having outlined the programme for the whole year by entering the planting and flowering dates according to the total cropping time, the lighting and blackout dates will depend on the response groups of the varieties chosen.

The term 'response group' refers to the number of weeks to flowering from the commencement of short days in a night temperature of 15·6° in light conditions near to those prevailing for natural flowering (September and October). Varieties suitable for controlled growing have been classified into eight response groups, ranging from 8 to 15 weeks. The response group classification is not necessarily valid at all seasons of the year, because with most varieties the response changes with the light available.

The correct choice of varieties round the year largely determines the success or failure of the enterprise. The main criterion is the varietal tolerance to the amount of light available for photosynthesis. American workers have divided chrysanthemums into two classes, 'light efficient' and 'light inefficient'. Light efficient varieties are those which are able to make the most use of the limited light available for growth during winter and early spring, to produce high-quality flowers during these seasons. Many 12- to 14-week varieties are light efficient probably because they are naturally adapted to relatively low light conditions for flowering. Conversely, light inefficient varieties are often the 8-, 9-, 10- and 11-week varieties which flower naturally during seasons of higher light intensities. A number of the light inefficient varieties grown as standards and flowered during the winter produce flowers which contain relatively few petals and in which the disc florets can be readily seen.

Fig. 34 A mid-February crop of Elegance in Britain grown in 18 weeks. Uniformly high quality was produced in the east–west house.

Not only do early flowering spray types subjected to low light conditions behave similarly but an undesirable tightly clustered spray also results, since pedicels do not elongate normally. However, it may be misleading to generalize too much because the two best varieties for response in poor light conditions are Elegance (Fig. 34), a 14-week variety bred in America, and Snowdon, a 10-week variety bred in Britain.

The 10-week varieties are the backbone of the year-round programme, since they are flowered from April until November. Indeed some 10-week varieties such as Snowdon, Hurricane, Fandango and Robeam can be flowered successfully round the year. Apart from the November to February flowering period, plants of most varieties produce better quality flowers than they do on their natural flowering dates. In these plants the stems are stronger and the flowers larger and more numerous. The only exceptions are a few varieties which lose colour or are subject to petal scorch on hot summer days (Flamenco and Red Fandango).

Varieties for Europe

The varieties for use in the direct longday planting system depend not only on their suitability for the system but also to a large extent on the market requirement. This will vary according to the country in which the flowers are to be sold, the use to which they will be put and on the time of flowering.

A large percentage of the Dutch year-round crop is sold in Germany so that the requirements of both countries have to be taken into consideration by the Dutch growers. The spray varieties of spider* form popular in the Netherlands also sell well in Germany, where large standard varieties are also required in some quantity. Long stems (90 cm) are necessary in these two countries where a large percentage of flowers are used for house decoration. This will require a programme allowing more long days than shown in the programmes on pages 90 and 92 so that the number of crops possible per year is reduced.

In Denmark, Sweden and especially Finland, spray varieties with single flowers are favoured, while in Britain it is the decorative* form, especially in spray varieties, which is predominantly required. In this country a very high percentage of chrysanthemum flowers are used in wreath work so that the length of stem is not so important as on the continent. Hence fewer long days have to be allowed in the planning of the programme.

Spray Varieties

The ideal spray variety should display between 6 and 12 equally sized lateral flowers at a similar stage of development arranged attractively on the main stem.

The great variation in colour and form of spray varieties is an indication of the popularity of this type, and in Britain they now form about 90 per cent of the year-round crop. However, in the 9- and 10-week groups, out of hundreds of spray varieties listed, probably not more than 30 are used extensively for year-round production.

SUMMER FLOWERING

During the summer the choice is limited to those varieties which grow consistently well in a hot dry atmosphere. In night temperatures of 27°, which are quite usual in the early evening under the blackout, and day temperatures that frequently exceed 38°, the plants have to maintain a rapid growth rate and produce high-quality flowers resistant to burning.

Certain of the 10-week varieties, such as Polaris, Flame Belair and Pink Gin (Plate 15), are consistently good throughout the summer period. Others, such as Fandango (Plate 19) and White Spider, are mainly used in the spring and autumn, because their quality can be impaired by continuous high temperatures. Other 10-week varieties, including Hurricane (Plate 5) and Tuneful, fail to develop buds quickly and evenly in very high temperatures, and under these conditions flowering may be delayed by up to 10 days. Certain, bronze and pink varieties readily lose colour during the late summer. Varieties in this category include Pollyanne and Bronze Nero (Plate 20). In summer, use is also

* Chrysanthemums are classified according to flower form in Appendix 1.

made of a number of 9-week varieties which are in general more tolerant of high temperatures. Blue-chip and its sports, notably Southdown Chip (Plate 13), are consistent performers in this group, as are the Marble family, Dolly, Rosado (Plate 21), Judith and Arctic.

Polaris (Fig. 35), although a 10-week variety, flowers during the summer as a 9-week variety and can actually be flowered $10\frac{1}{2}$ weeks from planting, with 10 long days for vegetative growth. The development of a range of varieties of this type, vigorous and not delayed by high summer temperatures, would improve the efficiency of the summer programme.

AUTUMN AND SPRING FLOWERING

A few of the 11-week varieties including the Taffetas and Jubilee have been found suitable for flowering from October until December while the bronze Galaxy (12-week) and its sports are occasionally grown for the Christmas market.

In the autumn a larger proportion of the red and bronze types is normally used.

In spring all of the 11-week varieties have to be discarded, not only because of the more limited colour range needed but also because certain of them, particularly Shane and the Taffetas, are very sensitive to temperature in low light conditions. They require a night minimum of 16·5° to 18·5° for bud formation and early development. This temperature is costly to provide and may be difficult to maintain consistently in January and February.

It is now usual for the best 10-week varieties, which are tolerant of low light for growth and flowering, to be used for autumn and spring production. These varieties include Snowdon (Plate 14), Yellow Snowdon, Fandango and Robeam (Plate 16).

WINTER FLOWERING

It is most difficult to find suitable spray varieties

Fig. 35 A uniform crop of Polaris in mid-summer.

for flowering from early January to mid-March. Not only must the variety maintain a reasonable quality during this period of poor light but its sensitivity to temperature and other factors such as light spill, must not be too critical. In some varieties sensitive to high temperature, such as Christmas Greeting and Minstrel, rosetting occurs even at 15·6° during periods of low light intensity. Although normal growth may be made by these varieties if given a lower night temperature, the performance of some other varieties in the same greenhouse would be adversely affected.

Some varieties in short days are extremely sensitive to light spill from nearby units in artificial long days, and a delay in bud development occurs.

Thermonegative varieties such as Debutante will set buds at 12·5°, while flowering is seriously delayed if the night temperature rises above 15·6° for any length of time during the early bud development stage. High day temperatures which are not always easily controlled can cause this delay. Consequently, during the winter it is not always possible to use the varieties required by the markets. It is therefore, much more important to select those of reasonable quality which will flower on time under the conditions which the grower is likely to encounter.

Experience with winter cropping especially has shown that the suitability of each particular variety is much more important than the conception of restricting the choice to varieties within a given response group. Thus, in January and February the 14-week varieties Elegance, Cream Elegance and Golden Elegance are used in the standard year-round programme. Particular care has to be taken to avoid temperatures above 16·5° with these varieties, otherwise high-temperature delay occurs especially in low light conditions. However, for fast programmes of 15 to 17 weeks the 10-week varieties Fandango, White Spider and Hurricane and their sports and Robeam are amongst the most successful and can be continued with in March and through the spring.

It is a measure of the rarity of good winter spray varieties that the standard variety Snow-

don and its yellow sport form the backbone of spray programmes from January to April and have done so for some years. Snowdon is extremely reliable in both low light and low temperature conditions and represents an important step forward in the production of new, specially bred, varieties for the north European winter.

The first 20 years of production of winter crops have shown that with poor light prevailing in Britain it is unwise to allow any variety more than six weeks of longday treatment. Plants become too vegetative in winter with an excessive longday growing period and it is very difficult to induce a rapid and even bud-set, even where temperature and water regimes are strictly controlled. Usually it has been found that uniformity decreases proportionally with the increase in the number of long days.

It is usual for each grower to ascertain the correct length of the longday treatment needed for each variety in his particular programme and to plan accordingly. The best schedules for each of the varieties used at present for February flowering are shown in Table 13.

It will be noted that in the winter programme the response group of the variety is not necessarily the same as the number of weeks of short days for flowering, as would apply during periods of average light. The 12-week variety Galaxy, when flowered in January and February, assumes a 14-week response. The most reliable 10-week varieties require 10½ to 11 weeks of short days in winter, while the majority of 10-

TABLE 13   Varieties for Spray Production in February

Variety	Response group	Weeks of long days	Weeks of short days to flower	Total time in weeks
Elegance	14	5	14	19
Hurricane	10	6	11½	17½
White Spider	10	6	11	17
Fandango	10	5	11	16
Snowdon	10	5	10½	15½
Robeam	10	5	10½	15½

week varieties require 12 or even 13 weeks for flowering even when night temperatures are controlled at 15·6°.

Butters, working in Hampshire, has investigated the response and performance of a number of varieties in various night temperature regimes (Anon., 1976). Arctic, Fandango, Dolly and Light Melody were found to perform reasonably well with little or no delay at night temperatures of 13·3° during the winter of 1974–75. Arctic was the only variety that could be considered in night temperatures of 10° but quality was impaired and a two-week flowering delay resulted.

In a more recent experiment (Anon., 1978) the new variety Snapper (Plate 17) flowered in 9 weeks of short days at 15·6°, in 10½ weeks at 13·3° and in 12 weeks at 10° in February 1977. In the latter treatment, although response was not uniform throughout the bed, the quality and

weight of the flowering stems was greatly superior.

In view of the amount of capital needed for year-round growing and the high cost of running the programme, it is essential that only varieties with reliable responses be used in winter. The few varieties which are tolerant of low temperature and low light are being actively used in breeding programmes to create a wider choice.

A list of spray varieties suitable for each season under the climatic conditions generally experienced in southern England is given in Table 14.

NEW DEVELOPMENTS

The majority of spray varieties originally used in European programmes were American in origin. However, as programme planning and market requirements have become more specific, it has been increasingly difficult to breed varieties which can be used throughout the

TABLE 14   The Best Spray Varieties for Each Flowering Period

White	Yellow	Pink	Red/Bronze
	January to mid-April		
Elegance (to early March	Golden Elegance (to early March)	Fandango*	Bronze Nero* (Plate 20)
	Cream Elegance	Pollyanne*	
Hurricane		Snapper*	Red Fandango*
Snowdon*	Robeam		Dramatic*
White Spider	Yellow Snowdon*		
	Yellow Spider		
	Mid-April to Mid-October		
Arctic*	Yellow Arctic*	Pink Gin*	Bronze Nero*
Hurricane	Improved Yellow Hurricane	Pink Marble	Lara*
Polaris*	Yellow Polaris*	Rosado*	Tuneful
White Marble	Golden Polaris* (Plate 18)	Bluechip	Apricot Marble
	Yellow Marble		
	Yellow Tuneful	Rosechip	Dramatic
Snow Crystal	Yellow Crystal	Snapper*	Flame Belair
		Dolly	
		Judith	
		Belair	
	Mid-October to Mid-December		
			Bronze Nero*
Hurricane	Improved Yellow Hurricane	Flandango*	
Snowdon*	Yellow Snowdon*	Pollyanne*	Red Fandango*
White Marble	Yellow Marble	Snapper*	Dramatic*
White Spider	Yellow Spider		

* Bred by B. J. Machin in Sussex, England, for north European programmes.

world. This fact has become more apparent as experience has been gained with year-round cropping, especially in the winter. For example, light values in Britain from November to February are lower than in the USA and only some American-bred varieties can be flowered in Europe during the winter months.

Varieties are required to respond uniformly to controlled temperature regimes in poor light and at the same time to be vigorous, large-flowered and colourful. At present, the recommendations of Efford EHS are that night temperatures of 17·2° are required in December and January and 15·6° in October, November and February where varieties such as Hurricane, Heyday and Pollyanne are still grown.

Using a programme of Snowdon, Yellow Snowdon and Fandango for winter production, the night temperature requirement would be 13·3° throughout, representing a very considerable saving in fuel.

By careful selection of parent material it should be possible to raise new varieties with good response and quality in night temperatures of 10° even in areas of poorer winter light than southern England.

Standard Varieties

Disbudded blooms, or standards, are large single blooms on long stems. These represent about 85 per cent of the natural season chrysanthemum crops and about 10 per cent of the year-round crops grown in Britain. In the USA, standards represent about 50 per cent of the crop. Normally, the length of stem is controlled to between 76 and 91 cm by allowing the appropriate period for vegetative growth in the year-round programme.

It has been found, both in Britain and the USA, that very few of the standard varieties raised are suitable for year-round culture. The few varieties which are successfully grown are found in the 8- to 11-week response groups only (Snowdon and Escapade).

Most of the British standards have been bred for their slow-growing habit and have been selected for their performance under cool growing conditions and natural daylength. It is not surprising, therefore, that few British varieties respond favourably to year-round growing methods.

The 12-, 13- and 14-week standards are less suited to year-round growing methods, because they do not respond uniformly to artificial daylength and controlled night temperature conditions. It is possible, of course, to grow these varieties out-of-season and to obtain good blooms, but flowering is sometimes spread over a period of weeks, and they cannot economically form part of a year-round programme.

The 10-week standard varieties are normally used for year-round growing, but even in this group very few varieties have the necessary qualities of fast, strong growth with a rapid response to changes of daylength.

One of the most popular and reliable varieties has been Indianapolis White and its sports. The fact that this chrysanthemum was raised nearly 50 years ago emphasizes the scarcity of suitable year-round standards. In the USA the Indianapolis group is flowered round the year in many areas, but interrupted light treatment (page 108) has to be given to obtain good quality blooms during the winter months in the north. Where hot summers are the rule, other varieties, such as Good News, Detroit News, Giant Betsy Ross and Albatross, are more reliable.

In Europe, it has been found that Indianapolis varieties are at their best in October and November and again in April and May. The light is too poor for producing uniformly high-quality blooms of these varieties from December to March. The flowers tend to fade or scorch in bright weather in the mid-summer months although a few growers produce them very successfully through the summer using fan ventilation.

Mefo, Fred Shoesmith and their sports have been used extensively, especially in November, December, March and April when high-quality blooms can be produced.

The most successful standards for year-round production in Britain since 1970 have been the white flowered Snowdon (Plate 1) and its yellow sport. These were bred and selected for response and performance during poor light conditions in the English winter and have given excellent results both as medium-sized standards and following removal of the apical bud, as sprays.

High summer temperatures lead to slight crinkling of the surface of petals, but this is not a sufficient drawback to prevent the Snowdons from being extensively grown as standards throughout the summer and autumn. Escapade, a 10-week pink American standard, is the best companion for the Snowdons during periods of average to good light conditions for flowering in spring and autumn.

NEW DEVELOPMENTS

It is probably in the field of year-round standards that most effort is required to raise new varieties. The Americans are handicapped to some extent by the shortage of good year-round standards from which to breed.

The problem in North America is to provide varieties which can withstand the high temperatures of much of the USA and Canada during the summer months.

British raisers have a great opportunity, because they are fortunate in having both a wide range of varieties for breeding purposes and a long experience with standard varieties.

In Britain, summer temperature problems are not so severe and a more important consideration with standards is to produce varieties which do not 'damp' (due to botrytis, page 163) under conditions of high relative humidity. Varieties with small petals are more resistant to damp conditions, but give rise to small blooms. Large-flowered responsive varieties of good texture are urgently required.

There is a wide range of colour in British standards, but the raising of these varieties has been due in no small part to the intercrossing of early and late varieties. Thus, some of the excellent varieties raised in this way such as Princess Anne and Woking Scarlet are prone to produce unwanted buds even in longday conditions due to their 'early blood'. American varieties are less colourful but much more dependable in their vegetative characters. The future with year-round standards lies, therefore, with the amalgamation of American response and vigour with British form and colour.

There is a steady market for standard varieties throughout the year, but with those currently grown it is not easy to obtain such a high percentage of marketable flowers as with spray varieties. Also flower size is often a problem especially in Germany where the Snowdons are considered to be too small despite their other outstanding qualities. Breeders must aim to meet these requirements as soon as possible.

Disadvantages of the Direct Longday Planting System

Despite the introduction of improved varieties and better methods of environmental control and husbandry, together with the use of carbon dioxide enrichment and chemical growth regulators, year-round chrysanthemum cut flower production, using the direct longday planting system, has not substantially increased, in terms of stems per hectare per annum, since 1955. At that time crops planted in October required a total of 20 weeks to flower. In 1977, with improved varieties, the standard programme still requires 18 or 19 weeks for winter cropping. During the summer, cropping time has been reduced by only one week, or two in very exceptional cases.

In 1955 it was possible, by careful varietal choice, to achieve up to $3\frac{1}{4}$ crops per annum from a flowering area. The fastest crops in 1977, using a similar direct longday planting production system, average between $3\frac{1}{2}$ and $3\frac{3}{4}$ crops per annum, while in the normal programmes, although quality has undoubtedly improved, production remains static (consult programmes on pages 90 and 92).

Since 1955, with little or no increase in the number of flowering stems produced, production costs have risen steadily up to 1973 and very steeply since then, owing mainly to the cost of fuel. During this period the average price per stem received by the grower has lagged behind in the inflationary spiral since 1973. In view of this trend Machin, during 1968 (Machin, 1973), critically examined the direct longday planting system with the object of increasing the output of good quality cut flowers round the year from a given area.

An economically sound horticultural flower crop must proceed from the seed or vegetative cutting stage to the harvested flower at the most rapid rate of growth conducive to a high-quality product. An examination of the production methods used in the direct longday planting system will show that, although a rapid rate of plant growth is normally maintained, there are certain periods in the production cycle when plant growth is very slow or negligible.

ROOTING CUTTINGS

It is unusual for commercial propagators to use base or liquid feed during the rooting stage. It is assumed that the nutritional requirements of the rooting cutting will be supplied from within the cutting itself and that this will be sufficient for good growth. However, even when stock plants have been adequately fed with nutrients in correct balance, and this is not always the case, the unrooted cutting is fully supplied with nutrient only at the commencement of the rooting period.

Two factors affect the amount of nutrient retained in the cutting; the rate of utilization of nutrients during the rooting process and the leaching effect of the overhead watering system normally employed. Unless nutrients are supplied to the cutting during its rooting period of two to three weeks, the nutritional status of the rooted plant will be less than that of the unrooted cutting. This deficiency may, in some cases, reach a starvation level, and will seriously affect the subsequent rate of growth of the flowering crop.

LIFTING AND PACKING OF ROOTED PLANTS

In large commercial propagation installations rooted plants are given less water than that required for optimum growth for a few days prior to despatch, to facilitate this operation and to enable plants to travel long distances without rotting. This partial drying out leads to some loss of rooting medium around the roots, the amount of loss depending on the travelling time

to the grower's nursery. Although every care is normally taken by the propagator to ensure that rooted plants arrive safely at the flowering area, the fact that they are usually packed in boxes of 500, which may take two or more days to travel, means that a certain amount of physical damage either to the roots or the leaves is almost inevitable.

THE LONGDAY ENVIRONMENT

Immediatley on receipt of the rooted cuttings by the grower they are planted approximately 12·5 by 12·5 cm and watered in. Although air temperatures are similar to those in the rooting area, that is a minimum of 15·6° at night, both the temperature in the soil and the humidity of the air will be markedly lower than during rooting and, even with first-class husbandry, the plant will not normally achieve its optimum growth rate for at least seven days after planting. The first objective has to be to encourage rapid and healthy root growth, and only when this occurs can nutritional deficiencies be made good.

Thus, in the longday planting system, the optimum growth rate of the flowering plant is not normally achieved between the time it is removed from the stock plant as an unrooted cutting and the time it has been planted in the flowering area for approximately a week. This period, not allowing for cold storage of either the unrooted or the rooted cutting, may be as long as four weeks and constitutes an average of 25 per cent of total crop time if this is calculated from the date of commencement of rooting the cuttings.

THE DIRECT SHORTDAY PLANTING SYSTEM

In view of the weaknesses in the direct longday planting system Machin devised a system which eliminated the periods of checked growth and nutrient deficiency described above.

Basically, the new system is one in which cuttings are rooted and grown on in long days at close spacing until large enough to plant directly into short days.

Following a series of pilot trials in 1968

(Machin, 1973), it became clear that a much faster growth rate than in the current system could be achieved if the cuttings were rooted in small containers either filled with or made from a compost containing adequate nutrients. It was found that, by using 60 mm containers in winter and 50 mm containers in summer and by keeping them pot-thick, growth rate was so improved that, after a period of three to four weeks from the insertion of unrooted cuttings according to season, plants could be planted directly into short days for flowering. At no time of the year was the quality of the flowering stems of plants rooted and grown in containers inferior to plants rooted and planted into long days in the flowering area. Indeed, in the new system, flowering plant quality was generally improved in terms of number of flowers per spray and size and form of spray, and appreciable reductions in the number of short days required for flowering resulted.

The fact that cuttings could be rooted and grown on in the same area, at a spacing of not more than 60 mm square, until the plants were sufficiently large to be planted directly into short days meant that an entirely new concept of year-round production of cut flower chrysanthemums could be envisaged.

One immediate advantage was that the long-day and shortday areas could be in separate houses, facilitating daylength control and avoiding the problems of light spill of the direct long-day planting system. The shortday flowering area could have 100 per cent automatic blackout, a situation much easier to organize than in the normal system, where up to a third of the beds remain in natural longday conditions during the summer period. Work at Efford EHS (Anon., 1973) has shown that there is no measurable effect from continuing blackout to the end of the crop instead of stopping at the bud colour stage.

With longday and shortday areas in separate houses, optimum environmental conditions for the different phases of crop growth could be given, with obvious advantages to both the quality and quantity of flower production.

The limitation of root growth within a small container during long days appeared to be beneficial, because, particularly during seasons of poor natural light, the plants were not so strongly vegetative at the commencement of short days as plants planted directly into long days as rooted cuttings.

The latter have a free root run, sometimes in cool ($10°$) soil conditions, and find an immediate change from vegetative to reproductive growth difficult compared with direct planting into short days with restricted roots near the surface of the soil.

A further benefit is that grading at planting time is done only 9 to 11 weeks from flowering, compared with 12 to 19 weeks in the older system, which results in a higher percentage of good flower grades.

It was in total production that the advantage of the new system appeared significant. In the direct longday planting system, assuming a 70 per cent planting in the flowering area, 0·4 ha will produce a potential of 572,000 stems per annum, the equivalent of $3\frac{1}{4}$ crops.

In the direct shortday planting system about one-tenth of the total area has to be allowed for rooting and growth in long days but from the remaining 0·36 ha a potential of 792,000 stems are possible, that is an increase of 35·5 per cent. This is because five crops per year can be grown (Table 15). If 0·4 ha of flowering area is used, and an additional area used for longday growth, then 880,000 stems may be produced, an increase of 54 per cent over the conventional system. Of course, the extra cost of labour and heating in the longday area have to be taken into consideration, as have the extra costs of the increased production. However, the potential for increased profitability in year-round chrysanthemum cut flower production is undeniable.

One further advantage of the new system is that, because young plants are closely spaced for at least three weeks in the longday area, supplementary lighting which is beneficial to growth (page 107), can be used economically during this period of active growth.

Important Phases of Growth

Early research relating to the direct shortday planting system had indicated that certain phases

TABLE 15   Year-Round Programme for the Direct Shortday Planting System: 10-Week Varieties (10 Units. Single Stem Crops)

Unit No.	Plant date	Response	Flower date	Plant date	Response	Flower date	Plant date	Response	Flower date
1	3 Nov	10	12 Jan	19 Jan	10	30 Mar	6 Apr	9	8 Jun
2	10 Nov	11	26 Jan	2 Feb	10	13 Apr	20 Apr	9	22 Jun
3	17 Nov	11	2 Feb	9 Feb	10	20 Apr	27 Apr	9	29 Jun
4	24 Nov	11	9 Feb	16 Feb	10	27 Apr	4 May	9	6 Jul
5	1 Dec	11	16 Feb	23 Feb	10	4 May	11 May	9	13 Jul
6	8 Dec	11	23 Feb	2 Mar	10	11 May	18 May	9	20 Jul
7	15 Dec	11	2 Mar	9 Mar	10	18 May	25 May	9	27 Jul
8	22 Dec	11	9 Mar	16 Mar	9	18 May	25 May	9	27 Jul
9	29 Dec	11	16 Mar	23 Mar	9	25 May	1 Jun	9	3 Aug
10	12 Jan	10	23 Mar	30 Mar	9	1 Jun	8 June	9	10 Aug
1	15 Jun	9	17 Aug	24 Aug	10	2 Nov			
2	29 Jun	9	31 Aug	7 Sep	10	16 Nov			
3	6 Jul	9	7 Sep	14 Sep	10	23 Nov			
4	13 Jul	9	14 Sep	21 Sep	10	30 Nov			
5	20 Jul	9	21 Sep	28 Sep	10	7 Dec			
6	27 Jul	9	28 Sep	5 Oct	10	14 Dec			
7	3 Aug	9	5 Oct	12 Oct	10	21 Dec			
8	3 Aug	10	12 Oct	19 Oct	10	28 Dec			
9	10 Aug	10	19 Oct	26 Oct	10	4 Jan			
10	17 Aug	10	26 Oct	2 Nov	10	11 Jan			

of growth in the life-cycle of the chrysanthemum plant were more important than others and merited closer study.

LEAF PRODUCTION IN LONG DAYS

The rate of leaf production in long days appeared to be critical for the success of this new system. At the end of long days, plants, which for ease of handling and uniformity of production, should not be longer than about 20 cm at planting time, must have sufficient leaves to produce a flowering stem of suitable length for market purposes. In Britain, the minimum length of stem is considered to be 81 cm. Length of plant is a product of the number of leaves on the main stem and the mean internode length, and this varies with the amount of light available. Machin (1973) found that the rate of leaf production per day in long days varied between summer and winter in the two varieties he used in the direct shortday planting system:

	Summer	Winter
Heyday	0·36	0·30
Polaris	0·21	0·14

The figures also illustrate the differences in rate of leaf production in long days between varieties. Polaris was found to have internodes 30 per cent longer than Heyday and this compensated to some extent for the lower leaf production in the former.

REPRODUCTIVE MORPHOGENESIS

Reproductive morphogenesis is the transformation of the apical and lateral buds from the vegetative to the reproductive condition. The rate of this process, and the subsequent rate of flower development, determines not only total flowering time in the shortday area, which is critical for crop planning, but also the number of flowers per spray and the type of spray. Ugly compound sprays frequently result from a delay in the change from the vegetative to the reproductive state.

Consequently, the factors affecting both the rate of leaf production in long days and the rate of reproductive morphogenesis were studied in detail in relation to the direct shortday planting system.

Special Aspects of Production

A number of factors concerning both husbandry and the control of the environment were found to be especially important in the new system.

THE UNROOTED CUTTING

The nature of the unrooted cutting is important with every vegetatively propagated crop but in the direct shortday planting system it is especially so. The time from the date of insertion of the unrooted cutting to the date of marketing the crop (11 to 15 weeks) is several weeks shorter than with other systems of production and the effect of the nature of the unrooted cutting on the growth and quality of plants in the system is, therefore, likely to be greater.

The variability of plant material, even between closely related clones, has been discussed and it is re-emphasized that great care is needed to ensure the selection of uniform plant material for use in the production system.

Microscopic examination of a typical vegetative unrooted cutting, 50 mm in length, shows that it contains approximately 15 leaves, roughly 50 per cent of the leaf number of the flowering plant. The final size and quality of these longday leaves will, to a large extent, govern the subsequent response and quality of the flowering plant. It is essential, therefore, that the stock plants from which the cuttings are derived are kept free from pests and diseases.

Unrooted cuttings should be of good quality (high total wet weight) and cuttings of up to 75 mm are beneficial if the extra length incorporates an extra number of leaves. This is particularly important in seasons of low light when the rate of leaf production in long days is slowed down. One extra leaf on the unrooted cutting can reduce the time required in the longday area by three to seven days.

INSERTION OF CUTTINGS

Although the physical conditions in a compressed peat block are slightly less favourable to rooting than the relatively loose peat and grit mixtures used in a conventional rooting bench, direct sticking in closely spaced peat blocks has proved successful in most situations. However, in seasons unfavourable to rapid growth and where peat blocks are either too compressed or too wet, it has sometimes been found to be advantageous to 'callus' the unrooted cutting prior to insertion in the blocks. Cuttings are stuck 30 to 35 mm apart in conventional rooting benches and removed after approximately five days when root primordia are emerging around the circumference of the base of the stem. They are immediately inserted into freshly made peat blocks and watered in. The rooting blocks are misted frequently until the roots emerge at the sides and this occurs after a further five days in good conditions.

TYPE AND SIZE OF CONTAINER

Proprietary peat pots of 44 and 56 mm are found to produce satisfactory results, provided the compost used is of good physical quality and contains sufficient nutrient.

Blocks of compost, rather than containers filled with loose compost, are preferable for the rooting and longday period because the compressed compost of the former contain up to three times the nutrients of the latter. These nutrients are less readily leached during rooting from blocks compared with peat pots.

Because of the current use of peat compost blocks in the longday area the direct shortday planting system is sometimes erroneously called the 'blocking system'.

From mid-October to the end of January peat compost blocks 60 mm square are used because growth during long days will take place through the poorest light period of the year. Root growth will also be less than at other times and so the depth of the blocks need not be more than 40 mm. This also allows warm air from under the rooting plants to penetrate the blocks more uniformly.

During the remainder of the year 50 mm square peat compost blocks, 50 mm deep, are used.

LONG DAYS

Whether in the 50 or 60 mm blocks all plants

Fig. 36   Direct shortday planting system: plants ready for planting into the shortday area.

remain unspaced until they are ready for planting directly into the shortday area for flowering (Fig. 36). The criterion for deciding the correct size of plant for planting into short days is an important one and will determine the success or failure of the crop.

The heavier the dry weight of the plant at the start of short days, the faster the rate of change to the reproductive state, and the earlier the flowering date, especially in low-light conditions.

Because dry weight measurements are inconvenient on a busy nursery Machin has devised a simpler criterion for the measurement of adequate growth prior to short days. If a plant contains 20 leaves at the end of longday treatment (Fig. 37) then, according to the rate of change to the reproductive state, which will depend on the time of year, a further 5 to 10 shortday leaves will be formed on the main stem beneath the apical flower. A total of 25 internodes in the summer and 30 internodes in the winter will generally add up to the minimum

length of stem (81 cm) required for market purposes. Also, if grown well, a plant containing 20 leaves will be of sufficient dry weight to produce a reasonable flowering response in short days even in winter.

Microscopic examination has shown that the growing points of chrysanthemum shoots in a vegetative state and grown at 15·6° contain approximately 11 leaves counting those up to 12 mm in length. It is, therefore, a simple matter to count the leaves either on an unrooted cutting or a plant ready for planting into shortday conditions.

Table 16 gives figures for the variety Snowdon for summer and winter conditions. It can be seen that, provided information is available on the rate of leaf production in long days, and on mean internode lengths for the most important varieties at each season, stem length can be closely controlled in the direct shortday planting system. This information can readily be worked out by the grower himself. This facili-

Fig. 37   20-leaved plant ready for planting into short days.

tates not only the supporting of the crop but the clearing of the beds for the next batch of plants.

NUTRITION

Correct nutrition of the stock plants from which the cuttings for the crop are derived is important and establishes the growth rate in the shoot which will ultimately affect the rate of produc-

tion of leaves on the vegetative plant during long-day conditions. If leaf production in long days is too slow, due to poor nutrition of the stock, and immature plants are planted into short days, a lowering of flower quality and a delay in flowering will result.

Inadequate stock plant nutrition can lead to delays of up to six days in flowering with up to a 30 per cent reduction in the quality of the flowers compared with plants which are derived from well-fed stock plants. This can occur despite the fact that adequate nutrition is given during the longday period, which commences with the insertion of cuttings into the peat compost blocks (Machin 1973).

The effect of nutrition during the longday period is even more important than the effect on stock plant growth. Poor nutrition during long days can delay flowering by up to 10 days and reduce flower quality by up to 40 per cent compared with adequate nutrition during this period.

In contrast, nutrition in the shortday area is not of great importance provided that adequate nitrogen and potash is available for the final stages of flower development. Any harmful effect on flowering induced by inadequate stock or longday nutrition cannot be corrected by the addition of fertilizer after planting directly into short days. The balance between nitrogen and potash and the actual quantity of nitrogen available appear to be the most important factors of nutrition, provided that phosphate and the trace elements are present in sufficient quantity for optimum growth.

In stock areas the availability of nitrogen to

TABLE 16   Leaf Production and Mean Internode Length for the Variety Snowdon over Two Seasons

	Leaf number in unrooted cutting (60 mm)	Number of leaves formed per day during long days	Leaf number at planting into short days	Number of leaves formed in short days	Total leaf number	Mean internode length (mm)	Total stem length (cm)
Summer 16 long days	16	0·25	20	6	26	33	85
Winter 28 long days	15	0·18	20	9	29	28	82

potash should be 3N : 1K$_2$O with a soil analysis of 80 to 100 ppm N.

The best combination of nitrogen and potash in the peat used for blocking is 250N : 360K$_2$O in g/m^3. Liquid feed—which should contain 275 ppm N : 150 ppm K$_2$O—must be applied to the plants in the longday area at least every other watering from five days after insertion of the cuttings until planting.

SUPPLEMENTARY LIGHT

Supplementary light is beneficial in several ways when used to raise the levels of natural winter light. First, it can be used to reduce the number of long days required for vegetative growth during the winter months, leading to immediate economies in production costs. Second, in many of the varieties which are proving useful in the new system (Snowdon and Fandango), the improvement in leaf quality and rate of bud formation, due to higher light levels during the longday period, are reflected in faster response and higher quality flowers. Higher light levels during the first 14 short days are even more beneficial to flower response and quality but it is difficult at present to apply this technique in commercial programmes. However, the use of supplementary light in winter during the last 14 long days is successful in practice on commercial holdings employing the direct shortday planting system by ensuring that the minimum length of stem required is achieved, and by improving the market grades and substantially reducing waste.

PLANTING INTO THE SHORTDAY AREA

Apart from planting, all husbandry techniques carried out in the shortday area are similar to those already described in Chapter 7.

Plants removed from the longday area must be planted quickly to avoid any check to growth. When the peat compost blocks are separated an expanse of new root covered in root hairs will be exposed and this must be covered with soil and watered as soon as possible. Because the cutting was inserted into the block to a depth of 12 mm, roots will generally emerge from the sides at about the same distance from the top edge of the block.

If the soil is prepared loosely the blocks are simply pressed into the soil, leaving 12 mm of the block above the surface. After watering in, preferably by mist spray line, the roots of the newly planted crop should have adequate moisture, aeration and temperature to enable them to grow away rapidly.

VARIETIES

Since 1973 all the most important year-round varieties such as the Snowdons, the Hurricanes, Fandango, Pollyanne, and the Bluechip, Polaris and Pink Marble families as well as many others, have been grown successfully in the direct shortday planting system. Varieties with especially short internodes, such as Bonnie Jean, are best avoided. New varieties which fit the ideotype set out on page 32 will do well in the new system, especially if they have a very high leaf initiation rate in long days, long internodes and a rapid change from vegetative to reproductive growth.

ORGANIZATION

Apart from the conventional rooting benches,* which may be required for callusing the cuttings, the longday area consists of a number of bench tops along which mobile trays can be moved from the sticking area through the supplementary light area, if this is provided, to the end of the house, whence they are removed for planting into short days. Therefore, the correct number of benches required for each season needs to be carefully planned. Normally, one-third of the area of mobile trays is equipped with mist spray lines for use during the first five days after insertion of callused cuttings. The trays are approximately 60 cm by 180 cm and each hold approximately 450 50 mm and 310 60 mm blocks respectively. They are readily pushed along the benches in the longday area by hand but an efficient mechanical system for moving them to and from the shortday area is essential on large nurseries.

---

* If rooting benches for callusing are necessary they must be taken into account when costing the direct short-day planting system.

IMPROVEMENT OF CUT FLOWER QUALITY

A number of techiques for the improvement of the quality of flowering stems have already been mentioned but it is convenient to discuss them in more detail at this point. They are generally concerned either with the use of light, by manipulations of daylength or the application of high-intensity artificial light for better growth, carbon dioxide enrichment or various chemical growth regulators. In some nurseries all three methods are used for the improvement of the winter crop in Britain.

Interrupted Lighting

Interrupted lighting is a technique in which a short period of artificial long days is given (by night-break lighting) following a period of short days for bud initiation.

The technique has been developed following the understanding of the natural processes involved in flower initiation and development. Following the onset of short days the apical meristem enlarges to form a receptacle which, three to four weeks after the start of short days, is covered with florets. If, during this period, the plants are briefly returned to long days, and this often occurs naturally, the receptacle continues to grow and on its enlarged area more florets are later initiated. The result is an improvement of flower quality.

The effect of alternate short and long days on flower quality was noticed by Post (1947a). As a result Post and Lacey (1951a) attempted to control the number and types of florets present in flowers of several disbudded varieties by alternate shortday and longday treatment. It was found that by interrupting the normal shortday treatment by a period of longday treatment, this effect was produced. Recent work has shown that nine short days should be given to initiate the terminal bud, 12 long days for the growth of extra ray florets and then continuous short days for flower development. This technique is especially important when varieties of the earlier (light inefficient) response groups are grown in seasons of low light intensity, but interrupted lighting cannot safely be employed with all varieties. In all but the single varieties a greater number of disc florets is desirable but some varieties are benefited more by this treatment than others. The Indianapolis varieties and Fred Shoesmith and its sports are markedly improved, whereas only a very slight improvement has been noted with the Mefo varieties.

The most simple method for planning the schedule for a crop of standards with interrupted light treatments is as follows. Count back 12 days from the date when short days would have commenced without interrupted light treatment. From this date, give nine short days, followed by 12 long days, then commence shortday conditions for flowering. The final flowering date is delayed by about one week. A typical programme for Fred Shoesmith would be as given in Table 17.

Interrupted light has also been used with spray varieties to control the type of spray (Post, 1947a, 1948a and b, 1949a and 1950a; Kiplinger and Alger, 1948; Post and Kamemoto, 1950). A crown bud is initiated after four to eight consecutive short days, depending on variety. Various combinations of shortday and longday treatment, before consecutive short days for flowering are given, determine the length of the pedicel, the type, number and position of buds

TABLE 17 Programme for Interrupted Light Treatment for the Variety Fred Shoesmith Compared with Normal Programme

	Plant	Lights on	Lights off	Lights on	Lights off	Blackout	Weeks to crop	Response	Flower date
Normal crop	13 Sep	13 Sep	—	—	25 Oct	No	18	11	10 Jan
Crop with interrupted light treatment	13 Sep	13 Sep	13 Oct	22 Oct	3 Nov	No	18	12	17 Jan

on the pedicel, and consequently the formation of the sprays as a whole. Figures 27 to 31 illustrate the different types of spray produced by different daylength treatments.

Tightly clustered sprays with flowers containing open centres occur on many of the 9-, 10- and 11-week varieties grown in late autumn if interrupted daylength treatment is not given. However, modern breeding is gradually providing varieties in the 10- and 11-week response groups which produce adequate spray formation in winter without the help of interrupted lighting. The 13- and 14-week spray types do not require this treatment, because spray formation is usually good even during seasons of very poor light.

It should also be noted that interrupted lighting delays flowering by up to the number of long days used for interruption, so that unless planned carefully the smooth running of the year-round programme might be affected.

After Lighting

This technique has been suggested for the improvement of flower size in standard or disbudded varieties (Ben-Jaacov and Langhans, 1969). Following four weeks of shortday treatment for flower bud initiation and development, long days are continued until flowering. This, although resulting in flowering delay compared with control plants, increases flower size owing to an increased length of all individual petals. The number of petals is not increased as with interrupted lighting.

The improvement in flower size in the varieties used range from 4 to 20 per cent, but the delay in flowering over control plants kept in short days throughout was from 6 to 16 days. In view of the flowering delay and the different varietal responses, this is not a technique which can be used by the normal year-round grower, but it might be considered for spot crops of standards for special markets.

Pre-Dawn Lighting

This is a technique suggested by Cathey (1974) following an experiment in which a four-hour artificial light treatment either preceded, interrupted or followed a 12-hour dark period from the start of shortday treatment.

Cathey found that artificial light treatment which followed a 12-hour dark period and was continued until sunrise, promoted internode extension and increased fresh and dry weight of the flowering plant without delaying flower initiation and development. A number of types of lamp were tested but light (21·2 lx) from an incandescent-filament lamp which emits red and far-red light in equal proportions was the most effective. Length of stem in plants of the variety Improved Indianapolis White was increased by 41 per cent in comparison with control plants which received 16-hour dark periods until flowering, the latter flowering one day earlier.

Cathey's technique has been attempted experimentally in England with mixed results. Using the spray varieties Hurricane and Fandango for flowering in November, Machin (unpubl.) found that length of stem was increased substantially by pre-dawn lighting, but flowering was delayed by up to 10 days. However, with the standard variety Snowdon, grown as a spray for April flowering, pre-dawn lighting treatment induced longer internodes and pedicels with subsequent improvement to flower grade with no flowering delay compared with control plants.

Trials at Efford EHS (Anon., 1977) suggest that the dark period must be at least 13 hours. Considerable delays to flowering were experienced when 12-hour dark periods were used. When 13-hour dark periods were given, followed by three hours of low illuminance lighting, stem length increases of 10 to 12 cm resulted. Only a slight delay in flowering was experienced with no decrease in flower quality.

Clearly, more research is needed with pre-dawn lighting before it can be generally applied to the year-round crop, but it might develop into a very useful technique for the improvement of cut flower quality.

Supplementary Light

Supplementary light used to raise the level of winter light, either during the longday or shortday phases of the year-round chrysanthemum crop, has been proved to be beneficial to the quality of the flowering plant. The problem is that, because of the high cost of installation of high illuminance lamps, the high running costs and the type of cut flower programme used by the majority of growers, it is difficult to see how the use of supplementary light can be made to show a profit. Unless the grower is using an advanced technique, such as the direct shortday planting system in which plants are held at close spacing for sufficient time for supplementary light to be used economically, its use may be limited.

It is known that supplementary light used for the first 14 short days during the winter, will shorten flowering time by up to 13 days (Canham, 1975) and this could lead to a greater output from the flowering area. However, the quality of the flowers is not necessarily improved following this treatment. This is because during February, March and April in Britain natural light conditions improve almost daily. Plants which are induced to flower early by supplementary light frequently receive much less light during the final two weeks prior to marketing than plants with a slower flowering response. It is possible, therefore, that improved flowering response and improved flower quality cannot be achieved at the same time, although the uniformity of the crop is likely to be better, which will be reflected in a low percentage of waste.

It is also known that supplementary light used to raise light levels to $1 \cdot 25$ MJ/m^2/day in winter during the final two weeks of the crop will increase flower dry weight by up to 100 per cent depending on variety. However, there would need to be a great deal of change in the economics of year-round production before supplementary lighting, when the plants are at their final spacing, could be profitable.

Carbon Dioxide Enrichment

As with supplementary lighting, carbon dioxide enrichment can be beneficial to plant growth, but it is less easy to prove that it is profitable to the year-round grower. However, figures provided by Efford EHS (Anon., 1975) are use-

ful in this respect. They showed the percentage increase in yield in boxes of flowers per 1000 stems planted, due to carbon dioxide enrichment, to be as set out in Table 18:

TABLE 18   Percentage Increase in Yield due to Carbon Dioxide Enrichment

Flowering Weeks*	Per cent Increase in Yield	
	Hurricane	Heyday
2/3	11·9	17·1
7	14·9	—
11/12	14·0	13·7

* Week 1 was 1–7 Jan. and so on.

The report concluded that 'the results suggest that there will only be a response from using carbon dioxide from November to March on plants flowering in January to March. If a 13 per cent yield increase was obtained for those three months, the increase in returns could amply cover the cost of burning propane for the five months November to March, but would not cover the cost of using pure carbon dioxide. It should be emphasized that temperatures must be adequate for bud initiation where carbon dioxide is used, as it will not compensate for low temperatures, nor will flowering be advanced.'

Growth Retardants

Of the growth retardants available, Alar is best used for controlling the quality and type of growth on cut flowers, especially during the period of winter and spring production.

The beneficial effect of the use of Alar can be considered in two ways. First, there are those varieties on which Alar has a beneficial effect by reducing the length of and thereby strengthening the naturally weak pedicels. In winter the spray varieties Polaris, Delmarvel and Heyday have been particularly improved by spraying with an Alar solution of 66 g/100 l (or 33 g/100 l as necessary) approximately 10 days after the start of short days. Other varieties where spray formation is improved in this way are Flamenco, Surfside, Delight, Pink Marble and other varieties which normally have few flowers and long pedicels in winter. The effect of the reduction of growth in the top buds and pedicels in the spray encourages development of further buds down the stem. In one experiment, the number of flowers per stem on Heyday was increased from eight to 16 by spraying Alar as described above. When used for the purpose of reducing pedicel length one litre of solution will treat approximately 260 stems.

Second, its general effect of slowing down vegetative growth can be used on all varieties during poor light conditions to assist the change to reproductive growth. Trials in December and January have shown that a solution of 66 g/100 l applied to varieties such as Hurricane and Delight (33 g/100 l is sufficient in other varieties) markedly improves the uniformity of growth in the weeks after spraying. The weaker plants, invariably found in the centre of beds, benefit by the reduction in growth rate of their stronger neighbours. The reduction in growth rate leads directly to an increase in strength of stem. The best time of application of the Alar for this purpose is 10 to 14 days prior to the start of shortday treatment provided that the total longday treatment is four weeks or more. With this type of application one litre is sufficient to treat up to 440 stems.

HARVESTING

The objective of the year-round chrysanthemum grower is to produce flowers which, when sold to the consumer, will give good value for money. Presumably, the consumer will then buy again. In this way the year-round chrysanthemum industry can consolidate and prosper.

Methods used to harvest, pack and market chrysanthemums probably have more effect on the keeping quality of the cut flowers and therefore, indirectly on the consumer's good will, than most of the techniques of husbandry described hitherto. Yet, until recently, the harvesting of the crop has received comparatively little attention. However, as margins between returns and costs have narrowed, increasing thought has been directed towards the best and most efficient methods of harvesting, packing and marketing.

Harvesting changes the physiology of the flower completely. It is instantly removed from the source of food and water supply, the roots, and unless the correct treatment is given wilting will rapidly occur.

Cut flowers should be removed from the house as soon as possible after harvesting, especially during warm sunny weather.

To prevent undue colour loss (fading) it is normal practice, once colour shows on pink, red and bronze varieties, to shade with butter muslin or small-mesh nylon net until the crop is completely harvested in order to reduce the direct radiant heat on the flowers during periods of sunny weather.

Flowers should not be removed from the houses by hand in large bunches, because, not only is this practice inefficient, but will lead to increased amounts of damage and waste. It is desirable therefore, to use some form of bulk container to move flowers to the packing area. While effective use of trolleys has been made with chrysanthemums to move the harvested crop along the long axis of a widespan house, mono-rail and combined mono-rail and pallet systems have gained favour in year-round cut flower programmes (Fig. 38).

Factors Affecting Keeping Quality

Cut chrysanthemums have traditionally been placed in cold water in cool dark packing sheds following removal from the flowering area. A study of the factors affecting keeping quality indicates that these are not the best conditions for ensuring long vase life.

WATER

It is extremely important that crops receive adequate amounts of water during the two weeks prior to harvesting. This will not only allow the flowers to grow to their full potential but the flowering stem will have an adequate supply prior to cutting.

It is also necessary with all cut flower chrysanthemum crops, but particularly with the large-flowered standards, to ensure that an adequate and even supply of moisture is available to the crops throughout the harvesting period. Once the first cut has been made into a crop, the rate at which the soil dries is accelerated by the in-

Fig. 38   Mono-rail for transporting flowers through the greenhouse.

creased movement of air across the soil surface, and the development of the true potential size of many flowers on the later stems can be arrested by lack of moisture.

The first objective after cutting is to keep leaves fresh and turgid by both conserving the moisture already in the stem and by ensuring a rapid and unrestricted uptake of water when the cut flowers are placed in water containers.

It is known that warm water (approximately 38°) will be taken up into the stems of cut chrysanthemums more rapidly than cold water and this fact should be borne in mind when planning the facilities of the packing shed.

Also, physical changes occur in the stem following cutting, which directly affect the subsequent uptake of water. Partial blocking of the stem due to the leakage of the contents of damaged cells and the growth of bacteria and fungi leads to the wilting of leaves. This affects some varieties more than others, examples being Hurricane and Heyday. Chemical treatments can be used to improve water uptake by acting as germicides which reduce the microbial plugging of the conducting tissues in the stem. Silver nitrate solutions have been used for this purpose. Stem immersions for 10 minutes in a concentrated solution of silver nitrate (using tap water) (0·012 per cent) is effective for increasing the vase life of chrysanthemums. Alternatively, more dilute solutions (0·003 per cent) of silver nitrate can be used in which to keep cut flower stems continuously. Short treatment for four hours using the same concentration in distilled water is also effective. There is a 'carry over' effect into the following day even when the stems have been out of water (for example on the way to market) for a period. Care must be taken when handling silver nitrate because it is poisonous and slightly corrosive. Overdoses will lead to blackening of stems and foliage.

Chrysanthemums have a relatively large leaf area in comparison with other cut flowers so that water loss by transpiration can be reduced considerably by removal of all leaves not required for decorative purposes.

There are two reasons for ensuring that adequate light is available to the flowers after cutting. First, continuing development of the opening flowers will occur only if light conditions are sufficiently good for photosynthesis to continue. Unlike other flowers such as narcissus and tulip, chrysanthemums do not carry food reserves in the stems and leaves, and must manufacture food requirements for flower development day by day.

Second, leaves turn yellow prematurely in complete darkness at room temperature due to the breakdown of chlorophyll and will age more rapidly in poor light than in good light. It is an important point to remember that the vase life of leaves is less than that of flowers in optimum light conditions.

TEMPERATURE

Cut flowers have a high rate of respiration in conditions of adequate water and light and this adversely affects their vase life. Keeping flowers at low temperatures considerably reduces the rate of respiration and increases vase life.

Cool stores can, therefore, be used for short-term storage because this not only slows down respiration but also reduces water loss, arrests the development of bacterial organisms in the stem and generally prevents ageing. Optimum temperature is 2°. Temperatures lower than this ($-1°$) cause irreversible freezing damage, while in higher temperatures leaf yellowing would occur unless artificial light is provided.

Stage of Harvesting

The stage of harvesting is very important, and, if chosen correctly, will prolong the shelf-life of the flowers.

SPRAYS

It is difficult to be precise about the stage of harvesting spray chrysanthemums, as great variation occurs according to flower form and by variety within each form.

Single varieties should be harvested when the maximum possible number of flowers are open but before the pollen is shed in the outer row of disc petals of the topmost flower. Anemone-centred varieties should be harvested before the cushion rises on the topmost flower.

Decoratives should be harvested when the petals in the centre of the topmost flower are almost fully developed. (Fig. 39). This will ensure that adequate development has occured in the lower flowers. However, whereas it would be possible to allow one variety which had reached this stage, for example Hurricane, to stand for a further three days before harvesting, another, such as Fandango, would need to be harvested at once because the centre of the flowers contain fewer petals and in consequence passes the optimum harvesting stage more quickly.

STANDARDS

With standards, harvesting usually occurs when the outer petals have ceased to elongate and the central area of unfurled petals is between 15 and 20 mm in diameter.

Once-Over Harvesting

This concept of cutting whole units at one time is a very attractive one for year-round chrysanthemum growers in view of the economic advantages which would follow its successful application. However, year-round production has not yet progressed to the point where crops can be once-over harvested with all varieties in all environmental situations and with all flowers having reached the stage of development described above.

Opening Solutions

The development of bud-opening solutions has brought the practical application of once-over harvesting a great deal nearer. It has now been shown that flowers can be cut in bud and then opened in solution in warm, light conditions. This is important, not only for once-over harvesting but also for the growers who wish to avoid waste and delay caused by uneven flowering response.

A number of workers have reported on the use of various chemicals for opening chrysan-

Fig. 39   A uniform crop of Rosado ready for harvesting.

themums cut in the bud stage (Marousky, 1971, 1973; Kofranek and Halevy, 1972; Nichols, 1976). Stems are cut when the outer florets are showing colour and starting to unfurl. All unnecessary foliage is removed and the stems placed in containers of bud-opening solutions in warm (over 18°) illuminated conditions. The higher the temperature the faster will be the rate of opening of flowers. The containers should be non-metallic if a solution containing silver or hydroxyquinoline salts is used. Good results have been obtained by using solutions made up of 20 g sucrose per litre of water to which is added either silver nitrate (30 mg/l) or dichlorophen (25 mg/l).

For opening disbudded blooms solutions of hydroxyquinoline salts (200 mg/l) have been used. For standards silver nitrate (25 mg/l) and citric acid (75 mg/l) have been added to the sucrose solution described above. The sucrose in the solution provides the energy needed for flower opening and enlargement while the other additives either promote the uptake of solution or slow down the growth of micro-organisms in the solution which might otherwise block the stems. Because varieties differ in their metabolic activities one solution is not ideal for all varieties at all seasons, and the grower will need to try out various combinations and dilutions of the above chemicals. Care should be taken, however, when experimenting with concentrations of sucrose, because leaves will be damaged by excess amounts.

Results on the use of a bud-opening solution for once-over harvesting are available from Efford EHS (Anon., 1977). The opening solution used contained 2 per cent sugar, 1000 ppm citric acid and 25 ppm dichlorophen. Cut stems were placed in plastic buckets at a constant temperature of 18° in light levels averaging 1500 lx and the humidity was between 60 and 70 per cent.

Table 19 compares total production from the two harvesting techniques in the experiment. Normal harvesting, when each stem was cut at maturity, was compared with once-over harvesting when all stems were cut when the most backward plant showed colour in the lowest bud.

TABLE 19   Boxes per 1000 Plants from Two Harvesting Treatments

Variety	Cut in bud	Normal harvest
Hurricane	31·0	32·9
Yellow Hurricane	37·6	36·2
Yellow Snowdon (Sprays)	44·9	44·4
Yellow Snowdon (Standards)	40·9	38·4
Rosechip	41·4	41·9
Mean	39·2	38·8

Mature stems from the latter bed were harvested at once.

On stems cut at the tightest stage, flowers opened in solution in four to seven days depending on variety. In good light conditions for flowering, the marketing date for each variety was similar with each harvesting method and the time saved in the shortday area was 7 to 12 days, depending on variety. During the poor light of December and January it was found possible to open flowers faster in solution and these were of better quality than the controls. Despite the benefits of bud-opening solutions and flower preservatives it is important to emphasize the part played by certain factors of the environment. If transpiration can be kept to a minimum by the control of temperature and humidity much of the stress will be removed

Fig. 40   Bunched graded flowers standing in troughs of water in the packing area.

from the cut flower. Also, in optimum conditions for storage, flower preservatives are less likely to cause damage to foliage.

Grading

The purpose of grading is to sort the flowers which have been selected for harvesting into certain predetermined classes according to size and/or weight. In this way both the producer and the purchaser can appreciate more readily both the quantity and the quality of the flowers. The aim of grading must be to provide a consistent and reliable standard product throughout the year, upon which confidence between producer and purchaser may be built.

Grading has traditionally been done as a separate operation in the packing department after the flowers have been in water. However, there are advantages in making grading an integral part of the whole packing operation and where bulk packing is used, the flowers can be graded, bunched and wrapped before going into water (Fig. 40).

Another possibility associated with bulk packing is to cut by grade in the house and bunch at the same time (Fig. 41). This is satisfactory where the grade is fairly even, but it requires that a large proportion of the staff be skilled graders, and the more people involved in the grading operation the greater is the chance of a substantial variation in standard. On a large nursery it would seem preferable to restrict the grading to a comparatively small number of skilled staff.

SPRAYS

If grading is to be consistent round the year, as it must, then it is necessary to have a strict specification to which each of the graders can adhere. While it could be argued that not every variety will fit a given specification, the vast majority will do so. A useful specification which has been made to work extremely well for bulk packing is shown in Table 20.

TABLE 20 Metric Grade Specification for Spray Chrysanthemums

Grade	Stems per sleeve	Specification
Gold	(10)	6 flowers or more out and some to come
Silver	(15)	4 or 5 flowers out and some to come
Bronze	(20)	3 flowers out and some to come
Make-up	(—)	All stems not covered above, filling sleeves to same extent as other grades

Length of stem should not be less than 66 cm for British markets and stems less than 51 cm should be marked 'shorts'.

STANDARDS

Standard chrysanthemums grown in Britain are still usually packed into traditional display boxes. They are graded for size by bloom diameter and are grouped together under the counts which

Fig. 41   Cutting, grading and sleeving in the flowering area.

can be packed into the display box, for example 18, 24 or 30.

Standard varieties graded in this way may be packed into sleeves in which they are more protected from damage, but as the grading of these blooms is less easily defined, more skill is required when grade cutting, to maintain a consistent pack. Certain producers net incurving standard and spider varieties, when colour shows with a small open-mesh nylon sleeve. The blooms are then harvested at an earlier stage than that for normal harvesting, but consistent grading is more difficult for the inexperienced grader. However, the blooms are certainly better protected for handling and are well suited to bulk packs, such as those used in continental Europe.

PACKING

The method of packing will be determined largely by the type of sales outlet being served. Even where flowers are sold through the wholesale markets a low-density, display-type box has traditionally been used. These boxes are expensive and time-consuming to make up and pack. Moreover, this type of pack is costly to transport and does not protect the product to a satisfactory degree, and represents an outmoded method of primary packing. These factors combined with an ever-increasing spiral of costs and more or less static returns, have brought about a major swing to bulk packing with year-round spray chrysanthemum crops. The reduced area required for packing and storage facilities, where bulk packs are used, offers reduced capital investment in providing these facilities on new nurseries.

Sprays

With bulk packing 10, 15 or 20 stems are placed in sleeves according to grade. Six sleeves, three at each end, are normally packed in each box which measures 80 by 50 by 23 cm.

Standards

The majority of standard chrysanthemums are still packed in display type boxes which measure 91 by 43 by 15 cm. The blooms are placed in the boxes according to grade. Where some of the

larger, but rather loose blooms are packed it is usual to place a 'pillow', made from a strip of corrugated paper, under the necks of the bottom layer at each end of the box. With smaller, firmer blooms this may not be considered necessary. With all display packs an attempt is made to hold the stems in place with a metal tie strip.

MARKETING

The choice of varieties made by each grower should be intimately connected with his marketing arrangements. Most of the larger producers (more than 0·3 ha) send their flowers to the wholesale markets, which in Britain may be from 50 to 400 miles away. For the long-distance markets careful selection of varieties is essential.

Small growers (0·1 to 0·2 ha), who have local contracts for most of their produce, grow a wider range of varieties. Retailers tend to prefer the more unusual single and anemone-centred varieties, particularly during the summer months, and find ready sales if these varieties can be supplied by local growers with a minimum of travelling time. It is extremely important, therefore, that the grower, before selecting varieties, should contact his salesman or florist and be guided to some extent by their suggestions.

Sprays

Spray varieties must take water well after cutting and arrive at the market in good condition. The strong-growing, rather soft varieties such as Polaris and Fandango are ideal travellers. As a general rule the decorative types and the pompons travel well, but some of the pompons are inclined to break just below the flowers due to their brittle pedicels. Woody types such as White Sands and Heyday and many singles do not take water readily and cannot be sent long distances with complete confidence at all seasons.

There is some preference for the decorative types in the British wholesale markets. This may be due to some extent to their good travelling qualities or to the fact that the decorative varieties usually form larger sprays than do the pompons. The latter are more likely to flower unevenly and appear untidy if low crown bud formation leads to a compound spray.

Another factor in the choice of spray varieties is colour. Red, bronze and gold are generally considered to be autumn shades and these colours are usually grown in limited numbers after Christmas. In the spring and early summer the emphasis is on white, lemon and pink shades with an increase of yellow and gold in mid-summer.

Standards

Traditionally there is a market in Britain for well-grown standard blooms from June until January, but particularly in the autumn months. The proportion of standard varieties included in the year-round programme from early October may, with advantage, be steadily increased to about 30 per cent of the crop at Christmas.

Experience has shown that standard blooms sell remarkably well in the spring if the colours are carefully chosen. Bronze shades are unwanted at this season, but white and all shades of yellow and a small proportion of pink and red blooms can be profitable to the year-round grower until the end of May. After this date there is an increasing competition from the English early varieties commencing with those flowered under glass in June and July. These are followed by blooms produced out-of-doors in August and September, which during periods of fine weather can reach a high standard of quality.

NEW TECHNIQUES OF CUT FLOWER PRODUCTION

In a viable and important cut flower industry such as year-round chrysanthemum production, new techniques are constantly evolving from scientific and other research. Following the development work, often carried out in one or more of the Experimental Horticulture Stations, these techniques are usually tried out in commercial installations.

Production in Pots

One such technique is the production of cut flower spray varieties in pots.

Much of the development work on this system has been carried out at Efford EHS although the technique was originally tried at Framptons Nurseries Ltd.

Basically the system is for use on mobile benches with the object of reducing the cropping time and costs of the standard (direct longday planting) system of production.

Unrooted cuttings are stuck directly into pots and after the rooted plants are given a sufficient period of longday growth for stem length, the benches are moved into short days for flowering. In many ways the concept of the system is similar to that of the direct shortday planting system which seeks to eliminate checks to growth and to provide optimum growing conditions from insertion of cuttings to flowering.

A number of trials using the pot production system have been reported (Anon., 1975, 1976, 1977) and details of propagation methods, composts, containers, longday treatment, spacing, feeding and supplementary lighting are given. The main problem is to ensure that sufficient nutrition for quality of flowering stem is possible in the pots which necessarily restrict root run compared with crops flowered in ground beds. However, Efford EHS suggest that the pot production system for cut flowers is an acceptable alternative method to crops grown in greenhouse beds.

Culture in Nutrient Film

Plants have been grown in hydroponic culture for many years, but following recent work by Cooper at GCRI, Littlehampton, a method in which plants are grown in plastic troughs supplied with aerated nutrient solution has been developed. This is raising a great deal of interest with commercial growers of a range of crops all over the world. The interest is greatest in the arid areas where evaporation losses are high with soil-grown crops.

The main research effort has been on tomatoes, but growers have been producing cucumbers, sweet peppers, chrysanthemums and carnations on a small scale during the last two years.

PRODUCTION SYSTEM

The production system has been fully described by Potter (1975). The technique is to grow the plants with their root systems contained in black polythene film 45 mm wide clipped with clothes pegs at the top to form a channel, in a rigid channel using asbestos guttering, or in rigid plastic gutters. With all methods a nutrient solution containing all the elements required for plant growth is continuously circulated by a submersible pump in a catchment tank. This tank is covered with black film to prevent the build-up of algae. A water supply controlled by a ball valve is connected to the tank to replace water lost by transpiration, otherwise the nutrient concentration could increase due to this water loss. Ideally the ground should slope not less than 1 : 25 towards the tank and be evenly smooth to prevent localized deep stagnant areas where the roots would die.

The plants are then set out in the channels at normal spacing. Either rooted cuttings or plants in peat compost blocks or pots may be used.

Fig. 42 illustrates one possible layout.

NUTRIENT SOLUTION

In trials carried out at Fairfield EHS in Lancashire in 1973 and 1974, the nutrient solution used was:

Potassium nitrate	10·2 g/10 l
Calcium nitrate	4·9 g/10 l
Ammonium di-hydrogen phosphate	2·3 g/10 l
Epsom salt	4·9 g/10 l
Iron sequestrene	0·2 g/10 l
Manganese sulphate	10·0 mg/10 l
Copper sulphate	0·8 mg/10 l
Zinc sulphate	2·2 mg/10 l
Boric acid	28·6 mg/10 l
Ammonium molybdate	1·0 mg/10 l

Measured amounts of the above solution were

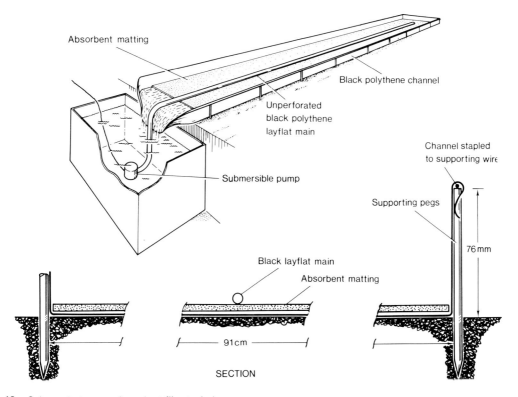

Fig 42 Schematic layout of nutrient film technique.

added to the tank two or three times a week, depending upon the readings from a conductivity meter. Generally a conductivity reading of cF 18 to 20 is desirable for chrysanthemums. There are several other good nutrient solutions available and it appears from current research at the GCRI that plants will tolerate quite a wide range of nutrient levels and still perform satisfactorily.

Twenty-seven year-round spray and standard varieties were grown for autumn flowering at Fairfield in channel widths of 45 and 60 cm. To overcome any unevenness in the gradient where the roots could become waterlogged or where dry areas occur, an absorbent mat was placed at the bottom to even out the supply of the solution. Rooted cuttings were potted up into 90 mm pots in mid-July and the pots placed in the beds in late August to flower in late November and early December. The beds were covered with a thin layer of black polythene to exclude light, and holes were cut to take the pots containing the plants.

Results were very promising for most of the varieties grown, but there was a tendency for the variety Tuneful to suffer from iron deficiency.

During the winter of 1974 five spray varieties were grown in nutrient solution to flower in February and March. One object was to note whether flowering would be delayed due to the plants being grown wet at the roots, which would rule out the use of hydroponics for the winter. The nutrient solution was maintained at two concentrations, weak and strong. The electrical conductivity readings for the solutions were cF 18 and cF 30, respectively. Unrooted cuttings were placed in rock-wool blocks which were then placed in the nutrient solution flowing down the channels. The plants grown using the nutrient film technique flowered about nine days earlier than a comparative crop grown in soil beds, presumably because the plants became established and grew away more quickly in the nutrient solution.

Two years of trials of nutrient film culture have also been carried out at Efford EHS (Anon., 1976, 1977).

The technique is in the early stages of development and improvements are needed to simplify the methods used to replace the nutrients recommended for commercial use on a large scale. Equipment is required to monitor the pH and cF of the solution automatically and to inject a given quantity of nutrients when required. If this system became established soil preparation and sterilization would be eliminated, watering reduced and crop production increased.

Future Techniques

Current research into factors affecting the growth and flowering of chrysanthemums could lead to more advanced systems of production of cut flowers than those described in this chapter. New knowledge constantly becoming available leads to new ideas and there is no shortage of genetic material for the breeding of varieties for use in future systems.

The limiting factor to progress is, as always, the current economic situation. New developments progress at a rate proportional to the rate of financial investment possible for capital equipment, and this is in turn dependent on the profitability of the enterprise at any given time.

From the knowledge available a completely automated system of chrysanthemum cut flower production could be devised in which each growth phase received the optimum environmental conditions. Using present varieties, six crops per year would be possible from at least 95 per cent of the production area. This area would probably be a very large growing room where it would be easier to control the environment than in a greenhouse. Staff would operate in the most efficient working conditions in which benches for either planting or harvesting would be bought to them by conveyor belt. This may occur in 5, 10, 15 or 25 years, depending on the economic climate then prevailing.

9 Pot Plant Production

There has been a steadily increasing demand for pot plants for house decoration and for use in amenity horticulture during recent years. Modern architectural design, which generally allows excellent light admission into all types of building, coupled with the increasing desire to enjoy plants, suggests that this trend will continue. The chrysanthemum is a plant which, if grown in a pot and controlled in size, is eminently suitable for this purpose.

For several reasons, chrysanthemum pot plants have become popular round the year. An excellent range of colour and form is available and the lasting quality of the plant in the home is extremely good provided that reasonable care is taken, especially with watering, Different shapes and sizes of plant and pot are available to suit the different and widely varying requirements of the consumer. Also, the crop is usually satisfactory for the producer. A high return per square metre is possible especially when efficient up-to-date growing techniques are used. With selected varieties five crops per year can be produced in the same area.

However, the growing requirements for the crop are extremely exacting and only slight deviations from the optimum conditions can reduce the quality of the plants substantially. A grower who understands the principles of production, who is well organized and who watches the crop carefully from day to day, has little to fear, but results can be disappointing where any of the factors necessary for optimum growth are not under strict control.

The generally accepted standards for pot plant measurement are that the height of the plant, as measured from the rim of the pot, should nearly equal the diameter of the flowering head, and the height of the actual plant should be three times the height of the half-pot normally used.

Some markets, particularly in the north of England, require plants rather taller than the measurements outlined above. The London market and other southern areas favour a shorter habit. With the control of environment possible, with choice of varieties and the many cultural aids available, the pot producer can 'tailor' his plants to the market requirement.

Pot plant production in Britain has been established on two broadly defined levels. First, there are many producers in the range of 200 to 500 14 cm half-pots per week using 0·04 ha of greenhouse or less. Usually these growers supply their own immediate neighbourhood and have the advantages of a regular requirement for their product and a low marketing cost. The quality of plants in these programmes is generally very good. Second, there are the large producers who may supply local markets, but much of their production has to be sent long distances to the large towns or cities.

Before commencing production, the pot plant producer must discuss with his markets the type and size of plant required. The aim should then be to produce a regular supply of as many plants of this quality as possible from a given area. All aspects of husbandry and production organization should be considered from this point of view.

It should be emphasized again that high-quality pot chrysanthemums can only be produced by growers who fully understand the various techniques for controlling the greenhouse environment and who are fully aware of all the intricacies of husbandry required. Very careful choice of varieties is necessary, while the methods used for harvesting, packing and marketing should be carefully considered. Finally, an extremely efficient organization of the flowering programme is essential for chrysanthemum pot production to be a profitable venture.

CONTROLLING THE ENVIRONMENT

A great deal of thought must be given to the suitability of the nursery and the particular houses for year-round pot chrysanthemum production.

Greenhouses, with good light admission, should be well oriented, preferably with a good southern aspect, and never over-shadowed. Single east–west houses are usually ideal. Light values are sufficiently high in all areas of Britain for the production of high-quality pot plants from mid-March to mid-December, but for flowering in mid-winter only the best growing conditions will produce marketable pot plants. Not all varieties can be grown in mid-winter in northern England, Northern Ireland and Scotland. However, the continual improvement in growing techniques together with the introduction of new varieties more tolerant of relatively poor winter light conditions, are improving this position.

Daylength

With chrysanthemum pot plants it is imperative that daylength should be under complete control round the year. A shaft of light piercing a torn blackout in the summer may delay one or two stems in a cut flower crop, but in a pot plant programme far more damage can result because several pots may be rendered unmarketable. Similarly if the lights fail for two or three days during the longday period of a cut flower crop little harm is done. In a pot plant crop, two or three days may constitute 33 per cent of the total longday period allowed and a light failure will seriously affect the quality of the plants.

LIGHTING

The main difference between the lighting requirements for a year-round pot programme and those for cut flowers is that only the nurse area, and in some cases a small part of the intermediate spacing area, needs lighting equipment. This is because the number of long days necessary to produce a suitable pot plant, even in winter, are comparatively few.

For benches 1·8 m wide a single line of 100-watt tungsten-filament coiled coil pearl lamps, spaced 1·8 m and 71 cm above the bench will provide the necessary 50 to 100 lx satisfactorily. The normal nightly lighting periods are shown on page 15.

BLACKOUT

Normally, all benches are equipped with blackout material because, during natural long days, all or most of the area will be in artificial short-day conditions. At other times of the year benches with lights can be screened from those in natural short days by covering the lighted benches only. Also, where heating pipes are under the benches these can be enclosed by the blackout to conserve heat during the winter months. Where benches are blacked-out individually the material should be supported 71 cm above the bench on 12 mm galvanized light barrel arches spaced 2·4 to 3·0 m apart with five wires running the length of 1·8 m wide bench, The width of the blackout material needed will depend on both the width of the bench and the nature of the bench top. Where the top is of wire mesh or some other open-work construction the blackout material must be long enough to exclude light from the plants on the bench. Where a solid top is used the blackout need only extend a few centimetres below the bench top.

Year-round pot plant production, especially in clearspan houses, lends itself to automated blacking-out more readily than does any other form of production, and throughput may well be increased with automatic blackout.

Blacking-out should cease on all plants once the buds start to show colour. Excessive temperatures under the automatic blackout are far less of a problem with the greater volume of air enclosed, but approximately one-fifth of the final spacing area could be left without blackout and plants in colour moved to this area before marketing. Larger and brighter flowers will result from the cooler longday finish, but this extra move must be highly organized or the cost will outweigh any increased revenue.

Temperature and Humidity

Most plants respond to closely controlled and

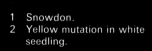

1 Snowdon.
2 Yellow mutation in white seedling.

3 Lemon Polaris
4 Yellow Polaris

5 Hurricane.
6 Mutations to shades of pink white and bronze in Popsie (pink) following radiation.

7 Rory Ⓟ
9 Wye Sylph raised by Mr. A. A. Jackson.
11 Rufus Ⓟ

8 Yellow Popsie Ⓟ
10 Rascal Ⓟ
12 Reaper Ⓟ

13 Southdown Chip.
16 Robeam Ⓟ
19 Fandango.

14 Snowdon grown as a spray.
17 Snapper Ⓟ
20 Bronze Nero Ⓟ

15 Pink Gin Ⓟ
18 Golden Polaris.
21 Rosado.

22 Magnesium deficiency symptoms.
24 Yellow Tokyo – a spider variety
    as a no-pinch pot plant.
26 Rosado in summer. Almost a
    once-over cut.

23 Boron deficiency symptoms.
25 Pink decorative spray seedlings.
27 Spic ℗

interrelated temperature and humidity conditions for starting off, growing on and finishing, and chrysanthemums are no exception.

Immediately after potting, the pots are stood pot thick, or almost pot thick, in a nurse area for one or two weeks. The starting climate should ideally have an 80 per cent relative humidity, full light and a temperature controlled at 18·3° minimum at nights, 18·3° on cloudy days, and up to 24° on bright days. The nurse area of a year-round pot programme is relatively small and unless the production unit is very large, nurse areas are generally in the same houses as the growing on and finishing areas. The ideal environment is therefore hard to achieve, but in order to maintain humidity and prevent rapid drying of plants, polythene or muslin tents can be used over the nurse area during the day.

Normal humidities with controlled air movement and a minimum night temperature of 15·6° are the rule in the growing-on area in which the plants remain for two or three weeks at half final spacing. A 5·6° rise in temperature is allowed on bright days.

The finishing climate should ideally have night temperatures controlled at a minimum of 13·3°, with cloudy days at 13·3° and bright days up to 16·7°. Plenty of ventilation should be given to keep humidity low. Relatively cool, dry conditions in the final stages lead to high-quality pot plants.

Recent work at Efford EHS has shown that, for certain varieties, lower night temperatures than those outlined above can be given with little or no delay to flowering even during periods of poor natural light. During flowering trials from December to July very few differences were recorded for the variety Bright Golden Anne between night temperatures of 15·0°, 16·7° and 18·3° (Anon., 1975). In practice, a night temperature of 15·0° was found to be adequate because flowering time was only reduced by two days compared with plants grown in a night temperature of 18·3°.

Further experiments (Anon., 1976, 1977) which also included the variety Redcap (1976 only), showed that, according to the time of the year and the stage of the crop, night temperature could be reduced still further with no ill effect. From November to the end of February a night temperature of 15·0° was adequate for the first four weeks of short days followed by 13·3° night temperature until flowering. From March onwards night temperatures could be reduced to 13·3° and 10·0° for equivalent stages of growth.

PRODUCING THE CROP

The production techniques described are considered separately, but are, of course, closely interrelated throughout the production period. The grower has not only to follow the main environmental requirements correctly but also to choose methods which give the closest control over all stages of growth.

There are a number of different types of pot plant crop, each of which require specialized treatment.

Types of Crop

The types of chrysanthemum pot plant crop may be broadly divided into three categories:

1 Plants in 12·7 cm or larger pots, usually marketed in packs of six and used mainly for decorating trade exhibitions and public buildings, and as high-quality plants for the home. This crop is very popular in Britain and in North America. The majority of plants in this category are grown in 14 cm half-pots using five cuttings per pot, or four in some cases in the summer. Occasionally 12·7 cm standard pots are used. Pots 15·2 cm and larger, with six or seven cuttings, are used to produce large specimen plants for special markets.

2 Plants in 10·8 cm pots using three cuttings per pot are grown on some scale in Europe and increasingly in Britain for home decoration.

3 Single plant specimens pinched to produce at least three stems, with each stem usually left undisbudded. Pot size is from 76 to 90 mm. These plants are exceedingly popular in the Netherlands and Denmark and are used almost entirely for home decoration.

Compost

The basic requirements of a compost are:

(a) To anchor the plant firmly in the pot in such a way that the plant will remain upright if handled in a reasonable manner;

(b) To provide good drainage and an environment in which the roots will grow freely and take up the amount of water and nutrient necessary for optimum growth;

(c) To be reliable and consistent.

Growers in the past made their own special composts and a wide range of both organic and inorganic materials have been used. Loam, peat, sand, perlite, vermiculite, leaf mould, chopped straw, sawdust and more recently plastic foam, have played a part.

Some producers in Britain used John Innes potting compost (using $1\frac{1}{2}$ times the base fertilizer) (Appendix 5), but most have since changed to various types of loamless compost comprising peat and fine or coarse sand, and more recently the all-peat compost has been introduced. Others have altered the basic formula of John Innes by increasing the peat and sand content substantially. Good crops can be grown in all these types of compost and in mixtures of them.

Most soil composts satisfy the first requirement above, but care is sometimes needed with the lighter all-peat composts. The lightness of the latter, although advantageous to the movement of pots around the house and for marketing, is sometimes a disadvantage as plants are very easily knocked over if the leaves extend into the paths.

Pot chrysanthemums in particular need a very fast take-off after planting. The roots need warmth, air and water in the correct proportions at the outset. The compost must therefore be retentive of moisture, but at the same time have adequate pore space to allow the entry of air. Very close, tight composts must be avoided.

Drainage is important for two reasons. Impeded drainage leads to root loss due to stagnation and the build-up of salts in the base of the pot. Pot chrysanthemums require large quantities of fertilizer, and liquid feeds containing up to 300 ppm N and 200 ppm K_2O are applied with each watering during the summer. It is important to use sufficient water and feed each time to bring the compost to its field capacity. Partially wetting the compost will quickly lead to a build-up of salts in the pot.

The very regular watering necessary means that a compost must have the physical properties to stand up to large applications of water and feed. Some growers have found the ideal compost for their programmes by mixing a John Innes type of compost with equal parts of one of the peat/sand mixes. Others have found that the addition of 3 mm grit to some of the all-peat composts achieves the right mixture.

Consistency of mix is very important and although both peat and sand can be variable in nature it is generally loam which gives the most trouble in this respect.

When trying new composts it is important to give them a fair trial because each compost has its own characteristics and therefore needs different treatments. It is not adequate to pot up a few plants and place them here and there in the programme. This method is bound to be unfair to the new compost. At least a considerable part of a bench should be allocated, with the crop consisting of several varieties. Even this can lead to poor results unless a great deal of care is taken to treat the new compost in its own right and not to adopt in their entirety the same growing techniques used with the remainder of the crop.

Each growing technique—watering, feeding, spacing, use of retardants, daylength and temperature control and so on—is interrelated in producing an environment in which a certain type of plant emerges to suit the grower's market. Changing one factor, such as compost, means that some or all of the other factors will need to be adjusted to maintain the quality of the particular type of plant produced.

Watering is generally the main factor involved and it will be found that with all-peat composts, careful watering will be necessary to avoid waterlogging and loss of root in the base of the pot. Most growers now use plastic half-pots and this greatly increases the dangers of excess water and the exclusion of air, especially around the basal rim of the pot.

Some composts give rise to a fast take-off and generally favour the vegetative phase of plant growth. Unless other factors are adjusted a tall ungainly plant may be produced, flowering up to two weeks late. Sometimes this leads to the new compost being rejected out of hand, whereas a slight shortening of the longday treatment and an increase in strength of the growth retardant might have resulted in a much improved product.

The choice of compost should, therefore, be made in the light of the three basic requirements listed and must accord with the cultural and other environmental conditions of each situation.

There are now a number of excellent proprietary brands of compost available, formulated to a large extent with pot chrysanthemums in mind. Some manufacturers will supply the growth retardant Phosfon already in the compost, in some cases mixed specially to the grower's own requirements. Bunt (1976b) describes both the physical and chemical aspects of a good compost in detail and as a result of his work in recent years the GCRI Potting Composts have been developed (Appendix 5).

Grading and Potting

Rooted cuttings of the highest quality are required for pot plant production and, bearing in mind the overall dimension of the final product, they should not exceed 90 mm in height at potting time. Comparing cuttings of between 3·2 and 4·8 mm with cuttings less than 3·2 mm at the base of the stem, Butters at Efford EHS (Anon., 1971) found that the thicker cuttings produced plants which flowered earlier and had more and larger flowers than plants produced from the thinner cuttings. Machin (unpubl.) has since confirmed these results by grading cuttings by fresh weight prior to insertion into the rooting benches. There was evidence that the more uniform batches of rooted cuttings following weight grading prior to rooting led to an earlier more uniform response in the flowering plants.

In all methods of production where more than one plant per pot is grown, very strict grading of the rooted cuttings for length, general sturdiness, leaf area and amount of root is necessary to ensure a uniform flowering head. The importance of careful grading will be seen when it is realized that it is not difficult to produce a reasonable pot plant using five identical cuttings, but it is impossible for any grower, no matter how good his husbandry, to grow a top-grade product with five dissimilar cuttings.

When potting, the compost should only be firmed sufficiently to hold the plants upright. For the most uniform and rapid establishment the roots must not be buried below their original level in the propagating bench. The plants must be spaced evenly around the edge of the pot inclining slightly outwards. The level of compost must be within 12 mm of the top of the pot. This allows space for watering with the maximum quantity of compost to promote good root growth and nutrient uptake.

Of all the operations necessary in chrysanthemum pot plant production, grading and potting are those which most influence the quality of the end product. It is here where small growers usually have an advantage over large producers in that the care and attention to detail in this vital operation are more easily achieved.

In large programmes more emphasis has to be placed on organization, especially when potting, and the whole job has to flow and be completed to a strict time-table. It is therefore not so easy under these conditions to maintain a constant high level of husbandry, compared with a programme where only an hour or two each week of one person's time is involved.

Where large numbers of pots are involved it is important for management to plan carefully to ensure that the quality of the work does not suffer. Composts should be mixed and pots filled in a separate area and conveyed to the house ready for potting. Grading of plants can be done separately so that, at potting time, the entire emphasis can be on equidistant spacing, correct depth of planting and uniform inclination of cuttings and firming of roots.

Potting is either carried out on roller con-

TABLE 21   Longday Requirement in Number of Weeks from Potting for 14 cm Pots

Height category	0	1	2	3
Tall	15 March to 13 September	20 September to 8 March	—	—
Medium	—	15 March to 13 September	20 September to 8 March	—
Short	—	24 May to 12 July	15 March to 17 May and 19 July to 13 September	20 September to 8 March

veyors in a wide service path or on a small part of the nurse area. In practice, it is found ideal to use wire-mesh trays holding twelve 14 cm pots at pot-thick spacing. One worker feeding the trays on and off the rollers and supplying the plants can usually keep two workers fully occupied on potting.

After potting a thorough watering in, using a flat rose, is necessary to settle the compost round the roots. Further waterings during the first week should be aimed mainly at keeping the foliage turgid and this is best achieved by the use of equipment designed to deposit very fine droplets on the leaves. It is a common mistake to use for this the same rose used for watering in. The coarse droplets will not wet the foliage efficiently since much water will run off and the compost will then become too wet.

It is important to remember that each plant in the pot will respond to its own microclimate and it is therefore essential to produce the same conditions for each plant, especially during the early stages of growth.

Longday Requirement

Plants grown as specimen pot plants, either singly or in threes or fives, require a certain number of long days for growth according to time of year and variety. The number of long days determines both the height and the quality of the final product by affecting the number of leaves produced prior to flower bud formation.

Plants need to be sufficiently vegetative to produce a strong, free breaking action so that the final diameter of the pot plant is proportional to its height.

For the purposes of height adjustment by day-length control, pot plants are divided into three categories of varietal vigour. These are 'tall', 'medium' and 'short', and Table 23 classifies each variety accordingly. Longday schedules have been worked out for each type of variety, at each time of year in British conditions and for each type of crop. These are given in Tables 21 and 22. These recommendations must be

TABLE 22   Longday Requirement in days from Potting for 90 mm Pots Using Single Plants

Height category	0	4 to 7	7 to 10
Tall	21 December to 9 November	16 November to 14 December	—
Medium	16 February to 12 October	19 October to 9 November and 21 December to 9 February	16 November to 14 December
Short	16 February to 12 October	19 October to 9 November and 21 December to 9 February	16 November to 14 December

used only as a general guide and it is important that all growth regulating factors are correlated carefully and the use of counteracting controls avoided. If, for example, the period of long days given at a particular time of year on a given variety is too long the cost of chemical growth retardants subsequently used will be unnecessarily high.

Plants are normally held pot thick in a nurse area for one week or more and in an intermediate spacing area for a further period. The use of varieties in all three height categories in one programme rather complicates the practical details of longday treatment in these areas, and most programmes are restricted as far as possible to tall varieties. This not only simplifies daylength control but is much more economic in terms of production. Large producers generally have one programme for tall varieties set

aside from medium or short varieties. Frequently the tall varieties are grown in 14 cm pots and the medium and shot varieties in 10·8 cm and 90 mm pots.

Early Shortday Treatment

Plants which go straight into short days generally produce fewer breaks from the pinch than those started under longday conditions. Single plant pots especially are very dependent for quality on the number of breaks, and to increase both their number and uniformity a few long days given after potting may well prove to be worthwhile, in spite of the added difficulties in height control.

However, longday treatment given after potting inevitably increases the total crop time, and during a year this may reduce total productivity by half a crop compared with a programme in

TABLE 23   Guide to Pot Plant Varieties

Height category	Response group	White	Yellow	Pink	Red	Bronze
	9					Rascal*s
Tall	10		Bright Golden Anne[d] Cream Princess Anne[d] Lemon Princess Anne[d]	Princess Anne Superb[d] Regal Anne[d]	Crimson Anne[d] Red Anne[d]	Bronze Princess Anne[d] Gay Anne[d]
	8	Altis*d				
	9	Neptune[d]	Reaper*d	Hostess[d] Rose Hostess[d]	Rory*s Rufus*s	Copper Hostess[d]
Medium	10	Bonnie Jean[s] Garland[s] Snow Crystal[q]	Armelle[s] Golden Crystal[q] Sunny Mandalay[d] Yellow Bonnie Jean[s] Yellow Hector*d	Cerise Magnium*d Dark Maritime[d] Judith*s	Redcap[d] Red Torch[d]	Dramatic[s] Glowing Mandalay[d] Mandalay[d]
	8			Deep Louise*d		Gay Louise*d
Short	10	White Popsie*p	Yellow Popsie*p	Deep Popsie*p		Bronze Popsie*p

[d] Decorative   [p] Pompon   [s] Single   [q] Quill
* Bred by B. J. Machin in Sussex.

which plants are potted directly into short days.

The possibilities of reducing production time by starting shortday treatment in the rooting benches have been explored at Efford EHS (Anon., 1970). Longer than normal cuttings were used in an attempt to offset the loss of quality normally resulting from a reduction of long days. Using the tall variety Princess Anne in summer conditions cropping time was reduced by seven days by giving two weeks of short days in the rooting bench prior to potting. Compared with the controls the treated plants had fewer flowers per plant but this was compensated for by using a larger (44 mm rather than 32 mm) cutting. These results were later confirmed for December flowering (Anon., 1971). By leaving the cuttings in the rooting bench for a third week in short days a further seven days' reduction in flowering time was gained over the controls, but extra space was needed between each cutting and feeding was necessary, because the extra rooting period led to plants with larger root systems at potting time. For this and other reasons, rooted cuttings having received shortday treatment in the rooting benches have not been made available by commercial propagators.

Growers wishing to use early shortday treatment should, therefore, purchase unrooted cuttings. Full details of the development work on this technique are available (Butters, 1975).

Direct Rooting

A number of growers are now inserting unrooted cuttings directly into the flowering pots. Experience has shown that provided the cuttings are of high quality and uniform, they will root well and grow evenly in soilless composts containing fertilizers and a growth retardant. Cost of rooting cuttings and potting are saved.

The main drawback in comparison with the normal method of potting rooted cuttings is that the individual plants in the pot have a more upright habit of growth which reduces the diameter of the pot plant. When potting rooted cuttings it is normal to lean the plants outwards at an angle of 45° to induce the production of a wider-spreading plant but this is impossible with direct rooting. This problem does not arise, of course, for single plants in small pots and direct rooting is increasingly used for this type of crop.

Care has to be taken not to leach out nutrients during rooting especially where mist systems are used, and a high nitrogen liquid feed should probably be given soon after the roots have formed.

The use of direct rooting in combination with early shortday treatment has proved successful at Efford EHS. However, there is one extra cost in comparison with the normal method which has to be considered. Compared with the normal rooting area for cuttings spaced 38 by 44 mm, up to three times this area is required for cuttings rooted directly in the pots.

Pinching

The main reason for pinching is to increase the number of breaks, and hence flowers, on each pot plant. The timing of the pinch and the amount of growth remaining after the pinch affect the final height of the plants and the quality and uniformity of the breaks which grow as a result.

After several years of experience, it is clear that under most conditions pinching should occur between 10 and 14 days after potting in summer and 21 days after potting in winter. However, it is most important that the timing of the pinch should be adjusted to the speed of take-off, the size and vigour of the plant and the number of leaves developed on the plant.

During the winter, growth is slow and a pinch after only 14 days on many plants will result in uneven growth due to the pinch having been made into hard wood. Delaying the pinch for a few days may make all the difference to quality. Indeed, trials at Efford EHS in 1974 showed that plants given one week of long days and pinched after 21 short days were superior in quality for winter flowering compared with plants receiving other combinations of daylength and pinching treatments (Anon., 1975).

A common mistake is to pinch too early, especially when take-off has been good and the plants appear to have made sufficient growth after seven to ten days. Some growers pinch early because they feel that this will keep height down. In fact, it has the reverse effect.

The date of the pinch has to be decided in relation to daylength treatment. Even when plants go straight into short days at potting an early pinch will have a less restraining effect on growth than a late pinch. Breaks developing from a pinch made immediately after the start of short days will have more foliage and grow more vigorously than breaks from a later pinch. Thus, a slightly earlier than average pinch is likely to give a taller final product than may be desired. However, if the pinch is made too late in relation to the start of short days the individual cuttings are likely to develop too long a 'leg' in relation to sideshoot growth and the flowers will be clustered too tightly on each individual plant. A very late pinch gives an effect similar to the removal of the terminal bud of a spray variety.

A further and very useful guide to the correct time to pinch is given by the number of foliage leaves developed on the young plant. To obtain the maximum number of breaks from each plant at least seven or eight leaves should be left on the plant after the pinch. This is particularly important with the Princess Anne family.

In the winter, or at other times when growth is slow, care should be taken to remove only a small portion, say 12 mm, of plant material otherwise the pinch may be made into hard wood and uneven growth will result. At other times, when growth is rapid and soft, larger portions may be removed provided that a reasonable length of soft wood remains on the plant. For instance, it is sometimes necessary to pinch tall plants harder to correct uneven growth of cuttings in the pot. Also, where more than eight leaves are left on plants of the Princess Anne family the top one or two breaks will quickly assume dominance over the lower breaks and the two upper foliage leaves become too large and shade other parts of the plant.

For winter flowering especially, the pinch should be made to leave at least three internodes very close together at the top of the plant (this usually corresponds to a pinch down to eight leaves) so that each break develops in full light. If the origin of the third break is more than 12 mm below the top of the plant after pinching, it is likely to produce a much poorer flower than will the upper breaks. In summer there is sufficient light to maintain the growth of five or six equal flowers on each single plant.

The No-Pinch Method

The majority of pot plants produced in Britain are grown using the single-pinch method but at certain times of the year and for certain markets the no-pinch method gives excellent results (Plate 24).

The main difference is in the number and quality of flowers produced. Pinching induces about fifteen flowers per pot for January to March flowering. The no-pinch method naturally only gives as many flowers as the number of cuttings planted, which is normally six in a 14 cm pot with this method, but the flowers are of far superior quality. However, total flower cover is still greater with the pinched plants.

The no-pinch method encourages earlier flowering, because a pinch can delay flowering up to a week, and at certain times the no-pinch method will give more uniform flowering.

During January and February pinched plants frequently develop unevenly from the pinch. This is because of the limited light available for growth. Although four or five shoots may develop from the pinch only two or three may grow normally, the others remaining dormant. Also, the top shoot, because it is nearest to the light, will often grow more quickly than the second and third shoots and a very uneven pot results. The no-pinch method is therefore worth experimenting with for mid-December to mid-March flowering. However, when potting cuttings to flower on single stems special care must be taken to grade accurately. One taller or shorter plant will spoil a pot, and there are no means of corrective action. Finally, the extra cutting needed in each pot must be justified by the return.

Spacing

The average final spacing in spring, summer and autumn required to produce pot plants of adequate quality in southern England is 30·5 by 30·5 cm, increasing to 30·5 by 33 cm for winter production.

Ideally, for maximum quality, the plant should be allowed a little more room each week from the pot thick stage after potting to the point of maximum growth. In practice it is found that with good organization two moves are adequate to produce high-quality pots and can be worked into an efficient production schedule.

This aspect is discussed in detail on page 146.

It is normal practice to give only one week at the pot thick stage in the nurse area. At this spacing individual plants are crowded together in clumps as the pots fit closely together, and small differences in the microclimate affecting each plant can result in uneven elongation. The only exception to this is the single plant in a 90 mm pot which, owing to the wider and more uniform spacing between each plant when at the

TABLE 24   Space Requirements Per Pot

Pot size	Starting	Growing on	Finishing
14·0 cm	1 week at 14 by 14 cm	2 weeks at 20 by 23 cm	6 weeks at 30·5 by 30·5 (summer) Up to 10 weeks at 30·5 by 33 cm (winter)
10·8 cm	1 week at 11 by 11 cm	2 weeks at 15 by 18 cm	6 weeks at 23 by 25 cm (summer) Up to 10 weeks at 25 by 25 cm (winter)
90 mm	2 weeks at 90 by 90 mm	7 weeks at 13 by 15 cm (summer) Up to 10 weeks at 15 by 15 cm (winter)	

Fig. 43   Layout of 14 cm pots at intermediate spacing just prior to pinching.

Fig. 44   Layout of 14 cm pots at their final spacing about one week before marketing.

pot thick stage, can be held in the nurse area for two weeks.

After the first week, 14 cm pots are moved into the intermediate area (Fig. 43) and usually spaced 20 by 23 cm for the next two weeks or 23 by 23 cm for the next three weeks. This allows the foliage to expand and the stems to thicken before the plants are pinched. The pots are moved to their final spacing (Fig. 44) before the breaks are so large as to be adversely affected by lack of light.

Table 24 summarizes the average spacing requirements of various sizes of pot plants using 10-week tall varieties. These average spacings are varied by growers according to their exact requirements. For example, a wider spacing of say 15 to 18 cm each way for 14 cm pots might be preferred in the nurse area, leaving the pots at this spacing for up to two weeks. This is sometimes followed by a spacing of 25 by 25 cm for a further four weeks prior to final spacing.

Disbudding

The general practice is to disbud most varieties in 14 cm pots, leaving one bud on each lateral. Most of the leading pot plant varieties are either normal standard varieties, like the Princess Anne family, or are bred from standard varieties or large-flowered decorative spray types. They can therefore look rather untidy if all lateral buds are left to develop, especially if the apical bud, which flowers first, is not removed. Also, plants with all buds left to develop will mature up to a week later than disbudded plants.

Because of the high labour cost it is normal to allow the plant to develop to a stage where all lateral buds can be removed in one operation. Delaying disbudding too long will lead to loss of quality of the apical flowers.

It has been shown that late pinching (three weeks after short days) reduces the length of the lateral flowering stems and thus reduces the number of lateral buds (Anon., 1973).

The size and form of the apical buds is improved by disbudding. However, in an otherwise highly mechanized programme with rapid movement of pots, automated watering and shading, the labour required for disbudding can be up to 30 per cent of the total labour requirement. Because of this many growers do not now disbud plants during the summer months when delayed flowering is not a major problem. The reduced quality plants appear to have been acceptable to both markets and consumers. Single plants in 90 mm pots are rarely disbudded.

As reported earlier chemical disbudding has not reached the stage of full commercial use but there is evidence (Parups, 1976) that certain chemicals can be used to reduce the number of lateral buds. Disbudding the remainder by hand two weeks after treatment will ensure that flower size remains unimpaired.

Watering

While careful hand watering of individual pots may still produce pot plants of excellent quality the cost of labour for this single operation, especially in the late spring and summer, soon becomes prohibitive. Moreover, with the introduction of the 90 mm single plant pot the physical difficulties involved make any form of individual treatment for each pot a near impossibility.

Several distinct watering systems have now been evolved and leading growers are working on varying degrees of partial or fully automatic control.

The available systems may be divided into those which apply water over the top of the crop from spray lines, those which water each pot individually by means of small-bore tubes or trickle irrigation nozzles (Fig. 45), and those which allow the moisture to be taken up by capillary action through the base of the pot.

SPRAY LINE WATERING

Watering with overhead spray lines suspended above the benches became popular with the advent of the 90 mm single plant pot. The disadvantages of this system are that with the circular throw of water a certain proportion of the

pots are given more water than the others and crops of even growth are difficult to achieve. Moreover, as the crop matures the large bottom leaves overhang the rim of the pot and deflect the mist spray away from the compost. From the time the buds start to show colour until they are marketed, the grower has the additional worry of having to decide whether to continue to water from overhead and risk damaging the opening flowers or to switch to some alternative method.

Feeding from overhead spray lines can be accomplished successfully, within the limits of the above, provided a flush of clear water follows each application.

In spite of criticism of spray line watering, a mist line over the benches of the nurse area can be extremely valuable in assisting take-off, especially during the summer months in airy, bright houses with a dry atmosphere.

INDIVIDUAL POT WATERING

With all the individual irrigation systems available, each pot is watered and fed by its own small bore (spaghetti) tube connected to a hose running down the centre of the bench (Fig. 45). Because of the identical length of each of the tubes the same amount of water, and fertilizer when needed, is supplied to each pot, and the rate of flow may be regulated by means of a needle valve at the head of each main. The fact that each plant receives exactly the same amount of water tends to lead to uniform growth throughout the crop.

The use of these small-bore systems is generally confined to the 14 and 10·8 cm pots. Where programmes are run on a double spacing schedule it is usual for only the final spacing area to be equipped, although it would be perfectly possible to equip the intermediate area also. Ideally, these systems are at their best when one variety only is watered from a control point. However, this is by no means essential, and provided the plants are watered according to the requirements of the most water-sensitive variety, excellent crops can be produced. The spaghetti systems work extremely well on open wire-mesh benches and can provide a positive method of

Fig. 45   Small-bore tubes used for irrigation of pot plants on open-mesh benches.

growth control throughout the winter months.

A satisfactory adaptation of the small-bore system for watering 90 mm pots is hard to visualize, owing to the very large number of watering points that would have to be handled.

CAPILLARY METHOD OF WATERING

Many commercial capillary watering systems consist essentially of a layer of sand 25 mm deep laid on a surface of butted corrugated or flat asbestos sheets or 200 gauge polythene, forming the top of the bench.

This surface should be slightly higher at the centre than at the sides to allow free drainage and it is important that the polythene is not turned up around the sides to make a watertight bench. If the bench is watertight, a high salt concentration may become a problem and water-logging in the base of the pots is likely to occur.

Water is applied to the sand by means of trickle irrigation lines running lengthways down the bench or by a spaghetti watering system from underneath. On a bench 1·8 m wide the trickle irrigation lines are spaced about 38 cm from each side, with the nozzles 30 to 38 cm apart in each line.

It is important that the moisture level of the sand is kept constant and near field capacity, as too low a moisture level or infrequent topping up will encourage the plants to root through into the sand. Control of growth is then lost and the plant receives a severe check when moved. The commonest faults in using this method of watering are either allowing the sand to become too dry between waterings or running at too low a moisture regime.

Plants in all sizes of pot are grown with equal success on sand benches, but in general height control is more difficult than with plants grown on open-mesh benches using individual pot watering methods and higher rates of growth regulator may be required.

Plastic pots are generally used with sub-irrigation, because with their flat base and three or four drainage holes, water uptake by capillarity is easily established and maintained. Clay pots may be used on sand benches, but algae tend to be quickly transferred from the sand to the sides of the pots, giving the pots an unsightly appearance and making them slippery to handle.

Growers have experimented with other systems of sub-irrigation, ranging from polythene-lined corrugated sheets to strips of glass fibre, and more recently, to various types of matting. The latter are proving extremely useful for the sub-irrigation system of watering. The use of matting rather than sand is advantageous for the following reasons:

(a) It is lighter so that bench construction can be less substantial;

(b) It easier to keep clean and can be turned over and used many times with the aid of algaecides;

(c) It can be used round the year with no adverse effects in poor light conditions; when plants root into sand in seasons of poor light they become too vegetative for the most rapid flower development; roots do not penetrate matting to any extent.

Feeding

In order to produce chrysanthemum pot plants of high quality it is necessary to feed frequently and regularly. Although much will depend on the nature and strength of the compost, it is advisable to commence feeding between four and seven days after potting and to continue until the flower buds begin to show colour. Feeding will be of little benefit after this stage and may, in fact, have a detrimental effect in causing brittle foliage and rotting of flowers in poor light conditions.

From approximately mid-April to mid-October a feed of as much as 300 ppm N to 200 ppm K_2O has been found to be necessary with each watering. For the remaining months of the year the feed used should be adjusted to one of equal parts nitrogen and potash, except possibly with carbon dioxide enrichment, when nitrogen should again predominate. During seasons of poor light it is extremely important not to overfeed with nitrogen, and winter feeds containing 100 to 150 ppm nitrogen have generally been found to be satisfactory.

A wide range of proprietary fertilizers suitable for all seasons and for all composts is available, and should be used strictly in accordance with the manufacturers' recommendations. Growers who prefer to make up their own feeds can do so with the aid of the calculations shown in Appendix 7.

Feeding is a difficult subject on which to make specific recommendations as much will depend on the nature of the compost. Composts with very open textures, which allow rapid take-off and soft early growth, produce plants which break profusely. These have to be hardened slightly by the use of a feed with a relatively higher potash to nitrogen ratio.

The main problem is to achieve the correct balance between the various essential elements. Too much nitrogen, especially where the pH is high, is likely to lead to leaf chlorosis induced by a deficiency of trace elements such as iron or copper, or both. Excessive feeding of potash will result in magnesium deficiency and vice versa.

The correlation between phosphate deficiency and manganese toxicity, especially in acid composts, is well known, and brick earths which, when steamed, are liable to give rise to manganese toxicity, should be avoided. The adverse effect of high nitrogen in winter can be counteracted to some extent by the use of extra phosphate. Also, phosphate is more readily leached from soilless composts than from those incorporating loam, and this must be allowed for in the feeding programme.

With the increasing use of soilless composts, trace elements such as boron are becoming more important. Peat usually contains no boron, and unless this element is added and well mixed in the compost, boron deficiency can occur. This is more likely in conjunction with high nitrogen feeding. Conversely, the late irregular flowering of plants due to high nitrogen in poor light can be counteracted by feeding extra boron. Boron deficiency is easily recognizable in the flowering stage as the flowers lose colour and petals are thin and rolled (Plate 23), but it is very difficult to diagnose from the foliage symptoms before the flowers are fully open. Sodium borate incorporated into the compost at the rate of 9 g/m³ will prevent boron deficiency. Alternatively a liquid feed containing 0·5 ppm boron may be used. Care should be taken to avoid excess as the addition of 20 g of sodium borate to a cubic metre of compost will produce the boron toxicity symptoms of marginal leaf scorch (Bunt, 1965).

The acidity and salinity of the compost are very closely related to nutrition and their effect is markedly influenced by the buffering and base exchange properties of the medium. Both the buffer and base exchange capacities are lower in peat/sand composts than in loam, and thus there is more danger of high salt and pH problems in the former. In peat/sand composts the pH should be held in the 5·0 to 5·5 range. This is equivalent to a pH of 6·0 to 6·5 in loam-based composts.

Trace element deficiencies can be avoided by keeping the pH value down, using liquid feeds based on potassium and ammonium sulphate rather than on the more conventional urea/potassium nitrate combination.

Growth Retardants

The introduction of chemicals for controlling growth in pot plants coincided with the rise in popularity of the Princess Anne varieties and other 10-week tall varieties. These are far more efficient in production than the short varieties which, although producing very balanced pot plants, take longer to grow to the required size.

The 10-week tall varieties generally produce large well-shaped flowers. The problem is to restrict height while retaining flower size and quantity, and a well-shaped plant with good quality foliage. Reduction of longday treatment or late pinching can reduce height, but also frequently reduces flower size and the number of leaves on the flowering stems.

The action of chemical retardants not only reduces height but induces sturdier stems, darker and more luxuriant foliage and a more compact

habit, and at the same time does not reduce flower size. The Princess Anne family is particularly improved by chemical retardants used in conjunction with other height-control measures.

The rate and time of application depends to a large extent on other factors affecting growth rate. For example, a lower concentration of retardant is necessary to improve a plant grown on an open-mesh bench watered by the drip method than will be required by a plant grown on a grit bench with overhead watering or on a capillary sand bench.

Also, the rate of application of chemical growth retardant should vary according to the compost used. Generally, loam composts require less retardant than all-peat composts although if the latter incorporates a very young peat (Finn-peat) this may not be the case.

Height reduction usually means some decrease in diameter of the flowering head. This is acceptable if the market demands very small compact pots, but higher prices are usually commanded by plants of medium height with a large diameter, allowing space for the maximum display of each flower.

The spectacular effect on height to some extent masks the extremely beneficial effect of growth retardants on the uniformity of bud development. The reduction in rate of growth after application greatly assists the plant's change from a vegetative to a reproductive state and more uniform crops with better timing are produced.

PHOSFON

Phosfon (Phosfon 1·5 granulet) was the first growth retardant to be used with the pot chrysanthemum crop in Britain and is still very widely used, especially for the Princess Anne varieties in summer. The required amount of Phosfon must be thoroughly mixed with the potting compost. This point must be emphasized because uneven distribution of Phosfon in the compost could result in very irregular growth.

The rate of application of Phosfon varies with variety, the season, the type of compost used and the degree of control needed (Fig. 46). Experience is required to find the correct dose for each

Fig. 46   The effect of Phosfon 1·5 granulet on the variety Mandalay in all-peat compost. Dosage rates left to right:
900, 720 and 540 g/m³.

variety under all conditions. Suggested rates for application of Phosfon to some proprietary composts are given in Table 25. Guide rates of application of Phosfon for some of the main varieties are given in Table 26. Phosfon is an effective and persistent height regulator and the effects of overdoses cannot easily be counter-acted. However, growers experienced in the use of Phosfon with their own composts and growing conditions can obtain excellent results.

Phosfon is rather more than a regulant of plant height. The colour of all leaves is improved because Phosfon is available to the plant as soon as the roots begin to grow. This helps to improve growth generally, as well as increasing the aesthetic value of the pot plant. Also, Phosfon reduces apical dominance and this encourages lateral branching.

Under the influence of Phosfon the leaves develop thicker cuticles (skins), which improve both the drought and disease resistance of the plant. The general improvement in growth following Phosfon application leads to a longer shelf-life following marketing. Compared with plants treated with Alar, Phosfon-treated plants

TABLE 25   Rates of Phosfon 1·5 Granulet for Application in some Proprietary Composts

Brand of compost	Rate g/m³	
	Summer	Winter
John Innes Potting	450	300
Eff	450	300
J Arthur Bowers	600	450
Levington Potting	750	600

TABLE 26 Phosfon 1·5 Granulet. Guide Rates of Application for Pot Chrysanthemums. (If Alar is to be used in conjunction with Phosfon the quantities given below should be reduced by 17 per cent)

Varieties	All-peat g/m³		Soil g/m³	
	14 cm	9 cm	14 cm	9 cm
Altis	540	720	360	540
Bonnie Jean	720	720	360	360
Bronze Princess Anne	900	900	360	540
Cerise Magnum	540	720	360	540
Deep Louise	540	720	360	540
Dramatic	540	540	180	360
Mandalay	720	720	360	540
Neptune	360	720	180	360
Rascal	1440	1440	720	720
Reaper	900	900	540	540
Regal Anne	1440	1440	720	1080
Rory	720	720	360	540
Rufus	900	900	360	540
White Popsie	360	720	180	360
Yellow Hector	540	720	360	540

TABLE 27 Rates of Phosfon 10 per cent Liquid for Use with Each Category of Variety in Soil and Peat Composts

Variety category	ml/4·5 l water	
	All-peat compost	Soil compost
Medium (Mandalay)	2·0	1·5
Tall (Bright Golden Anne)	3·5	2·0 to 2·5
Very Tall (Regal Anne)	4·0 to 5·0	3·0 to 3·5

at Efford EHS had a 12·5 per cent increase in shelf-life (Anon., 1974).

Phosfon affects the metabolic activity of some proteins found in certain colour pigments, as well as reducing the levels of endogenous gibberellic acid (Stobart, 1974). This has the effect of enhancing the petal colour in certain red and pink varieties.

Phosfon is also available as a 10 per cent liquid formulation and can be used as a soil drench where Phosfon 1·5 granulet has not been used in the compost. But the active chemical in Phosfon, chlorphonium chloride, is toxic to chrysanthemums if sprayed on the foliage and care must be taken to avoid splashing when using it as a soil drench. To obtain optimum results from Phosfon liquid, the compost must be uniformly moist and the liquid applied as soon after the plants are turgid following planting, and preferably prior to pinching.

Rates of Phosfon 10 per cent liquid for use with each category of variety in soil and peat composts are given in Table 27.

Normally 100 ml of the solution should be applied to each 14 cm pot.

Phosfon may be used as the only growth retardant but is generally used in conjunction with a spray application of Alar which restricts elongation of peduncles of vigorous varieties in the final stages of growth.

ALAR

Alar (daminozide*) contains 85 per cent active ingredient as a wettable powder and is used as a foliar spray to assist in height control of chrysanthemums.

For the most effective and economic results a spray of small droplet size is required and is best applied 10 to 14 days after pinching when breaks are between 13 and 18 mm long. For late autumn and winter flowering it has been found better to delay application slightly to counteract the increased tendency for elongation during the final stages of flowering in poor light conditions. Thorough wetting of all leaves to the point of run-off is required. To ensure maximum absorption the chemical should be applied in warm water to turgid plants with dry foliage, and the foliage should not be wetted for 24 hours after application.

Thorough spraying of the lateral shoots can be as effective in controlling shoot elongation as complete spraying of all the aerial parts of the plant (Menhenett, 1976b).

As with Phosfon, different varieties respond to different doses of Alar and trials are required to find the best rate of application for each variety according to conditions. However, if it is found that the dose is insufficient, a second

* This is the common name and not the actual chemical name.

application of Alar (provided the plants are not showing colour) will still be in time to restrict the final elongation of the flowering stems. Care should be taken with any second application because Alar will cause colour fading, especially in red and bronze varieties, if applied too late. Indeed, in trials in which plant height has been controlled totally with either Phosfon or Alar, plants controlled with Alar have generally produced flowers with inferior colour.

For 14 cm pots concentrations from 66 g/100 l to 264 g/100 l* have been used successfully as the situation has demanded. Often it is found that two applications of 132 g/100 l at a three week interval give better results than one application of 264 g/100 l. Occasionally, a single application of 198 g/100 l has given the required result.

With the tall pot plant varieties, there appears to be little difference in varietal response to Alar. There does appear to be a seasonal effect and it is suggested that the concentration of the solution be varied accordingly. Production of a short, compact pot plant may need a concentration of up to 246 g/100 l during the growing period March until early October (flowering June to December), but for the growing period mid-October to the end of February (flowering January to May) a concentration of only 132 g/100 l or less may be needed. The closer the final spacing of pots the higher the concentration of Alar likely to be needed to produce plants of the required proportions.

For single plant specimens in 90 mm pots it is the practice in the Netherlands to use three or four applications of a very dilute Alar solution (33 g/100 l), so that growth is uniformly restricted throughout the crop. The first application is given prior to pinching.

It is emphasized that the effect of the same concentration of Alar will vary slightly from one nursery to another because of differences in growing methods, light intensity and atmospheric humidity. The dosage recommendation should therefore be treated as a tentative guide upon which to base individual trials.

* See footnote on page 64.

One litre of the diluted solution is sufficient to treat about seventy 14 cm pots.

OTHER GROWTH RETARDANTS

A number of other growth retardants for use with pot chrysanthemums have been developed recently but are still in the experimental stage, some of which have been reported by Menhenett (1976a).

One common problem with growth retardants is that a delay in the time of flowering is usually associated with a reduction in stem length and this varies from two to ten days depending on season, variety and the retardant and its rate of use. However, screening of new chemicals is continuing and it is reasonable to hope that this problem will be overcome. Also, current research at the GCRI suggests that it may soon be possible to use one growth regulator as both a disbudding agent and a retardant. However, any new growth regulator will need to be both more efficient and less costly to use than existing materials if it is to be successful.

Carbon Dioxide Enrichment

The application of additional carbon dioxide to the atmosphere has a beneficial effect on the growth of chrysanthemum pot plants, and is usually made during the period October to March. During these months when ventilators in heated houses are normally closed until mid or late morning, there are insufficient air changes to ensure adequate natural carbon dioxide for optimum growth, especially for a fast-growing crop.

When light conditions for growth are poor (less than 8000 lx outside the greenhouse), it has been shown that 600 ppm carbon dioxide, which is twice the normal atmospheric level, will give optimum results.

As light conditions improve the plants respond to higher concentrations of carbon dioxide up to 1500 ppm. The highest-quality chrysanthemum pot plants have been grown in the good light conditions of spring and summer using 900 to 1500 ppm carbon dioxide with day temperatures controlled at 18·3° and night temperatures at 14·4°. If the day temperature could be held at $18.3°$ in bright weather in summer without the use of ventilators, there is evidence that increasing the carbon dioxide level in the house to 1500 ppm would be economically beneficial.

It is important to ensure that during the winter additional carbon dioxide is given only where night temperatures are accurately controlled, and where there is an efficient and accurate watering system. Increasing the carbon dioxide concentration tends to make the plant more vegetative and the better foliage leads to improved flower quality. However, if other factors, such as low temperature or over-watering, are not conducive to flower bud development, then the effect of additional carbon dioxide could well be to delay flowering. Where all other factors affecting flowering are under control, then additional carbon dioxide will normally accelerate flowering and improve the quality and uniformity of cropping.

Supplementary Lighting

The possibility of using supplementary light during seasons of natural low light to improve the growth and flowering of chrysanthemum pot plants on commercial holdings followed the work of Cockshull and Hughes (1972) at Reading University between 1968 and 1970. Using the variety Bright Golden Anne they showed that, by transferring plants from a constant light level of 0.63 MJ/m²/day (the daily average in greenhouses in southern England for the worst twelve weeks of the year) to 1.25 MJ/m²/day for the first two weeks of shortday treatment, plants flowered earlier and much more uniformly.

Canham (1972a) supplementing winter light in a greenhouse by 0.99 MJ/m²/day, using the same variety, induced an improved response of nine days and obtained more uniform flowering compared with unlit plants. Later, Canham (1972) tested a range of five varieties under supplementary light treatment in late December and obtained earlier flowering and better quality in all but one (Festival).

Cockshull and Hughes's work has also been applied at a number of the Experimental Horti-culture Stations in different parts of the country. At Fairfield EHS in Lancashire, supplementary lighting for 12 hours each day for the first 14 short days reduced flowering time by between nine and 21 days, and increased both the number of flowers per pot and the uniformity of flowering during three winters (Fairfield EHS Reports 1969, 1971 and 1972). It was considered that supplementary lighting would be profitable for year-round pot chrysanthemum growers in northern England.

Good results were also obtained by supplementary lighting at the Lee Valley EHS in 1971 when plants under lights flowered earlier and more compactly than the controls, and produced more flowers of better quality.

However, between 1969 and 1971 work at Efford EHS, which is situated in one of the best winter light areas in Britain, showed that quality of the flowering plant was not improved by supplementary light, and the gain in earliness was not sufficient to cover the cost of the supplementary light (Anon., 1972). At Efford EHS work was then concentrated on reducing the cost of supplementary lighting and of making use of the lights in the 'early shortday' technique over the rooting benches (Anon., 1973).

In order to make full use of bench space and lighting equipment in this system, cuttings are in the rooting bench for a total of three weeks but are given light for only the last two. Lamps have to be sited carefully to obtain maximum efficiency. The use of supplementary lighting in this way makes it possible to continue to use short days in the rooting bench throughout the winter period, thereby saving at least 14 days in the flowering house. The quality of flowering is maintained compared with unlit plants potted directly into short days from the rooting bench. In the first experiments on supplementary lighting described above the lamps used were mercury-fluorescent (MBFR/U). Later trials showed that 180 W low-pressure sodium lamps (SOX) were equally successful and the cost of lighting per pot was reduced by half. More recently (Anon., 1975) 400 W high-pressure sodium lamps (SON/T) have given results equal to SOX and MBFR/U lamps and may, in some

TABLE 28 Christmas Pot Plant Programme

Response group	Height category	Pot	Pinch	Lights on	Lights off	Flower date
9 week	Short	20 Sep	4 Oct	20 Sep	11 Oct	13 Dec
10 week	Short	13 Sep	27 Sep	27 Sep	4 Oct	13 Dec
9 week	Medium	27 Sep	11 Oct	27 Sep	11 Oct	13 Dec
10 week	Medium	20 Sep	4 Oct	20 Sep	4 Oct	13 Dec
9 week	Tall	4 Oct	18 Oct	4 Oct	11 Oct	13 Dec
10 week	Tall	27 Sep	11 Oct	27 Sep	4 Oct	13 Dec

installations, improve the evenness of illumination over the growing area.

Spot Crops

Pot chrysanthemums may be produced as spot crops for specific markets such as Mothering Sunday, Easter and Christmas. However, it is important to remember, especially in Western Europe, that plants are produced for the first two of these festivals during the poorest growing conditions of the year, and these crops should not be attempted without experience of production at other times. Also, it is frequently in these markets that customers buy pot plants for the first time and it is therefore essential to produce plants of the highest quality to ensure further sales to these buyers.

Spot crops have one great advantage over a normal year-round programme where plants in all stages, from those newly potted, to those showing colour, are occupying the same house. With spot crops, exact control of the environment to suit each growth phase may be carried out with every prospect of improved final quality, especially in colour and size of flower, over plants produced in the normal year-round programme. This applies particularly to the Christmas and Mothers' Day markets.

Table 28 shows the potting dates suitable in southern England for each height category to flower for the Christmas market.

Varieties

Although year-round pot chrysanthemum production has been largely developed in North America, the varieties at present dominating the year-round programmes are English in origin. Princess Anne was released in 1951 by H. Shoesmith as a standard variety and this together with its many sports now forms up to 85 per cent of the varietal range in most programmes. A close, critical look at the Princess Anne varieties should therefore give a picture of the characters necessary for pot plant growing and indicate the future trend of varietal requirements.

The first impression given by a well-grown Princess Anne is the high quality of the individual flowers. Flowers are large, full and of good shape, with broad resilient petals. Flower quality is clearly observed because the flowers are usually well spaced on the plant. Growth is vigorous, and provided that height can be regulated to produce a balanced plant a top-grade pot is produced.

As tall category varieties in the 10-week response group, the Princess Anne varieties theoretically require only 10 weeks of total growing time for June to October flowering in 14 cm pots. In fact, from early July to late September, because of good light conditions, plants can be marketed in nine weeks.

For February flowering, the total crop time for Princess Anne is 12 weeks in good glass in the south of England, but at least 13 weeks in northern areas.

With varietal efficiency it is important to realize that both height category and response group should be taken into consideration. A 9-week medium variety can be produced in the same time as a 10-week tall variety and a 9-week short normally flowers with a 10-week medium variety.

WINTER PERFORMANCE

Apart from flower quality, a major factor influencing the choice of year-round pot plant varieties is their response, or lack of it, during the December to March growing period, especially in the northern areas of Britain and in northern Europe.

Until recently, even in the south of England, only a few varieties such as the Princess Annes and Neptune had a reasonably reliable response during January and February. In the north of England, the uniformity of response between each plant in the pot is less satisfactory because under very low light conditions slight differences in the microclimate surrounding each plant result in noticeable differences in growth.

Careful selection following mutation breeding has increased the range of the Princess Anne family (Princess Anne is a periclinal chimera). Since 1968 Princess Anne Superb, Gay Anne, Purple Anne, Regal Anne, Red Anne and Crimson Anne have been introduced and all are grown during the winter.

A number of new decorative and single flowered pot plant varieties have been bred by Machin in Sussex, with winter response and performance very much in mind. Altis, Aramis, Cerise Magnum*, Deep Popsie,* Gay Louise* and Yellow Hector* are decoratives which have a shorter habit than the Princess Annes and tend to flower slightly earlier and more uniformly in poor light conditions.

The singles, Reaper and Rascal, require only 11 weeks from potting for the production of good-quality pots in February and are the first varieties to prove more efficient for winter production than those of the Princess Anne family. Apart from the Popsie family, which were bred specially for small pot production Altis (white), Yellow · Hector (yellow), Deep Louise and Cerise Magnum (pink), Red Torch (red) and Gay Louise (bronze), all give excellent results round the year as single plants in 90 mm pots.

COLOUR RANGE

White Neptune is still a good compact decorative variety while Altis, another decorative, has an excellent breaking action and is very responsive and uniform. It is used extensively in the Netherlands for single pot plants. White Popsie is a mutation from the pompon flowered Popsie and is easy to grow and is long-lasting.

Yellow Currently the three most widely used yellow sports from Princess Anne are Bright Golden Anne, Cream Princess Anne and Lemon Princess Anne. In the medium height range of decoratives Sunny Mandalay, of American origin, is noted for its very good breaking action, while Yellow Hector is a uniform and very dependable pot plant round the year.

Yellow Popsie (Plate 8) is a clear yellow mutation induced from Popsie.

Reaper (Plate 12), a sulphur yellow 9-week single, has been bred specifically for year-round pot programmes. Plants can be marketed in eight weeks from June to October, nine weeks at Christmas and in $10\frac{1}{2}$ weeks in February following one week of longday treatment. Flowers are of good shape and size with little pollen and are borne profusely on well-shaped plants.

Pink Princess Anne Superb and Regal Anne now constitute the pink range of the Princess Anne family, the latter being especially useful in winter due to its vigour. Also in the decorative range Aramis gives good results round the year and has a shorter, stronger habit than Princess Anne Superb. Cerise Magnum has a deep rich colour and prolific and dependable flower production at all seasons. Hostess and its rose sport are also to be recommended. Deep Louise has an excellent 8-week response and if short plants are required is one of the most efficient varieties. The flowers are beautifully incurved with broad petals.

Deep Popsie, a pompon, is valuable in both 14 cm and 90 mm pot programmes.

Judith, a single flowered spray variety, has been used successfully.

Red Red Anne has been available for some years but tends to fade to bronze in high temperatures. Crimson Anne is a recent much-improved colour sport. Red Torch can be recommended as a decorative for the production of shorter plants or in 90 mm pots.

* Colour mutations induced from the original seedling by radiation treatment.

Two 9-week red singles are now available, both with excellent pot plant habit. Rory (Plate 7) is dark currant red with a short prolific branching habit and needs little disbudding. Rufus (Plate 11) has large well-shaped dark red flowers borne on strong, wide-branching plants of ideal shape.

Bronze Bronze Princess Anne and Gay Anne, both developed from radiation treatment, represent the Princess Anne range. Mandalay is a dependable American decorative and Gay Louise is an excellent orange-red variety, especiall useful for a fast crop.

Bronze Popsie has recently been released to add to the colour range in this useful pompon family.

Rascal (Plate 10), a new 9-week tall single, is one of the most efficient varieties yet bred, because for most of the year it can be potted directly into short days. Flowers are large and colourful, fading to a pleasant orange-bronze in summer.

HARVESTING, PACKING AND MARKETING

Plants must be marketed in the correct stage of development to ensure that the consumer enjoys the benefit of the fully mature plant for the longest possible time. Flowers must not, therefore, be fully out at packing time otherwise they will be deteriorating by the time they reach the consumer. The most common mistake, however, is to market too early. It is true that the plants travel well with the buds just showing colour, but one or two days spent in a box followed by several days in a shop window with at best only limited or directional light, will not lead to the best and most uniform development of the flowers. Each producer should ensure that the plants leave the nursery with some flowers at least three-quarters developed and the remainder at a stage where unfavourable light and temperature conditions will not seriously affect the final stages of flower development. Pots marketed too early will only lead to complaints and disappointment, eventually leading to a lack of confidence in a plant which normally gives excellent value for money.

Investigations over several years have revealed the main factors which affect the decorative life of the pot chrysanthemum in the home. The most important of these is to ensure that a healthy and active root system continues to function. The grower can best do this by avoiding excessive feeding because a high salt concentration in the compost at marketing time can soon cause root loss followed by premature senescence.

Recommended feeding rates should not be exceeded and all feeding should cease when the buds show colour.

The cost of marketing pot chrysanthemums beyond the locality of the nursery is relatively high, and it is therefore necessary, as indeed it is with year-round cut flowers, to fully investigate the various and possible sales outlets before commencing production. Marketing pot plants locally can achieve not only substantial savings in the cost of containers and transport, but it is often possible to negotiate forward contracts for regular weekly supplies and thereby avoid fluctuations in market prices.

Where produce is sent wholly or in part to primary or secondary wholesalers, it is essential that close co-operation with the salesman is maintained, and his advice and comments sought on all questions of varieties, colour, markets, packs and quantities.

A close study of the colour percentage requirement over several years in Britain indicates that yellow is by far the most popular colour in pot plants, even in the spring when there are frequently large numbers of other yellow flowers available. In a box of six plants, three plants of various shades of yellow and one each of pink, red and bronze make an attractive colour range for the autumn. At other times three shades of yellow, two shades of pink and either a red or bronze may be more suitable. White is required in only small quantities and for special markets.

The basic colour percentages to plan for are therefore approximately 50 per cent yellow, 25 per cent pink, 15 per cent red and 10 per cent bronze and others.

Plants are usually marketed in boxes of six

14 cm pots or twelve 90 mm sleeved pots. A good range of colour and uniformity of height and size of each plant in the box is required in order to obtain the best returns.

Pot chrysanthemums are normally packed into first and second grades according to the specific requirements of the market. It is generally accepted for markets in Britain that the flowering height of 14 cm pots should be 30 to 36 cm from the base of the pot, with the diameter of the flowering head in the region of 30 cm.

Single plants in 90 mm pots should have a flowering height above the base of the pot of 18 to 23 cm and the diameter of the flowering head should be 14 to 16 cm.

ORGANIZATION

Pot chrysanthemum production requires a high level of planning and organization. The flow of pots through a unit and the various cultural operations carried out during the growing period must therefore be controlled by a strict time schedule geared to the rate of plant development.

Every pot plant grower will agree that it is good management to allow a plant extra space immediately that it is required; but house construction and traditional bench layout often do not lend themselves to rapid movement of large quantities of pots at regular intervals. In these cases a compromise has to be reached on the number of times the pots can be moved because, quite apart from the effect on quality, extra production is achieved by employing two moves rather than one, or going to direct final spacing after potting. The labour costs of three or more moves probably outweigh the advantage of extra production, but this point should be considered in the light of each type of programme and the labour and equipment available.

Ideally, it is more efficient to work out a programme employing say two moves ensuring a rapid and smooth flow of pots, and then to choose the particular greenhouse which most readily fits the general plan.

Construction of Benches

Many types of bench have been used for this crop, but benches can be classified into two main types, solid and open topped.

Wood has been used for bench construction in the past, but its liability to shrinkage, warping and rotting has led to the increasing use of angle iron framework of varying types. Benches with solid tops are normally covered by various materials such as sand or gravel, which aid humidity control or form part of the watering system itself. They are ideal in the nurse and intermediate spacing areas where high humidities are required, medium-sized gravel being the most common covering material.

The use of solid benches with sand, gravel or matting for the entire crop leads to a reduction in the amount of watering required and, where hand watering is the practice, results in a substantial saving in labour. However, the tendency to rooting through and the probability of high humidity in the later stages of growth can lead to loss of control over growth and to tall ungainly plants unless great care is taken.

The use of 12 gauge galvanized wire with 25 by 75 mm mesh for bench tops gives more flexibility because in the early stages of growth the bench can be covered with polythene for holding the medium. At the final spacing the benches remain open, allowing adequate air circulation, low humidity and good temperature control around the plants. Benches are usually from 1·7 to 1·8 m wide for maximum utilization of house area and at the same time to enable the workers to reach the centre plants without undue effort.

The factors influencing the choice of material from which both the supporting framework of the benches and the bench surface are constructed are as set out below.

(a) Availability and cost of materials.
(b) Maximum load when bench is fully cropped.
(c) Dimensions of bench surface and height.
(d) The type of construction and spacing of the benches.
(e) Degree of mechanization, and the method of watering to be employed.
(f) The size of pot to be used.

In programmes where wire mesh trays are used to hold pots at the close and intermediate spacings the nurse and intermediate bench area used need not have a conventional top. If the size of the nurse and intermediate area for maximum summer production is worked out, then this area of bench can consist of angle iron spaced to the dimensions of the wire trays.

Layout of Benches

The advent of mechanized handling in the year-round pot plant programme has meant that bench type and layout have become increasingly critical. While the ultimate in mechanized handling may prove to be mobile benches covering up to 90 per cent of the area of the house, (Fig. 47) many operations are still carried out by hand. A path network adequate to allow access to all parts of the bench area is therefore essential in units with static benches.

It is impossible to lay down hard-and-fast rules on the subject of bench layout, as much depends on the type of house to be used. Two bench arrangements in common use are the longitudinal and lateral layouts, and with each the design of the bench will depend on:

(a) The shape and size of the house, including the position of the fixed internal obstructions and doors. If the house is to be built it is important to work out where the doors are needed before erection commences, for often the normal position is the least suitable.

Fig. 47 Mobile benches used to increase the total cropping area in the greenhouse.

(b) The degree to which mechanization is to be introduced. This includes the mechanization of watering, ventilating, blacking out and control of pests and diseases, as well as the mechanized handling of the pots themselves.

(c) The maximum width of bench over which the operator can reach using mechanical aids where available.

(d) The spacing of the pots for the greatest period of time and the area allowed per pot. Bench width cannot be decided because it fits conveniently into the house, but must be calculated according to the most suitable row spacings. Calculation of pot capacity for any given bench should be made using actual bench area. However, pot spacings may be varied slightly and by so doing it is sometimes possible to reduce the width of a bench by up to 10 cm without reducing its capacity. Where possible pots should fit neatly into the benches at each

of the required spacings throughout the life of the crop.

(e) The planned flower height of the bench. This will depend very much on the degree of mechanization possible and, if bench widths in excess of 2 m are planned, would involve tending the plants from trollies running above the crop. While a very low bench allows narrower paths, extra care must be taken to ensure a good circulation of air around the plants or loss of quality, especially in winter, could outweigh increased output.

The most efficient type of greenhouse for an up-to-date pot plant programme is an east–west single span house with no extended eaves. Two possible bench layouts in a modern aluminium/steel house of this type, 92 m long and 22 m wide (approximately 0·2 ha), are shown in Fig. 48.

The layout in both cases consists of benches

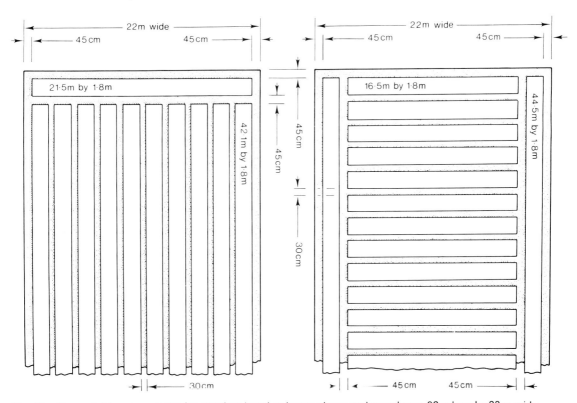

Fig. 48   Two suitable arrangements for pot plant benches in a modern metal greenhouse 92 m long by 22 m wide.

raised 30 cm above ground level, giving a potential flowering height of about 75 cm maximum. The working paths can be as narrow as 30 cm giving a bench area of 80·2 per cent and 79 per cent, respectively, of the total floor area of the house. With low-level crops the orientation of benches relative to light admission into the house is not as important as with cut flower crops.

The main advantages of the longitudinal bench system are that the nurse areas can easily be sectioned off from the rest of the house by a polythene or muslin tent, and separate microclimates maintained. It is also simple with this layout to cover the nurse area at night to prevent light spill to the remainder of the crop. Where automatic blackout is not fitted the labour to cover 20 benches 43 m long is less costly than that needed for 42 benches 16·5 m long.

The main advantage of the lateral arrangement of benches is that individual varieties can be accommodated more readily on separate benches and given individual watering and feeding treatment. It is well known that varieties such as Princess Anne and Mandalay have very different water requirements, and if grown on the same bench with the same automated watering system the former becomes too dry, or the latter tend to be over-watered.

Mechanized handling is essential in pot plant programmes of any size. One very efficient method is the use of the bench sides as railway lines supporting a truck with an open-mesh base travelling the length of the benches over the tops of the plants. Normally the nurse area will have a separate truck, but mobile bogies, which can be readily attached to the ends of the benches, can be used to transfer trucks from one bench top to another. This will reduce the number of trucks required. These bogies, which are essentially small detachable pieces of bench, can also be used as mobile potting areas.

Many types of houses are in use for year-round pot cropping and provided winter light is not too limiting and ventilation, particularly in summer, is adequate, efficient schedules can be maintained, provided a rapid means of pot movement can be worked out.

The size of pot plant produced, taking five cuttings in a 14 cm pot as an example, depends to a large extent on the final spacing of each plant, which can vary from 26·5 by 26·5 cm to 30·5 by 38 cm for summer production.

The pots produced from 700 and 1160 cm^2 respectively are obviously very different in overall diameter of the flowering head. They can both be of good quality if height is so regulated by cultural, daylength and chemical control measures as to produce a balanced plant.

Thus, 14 cm pot plants can be tailored by the final spacing to fit market requirements. The decision whether to grow a larger number of pots with smaller flowering heads, or fewer pots with larger heads, should not be made lightly. It is essentially a compromise between quality and quantity, because apart from the effect of spacing on the diameter of the flowering head, it is also more difficult to maintain uniformity of production at the closer spacings. Any mistake in watering, feeding, application of chemical retardant and so on, will show up more clearly the closer the pot spacing.

The important question is whether the extra revenue obtained from the larger pot plants makes up for the loss in quantity produced. The issue is by no means clear-cut, and it is probable that growers will have to make very different decisions to suit their own conditions.

Output

A few facts and figures are helpful in outlining the issues involved, taking as an example the 0·2 ha block with the bench arrangement as shown in Fig. 48, which gives approximately 1625 m^2 of bench area. It is assumed that 10-week tall varieties are being grown round the year, and that plants are spaced pot thick, 14 by 14 cm for one week and at 20 by 23 cm for the next two weeks before being moved to their final spacing. The area taken up by each pot during the first three weeks is therefore 0·11 m^2.

The response of plants varies with the quality of light and although 10-week varieties are being grown round the year, in reality the time taken for the plants to complete their development

TABLE 29 Variation of Pot Plant Production Round the Year

Period	Potting dates	Flowering dates	No. of weeks of production	No. of weeks at final spacing	Total cropping time (weeks)
1	3 May to 19 July	5 July to 20 September	12	6	9
2	26 July to 23 August 15 March to 26 April	27 September to 8 November 31 May to 28 June	12	7	10
3	30 August to 4 October 8 February to 8 March	15 November to 20 December 3 May to 24 May	10	8	11
4	11 October to 9 November 4 January to 1 February	27 December to 1 February 5 April to 26 April	10	9	12
5	16 November to 28 December	8 February to 29 March	8	10	13

in the final spacing area will vary from six weeks in summer to 10 weeks in winter. This takes into account that an extra number of long days must be allowed for good breaking action, especially during the autumn and winter production periods.

The total number of weeks allowed on average for development at final spacing at different periods of the year is shown in Table 29.

These are average figures, but they must be worked out carefully for each situation, using information obtained from actual cropping records. For instance, in modern east–west aluminium houses, period 5 may not exist at all, while for older greenhouses in northern areas this period may have to be extended to 14 weeks.

When year-round growing commenced in Britain the seasonal differences in production time were not adequately taken into account. The same numbers of cuttings were potted up each week until the reduced rate of development in the autumn and winter led to overcrowding at a time of year when it was least desirable. The effect of this on quality of plants and on

continuity of supply was serious, and it was difficult to maintain the confidence of the markets.

COMPARISON OF FINAL SPACINGS

It is interesting to compare production figures for the average summer spacing of 30·5 by 30·5 cm with the two extremes of 26·5 by 26·5 cm and 30·5 by 38 cm.

The bench areas required by each pot from potting to marketing in period 1 for the three spacings are:

A 26·5 by 26·5 cm (702 sq cm) = 0·53 sq m*
B 30·5 by 30·5 cm (930 sq cm) = 0·65 sq m
C 30·5 by 38·0 cm (1159 sq cm) = 0·78 sq m

The number of pots produced each week is obtained by dividing the bench area required for each pot into the total bench area. Thus the

* This figure is arrived at by multiplying the area of each pot at final spacing by six, this being the number of weeks at final spacing in period 1, and adding the requirement of each pot for nurse and intermediate area (0·11 m²). Each of the other calculations is made using similar steps.

numbers of pots per week at the three final spacings in period 1 are:

A   26·5 by 26·5 cm = 3017 pots
B   30·5 by 30·5 cm = 2427 pots
C   30·5 by 38·0 cm = 2027 pots

To find the annual differences in quantities a few more calculations and assumptions have to be made. A grower who is prepared to finish at a spacing of 26·5 by 26·5 cm in summer will not do so round the year.

Programme A could logically be:

26·5 by 26·5 cm for May to December flowering
30·5 by 30·5 cm for the remainder of the year.

Programme B is usually:

30·5 by 30·5 cm for May to December flowering
30·5 by 33·0 cm for the remainder of the year.

Programme C could retain a spacing of 30·5 by 38·0 cm round the year.

A series of calculations to find the weekly production figures for each of the final spacings and production times given above now have to be made. Following this, the annual production for each method is calculated by multiplying the weekly production figures for summer, spring, autumn and winter by the appropriate number of weeks of production and adding the figures for each season. These are shown in Table 30.

With method A, production is approximately 50 per cent greater per annum than with C, B gives 20 per cent more production than C and A 25 per cent more than B. The figures show wide differences between the numbers of pots produced depending on the final spacing, and a great deal of thought must be given to the subject before deciding on the method of production to adopt.

It could be dangerous, however, to stop at this point and draw conclusions, for it is probably wrong to assume that method A is com-

TABLE 30   Production Figures for Pot Plants

Flowering period	Total growing area for each pot in m²	Pots per week	Number of weeks of production	Total number of pots for each period (for 0·2 ha)
Method A				
1	0·53	3017	12	36,204
2	0·61	2665	12	31,980
3	0·68	2388	10	23,880
4	0·75	2161	10	21,610
5	0·82	1975	8	15,800
Total for year	—	—	—	129,474
Method B				
1	0·65	2427	12	29,124
2	0·76	2131	12	25,572
3	0·86	1900	10	19,000
4	0·95	1714	10	17,140
5	1·40	1561	8	12,488
Total for year	—	—	—	103,324
Method C				
1	0·78	2027	12	24,324
2	0·92	1774	12	21,288
3	1·03	1576	10	15,760
4	1·14	1435	10	14,350
5	1·25	1301	8	10,408
Total for year	—	—	—	86,130

mercially the best. While the costs of production per pot are obviously the lowest, many of the direct costs remain proportionately the same.

The pots produced under method C are unlikely to exceed the costs of those from method A by more than $17\frac{1}{2}$ per cent. But because the plants are markedly different in size and quality, it is found that many buyers are prepared to accept the additional cost and to pay proportionately more for the higher-quality article.

10 Pests and Diseases

Year-round chrysanthemum production systems demand a high degree of hygiene, pest and disease control. Therefore, control treatments should be routine rather than the occasional measure designed to clear up trouble after it has appeared. The programme should be regular, especially during the summer, and include chemicals toxic to any pest or disease likely to occur. This situation is, however, ideal and the over-use of chemicals during the last two decades has brought many problems.

PROBLEMS IN PEST AND DISEASE CONTROL

Wyatt (1966) demonstrated the presence of resistance in *Myzus persicae* to a number of organochlorine and organophosphorous insecticides. Since then, resistance problems, with both pests and diseases, have worsened. During 1977 the current mainstay of chrysanthemum pest control, aldicarb, did not control aphids and red spider mites as well as expected, and resistance in both these pests has been confirmed. The consequences of this development have not yet been fully appreciated. A leading authority has been heard to say 'resistance is a one-way street', so that new methods of control must be developed. General recommendations for control can no longer be given and pest management has to rely on selecting suitable chemicals which will be effective in the local situation.

The development of a new pesticide which may take seven years, may seem to be a solution but, since resistance already inbred into pest populations, can manifest itself even before a new pesticide is approved for use (cross-resistance), this is probably not the answer.

One way to delay the problem of resistance is to search for and screen alternative chemicals already available. For example, Gurney and Hussey (1974) found other suitable chemicals for the control of leafminer (*Phytomyza syngenesiae*) which was resistant to HCH (BHC) and diazinon (Hussey, 1969).

Obviously, the fewer applications of chemical used against a pest, the slower the development of resistance, with the result that the effective life of a pesticide is prolonged. It remains an open question whether it is better to alternate sprays of different types of chemicals, or to use one chemical repeatedly until it is no longer effective. The selection of resistant strains resulting from the regular use of chemicals may, in some cases, be reduced if the most troublesome pests are controlled biologically.

A bed of year-round chrysanthemums provides a dense canopy of foliage which is difficult to penetrate. There is a need, however, to cover the undersides of leaves with pesticides, especially when attempting to control caterpillars, red spider mites and some aphids, and it has been standard practice to achieve this with high-volume sprays. This is the most effective method available, but it is cumbersome in both labour and equipment, and wasteful in chemicals.

Alternative methods of application are widely used and include fogging, fumigating and the use of systemic materials.

When used in the manner intended, thermal fogging is a quick, simple and sometimes spectacular way of treating a greenhouse. Fogging machines were designed to be used with chemicals which vapourize when fogged (pirimiphos-methyl against whitefly) so that the application is essentially a fumigation, for which the correct time-concentration product of the pesticide must be achieved. However, these machines are also being used to fog non-vapourizing materials, although leaf coverage is not good. Residues can only be relied on to reach the upper leaf surfaces, and may not necessarily reach leaves in the middle of a crop at all. Results will be improved if materials with a translaminar action are applied, for instance dicofol and tetradifon mixtures against red spider mites.

Systemic pesticides applied to the soil may be translocated throughout plants, and for a number of years aldicarb applied in this way has given excellent control of a wide range of pests. A general guide to pesticide usage is given in Appendix 4.

PEST CONTROL

Since 1973 pest control has almost entirely relied on aldicarb applied to the soil (48 to 56 g*/100 m²), with other insecticide treatments being virtually non-existent. However, in 1976 and 1977 'clean-up' sprays had to be used prior to harvest to control aphids and red spider mites. The whole future of aldicarb on chrysanthemums is now questionable. because it is likely that 'clean-up' sprays will be increasingly needed. These sprays normally consist of pirimicarb against aphids and dicofol for red spider mites, this latter chemical sometimes being used as an aerosol.

It is common practice to omit aldicarb for a six- or eight-week period, around November, when the pest problem tends to be minimal.

When red spider mite is a continual problem, quinomethionate, dicofol or tetradifon are widely used, though the more recent introduction of cyhexatin should prove to be an effective replacement. Diazinon is widely used in routine spray mixtures against leafminers and aphids, though some control of red spider mites may be obtained.

Caterpillars are often troublesome in the spring and autumn, and control has relied on carbaryl, methomyl or DDT.†

Integrated Control

The problems of resistance to chemicals led to studies of the possibilities of controlling some greenhouse pests, particularly red spider mites and whitefly, with natural enemies. The capacity of lacewing (chrysopid) larvae to control aphids on chrysanthemums was studied (Scopes, 1969), but insect predators, in general, are not thought to be suitable for pest control in greenhouses (Scopes, 1975a).

The most important aphid (*Myzus persicae*) attacking chrysanthemums has been successfully controlled with a wasp parasite (*Aphidius matricariae*) in small greenhouse tests (Scopes, 1970) and from this work a practical integrated pest control programme was developed (Scopes and Biggerstaff, 1973), based on biological control of *M. persicae* with *A. matricariae* and red spider mite (*Tetranychus urticae*) with the predatory mite *Phytoseiulus persimilis* (Table 31). The programme depends on treating (seeding) boxes of cuttings with natural enemies prior to planting. This method has been used successfully in limited commercial trials. Other pests and fungi are controlled with chemicals that are compatible with the natural enemies, or by the careful use of chemicals which would otherwise be harmful to the natural enemies.

Some may feel that aldicarb still has a place. Some growers may wish to use aldicarb to control aphids and leafminers even though it may not control red spider mites. In such cases, *P. persimilis* can be used successfully following the application of aldicarb so long as seven weeks (more in winter) are allowed between introducing the predator and harvesting the crop, otherwise insufficient time will be available for the predator to control the red spider mites.

Specific Control

APHIDS

Aphids are perhaps the most injurious group of insects that attack chrysanthemums because they can not only transmit virus diseases, such as Mosaic and Aspermy virus, but they also suck sap from plant tissues which affects plant growth. They excrete honeydew on which sooty moulds develop.

Several species of aphid are regularly found

---

* Unless otherwise stated. all chemical rates refer to active ingredients (ai).

† Regulations for pesticide usage will vary between countries and states, therefore local advisors should be consulted before using any crop protection chemical.

TABLE 31   Integrated Pest Control Programme

| Pest or Disease | Treatment | |
	Biological	Chemical
Myzus persicae (Peach-potato aphid)	Prior to planting treat boxes of cuttings with aphids exposed to parasites at a rate of 10 aphids per 100 plants	—
Tetranychus urticae (Red spider mite)	Prior to planting treat boxes of cuttings with red spider mite and predators at rates of 100 and 2 per 100 cuttings	—
Phytomyza syngenesiae (Leafminer) Minor aphids	—	Dioxathion/pirimicarb spray (100 g and 25 g/100 l) misted over plants
Thrips tabaci	—	Thorough soil drench before planting (5 l/m² bed) with HCH (20 g/100 l) or diazinon (40 g/100 l)
Caterpillars	High-volume spray with *Bacillus thuringiensis* (30 g/100 l)	—
Botrytis cinerea (Grey mould)	—	Spray dichlofluanid (50 g/100 l)
Oidium chrysanthemi (Mildew)	—	Spray dinocap (6·3 g/100 l) or triforine (20 g/100 l)

on chrysanthemums, the most common being the peach-potato aphid (*Myzus persicae*), while the shiny brown chrysanthemum aphid (*Macrosiphoniella sanborni*) and the leaf curling plum aphid (*Brachycaudus helichrysi*) may be found feeding on stems and in growing points respectively. The cotton or melon aphid (*Aphis gossypii*) has also recently been found infesting chrysanthemum crops.

The peach-potato aphid is polyphagous (feeding on a wide range of plants), about 2 mm long and usually green in colour though it may be yellowish or even slightly pink. Unlike other aphids it does not live in dense colonies, but in loose aggregations wandering on the undersides of lower leaves and migrating to the apices of stems when buds develop or when aphid numbers are large. It develops throughout the year in greenhouses.

Varieties show wide differences in their susceptibility to attack, Tuneful, Rosechip, Heyday and Princess Anne being susceptible, while Portrait, Iceberg, Delmarvel and Hurricane are less so.

The chrysanthemum aphid is 2·0 to 2·5 mm long and may be easily recognized by its deep brown shiny body. It lives in dense colonies on stems, but migration to leaves occurs when colonies become too large.

The leaf curling plum aphid is small, 1·3 to 2·0 mm long and green in colour, and it lives in the tips of the vegetative shoots or later in the flowers, secreting dense deposits of crystalline honeydew. This aphid migrates into greenhouses from *Prunus* sp.

The cotton aphid is a variable species both in size and colour with individuals which may be bottle green or yellow, found in close proximity.

Other aphids are occasionally found infesting chrysanthemums and include the black bean aphid (*Aphis fabae*) and the mottled arum aphid (*Aulocorthum circumflexum*), which is a small (1·5 to 1·8 mm long) shiny green species. This latter species is commonly found on arums and cyclamen.

Contol Quick and effective control of aphids is essential, especially in stock beds, to prevent the transmission of viruses, and in this situation preventative treatments are recommended.

The peach-potato aphid has developed widespread resistance to organophosphorus insecticides, DDT, HCH and nicotine, while strains of the mottled arum aphid are resistant to HCH, nicotine, pyrethrum and many organophosphorus insecticides. On some nurseries the cotton aphid has been found to be tolerant to pirimicarb.

Soil treatments with aldicarb (48 to 56 g/100 m²*) are widely used to control aphids as well as other pests including mirids, leafhopper, leafminers, thrips and whitefly. It is not uncommon to find aphid outbreaks occurring prior to flowering as a result of migration from lower leaves. In these circumstances a wide choice of contact or systemic pesticides is available. They include HCH (12·5 g/100 l), demeton-S-methyl (22 g/100 l), malathion (113 g/100 l), parathion (10 g/100 l) or pirimicarb (25 g/100 l). When eradicant treatments have to be applied to open flowers nicotine smokes or pirimicarb sprays are least likely to damage petals.

Biological control of the peach-potato aphid with a parasitic wasp (*Aphidius matricariae*) (Figs 49 and 50) has been obtained experimentally and in commercial greenhouses. Aphid control is achieved following the introduction of small numbers of parasitized aphids into boxes of cuttings a few hours prior to planting (Scopes and Biggerstaff, 1973). Compatible chemical control measures for other pests and dieases are practicable (Table 31).

Research has shown that spraying spores of the entomophagous fungus *Verticillium lecanii* can provide effective control of aphids (Hall, 1975), but the system is still experimental.

CATERPILLARS

Many species of caterpillar have been recorded on chrysanthemums but the most common species are those of the angleshade moth

* All rates refer to amount of active ingredient.

Fig. 49 Adult *Aphidius matricariae*, a parasitic wasp which lays eggs in the peach-potato aphid.

(*Phlogophora meticulosa*), silver Y moth (*Autographa gamma*) and, occasionally, the carnation tortrix moth (*Cacoecimorpha pronubana*). Before the advent of year-round growing, attacks usually occurred in the autumn, but artificial lighting is attractive to moths on the wing. Recent research at Purdue University in Indiana showed that some types of light, especially high-pressure sodium lamps, are much less attractive to insects, including moths, than flourescent or mercury vapour lamps.

The green or brown caterpillars feed at night, resting by day, though day-time feeding may occur during dull weather. Young caterpillars feed on the undersides of leaves creating a 'window effect', as they leave a thin transparent layer of epidermal cells, while older caterpillars chew large holes in leaves and flowers. Black frass pellets on leaves indicate the presence of caterpillars though they may be difficult to find resting in leaf axils or on stems lower down the plant. It is often possible, however, to find caterpillars immediately after the blackout has been drawn back.

Control A few caterpillars can cause extensive damage, and it is sometimes possible to remove the culprits by hand picking, especially in dull

Fig. 50   Swollen aphid skins containing parasite pupae in a colony of healthy aphids.

weather when they may remain at the tops of plants.

DDT, as smokes, dusts or sprays (100 g/100 l), is a widely used control, while sprays of carbaryl (75 g/100 l) or trichlorphon (200 g/100 l) are also effective. The atomization of dichlorvos (3·5 g/100 m³) has given good control of young larvae. The new synthetic pyrethroids offer promise for the future.

Bacillus thuringiensis is a safe biological insecticide specific to caterpillars, which may be applied as a high-volume spray (30 g/100 l) bacterial powder (Burges and Jarrett, 1978, in press). Recent tests at the GCRI have shown that it can be applied through a thermal pulsejet fogger. *B. thuringiensis* is a stomach poison and so must reach the undersides of leaves where caterpillars feed in order to be effective. Therefore high-volume sprays must cover all leaf surfaces. Treatments should be repeated as the plants grow. *B. thuringiensis* is easily washed off foliage and so will not be effective where overhead irrigation is used.

The Mediterranean Climbing Cutworm (*Spodoptera littoralis*) does not normally live in Britain, being excluded by strict quarantine regulations. The greenish-brown caterpillars have conspicuous black and yellow markings along their bodies. The segments behind the head have two pairs of yellow spots.

This insect is common in the Mediterranean and the quarantine regulations require that all plant material imported to Britain is stored at 0·5° for 10 days to kill eggs and larvae.

In Britain, outbreaks of this pest must be reported to the Ministry of Agriculture, who will supervise the control programme. It is resistant to DDT, thus dichlorvos (atomised 3·5 g/100 m³), carbaryl (75 g/100 l) or trichlorphon (200 g/100 l) might be used. In other countries methomyl or endosulfan have been used as sprays.

EARWIGS

Earwigs, the most common being *Forficula auricularia*, need no introduction, and may, occasionally, be found in greenhouses where debris is left. They chew foliage and flowers, damage in the latter case resembling an attack by caterpillars, but no characteristic frass pellets will be found.

Control Earwigs are easy to kill with insecticides and thorough spraying with HCH (12·5 g/100 l), carbaryl (200 g/100 l) or trichlorphon (80 g/100 l) is commonly recommended, though smokes may also be used. Methiocarb pellets broadcast on to the soil (110 g/100 m²) appear to be effective.

EELWORM*

The importance of the chrysanthemum eelworm (*Aphelenchoides ritzembosi*) has declined dramatically in recent years because of the use of stock plants and sterilized compost. It is rarely found on year-round crops.

The colourless microscopic worm travels up the plant in a film of water, entering leaves via the stomata. Dark brown to black patches develop on leaves as they feed. The patches are often delineated by leaf veins, giving a characteristic triangular appearance. Damage is usually first seen on lower leaves, and spread of the pest up the plant depends on wet conditions.

Control Plants should be propagated from eelworm-free stock, but if this is impractical, infestations may be controlled by thoroughly drenching young rooted cuttings with thionazin (29 g/100 l), repeating the treatment after two weeks. Alternatively, aldicarb granules may be broadcast on to the soil (48 to 56 g/100 m²). Double rates should be used on stool beds. Such chemical treatments have largely replaced hot water treatments in which stools are immersed in hot water at 46° for 5·5 minutes, or in water kept at 43° for 20 to 30 minutes. Stools, after either treatment, should be immersed in cold water, prior to growing on. Some varieties are susceptible to this treatment and even if constant temperatures are maintained, stools may be killed or the production of cuttings delayed.

Drenching sprays of parathion have been widely used to control this pest but are un-

* See Appendix 2 for details of Advisory Leaflets in the Britain from MAFF.

likely to produce complete control because of inadequate penetration into the plant tissues.

GALL MIDGE

The chrysanthemum midge or gall midge (*Diarthronomyia chrysanthemi*), once a serious pest, is now virtually unknown on chrysanthemums. The larvae of these reddish-brown flies (2·5 mm long) hatch in leaf folds or among bracts, causing small thornlike galls on leaves, stems or buds. Infested cuttings produce weak plants. In the greenhouse, these flies will breed continuously throughout the year.

Control The regular use of pesticides has made this pest a curiosity and if an outbreak occurs several sprays with HCH (12·5 g/100 l) or diazinon (16 g/100 l) should eradicate an infestation. It is probable that control could be obtained with aldicarb, or any other broad spectrum insecticide.

LEAFMINER

Chrysanthemums are one of the many species of composite plants attacked by the leafminer (*Phytomyza syngenesiae*), and since widespread resistance to insecticides has occurred, it is a regular and troublesome pest.

The adult fly is 2·0 to 2·5 mm long with a grey head and thorax and yellow abdomen (Fig. 51). Adults usually feed on the upper surfaces of younger leaves, producing round white feeding pits. Eggs are laid singly within the leaf in some of these pits, and on hatching the small larvae begin to tunnel within the leaf,

Fig. 51   Adult leafminer fly: length 2·0 to 2·5 mm.

causing the characteristic trails which become larger as the larvae grow bigger. The larvae pupate at the end of the mine in the leaf. At 16°, the life-cycle takes about 12 days, while at 5° it takes 55 days. In greenhouses leafminers are active throughout the year.

Urophora zoe is a closely related species of fly whose larvae cause blotch mines in leaves. It is only rarely found attacking chrysanthemums. Another similar fly, *Paroxyna misella*, has been recorded locally in Britain. Larvae cause galls on the terminal shoot and blotch mines within leaves.

Control There is widespread tolerance among leafminers to both HCH and diazinon.

Aldicarb (48 to 56 g/100 m²) is currently used to control this pest and its effects are long-lasting. The recent failures of aldicarb to control some pests satisfactorily throughout the growing period may reduce its use, so that control of leafminer will have to rely on sprays. Research at the GCRI has shown that there is a wide range of alternative chemicals (Gurney and Hussey, 1974). They include azinphos-methyl (100 g/100 l), bromophos (100 g/100 l), cartap (100 g/100 l), dimethoate (100 g/100 l), dioxathion (100 g/100 l), pirimiphos-methyl (100 g/100 l), pirimiphos-ethyl (100 g/100 l) and trichlorphon (100 g/100 l). Dimethoate granules, applied to the soil at 2, 5 and 10 ppm, controlled this pest for eight weeks.

Where biological control of aphids and red spider mites is being used, dioxathion (100 g/100 l) should be applied as a fine spray on to the apical foliage every two weeks. Leafminer control is then obtained without harming any natural enemies.

Pirimicarb, a safe selective insecticide, will give some degree of control if applied as a fine spray (15 g/100 l).

Biological control of leafminers with parasites is possible, but no commercial source is yet available in Britain. Suitable parasites may be found attacking leafminers on sow thistles (*Sonchus* sp.).

Another leafminer, *Liriomyza trifolii*, was introduced into Britain in 1977. This leafminer is a potentially serious pest of tomatoes as well as chrysanthemums. It may be distinguished from *P. syngenesiae* by the yellow pupa, which forms outside the leaf and falls onto the soil.

In the USA, *L. trifolii* is difficult to control because of resistances to a wide range of insecticides. Permethrin has been used in Britain, either as a fog or spray.

MIRIDS (CAPSIDS)

Mirids primarily cause damage to chrysanthemums grown outdoors although they may occasionally occur in greenhouses. The two most common species in Britain are the bishop bug (*Lygus rugulipennis*) and the common green capsid (*Lygocoris pabulinus*). These true 'bugs' have shiny bodies, the green capsid being green, while the bishop bug is mainly brown.

They insert their stylets (mouthparts) into leaves and stems, sucking out the plant juices; the plant forming brown calluses as a result of toxic salivary juices injected into plant cells. As the plant grows, leaves and flowers become twisted and stunted and shoots become blind.

These insects fly off at the slightest disturbance and are thus difficult to find and spray.

Control Aldicarb (48 to 56 g/100 m²) will give effective long-term control. HCH or DDT are commonly recommended to control mirids either as sprays (HCH 12·5 g/100 l, DDT 100 g/100 l), smokes (HCH 12·5 g/100 m³, DDT 10·5 g/100 m³) or atomized solutions (HCH 3·5 g/100 m³, DDT 10·5 g/100 m³).

There is no resistance problem with mirids and it is reasonable to suppose that most broad spectrum insecticides would be effective, but the best results would be expected from fumigants or persistent materials.

RED SPIDER MITE

Red spider mites (*Tetranychus urticae*) are serious pests on most greenhouse crops and chrysanthemums are no exception. Mites will breed on the crop throughout the year because winter diapause is inhibited by the artificial lighting used for longday treatments.

Mites damage foliage by feeding on the undersides of leaves, causing a white speckling, but as numbers increase webbing may be spun round leaves and buds. Small populations may remain undetected until flowers open, when the mites will swarm into them. It is likely that many infestations begin from a very few individuals on cuttings at planting, or from migration as adjacent beds are cleared after flowering.

Control Strains of red spider mites are resistant to most of the conventional acaricides such as dicofol and tetradifon. Aldicarb (48 to 56 g/100 m²) has been extensively used to control spider mites in Britain but results are now erratic, as resistance has been confirmed on some nurseries during 1977.

Where mites are a persistent problem, high-volume sprays of demeton-S-methyl (22 g/100 l), diazinon (16 g/100 l) or quinomethionate (12·5 g/100 l) should be tried. Parathion or propoxur smokes or vaporizing naled could be useful alternatives, especially in smaller houses.

Organotin compounds such as cyhexatin (25 g/100 l) are proving invaluable in controlling this pest, as resistance has not yet been reported. There have, however, been reports of leaf damage when using this chemical, though it has the interesting property of not harming *Phytoseiulus persimilis*, the predatory mite.

Biological control of red spider mites using *P. persimilis* has been shown to be very effective (Scopes and Biggerstaff, 1973) on commercial nurseries. Ideally, small numbers of predators, together with some spider mites as food, should be introduced on to the cuttings prior to planting. The subsequent interaction will ensure complete control for the duration of the crop.

In cases where aldicarb has failed to control this pest, predators may be successfully introduced on to the crop so long as at least seven weeks are allowed before harvesting. If shorter periods of time are allowed, incomplete control will result, unless massive introductions of predators are made. A complete integrated pest control programme has been devised for use with this predator (Table 31).

SCIARID FLIES (FUNGUS GNATS)

The larvae of sciarids feed on young roots and serious attacks can kill young plants. One of the most common species (*Bradysia paupera*) appears to be attracted to freshly steamed soil,

Fig. 52   Adult sciarid fly: length 2·5 to 3·0 mm (compare with adult leafminer in Fig. 51).

while the trend to peat composts has increased the occurrence of this pest.

The greyish-black adult fly (2·5 to 3·00 mm long), with long antennae (Fig. 52), may be seen running over compost. The larva which lives in the soil is translucent white with a shiny black head.

Control Adult flies are readily killed by a wide range of insecticides but effective control relies on the use of persistent soil-applied chemicals to kill larvae and emerging adults. Diazinon incorporated into compost (170 g/m³) should give protection up to six weeks. Subsequent attacks can be controlled with a diazinon (16 g/100 l) or parathion (10 g/100 l) drench. Malathion (113 g/100 l) may also be used but is not persistent.

Recent trials have shown that spectacular control may be obtained by drenching soil with diflubenzuron. This insecticide appears to inhibit moulting.

SLUGS

Slugs should not be a problem in the greenhouse where regular hygiene measures are practised, but infestations, usually of the grey field slug (*Agrolimax reticulatus*), may occur from chance introductions, or from uncultivated land adjoining houses. They chew irregular holes in foliage and leave slime trials on foliage and soil. *Control* Slugs may be controlled by broadcasting metaldehyde (17 to 34 g/100 m²) or methiocarb (1 g/100 m²) pellets. The former chemical is available as a suspension for spraying (68 g/100 l) over the soil.

STOOL MINER

This small fly (*Psila nigricornis*), related to the carrot fly, is a pest on chrysanthemums but its importance has declined with the increasing use of up-to-date stock production techniques.

The larvae feed on the roots of young plants, reducing their vigour, and, consequently, infested plants produce few cuttings. Adult flies are active in summer, laying eggs round the stems of newly planted chrysanthemums. Damage is caused primarily by the larvae tunnelling in roots, especially at the base of the stem.

Control Adults and larvae are readily killed by thorough sprays of HCH (10 g/100 l) so long as larvae have not tunnelled into the roots and stem bases. In such cases sprays of demeton-S-methyl (14 g/100 l) are to be preferred. Aldicarb or thionazin is also likely to be effective.

SYMPHILIDS

Symphilids are white, active, centipede-like creatures which live deep in the soil. The most common species (*Scutigerella immaculata*) is about 6 mm long with twelve pairs of legs and long antennae. They feed voraciously on young roots, individuals eating their own weight in a day. The first sign of attack is a wilting of isolated plants or groups of plants, associated with a severe check to growth.

Control Soil sterilization treatments are unlikely to give completely effective control unless they penetrate deep into the soil. Once attacks have developed they are likely to recur. The most satisfactory treatment has been to drench the soil around the plants with parathion (12·5 g/100 l) or diazinon (10 g/100 l). Thorough incorporation of HCH dusts (2·7 kg/ha) into the top soil has also given satisfactory results.

Recent tests with dazomet incorporated into the soil (38 kg/ha) gave 97 per cent control, but such a treatment should only be used as a last resort, as residues may persist for up to three months.

THRIPS

Thrips, or thunderflies as they are commonly known, may migrate from grasses and damage plants during hot weather in late summer. They may feed on the growing point, causing distortion, while damaged petals may show silvery flecks.

Thrips tabaci, the onion thrips, can breed all the year round in greenhouses, feeding on the growing point. As the leaves expand they become mottled and distorted, but by this time the insect has pupated in the soil. Adults are about 1 mm long and brown to black with two pairs of fringed wings; larvae are yellow and eventually pupate in the soil.

Other signs of attack may include small callus trails up the stem as a result of feeding. In severe infestations, leaf silvering occurs where the upper epidermal tissues become separated from the remainder of the leaf.

Control Where a routine treatment of aldicarb has not been used, thrips may be controlled by a wide range of insecticides applied as sprays, aerosols or smokes. Such treatments will be needed to control infestations arising from grasses and cereals in late summer.

As *T. tabaci* pupates in the soil, populations may be controlled by applying soil drenches of HCH (20 g/100 l) or diazinon (40 g/100 l), using 5 l/m². Where thrips are damaging open blooms control is difficult, as the sprays may be phytotoxic (page 164). Nicotine smokes or sprays (50 ml/100 l) are also effective.

WHITEFLY

The greenhouse whitefly (*Trialeurodes vaporariorum*) is a common pest of many crops and may, on occasions, be troublesome on chrysanthemums, although it is unusual for it to breed on this plant. Infestations that do occur are often the result of mass migration from other crops such as tomatoes.

Control The routine use of a persistent

systemic insecticide such as aldicarb (48 to 56 g/100 m²) should give effective control. White-flies are difficult to control with sprays because of their long life-cycle, part of which is relatively immune to pesticides. Resistance to insecticides is widespread and where this occurs treatment with a pyrethrum/resmethrin mixture or pirimiphos-methyl should be tried.

Biological control with parastic wasp *Encarsia formosa* is unlikely to be successful because of the short growing period of individual crops.

DISEASE CONTROL

Chrysanthemums are attacked by fewer pathogens (fungi and bacteria) than many other greenhouse crops, but the same organism may attack several parts of the plant causing different symptoms, as, for example, when *Pythium* root rot spreads to stems. On the other hand, similar symptoms may result from infection by different pathogens (*Phoma* and *Verticillium*).

Bacteria are single-celled micro-organisms, often mobile in water, which can multiply very rapidly. The optimum conditions of temperature and pH for growth of bacteria are higher than for most fungi. Fungi produce a multicellular filamentous mycelium which spreads through plant tissues. The reproductive spores are produced on aerial branches (*Botrytis* grey mould), within thick-walled fruit bodies (*Didymella ligulicola*) or in pustules (rusts) erupting through leaf tissue.

Early detection of symptoms and identification of the causal pathogen is essential if the correct control measures (Appendix 4) are to be applied and a disease outbreak controlled, because most fungicides are protectants and few will eradicate a disease completely.

Varieties vary in susceptibility and a disease may remain undetected when only resistant cultivars are grown, severe symptoms subsequently appearing when susceptible types are planted.

Frequent soil steaming normally keeps soil-borne pathogens at a low level, and together with good hygiene and growing methods, providing optimum conditions for roots and shoots, constitute a major defence against disease.

Powdery mildew has become a local problem because aldicarb has removed the need for regular insecticide sprays. with which fungicides were often combined. Dinocap has been used against mildew but some varieties have been badly damaged, and triforine, thiophanate-methyl or benomyl are now used.

Mancozeb or zineb are often used when *Didymella*, *Pythium*, *Phytophthora* or *Septoria* are present, while quintozene is applied to the soil against *Rhizoctonia*.

Botrytis has become more troublesome in recent years in the early summer; the need to save fuel and the use of blackout results in lower temperatures and higher humidities, conditions conductive to fungal development. In some cases the fungus has developed strains tolerant to benomyl and related fungicides.

If a rust disease, especially Japanese White Rust (*Puccinia horiana*), is suspected, then a regular spray programme is used, based on benodanil, oxycarboxin or triforine.

It is common practice to mix insecticides and fungicides to save labour, and care must be taken to mix only chemicals that are compatible. The use of thiram, DDT and malathion and other combined sprays is not always possible because chemicals are occasionally withdrawn by suppliers, while others may be less effective because of resistance.

Bacterial Diseases

Bacterial diseases are not very common in Britain but, severe outbreaks have been recorded in the USA.

BACTERIAL WILT

Virulent strains of *Erwinia chrysanthemi* can cause wilting of mature plants, associated with vascular discoloration and a blackening of external stem and leaf tissues. If the infection is slight these symptoms may not develop but growth will be retarded. Cuttings may be infected when planted or bacteria may have survived in the soil.

Different strains of other bacteria, reported to be pathogenic on carnations and other crops, may attack chrysanthemums, producing mild symptoms.

PSEUDOMONAS SP.

Pseudomonas disease was first noticed and identified on chrysanthemums in the spring of 1970, using the methods of Lelliot, Billing and Hayward (1966). The damaging organism was identified as *P. fluorescens*, a species which is normally saprophytic. Symptoms seemed to occur when cuttings from stock plants grown in warmer climates were rooted in the poor winter light conditions in Britain. The bacteria multiply quickly, blocking the vascular tissues, producing a weak plant.

Cuttings are seldom killed but because of the serious delay in rooting and development, diseased cuttings normally have to be discarded. The disease may be recognized by the reddish coloration at the base of, and inside, the hollow stem.

ERWINIA SP.

Several closely related *Erwinia* sp., which are common soil inhabitants, occasionally attack weak plants, causing rotting or splitting at the base of the stem. Internal tissues may turn into a jelly-like mass and reddish-brown sticky drops may exude from infected tissues. *E. carotovora*, a soft rot bacterium, may produce a secondary infection, causing wet rots.

CROWN GALL

Agrobacterium tumefaciens stimulates the abnormal growth of plant tissues, producing galls on many plants and has been locally troublesome on chrysanthemums in Britain, Germany and the USA in recent years (Miller, Miller and Crane, 1975). The aetiology of infection has not been studied extensively, but the bacterium is a frequent soil-inhabitant, and galling presumably occurs when a virulent strain infects a plant. Galls are usually formed at or near soil level, but they can occur on shoots or leaves. Although they are unsightly, it is not known whether they harm normal plant growth.

CONTROL

There are no chemical controls for bacterial diseases of chrysanthemums, so control must rely on hygiene. Destruction of infected debris is essential and infected soil or compost must be steam sterilized to prevent carry-over from one crop to another.

These diseases tend to be more troublesome in high temperatures and humidities, and cultural conditions that favour soft growth should be avoided.

All new plant material should be carefully examined for infection, while stock plants should be tested for freedom from disease if there is the slightest risk of its introduction.

Fungal Diseases

ROOT ROTS

Root lesions and root death may be caused by several fungal pathogens, and more than one may be present in the soil at any one time.

Phoma root rot (*Phoma chrysanthemicola*) is likely to occur only in unsterilized or poorly-sterilized soil. First indications of the disease can be seen when groups of plants appear stunted, often with chlorotic lower leaves, which may eventually show necrotic spotting. These necrotic areas enlarge until the whole leaf is affected, hanging limply on the stem. Younger leaves become progressively affected in a similar way. Eventually, the whole plant will wilt and die.

The infection is usually confined to the roots, but it may, occassionally, invade the base of the stem when lesions occur. Reddish lesions may also be found on larger roots, while smaller ones may be rotted away.

The disease is favoured by adverse soil conditions. These include wet badly drained soil, high pH and inadequate nutrients, especially nitrogen and phosphorus (Peerally and Colhoun, 1969). Highly susceptible varieties include Fred Shoesmith and sports, Portrait, Bluechip and Loveliness. Heyday, Snowcap and Princess Anne have all shown a high degree of resistance to most strains of the disease.

Phoma root rot may be controlled with pre-planting soil drenches of nabam (140 g/100 l, using 22 l/m²), but planting cannot take place for at least 14 days.

Species of *Phytophthora* and *Pythium*, both

water moulds, can invade sterilized soil and infect roots, killing them. This will result in poor, uneven growing plants. *Pythium* sp. may also infect cuttings in the rooting bench, causing damping-off and a rot at the base of the stem.

Spores of these fungi are readily produced in wet soils and rapidly invade other plants, especially those with damaged roots. Optimum temperatures for these fungi are above 25° but damage may be caused at temperatures as low as 10°.

Control of root rots. Root rots may be prevented by regular soil steam sterilization, The likelihood of attack is reduced by avoiding over-watering, especially on heavy or poorly drained soils, by improving air circulation to reduce humidity and by planting cuttings no deeper than they were in the rooting bench.

Chemical control of *Phytophthora* and *Pythium* relies on soil drenches with a thiram/captan mixture each at 2·5 g/m². Chemicals which may prevent spread of the disease include drazoxolon, etridiazole or copper compounds.

FOOT ROTS

Foot or basal stem lesions often follow root infection, or they may develop when pathogens are reintroduced superficially on to sterilized soil.

Rhizoctonia solani may infect roots but is more frequently found attacking the base of stems of young plants, particularly in warm, moist conditions, Growth may be retarded before lesions are seen, and eventually the whole stem collapses. Lesions are brown and dry, and brown fungal threads may be seen on close examination.

Sclerotinia rot caused by *Sclerotinia sclerotiorum* is uncommon and rarely causes serious losses. The fungus can develop at a temperature as low as 10° and causes light brown lesions on stems, which become covered with fluffy fungal growth in which black sclerotia or resting bodies are embedded. The sclerotia bodies are extremely hardy and can survive prolonged adverse conditions in the soil.

Control of Foot Rots Soil sterilization is the key to preventing these diseases. It appears that peat may sometimes be a source of the disease, so the incorporation of the peat into the bed should precede steaming. The spread of *Rhizoctonia* is slowed down by drying out the soil, while drenching with thiram (150 g/100 l) or dusting quintozene (13 g/m²) should give control. Spraying or dipping in benomyl (240 g/100 l) has been found to protect young plants.

The spread of *Sclerotinia* may be checked by raking quintozene dust into the soil (13 g/m²), but once sclerotia have formed, even soil sterilization may not be effective.

STEM ROTS

True stem rots generally result from infection by aerial spores of fungi such as *Botrytis cinerea* (grey mould), although root infections by fungi such as *Pythium ultimum* and *Didymella ligulicola* may develop into stem rots.

Botrytis cinerea is an ubiquitous pathogen infecting all stages of growth. Stems of young plants may be infected while on the rooting bench, due to lower leaves in contact with moist compost becoming infected, and this can result in serious losses.

Infection occurs more easily through damaged tissue, especially on soft plants, and prolific sporulation takes place on dying or dead tissues. Rapid spread of the fungus occurs in warm humid conditions.

Ray blight (*Didymella ligulicola*), previously known as *Mycosphaerella* or *Ascochyta*, was originally found on the ray florets of chrysanthemums, but it can also cause blackish lesions on stems and lower leaves when the roots and stems of young plants have been contaminated with the pathogen. At the pre-bud stage, spores spread by insects or by water may germinate on leaves, producing irregular black blotches.

The fungus may also attack stems and leaves about the time flowers open, the infection developing from the point of attachment of the ray floret. It may then develop within the flower stalk, which turns black and droops, or it may spread to adjoining florets, resulting in flower distortion.

Pythium ultimum causes a stem rot sometimes known as 'Iceberg disease'. The first symptoms, lesions occuring at ground level, are not always noticed, but 6 to 10 weeks later the reddish-brown streaks may be seen extending up the stems, being particularly noticeable at leaf nodes. Plants may flag and die. Internal tissues are often discoloured beyond the area of the external lesions. Infections originate from the soil and the rate of development is influenced by softness of the plant, varietal resistance, temperature and humidity. Mature plants are not so easily infected as young ones.

A stem rot caused by *Fusarium solani* has been reported from the USA. Symptoms can occur on cuttings, stock or flowering plants, and are sometimes not unlike those caused by *Erwinia chrysanthemi*, *Pythium* or *Rhizoctonia*. On cuttings reddish discoloration and decay of the pith occurs, necrotic streaks develop on stems of older plants, and dieback of stub wounds on stock plants occurs. Wilting occurs in the later stages of the disease (Engelhard, Crane and Mellinger, 1976).

Control of Stem Rots. Decreasing the humidity and encouraging air movement around plants will help to limit stem rots. Where *Botrytis* is found to be the cause, thorough spraying with captan (100 g/100 l), dichlofluanid (50 g/100 l), thiophanate-methyl (50 g/100 l) or thiram (300 g/100 l) has given good results; while watering cuttings with captan (200 g/100 l) reduces rotting. High levels of nitrogen increase the susceptibility to infection.

Didymella is difficult to control once established. All soil should be regularly steam sterilized, and the use of clean plant material and the destruction of infected plants will also help to prevent the spread of this disease. Recommended chemical treatments include dipping or spraying cuttings with benomyl (50 g/100 l) and sprays of captan (100 g/100 l), mancozeb (80 g/100 l) or triforine (30 g/100 l) on older plants.

Recommendations for the control of *Pythium ultimum* are the same as for Pythium root rot (page 161). In the USA etridiazole and fenaminosulf have been used effectively.

LEAF DISEASES

Perhaps the most common disease of chrysanthemums is powdery mildew (*Oidium chrysanthemi*), an obligate parasite. White powdery patches of spores appear on the upper leaf surfaces, sometimes spreading to the undersides and on to stems. Spores spread quickly through the crop in the air and may be carried from outdoor plants, through vents or wherever draughts occur.

Rust (*Puccinia chrysanthemi*), another obligate parasite, produces pinhead size blisters on the lower leaf surfaces which break open, releasing powdery masses of dark brown spores. Viewed from above, the pustules show as yellowish spots on the leaves. The disease may spread rapidly in humid conditions, but is, nevertheless, relatively uncommon.

Septoria leaf spot (*Septoria obesa* and *S. chrysanthemella*) is now an uncommon disease causing circular greyish-brown leaf spots which become brittle in the center. Badly affected leaves may turn yellow and die. The symptoms may be masked by secondary infections, often of grey mould. Spores produced on the spots can spread in water and lush plants are more susceptible to attack.

Control of Leaf Diseases The incidence of these diseases is reduced by providing dry airy conditions. Mildew is controlled with triforine (30 g/100 l), thiophanate-methyl (50 g/100 l), pyrazophos (15 g/100 l) or a carbendazim fungicide (25 to 30 g/100 l). Until the development of modern chemicals sulphur was used to control mildew, either as a dust, vapour or spray.

Rusts are exceedingly difficult to eradicate and a regular spray programme (every 10 to 14 days) with benodanil (50 g/100 l), oxycarboxin (71 to 94 g/100 l), thiram (300 g/100 l) or zineb (125 g/100 l) must be used.

Thorough spraying with benomyl (25 to 50 g/100 l) will control Septoria leaf spot, and ideally diseased foliage should be removed and destroyed.

JAPANESE WHITE RUST

Japanese White Rust (*Puccinia horiana*) is not an indigenous disease in Britain but outbreaks

Fig. 53   Whitish pustules of Japanese White Rust on the underside of the leaf.

do occur occasionally, the first being in 1963. It is endemic in Europe, thus the importation of plant material involves some risk. It is kept out of the country by quarantine and strict measures are taken to eradicate outbreaks.

Japanese White Rust produces small whitish blisters or pustules on the undersides of leaves (Fig. 53) which when viewed from above appear as yellowish spots through the leaf. The pustules break open, releasing a mass of light brown spores. The interval between infection and the appearance of symptoms may vary from eight days to eight weeks but is normally two to four weeks (Grouet and Allaire, 1973). There appear to be different strains of the fungus which attack different varieties because varieties resistant in earlier outbreaks are not the same as those found resistant recently.

Control   Cultural control is important in preventing the spread of this disease. Foliage must be kept dry, as infection can occur if spores remain in a water film for at least five hours. It is thus unwise to water before covering the crop with blackout material.

As with most fungal diseases a routine spray programme must be used to protect plants and it is common practice to alternate benodanil (50 g/100 l) and oxycarboxin (71 to 94 g/100 l). Some protection will be obtained with zineb, mancozeb or a mixture of the two chemicals.

Trials in Germany suggest that triforine (25 g/100 l) will also give control.

Resistance to oxycarboxin has been reported in Japan.

FLOWER DISEASES

Grey mould (*Botrytis cinerea*) can be recognized by the brown water-soaked spots which form on petals. This is commonly known as 'damping'. Part or all of the flower head may subsequently rot and become covered with the characteristic spores from which the fungus takes its name.

Flowers infected with ray blight show tan or light brown specks at the base of florets, which may rot completely. Spores are produced in large numbers under blackout when temperatures and humidities are high (McCoy and Dimock, 1972). Buds fail to open properly and flowers become distorted, even if the fungus is checked by lowering the temperature and humidity or by spraying.

Petal blight (*Intersonilia perplexans*) rarely occurs on heated crops and unlike ray blight the tips of petals become infected first. The disease then develops into an irregular brownish rot. The symptoms are often masked by *Botrytis*, which invades the damaged tissue.

Control of Flower Diseases   Because flowers are sensitive to chemical sprays, the lowering of humidity plays an important part in preventing disease spread. Zineb applied as a fine spray (125 g/100 l) should, however, control petal blight. Where *Botrytis* or ray blight are the cause of damage, control measures are the same as for stem rots caused by these organisms. Great care should be taken when using chemical sprays on open flowers.

WILT DISEASES

As a result of culture indexing to exclude wilt pathogens from stocks, wilt diseases are not very commonly found. Two fungi cause wilt symptoms by invading the vascular tissues in the first stages of an attack.

Fusarium oxysporum has only rarely been found in Britain on chrysanthemums. Wilting is accompanied by a browning of the vascular tissues. Symptoms may not be detected below 15° but are severe above 26°.

Verticillium dahliae and *V. albo-atrum*, although common in garden soils, occur only rarely where soil sterilization is frequent. The disease shows itself in two ways; first, the plants may be stunted, with interveinal yellowing of lower leaves associated with browning of the petioles; second, more severe symptoms develop with general wilting, leaves turning brown but often remaining attached to the plant. Vascular tissues may be brown and discoloured, although wilting may not occur until the flower buds are developing.

Control of Wilt Diseases   Routine soil sterilization is essential and infected plants must be destroyed, because the disease spreads from infected plant material. Thorough drenches of carbendazim (25 to 30 g/100 l) should prevent spread. It has been claimed that high lime and nitrate nitrogen fertilizer treatments, together with benomyl drenches, will control Fusarium wilt (Englehard and Woltz, 1973).

PHYTOTOXICITY

Information on phytotoxicity is sparse because of the wide choice of chrysanthemum varieties and pesticides available. Great care should be taken in applying pesticides in view of the damage to flowers which can occur due to phytotoxicity. As a general rule pesticides should not be applied to plants which are dry at the roots or during periods of bright sunlight, because damage may occur. Also pests and diseases should be controlled before buds show colour, because the choice of chemicals which can be used safely becomes more limited after this stage.

Fungicides do not seem to damage plants as much as insecticides, and many have been used on open flowers without harm.

HCH has been known to damage young growth, the solvents used being thought to be the phytotoxic material. Diazinon, although normally safe to use, should not be sprayed on open flowers, and dicofol, similarly, may cause petal scorch. Dichlorvos has been widely used on open flowers without harm but the foliage of a few varieties now largely superseded, such as Dawn Star, Shasta and Taffeta, has been distorted and stunted.

Nicotine often causes marginal chlorosis when used in humid conditions or when the foliage is wet. When dry conditions prevail no damage results. It has been used safely on crops in bud.

Parathion, pirimicarb, pirimiphos-methyl and propoxur, are generally regarded as safe chemicals even on flowers, though pinks and reds seem prone to fading after spraying.

Pynosect and resmethrin both appear to be relatively safe pesticides, and it has been suggested that fogging or aerosol treatments are less likely to be phytotoxic than their equivalent high-volume sprays.

Trials in the USA (Poe, 1971), showed that cyhexatin damaged flowers of all varieties tested, but did not injure foilage.

Some pesticides are not recommended for use on chrysanthemums because of the risk of damage; they include binapacryl, carbaryl, dimethoate, dinobuton and formothion. Their use then becomes an individual's decision. Carbaryl, for instance, is widely used against caterpillars, while tests with dimethoate at the GCRI (Gurney and Hussey, 1974), on 26 varieties revealed only minor yellowing of lower leaves, certainly not enough to reduce market quality.

Care must be taken when spraying oxycarboxin, as a marginal leaf scorch can develop if the chemical drips on to the soil where it will be taken into the plant from the roots.

Where new varieties are being grown or new pesticides used, it is often best to conduct a small trial before spraying the whole crop. The decision as to whether high-volume or low-volume sprays, fogs, aerosols or smokes are to be used must be made according to weather conditions and the state of the crop at the time.

Growers not familiar with spraying out-of-season crops would be well advised to call in their local advisory officer.

MISCELLANEOUS DISORDERS

Chrysanthemums may be affected by several disorders, the causes of which are obscure or can be attributed to one or other of a wide range of cultural defects.

Chlorosis

Leaves with this condition become deficient in chlorophyll and turn whitish (chlorotic). Chlorosis may be induced by nutrient deficiencies, especially of magnesium or manganese. A lack of light or the exposure of growing plants to cold conditions may also cause a general chlorosis. The misuse of pesticides can produce chlorosis of the leaf margins.

Leaf scorch

This may be regarded as a more severe reaction to the cultural environment or to pesticides. Random spots or blotches on leaves may reflect misuse of sprays, while symmetrical scorching, round leaf edges or between veins, is suggestive of adverse soil conditions, either nutritional or due to soil-applied pesticides.

Rotted Flower Centres

These may be caused by fungi (ray blight), but heavy feeding and excess nitrogen can also cause cell breakdown in flowers. Fungi subsequently invade the rotting tissues, often obscuring the original cause of the disorder.

Stem Splitting

Horizontal splits occasionally occur on flower stems just beneath buds or opening flowers. Such splits, through more than half the stem, are sharp and clearly defined and cause the flower to topple over. Although such symptoms have never been induced experimentally, it is thought that this damage is due to incorrect water relations in the plant such as may be induced by over-watering a dry plant in hot weather.

Blind Shoots

Blindness of the shoots may be caused by insects or by a nutrient deficiency such as a severe lack of copper, but in this case other symptoms, such as chlorosis of the terminal veins of the middle leaves, would be evident. Pesticides may also cause blindness.

PART FOUR

Factors Affecting Growth and Flowering

11 Environmental Factors

The most important factors of the aerial environment are light (daylength, amount and spectral quality) and temperature. In the substrate environment soil air and water are of paramount importance together with nutrients and their availablity.

A brief account of the experimental work on the effect of light and temperature on chrysanthemums is given here because it should be helpful for a complete understanding of the principles of year-round chrysanthemum production. Recent work (Machin, 1973) has shown that for normal growth and flowering of chrysanthemums some aspects of nutrition are just as important as light and temperature. An account of the research on certain elements of nutrition is therefore included for the first time.

LIGHT

Both the photoperiod and the amount of light (daily radiation integral) are known to have major effects on the growth and flowering of chrysanthemums and these have been studied in some depth. The effect of spectral quality of light on chrysanthemums is generally more subtle and information is constantly being revealed which makes its importance more fully appreciated.

Daylength

The natural flowering season of the florists' chrysanthemum occurs between late summer and late winter according to variety. It was believed that flowering was induced by the falling temperatures of late summer and autumn, until the classical experiments of Garner and Allard (1920) appeared to show that for many plants the most important factor governing flowering was the length of day. Daylength is normally defined as the duration of the light period from sunrise to sunset. It was subsequently found that chrysanthemums flowered when the days were decreasing in length, and this led to their classification as 'shortday' plants. This important discovery led to many further investigations regarding this 'photoperiodic' effect, especially in the USA, where, with carnations and roses, chrysanthemums are the most widely grown cut flowers. It was inevitable that, owing to the impact of the work of Garner and Allard, most of the subsequent research was concerned with the response of chrysanthemums to various daylength regimes.

SHORTDAY TREATMENT

It soon became apparent that refined techniques for controlling the length of day would be required. Allard (1928) found that by restricting plants to 10 hours of light from 5.30 am to 3.30 pm commencing in May and placing the plants in a dark chamber for the rest of the day, flowering occurred on 15 July, whereas, by comparison, plants under natural conditions flowered in mid-October. Allard (1928) and Tincker (1929) used potted plants, which were wheeled in and out of darkened and specially ventilated huts according to the daylength regime required. From this beginning more efficient methods of producing daylength regimes on both a large and small scale have been developed.

For large-scale experiments and for commercial production under controlled daylengths, cloth covers have since been used for blacking out the plants *in situ*, a technique introduced by Laurie (1930) and Post (1931, 1932). This is still the standard method.

Black cloth was found to be superior to white (Poesch, 1931) because the latter reflects light through small spaces between the threads, while the former absorbs it. Post (1932), experimenting with various types of black cloth, obtained the best results with black sateen owing to its close texture. Later work showed that during periods of very high light intensity (March to July, at Ithaca, New York) either double thickness of black sateen or an entirely opaque cloth should be used (Post, 1947).

In view of the cost and weight of black cloth, dense black polythene sheeting (150 to 200 gauge) has been used in Britain for many years. It is effective for shortday treatment provided that light of no more than 22 lx filters through it.

It was also found that blacking-out is best carried out at each end of the light period. At these times, light rays strike the cloth more obliquely than in the middle of the day and less light passes through.

Poesch's method (1931) of blacking-out overhead without also blacking-out the sides caused plants in the centre of the plot to flower, but had little or no effect on those near the edges, which remained vegetative. Cailachjan's work (1945) has since explained this, for he demonstrated that it is only the leaves experiencing short days which receive the flowering stimulus and blacking-out at the apex only will not, therefore, cause flowering.

Much of the earlier research work was concerned with the effect of artificial shortday conditions on flowering time, and numerous examples are to be found in the literature. Post in 1931, by commencing various shortday treatments on 15 July to give plants 11-hour light periods, advanced flowering from 39 to 57 days compared with that of plants under natural daylength conditions. It is interesting to note that most of these early investigators attempted to accelerate the flowering time of varieties which flowered naturally during late October and November, because the range of early chrysanthemums (July to October), as known in Britain, is not grown to any extent in the commercial programme in the USA.

Various shortday regimes were tried out to accelerate flowering and included variations of the length of shortday treatment, the time of treatment during the day and the time of treatment during the season.

The Length of Shortday Treatment Shortday treatments, during which plants received either 10 or 11 hours of continuous light, were shown to produce earlier flowers than either shorter or longer light periods (Laurie, 1930; Poesch, 1931; Post, 1931).

The Time of Treatment during the Day When it was found necessary to shorten the natural light period by four hours in order to provide shortday conditions, it was shown to be better to blackout for two hours at each end of the day than at any other time. Post (1931) found that black cloth treatment from 6 pm to 7 am was more effective in hastening flowering than from 4 pm to midnight, which was in turn more effective than a similar period in the morning.

The Time of Treatment during the Season Laurie (1930) and Poesch (1931) reported that the earlier in the season the blackout was used the earlier was the flowering date, provided the treatment continued until the buds were visible to the naked eye. Laurie found that when plants received shortday treatment from 26 June to 3 September, the acceleration of flowering over control plants was 22 to 56 days compared with seven to nine days for plants blacked-out from 5 September to 9 October. He recommended that blackout should be used from one month after planting until the appearance of buds.

After nearly half a century, the recommendations of the above workers can hardly be improved upon for year-round production. Blacking-out after three to four weeks of growth from 6 pm to 7 am for seven nights a week until the appearance of buds will result in the most rapid flowering from late spring to early autumn while maintaining good quality.

Economic problems in recent years have led to the practice of using blackout for only six nights and, in extreme cases, five nights each week. Work at Efford EHS (Anon., 1972, 1973) has shown that six nights of blackout causes a three to seven day flowering delay compared with seven nights of blackout each week. It was thought that this was acceptable commercially but five nights of blackout caused both delay in flowering (11 to 14 days) and an inferior flowering stem so could not be recommended in summer. The work also showed that it is unnecessary to blackout until buds show colour and the earliest date that blacking-out can cease, without causing a flower delay, is one week after disbudding. This is normally after six or seven weeks of short days depending on variety. It often results in flowers of large-diameter in comparison with those borne on plants blacked-out until the bud colour stage.

LONGDAY TREATMENT

Since the experiments to accelerate flowering in natural long days by using artificial shortday conditions had proved so successful, it was argued that it should be a simple matter to retard flowering in natural short days if methods for producing artificially long days could be devised.

It has been shown (Green, Withrow and Richman, 1932) that very low light intensities may be considered as daylight for most plants which show daylength responses. Low-wattage incandescent lamps, arranged so that plants furthest from the light source received 55 to 110 lx at their tips, were shown by Poesch (1935) to be as satisfactory as any other type for retarding chrysanthemum flowering. They were used to supplement normal daylight and not, of course, to replace it.

Originally, lights were switched on at dusk for a period sufficient to give a daylength of 15 to 17 hours (Tincker, 1929; Poesch, 1936) and adjusted according to the seasonal fluctuation of daylight.

It was later shown that a period of light given in the middle of the long night had the same effect as a long day (Emsweller, Stuart and Byrne, 1941; Stuart, 1943), so lights are now usually switched on about 10 pm for four hours by means of a time-switch.

The reason for this effect was provided by Borthwick in 1947, who showed that it was the length of the dark period, not the length of the light period, that determined the reaction of plants to daylength. This means that, to retard flowering dates, a minimum dark period must be produced artificially if the natural nights are too long. This minimum dark period was shown to be from 9 to $9\frac{1}{2}$ hours, depending on variety (Post, 1953b), Thus, so long as a sufficient light period was given to ensure that not more than $9\frac{1}{2}$ hours of continuous darkness occurred each night, bud initiation was retarded.

The actual length of the artificial light period (when applied in the middle of the night), in contrast to shortday treatment, was shown to be of little concern provided that the minimum dark period was not exceeded. For the same reason the time of treatment during the night was not rigid, although the maximum effect occurred when the treatment was given near the middle of the dark period.

Amount of Light

The amount of light can be considered to have two primary effects on shortday plants. First, the total daily amount of visible radiation (wavelengths of light between 400 and 700 nm) received by the plant is an important factor in determining the rate of photosynthesis, and this in turn determines the vigour of growth and the rate of reaction of the plant to other factors of the environment. Relatively high light levels (for example 12,000 lx for 16 hours) are necessary for adequate photosynthesis.

Second, much lower light levels (for example 100 lx for 5 hours), if applied in addition to a natural short day, will induce longday response in shortday plants.

A description of experimental work regarding the effect of light on photosynthesis is outside the scope of this book, although some of the reactions of chrysanthemums to the environment which result from it directly or indirectly are discussed.

DAILY RADIATION INTEGRAL

Chrysanthemum plants develop at a rapid rate during each growth phase and from one growth phase to another only if the level of radiation received at the time is adequate. Flowering is normally delayed and variable during the winter months (Schwabe, 1953; Mason and Vince, 1962).

It is thought that a daily radiation integral of between 1·2 and 1·6 $MJ/m^2/day$ is necessary for adequate growth in chrysanthemums (Lawrence, 1950; Hassan and Newton, 1975).

Chrysanthemums can, however, make use of much higher daily levels of light. By growing plants of Bright Golden Anne in light levels of 2·5 and 3·75 MJ/m²/day, Hughes and Cockshull (1971a and b) recorded significant increases in dry weight compared with plants grown in a light level of 1·25 MJ/m²/day.

Average visible radiation levels received in greenhouses on the south coast of England from November to February have been given (page 14). It will be seen that only during February does the daily light level rise to near the requirement for adequate growth. Raising the light level to say 1·25 MJ/m²/day from November to February by means of supplementary lighting would undoubtedly solve many of the problems of winter production but the cost would be prohibitive. However, Cockshull and Hughes (1971, 1972) have shown that the main effect of low light (0·31 MJ/m²/day) is to delay the change from vegetative growth to flowering. They found that rapid and uniform bud development could be achieved by transferring plants from low light to a light level of 1·25 MJ/m²/day for the first 14 short days. This accelerated flowering response was retained by the plants even when they were transferred back to low (0·63 MJ/m²/day) or very low (0·31 MJ/m²/day) light levels after the treatment. Moreover, the results indicated that the chrysanthemum is capable of integrating light energy over a short period of time (two days). This means that with a good light meter and some simple arithmetic, accurate light supplementation can be achieved by the grower provided the treatment ultimately proves economic.

AMOUNT OF LIGHT FOR LONGDAY TREATMENTS

It was discovered by Poesch (1936) that the intensities of light necessary for extending the period of vegetative growth by artificially lengthening the day were very low. He stated that illuminances of 21·5 lx retarded flowering but not as successfully as illuminances of 43 lx.

The minimum nightly duration of artificial light necessary to maintain vegetative growth was found to be dependent on its illuminance. Two hours of light applied in the middle of the long dark period at an illuminance of 86 lx was insufficient to prevent initiation of crown buds (Post, 1953b). Three hours of light of this illuminance completely prevented bud initiation. He suggested that the following treatments similarly prevent bud initiation provided that each dark period did not exceed the critical minimum:

$$53 \text{ lx for five hours} = 265 \text{ lx-hour}$$
$$266 \text{ lx for one hour} = 266 \text{ lx-hour}$$
$$1064 \text{ lx for } \tfrac{1}{4} \text{ hour} = 266 \text{ lx-hour}$$

The general recommendation now is for the lamps to be arranged so that the plant tips furthest from the light source receive not less that than 110 lx and should be given for five hours in the middle of the dark period from November to February in Britain. Four hours of treatment are recommended from March to May and August to October.

Spectral Quality

The effectiveness of light for influencing plant growth depends both on the spectral quality (colour) of the light and on the response of the plant in question. For example, the spectral quality of light most efficient for photosynthesis is not necessarily the best for inducing photoperiodic responses, such as the induction of longday effects in shortday plants.

The different wavelengths of radiation which are visible (between 400 and 700 nm) also correspond closely to the wavelengths involved in plant growth and development.

PHOTOSYNTHETIC EFFECT

For photosynthesis the most active wavelengths are in the red (660 to 700 nm) and the blue (400 to 500 nm) regions. This is because chlorophyll, the green pigment which absorbs the light and converts its energy to chemical energy, absorbs best at these wavelengths. For this reason it has been thought that lamps combining red and blue wavelengths (for example white fluorescent) were superior to others. Canham (1972) showed that growth and flowering responses depended on total radiation rather than on spectral quality of light within the visible part of the spectrum. Low-pressure sodium lamps which are more economic to use than fluorescent lamps, but which are virtually monochromatic (only one wavelength), give excellent results for supplementing natural daylight.

PHOTOPERIODIC EFFECT

Poesch (1935) found that incandescent lamps were superior to others, such as neon and mercury, for inhibiting the flowering of chrysanthemums in natural short days when the lamps were switched on at dusk for several hours rather than for a shorter time as a night break.

When given in the form of a night break Borthwick (1947) found that the most effective range of light wavelengths for the inhibition of flowering of shortday plants was from 600 to 680 nm (red). Wavelengths of light of 400 nm (blue) were less effective, the least effective wavelength being near 480 nm.

Light from warm white fluorescent and mercury fluorescent lamps is effective for night-break lighting of chrysanthemums (Canham, 1966a and b) because the lamps emit wavelengths of light near both the red and blue wavebands.

Further work by the United States Department of Agriculture (USDA) established that red light (660 nm) set a particular response in motion and that this response could then be reversed by subsequent irradiation with far-red light (730 nm). This particular photoreactive mechanism controlled many processes in plants from germination in lettuce to flower development in chrysanthemums.

PHYTOCHROME

The fact that one photochemical reaction controlled growth responses such as germination, stem elongation, leaf expansion, tuberization and flowering in a wide range of plants indicated that a single photoreceptor was responsible and in 1959, Butler, Norris, Siegelman and Hendricks finally isolated a plant pigment with the necessary properties. They called it phytochrome.

Phytochrome is a photoreversible pigment existing in two forms. One form absorbs maximally at light wavelengths of 660 nm (P_{660} or P_r) and the other, the physiological active form (P_{730} or P_{fr}), at wavelengths of 730 nm.

It is generally accepted that during the day much of the phytochrome is present as P_{fr}. During darkness P_{fr} begins to revert to the more stable but inactive P_r form and at some stage reaches a threshold below which it no longer prevents flowering. A continuous 12-hour dark period is generally sufficient with chrysanthemums for rapid initiation and development of flowers. Red light given in the middle of the dark period reconverts phytochrome to the P_{fr} form and prevent flowering provided that P_{fr} is allowed to act for at least an hour after conversion. Far-red light can re-promote flowering by converting P_{fr} back to P_r any time within an hour of the red treatment.

Fluorescent light, provided it is of high intensity (several thousand lux), given for only one minute each night will completely inhibit flowering in chrysanthemums (Cathey and Borthwick, 1964, 1967). This is because fluorescent lamps emit light rich in the red compared with the far-red region of the spectrum.

Light from tungsten-filament lamps, which contains approximately equal proportions of red and far-red light, delays flowering only when it is given for several hours each night (Borthwick and Cathey, 1962), because it is only then capable of maintaining P_{fr} in a low photostationary state. This explains Poesch's early success when using light from tungsten-filament lamps for several hours at the beginning of the dark period. Following light treatment P_{fr} had only partly reverted to P_r and was still present in sufficient quantity to prevent flowering. Short periods (30 minutes) of illumination with tungsten-filament lamps given in the middle of the dark period, although adequate to prevent flowering of some other plants (soy bean and cocklebur) are therefore completely inadequate for chrysanthemums.

Canham, Cockshull and Hand (1977) have

effectively used low-pressure sodium lamps to delay flowering in chrysanthemums even though these lamps emit virtually monochromatic radiation of a wavelength 589 nm. However, this wavelength falls within the broader peak of the active spectrum for night-break lighting for shortday plants (Parker, Hendrick, Borthwick and Scully, 1946). Canham *et al.* found that lamps switched on for five hours each night were completely effective for delaying flowering at intensities varying from 10 to 40 lx depending on variety. This is important economically because low-pressure sodium lamps have an efficiency (percentage energy appearing as light) of 32 per cent compared with incandescent lamps.

Cathey (1974) has demonstrated a further function of phytochrome other than that of controlling flowering in chrysanthemums. Internode elongation occurred when low levels of light were given from the thirteenth to the sixteenth hour of the night following 12 hours of darkness for flower initiation and development. There was no effect on flowering provided that light equal in red and far-red rays (for example frosted tungsten-filament) was used.

Cathey assumed from this work that light treatments as low as five to 20 lx, applied after a 12-hour period and continuing until natural daylight, caused higher levels of P_{fr} to be present in the leaves at the onset of the next dark period. Following only 12 hours of darkness, low levels of P_{fr} remain and this is maintained by equal red/far-red light of very low intensity through the remainder of the night. This promotes internode elongation without delaying flowering, compared with plants given 16 hour dark periods.

TEMPERATURE

After Garner and Allard had suggested that in many plants certain growth responses could be attributed to the effect of daylength, experimental work on chrysanthemums tended to be directed mainly towards the effect of light on growth and flowering. Consequently, the im-

portance of temperature tended to be overlooked by some of the earlier workers and some of their experimental results must therefore be open to misinterpretation.

However, recent investigations have shown that, in many plants affected by daylength, including chrysanthemums, temperature is as important as daylength in determining plant responses. It is probable that all chrysanthemums are affected by both temperature and daylength, but in some varieties the former is the dominating factor (summer-flowering varieties) and in others the latter is the more important (autumn-flowering varieties).

Temperature affects the rate of photosynthesis, respiration, water and nutrient absorption, translocation and transpiration in plants. The importance of temperature on growth and flowering responses and dormancy reactions are mainly considered in this book.

Vegetative Growth

The comparative effects of light and temperature on the growth of young plants has been demonstrated (Machin, 1955). When the difference in temperature was in the order of 11° temperature had a more significant effect on growth than light.

Cockshull (1976b) has since reviewed the effect of temperature on vegetative growth. Chrysanthemums grow slowly at temperatures of 10° but growth increases rapidly in terms of both stem extension and weight of plant as the temperature is raised to 15°. Above this temperature stem elongation and leaf expansion continues but with no additional plant dry weight, because growth is mainly in the form of cell enlargement due to the uptake of more water. Thus, growth at very high temperatures (25° to 29°) is usually thin and weak and undesirable to the chrysanthemum grower.

The effect of temperature on the vegetative growth of stock plants can be carried over when the plant enters its reproductive cycle (Anon., 1975). Stock plants of the variety Heyday grown at night temperatures of 10° in January produced cuttings which flowered three days later in May compared with cuttings produced from stock plants grown at 15·6°. This occurred irrespective of the night temperature in the flowering house which varied from 13·3° to 18·3°.

Flowering delays have been recorded following low temperatures during the longday period following rooting (Anon., 1975). The varieties Heyday and Hurricane were delayed by 3·5 and 2·5 days respectively by night temperatures of 13·3° compared with 16·7° during long days in November and December. Low night temperatures in long days ceased to affect flowering from mid-May onwards. Later work at Efford EHS (Anon., 1976) showed that no flowering delay occurred with the variety Yellow Snowdon when given a longday night temperature of 11·5° if temperatures were kept at 16·7° in the flowering house.

Cathey (1954b) showed that in the variety Encore, cuttings from stock plants grown in a temperature of 16° produced normal vegetating and flowering plants. If the temperature given to the stock plants was raised to a minimum of 21°, premature budding and delayed flowering resulted. Plants grown from cuttings produced at a minimum night temperature of 10° or 13° produced a greater number of flowers, longer stems and heavier sprays than the plants grown from cuttings produced at 16°.

Stock plant temperatures of 21° and 27° produced plants which did not readily form lateral shoots when they were pinched and irregular flowering resulted. Flower bud initiation, the number of days to flower and the spray type were more easily controlled when cuttings were grown at a constant 16°.

Varieties responded differently and Shasta showed little response to different temperature conditions given to the stock plants. Revelation produced few cuttings in a temperature of 16° owing to blindness, but at higher temperatures (21° and 27°) rapid growth and large numbers of cuttings were obtained (Cathey, 1955b).

Flowering

Owing to the chrysanthemum's importance as a cut flower, the effect of temperature on its flowering has been studied more fully than the effect of temperature on vegetative growth. The effect of temperature on the various stages of flower formation is not so obvious as the photoperiodic effect on similar stages because most of the results of experimental work have been recorded as the effect of temperature on flower formation as a whole, that is, bud initiation, development and floret elongation combined.

Post (1953c) described the chrysanthemum as a 'high temperature' plant since buds are initiated and developed above a critical temperature. Below this temperature, which varies with variety, only vegetative growth occurs. Post's work suggested that for the American varieties, the critical temperature for flowering is about 16°.

Using the variety Gold Coast, Watson and Andrews (1953) showed that under a similar light intensity and after a similar period of 27 shortday treatments no bud initiation occurred at a night temperature of 10° compared with 99 per cent initiation in 16°.

Very high temperatures (40°) delay flowering in some varieties even if this period lasts for only two days. (Post and Kamemoto, 1950). Furuta and Nelson (1953) have also demonstrated the adverse effect of very high temperatures on bud development using the variety Seagull. Average temperatures of 24° and 27° did not delay flowering, 29° retarded flowering by 11 days, while plants grown at a mean temperature of 38° never flowered. However, during the latter stages of flower formation, that is during floret elongation and growth, temperatures as low as 10° do not delay flowering in most varieties (Vince, 1953; Cathey, 1954a). The response of chrysanthemums to temperature depends largely on varietal characteristics. As a result of his investigations in 1954, Cathey divided chrysanthemums into three distinct groups according to their response to temperature. He has since published (1955a) a more complete list of North American varieties and their temperature classification.

Certain varieties flowered at any temperature ranging from 10° to 27° but most consistently at a constant 16° night temperature. At either end of the range flowering was slightly delayed.

This group he classified as *thermozero* exemplified by the variety Shasta.

Other varieties required a minimum temperature of 16° for all stages of flower formation. Bud formation was rapid at higher temperatures (27°) but flowering was delayed. Continuous low temperature (10° to 13°) completely inhibited bud initiation or seriously delayed it. In this group, the temperature conditions before bud initiation affect plant response after the commencement of shortday treatment. Flowering is considerably delayed in plants grown at 16° and transferred to 10° at the commencement of shortday treatment. Those grown at 10° both before and after short days commence fail to flower at any time. Cathey classified this group as *thermopositive* and quoted as examples the varieties Encore, Dreamboat and Cameo.

In the third group, bud initiation occurs at all temperatures from 10° to 27°, but continuous high temperatures delay bud development. Most rapid and uniform flowering occurs in a constant 16°, but initiation of buds at 16° and

development at 10° results in almost negligible delay. The varieties Defiance and Revelation are representatives of this *thermonegative* group (Fig. 54).

The chrysanthemum varieties classified by Cathey consist mainly of those types grown in America. Vince (1955c) has carried out trials to test the temperature requirements of certain British varieties using a 16° day temperature combined with night temperatures of 10° and 16°. In seven varieties the three temperature groups identified by Cathey were detected. The results indicated that the varieties Rose Harrison, Imperial Pink and Finale require a minimum night temperature of 16° for bud initiation, but for the most rapid and uniform development 10° to 12° is desirable after the buds are visible (thermopositive varieties).

The formation of buds in the variety American Beauty was less affected by temperature, being slightly accelerated by 16° compared with 10°. However, for normal expansion of the flower it is necessary to lower the temperature

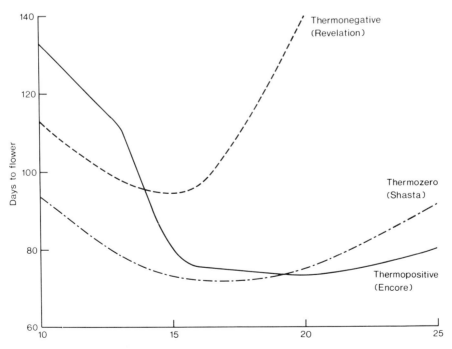

Fig. 54   The number of days from the start of short days to flower for a thermopositive, thermonegative and thermozero variety planted in early January from stock kept at 16°. The plants were grown in a night temperature range 10 to 27° as shown above. (After Cathey, 1955.)

after the bud becomes visible (thermonegative variety).

Crensa, Mayford Crimson and Balcombe Perfection initiated buds at the lower temperature (10° to 12°) and most rapid and uniform development occurred in similar conditions (thermozero varieties).

THERMOPERIODS

Roberts and Struckmeyer (1938) suggested that thermoperiodicity was an important factor in the flowering of chrysanthemums, and that control of night temperatures is most important because these affect the response of the plants to the photoperiod more than do the day temperatures. Subsequently, Post and Lacey (1951b) confirmed this view. Plants were grown under four temperature regimes. The treatments and results are recorded below:

16° night and day —most rapid development of flowers

16° night, 32° day—less rapid development of flowers

32° night, 16° day—still less rapid development of flowers

32° night and day—least rapid development of flowers

Post (1953c) has since confirmed that an optimum constant temperature is more beneficial for bud development in the chrysanthemum than a fluctuating temperature.

In all cases, Cathey (1955a) found that it was more important to control night temperatures than day temperatures. With plants of the thermopositive variety, Encore, grown at 21° day and 4°, 10°, 16°, 21° and 27° night temperatures, the flowering period extended over 36 days, whereas the flowering period of plants grown at 21° night and 4°, 10°, 16°, 21° and 27° day temperatures was reduced to 11 days. The night temperature was, therefore, found to be three-and-a-half times as effective as the day temperature in determining the flowering response, although high day temperature does counteract to some extent the effect of the low night temperature.

VERNALIZATION

It is convenient at this point to discuss the work of Schwabe (1950) on vernalization of chrysanthemums. He observed that differences in average flowering time and the numbers of leaves formed before bud initiation between plants in temperate and warm conditions, suggested that temperature might be an important factor affecting flowering responses. From the results of subsequent experiments on the varieties Sunbeam, Cossack, Godfrey's Gem and Blanche Poitevene, he concluded that chrysanthemums require a temporary exposure to low temperatures for normal and rapid inflorescence initiation. He demonstrated that in these varieties an absence of this vernalization period would increase considerably both the number of days of growth necessary before bud initiation and consequently the number of leaves formed before this stage was reached. He suggested that if plants were subjected to a period of three or four weeks of temperatures from 4° to 7°, or to the normal outdoor temperatures of January to March in Britain, their vernalization requirements would be fulfilled. This requirement had not been noted by earlier investigators because stock plants are usually exposed to cool conditions in normal horticultural practice.

Further research showed that the cold treatment could be interrupted by daily exposures to temperatures of 16° for as long as eight hours without annulling the low temperature effect, but only if the higher temperatures were applied during the normal light period (Schwabe, 1953).

Low temperature treatment was found to be necessary after each reproductive cycle although the chilling effect remained in shoots which had been severed from the stock plants as propagating material. Schwabe concluded that the vernalization requirements of the chrysanthemum were completely satisfied by normal horticultural practices in Britain, but suggested that his results might explain some abnormalities in plants grown commercially under certain conditions in America. Post observed (1939) that 'the late propagation of plants increased the amount of blind growth, and that shoots which failed to form flower buds during the autumn at high temperatures remained blind during the winter even though the temperature was increased'. This suggested to Schwabe that these plants had received no low temperature treatment prior to propagation, and that continuous high-temperature treatment of the stock plants had produced the observed effect. After later work (1959) Schwabe showed that chilling affected the 'true plastochron' (the rate of leaf initiation) of the vegetative apex but that temperatures in the range 17° to 22° had no effect.

It seems likely that while vernalization is essential for normal development in some varieties, others do not respond to low temperature treatment, or respond to a lesser extent. Unvernalized plants of the variety President developed a markedly rosetted type of growth. The variety Sunbeam developed not only a rosette habit but also a diageotrophic (horizontal) type of growth. In these two varieties flowering was delayed several months in the absence of vernalization. Godfrey's Gem was not prevented from flowering by constant high temperatures but initiated buds only after reaching high leaf numbers.

Vince (1955a) found that the commercial variety Magnet showed only a limited low temperature requirement and vernalization merely accelerated flowering time by about two weeks and did not markedly reduce leaf numbers.

Vince suggested that in view of the tendency towards the cultivation of plants from cuttings propagated during early summer when temperatures are naturally high, it would be advisable to ascertain the vernalization requirements, if any, of all commercial varieties. Breeders of year-round chrysanthemums today screen all seedlings against any vernalization requirement. Her later work with Mason (1959) confirmed that the low temperature effect varies with the variety. Okada (1959) also ascertained that the factors responsible for rosetting varied with the variety.

NUTRITION

The effect of nutrition on the growth of chry-santhemum plants in year-round production systems had been widely studied (Joiner and Smith, 1962; Leiser, Sanborn and De Rolf, 1966; Joiner and Poole, 1967; Adams, Graves and Winsor, 1971, 1975b; Butters and Wadsworth, 1974).

However, a number of cultural and environmental factors, particularly the choice of substrate, the number of long days allowed for vegetative growth, the type of crop (pinched or single stem) and the total quantity of light available for growth, have differed considerably in their investigations. It is not surprising, therefore, that many results and subsequent recommendations for nutrition have also differed, and in many cases are apparently opposed.

Much of the work has been applied to the crop as a whole or during the later stages of growth after the commencement of short days. Relatively little has been done to investigate the effects of nutrition on particular stages of growth especially during the later stages of vegetative growth and the period of transition to reproductive growth.

The importance of nutrients in the shoots prior to their removal from the stock plants as cuttings has been emphasized in relation to their growth rate during rooting (Good and Tukey, 1967). Apart from this there appears to have been little research on the nutrition of stock plants.

Rooting

The increase in dry weight in the rooting cutting occurs mainly in leaves and roots, the required nitrogen being utilized from the lower, more mature leaves of the cutting (Good and Tukey, 1967). Nitrogen is easily leached from these lower leaves during mist propagation but is less readily leached from the young tips of cuttings after translocation.

Mist propagation leads to an appreciable amount of leaching of mineral nutrients from the foliage and nutrients in the young plants are rapidly reduced still further by the demands of the growing plant itself (Good and Tukey, 1966). These writers and others (Morton and

Boodley, 1969) demonstrated the value of applying fertilizers in the mist for improving the rate and quality of growth. The plants responded to nutrient mist propagation by improved flowering response and increased size and number of flowers.

Flowering Plants

Most of the nutritional experimental work to be found in the literature relates to the use of different base fertilizers and subsequent liquid or foliar feeds which are given throughout the crop or until the buds show colour. The value of this work is limited because it does not allow for differential nutritional requirements according to the stage of growth of the crop. It is unlikely that the optimum level of nutrition or the correct proportion of major elements of nutrition to each other are the same for the production of leaves during the longday period, and for the development of flowers during the shortday period.

The particular importance of nutrition during the longday period has been noted. For instance, Lunt and Kofranek (1958) grew a single stem crop of three standard varieties in a loamy sand compost giving the plants eight weeks of long days. They found that nitrogen deficiency during the first seven weeks of the crop affected the quality of the flowers adversely and that extra nitrogen given after the ninth week of the 16-week crop could not compensate for this trend, even though 60 per cent of the dry weight of the flowering plant was produced during the final seven weeks.

Winsor and Hart (1965) noted the vital importance of nitrogen in the early stages of a crop of the variety Fred Shoesmith planted in August in a soil bed. Increasing levels of nitrogen resulted in plant lengths of 36, 64, and 81 cm, measured in early October. Joiner (1967), who used a gravel substrate, was aware of the importance of nutrient levels during the early stages of the crop and compared nutrient levels in the plant at two weeks after the start of short days with those at flowering.

There are a number of conflicting reports on the effect of nutrition on flowering responses.

Chan (1955) found that low mineral nutrition levels, particularly low nitrogen, delayed flowering in some varieties of chrysanthemum by 11 to 14 days, while other varieties were delayed by high nitrogen rates. However, different N : K combinations did not affect the flowering response of a third group of varieties. Lunt and Kofranek (1958) found that wide variations of the N : K ratio were possible without affecting response, but that severe potassium deficiency delayed flowering by 10 to 15 days in a soil/peat substrate. Their later work (Lunt, Kofranek and Oertli, 1964) using a pure sand substrate, confirmed that only very severe deficiencies of nitrogen and potassium delayed flowering and then only to a small degree.

Experiments at Efford EHS (Anon., 1971, 1972), using the 10-week spray varieties Heyday and Hurricane, showed that in several peat/sand substrates there was a significant early flowering response (up to seven days) to high levels of potassium applied as a base dressing for a March flowering crop. Conversely, high rates of nitrogen in the base fertilizer led to delayed cropping with a difference of four days between high and low nitrogen treatments.

When the varieties Hurricane and Polaris were planted in soil beds for flowering in February 1970, using two levels of potassium in the base dressing, a negligible flowering response to the high rate of potassium was recorded. An experiment using different rates of nitrogen in the liquid feed was carried out at the same time in a soil substrate and this also showed no significant differences in the time of flowering. Clearly, the flowering response to nitrogen and potassium levels in cut flower varieties studied differs according to the nature of the substrate during periods of poor light.

There are other examples of differential plant response in chrysanthemums to similar nutrition treatments in different substrates (Massey and Winsor, 1970). They noted that deficiencies of most major and minor elements occur more easily in soilless than in soil substrates.

Summarizing the results of several years of work at Efford EHS Butters and Wadsworth

(1974) have given figures for the optimum nitrogen and potassium application at various times of the year (Table 32).

TABLE 32 Suggested Application Rates of N and K for Spray Chrysanthemums Flowering at Different Periods

Planting date	Flowering time	Optimum application kg/ha/crop	
		N	K
Feb to Aug	May to Nov	448	448
Sept to Dec	Dec to Mar	168	672
Jan	Apr	336	560

Bunt (1973) using peat/sand substrates for the production of pot plants, found that delays in the flowering response in winter are primarily of a chemical rather than a physical nature. They can be classified under two headings: (a) minor element deficiencies and (b) nitrogen excess. Treatments resulting in high nitrogen levels in the leaf tissue delayed winter crops of one variety (Dark Red Star) up to 28 days and with the variety Golden Princess Anne each increase of one per cent in the nitrogen in the leaves delayed flowering by four days.

Of the numerous references concerning the effect of nutrition on the quality of the flowering plant the work of Lunt, Kofranek and Oertli (1964) was particularly comprehensive and deficiency symptoms for all the major and minor nutrients were described. However, the work was done on one variety (Good News) and was necessarily carried out in a pure sand substrate.

Of particular interest are the conflicting reports of the effect of different levels of nutrient using different ratios of nitrogen and potassium. Cathey (1969) reported that increased potassium nutrition had little effect on growth other than increasing the potassium content of leaf and flower tissue. Increasing nitrogen led to a decrease in yield and post-harvest keeping quality. Cathey concluded that chrysanthemums tolerate relatively large amounts of nitrogen and potassium, with no interrelation in the effects of the two elements. Lunt and Kofranek (1958) also found that when adequate levels of nitrogen and potassium were supplied to plants in a factorial experiment in a peat/sand substrate, there were no important interactions relative to flower quality when the level of the two nutrients was altered as much as five-fold. However, other workers have reported that increasing the level of nitrogen up to an optimum increased the size of foliage, the quality and length of stem, and the size and quality of the flowers (Winsor and Hart, 1965; Adams, Graves and Winsor, 1970; Massey and Winsor, 1974) in both soil and peat/sand substrates. In the same experiments it was demonstrated that, not only low nitrogen, but low levels of potassium and phosphorus reduced the quality of the flowering plant.

Some of the anomalies in plant response to nutrition in cut flower crops reported above can be explained by the differences in the experimental procedures used, in the cropping programmes followed and in the actual assessment of results. Massey and Winsor (1974) found that the variety Hurricane was surprisingly tolerant of low nitrogen levels in the soil. They found that plants treated with high nitrogen had a limited root formation and that low nitrogen treated plants had developed large root systems. Subsequently they showed that, by limiting root production by growing plants in pots compared with soil beds and using a similar substrate, the former were more affected by low nitrogen treatment than the latter.

The pH of the substrate is especially important and Bunt (1967) considered a value of 5·5 to be optimum for chrysanthemums in a peat/sand compost. Higher values of pH could cause problems with minor element deficiencies, particularly iron. It is known that in soil composts a higher pH (6·5) will not lead to these deficiencies.

It has also been reported (Leiser, Sanborn and De Rolf, 1966) that the use of certain slow-release fertilizers, such as magnesium ammonium phosphate, may give problems connected with the balance between magnesium and potassium.

INTERACTION OF FACTORS

Although it has been convenient to discuss the

effects of various factors of the environment separately, it is important to realize that for most varieties of chrysanthemum, only certain combinations of these factors give the optimum conditions for normal growth and flowering. Furthermore, different combinations of factors are essential for the maximum development of each stage of growth.

Experimental results have indicated the complex nature of the interaction of these factors on plant growth, and, as Schwabe commented in 1953, 'the complexity of effects argues against any simple explanation'. Morphological and anatomical responses have been demonstrated, but some of the physiological reactions of *Chrysanthemum morifolium* to its environment remain obscure. The photoreversible pigment phytochrome is thought by some authorities to be an enzyme which triggers off a complicated series of chemical changes in the plant. However, there is no experimental evidence for this possibility.

Another way in which the sort of morphological changes which are regulated by phytochrome can be directed is through the control of gene activity, leading to the synthesis of new enzymes. This possibility has been widely explored as far as phytochrome is concerned, and its action as a gene de-repressor has been considered. Unfortunately, there is no evidence that in the morphological control exerted by phytochrome any new nucleic acids or proteins are synthesized soon after the photochemical production of the active P_{fr}, although such synthesis might well occur later. Also, the nature and speed of some of the plant responses to phytochrome appear to rule out gene activation as a primary action of phytochrome.

Phytochrome is now associated with changes in the permeability of cell membranes to water. This action of phytochrome on cell permeability might well result in numerous changes in metabolic activity and hence cellular development. When the permeability of cell membranes is changed, enzymes and their substrates, which were previously isolated, can be brought into contact. This could lead to an increase in cell growth, as occurs in the stimulation of germination, or in the case of leaf expansion or flowering, to the synthesis of hormones.

However, some of the direct effects of the interaction of factors of the environment on chrysanthemums have been demonstrated and three of them are reported here.

Daylength and Temperature

Temperature profoundly affects the reactions of chrysanthemums to daylength. Roberts and Struckmeyer (1938) grew plants of the variety Lilian Doty under both long and shortday conditions at three different temperatures (13°, 17° and 21°). While flowering was retarded by long days in each temperature regime, short days induced flowering only if combined with a temperature of 21°. The lower temperatures, even when short days were given at the same time, induced a longday response, as manifested by continued vegetative growth.

However, short days combined with very high temperatures may also retard flowering (Post and Lacey, 1951b). It is apparent, therefore, that bud initiation and development under shortday conditions is dependent on the prevailing temperature regime, the optimum temperature depending on the variety.

Schwabe considered the temperature effect to be even more important than the daylength effect in certain varieties. Vernalization by low temperature treatment hastened bud initiation both in long and shortday conditions, although he agreed that short days were necessary for bud development. He likened the longday effect to the effect of non-vernalization but showed that failure to flower could be due either to lack of vernalization preventing the formation of a bud, or to longday conditions preventing the continuation of its development after formation. On the other hand four to six weeks of long days given to young plants immediately after vernalization had a favourable effect on bud initiation. Such limited longday treatment resulted both in a reduction of leaf numbers and of the length of time before bud initiation, compared with plants exposed to continuous shortday treatment after vernaliz-ation.

Daylength and Amount of Light

Significant reductions in the rate of photo-synthesis, due to very low light, may alter the responses of plants to daylength. Flower bud initiation is delayed by low light even when shortdays are given. Flower bud develop-ment in shortday conditions can be arrested if light levels are seriously reduced before the buds reach a certain diameter (Schwabe, 1953).

Post noted in 1941 that plants grown under daylength and temperature conditions con-ducive to rapid bud development did not flower normally in light intensities below 500 lx. The effects of low light in short days have been summarized by Cockshull (1972).

Although photoperiodic reactions are in-duced by very low light intensities (60 lx) a certain minimum duration of this low light is essential in order to induce longday responses by interrupting the long dark period with artificial light; in other words, the duration of artificial light for this purpose is dependent upon its intensity.

Temperature and Amount of Light

The most important environmental factors affecting vigour are temperature and the amount of light. The effects of temperature and light should never be considered separ-ately because the vigour of the plant is largely dependent on the balance between these two factors. Rising temperatures increase the rate of photosynthesis and respiration. Falling light intensities, while decreasing the rate of photo-synthesis, have little effect on the rate of res-piration. High temperatures increase the rate of respiration more than the rate of photo-synthesis. Therefore, high temperatures, com-bined with low light, decrease the rate of food production and increase the rate of food loss.

Watson and Andrews (1953) showed that, although the variety Gold Coast did not form buds at 16° at low light intensity, high light intensity at this temperature induced 100 per cent budding.

This correlation between temperature and light is now fully exploited by year-round chrysanthemum growers. Work at Efford EHS (Anon., 1977) has resulted in recommendations for night temperature control according to the light available for growth month by month (page 19).

The extreme importance of the interaction of all these factors has only gradually been realized. It is possible, therefore, that many of the earlier results may need modification because the interaction of these factors may not have been fully appreciated. Many of the experiments regarding reaction to temperature were carried out under the low light con-ditions of winter months. Photoperiodic re-actions were studied under light intensities either of summer or of winter, but generally not under both. Future researchers, and also all chrysanthemum growers, should take into account the interaction of all the environmental factors on each separate growth phase.

12 Plant Response

The response of a plant to its environment is dependent to a large extent on the particular stage of development reached. Post (1942) has postulated seven distinct periods in plant growth; propagation, vegetative growth, flower bud initiation, flower bud development, elongation and growth of flower parts, flower fertilization and seed growth and ripening.

Similar combinations of environmental factors may produce different responses according to the growth stage on which they react. It is necessary, therefore, to study in some detail the effect of these factors on each distinct phase in the life-cycle of the chrysanthemum.

The propagation stage has been discussed and the subjects of flower fertilization and seed growth and ripening are omitted, since it is the stages of growth prior to these that growers and users of chrysanthemums are primarily concerned.

VEGETATIVE GROWTH

In higher plants, such as the chrysanthemum, the active stem apices or meristems give rise to the leaves and their associated lateral buds in an orderly sequence while in the vegetative condition. The distances between the leaves (internodes) depend to some extent on the variety. This orderly vegetative growth pattern continues until the plant is caused to change into a completely different sequence of growth by a change in certain environmental factors or until it reaches a certain physiological age (page 186).

The vigour of growth and the rate of development of leaves and stems are largely controlled by the amount of light and temperature.

Daily light integrals of approximately 1·4 $MJ/m^2/day$ are adequate for vegetative growth in chrysanthemums, but growth improves (increased dry weight) as the light levels increase to at least 3·75 $MJ/m^2/day$ (Hughes and Cockshull, 1971b).

A light level of 12,000 lx improved the rooting performance and early growth of cuttings compared with low (6000 lx) and very low (3000 lx) light levels if the cuttings were compared 14 days after insertion. Also, artificial light for 24 hours per day was more effective than light for shorter periods (Canham, 1973). It is also known that low light levels adversely affect the rate of subsequent vegetative growth. Kiplinger and Rose (1951), experimenting on commercial methods used to secure a year-round flowering programme, discovered that more time had to be allowed for adequate vegetative growth to be made during the winter months, than during seasons of higher light levels. Schwabe (1953) and Chan (1955) confirmed this.

Various periods of reduced light applied during long days, delayed but did not prevent flowering (Chan, 1955). This was true using a wide range of varieties from 8-week to 14-week response. Chan remarked that his results agreed with those of Schwabe (1954) in whose experiments flowering was delayed by the reduction of light up to 10 to 15 per cent of natural daylight.

However, the effects of low light during the vegetative period in the experiments of Chan and Schwabe were probably quite distinct. The varieties used by Chan were American spray varieties such as Popcorn, Shasta and Gold Coast, and they are known to have no annual or post-flowering vernalization requirements. The effect of reduced light intensity in this case was likely to have resulted from a reduction in the rate of change from the vegetative to the reproductive condition.

In Schwabe's experiments, the variety Sunbeam, in which the basal shoots have an annual vernalization requirement for normal flowering, was used. Plants which had been vernalized by low temperature treatment could be de-vernalized by three or four week periods of very much reduced light (about 270 lx) and they then produced a completely rosetted habit of growth. Rosetted growth of this type, which is normally associated with de-vernalization or with non-vernalization, has been noted on many occasions during very poor light periods in some American spray varieties. (Tuneful). They do not require post-flower vernalization when they are grown at high temperatures (16°). Sometimes, a complete rosette is formed with very short internodes and only the removal of the apical meristem will induce normal vegetative growth. On other occasions, with the same variety, a partial rosette will occur; but with the improving light, the apex resumes normal vegetative growth.

It is important to differentiate between these two effects of light on vegetative growth.

Chrysanthemums respond extremely rapidly to increases or decreases in the total light levels available each day. Machin (1973) grew plants of the variety Heyday in light levels of 2·02 and 0·86 MJ/m²/day and after 14 days transferred some plants from high to low light treatments and vice versa. Despite a difference in total plant dry weight of 37 per cent at the time of transfer, plants transferred from high to low light and vice versa were equal in weight after only a further 12 days.

Daily light levels continue to affect the vigour of growth even after plants are given shortday conditions to induce flowering. The stems of plants subjected to photoperiods six hours in length were much less vigorous than those of plants in a 10 or 12 hour day (Tincker, 1929). Weak growth was the result of decreasing the total amount of light available for photosynthesis. The time of shortday treatments has also been shown to be of importance for the same reason. Where the plants were heavily shaded in the middle of the day (9 am to 1 pm) weaker growth occurred than when plants were given blackout at either end of the day (6 pm to 7 am) (Post, 1934). Indeed, results from Efford EHS (Anon., 1977) showed that flowering was delayed when plants received 10 hours of light compared with those receiving the optimum of 11 hours of light each day. The delay was attributed to the lower total radiation received during the shortday period.

Leaf Production

Gregory and Purvis (1938) suggested that the number of leaves up to the inflorescence may be taken as a measure of total vegetative growth of a plant before bud initiation. Since then Schwabe (1950), Vince (1955a), Machin (1955, 1973) and Cockshull (1975, 1976a) have used this criterion to determine the effects of various environments on flowering.

In an experiment on the variety Baldock's Crimson (Machin, 1955), the average leaf number from break to bud on plants receiving the normal daylengths of August and September was 36·2. On plants receiving longday conditions from 23 August to 19 September, the corresponding number was 45·3. All plants were pinched on the same date. This increase in leaf number resulted in a corresponding increase in stem length, since internode length did not vary between treatments.

Clearly, leaf number is especially important in cut flower crops owing to its effect on stem length. However, in the fast-growing year-round crop, the rate of leaf production is just as important. This is because of its effect on the total time required for vegetative growth to achieve the minimum length of stem.

Vegetative chrysanthemum plants grown in a longday controlled environment will normally (although by no means always) remain in a vegetative condition, producing leaves for the period of time required for optimum length of stem. This vegetative growth pattern has been described in some detail by Schwabe (1959), although he stressed that for his work he used a variety (Sunbeam) which is nearer to the 'wild type' than varieties of current commercial value. However, similar growth patterns for the vegetative phase have been described by other workers using completely different varieties (Popham and Chan, 1950; Popham, 1963; Cockshull, 1976b).

Each vegetative growing point consists of a small (0·2 mm in diameter) bare apex from which leaf primordia are initiated at a regular interval, this interval being known as the 'true plastochron'. This, for the variety Sunbeam, varied from 3·2 to 2·2 days. The 'true plastochron' can vary according to the previous history of the plant and the prevailing environment. Schwabe showed that, for Sunbeam, the rate of leaf production was dependent on whether or not the plant's vernalization requirements had been satisfied.

Machin (1973) established the plastochron for the varieties Heyday and Polaris under several different longday and nutritional regimes. The daily radiation integral affected the rate of longday leaf initiation as follows:

Longday light level (MJ/m²/day)	Plastochron (days) Heyday	Polaris
2·02	2·4	5·1
0·86	3·3	7·1

Longday nutrition (natural May light levels)	Plastochron (days) Heyday	Polaris
Liquid feed (ppm) 200N : 100K₂O	3·3	3·6
No liquid feed	5·7	6·7

Cockshull (1975, 1976a) has also found that light levels markedly influence the rate of leaf production in long days. Working with 12 year-round varieties he also concluded that there is a genetic control on the rate of leaf initiation but that this can be modified by environment. Increasing temperatures up to 25° increase the rate of leaf initiation (Cockshull, 1976b). Above this temperature, leaf initiation slows down again.

Stem Length

Stem length is, as already discussed, directly influenced by the rate and number of leaves initiated during vegetative growth. Leaf production ceases when plants form flower buds, so it follows that the factors which affect bud initiation also affect stem length.

Stem length is equal to the total number of leaves (and bracts) beneath the apical flower bud multiplied by the mean internode length. Thus, factors which affect the mean internode length are important and include temperature, amount and quality of light and nutrition.

Internode length in plants grown at 5° is doubled if the temperature is raised to 16° and increased by a further 50 per cent at a temperature of 29° (Cockshull, 1976b). At this latter temperature internode length increases faster than the formation of carbohydrates from photosynthesis so that very long, weak stems are produced.

The daily radiation integral is an important factor affecting the length of internodes. Table 33 gives values of mean internode lengths for Polaris and Heyday for summer and winter crops. Machin (1973) has used these figures, together with the rate and number of leaves produced during longday and shortday conditions, to calculate the number of long days required to produce sufficient length of plant in cut flower crops according to the amount of light available for growth at each season.

TABLE 33   Mean Internode Length at Two Seasons (from Machin, 1973)

Crop	Mean internode length (mm)	
	Polaris	Heyday
Summer	34	28
Winter	29	21

The quality of light influences the length of internodes. Light from certain incandescent lamps, of roughly equal red and far-red wavelengths, increased internode length without delaying flowering if given for four hours following 12-hour dark periods (Cathey, 1974). Table 34 shows the effectiveness of a number of lamps emitting light of different red/far-red ratios for this purpose.

Nutrition also affects the length of internodes especially during the longday period. Using high, medium and low rates of N : K₂O (1 : 1) nutrition during long days Machin (1973) found that mean internode length at the end of long days was 9·1, 6·7 and 4·3 mm respectively in the variety Heyday.

Morphology

Certain environmental factors, especially temperature and light quality, significantly influence the morphology of vegetative growth.

The morphology of the young leaf primordia is determined at a very early stage in the veg-

TABLE 34   Response of Improved Indianapolis White to Quality of Light when Irradiated During the Last 4 Hours of a Daily 16-hour Dark Period

Lamp	R/FR*	Height (cm)	Number of nodes	Mean internode length (cm)	Days to flowering
Fluorescent—cool white	9·30	58	30·8	1·9	64·0
Incandescent—frosted	1·07	62	29·8	2·1	64·2
Incandescent—ruby red	0·37	62	29·8	2·1	63·2
Incandescent—BCJ	0·19	66	30·2	2·2	73·2
Dark control	0	50	30·1	1·7	63·8

* R/FR = Ratio of radiant energy 600–700 nm/700–770 nm in μW/cm² (from Cathey, 1974).

etative apex of the shoot and this will vary with variety. The external environment may then modify final leaf shape. The degree of dissection of the leaf margin varies to a great degree depending on the temperature prevailing during initiation. Leaves initiated at high temperatures (27°) become much less dissected than those initiated at 17° (Schwabe, 1959) (Fig. 55).

Leaf shape and size differ in plants grown under short and longday conditions (Vince, 1955a). In short days, leaf blades fail to expand normally and their edges curl under. Leaves under longday conditions, however, are broader and larger although the leaf area increases proportionately more than the leaf length.

It is well known that plants grown entirely in artificial light from some types of lamp are morphologically different from those grown in daylight, even though the daily light levels received are similar. For instance, chrysanthemums grown under warm-white fluorescent lamps (Mazda universal), which have a high percentage of light in the blue region of the spectrum, have short internodes, small leaves and flowers and the foliage is very dark green. In contrast, plants grown in natural daylight, a higher proportion of which is red light, have longer internodes, larger leaves and flowers and are relatively soft in appearance. It is interesting to note that, despite morphological differences, total plant dry weight, and indeed the dry weights of individual plant parts such as leaves, stem and flowers, were similar for each plant (Machin, 1973).

FLOWERS

When grown under natural daylength conditions chrysanthemums produce terminal flower bud initials after having made a certain amount of vegetative growth. In plants of any particular variety grown at a similar latitude, this phenomenon occurs on approximately the same date each year (Post, 1936). These and other early findings led to the conclusion that

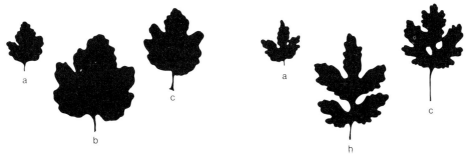

Fig. 55   Temperature effect on leaf shape. Left: from a plant grown at 27°; right from a plant grown at 17°, a) young leaf, b) mature leaf, c) senescent leaf. (From Schwabe, 1959.)

vegetative growth continues until daylength becomes short enough to cause bud initiation, after which no further vegetative organs are laid down.

However, in natural season chrysanthemum crops flower buds (break buds) are normally produced relatively early in the growing season prior to the onset of natural short days. Also, in stock plants of many year-round varieties premature flower buds have been formed in long-day conditions.

Budding in Long Days

Some workers have suggested that this premature budding could only occur due to an unintentional exposure to short days (Post, 1950a; Popham and Chan, 1952; Okado, 1963). Others have shown that flower buds can be formed in the absence of short days (Schwabe, 1950, 1953; Furuta, 1954; Vince, 1955a; Kofranek and Halevy, 1974). Furthermore, the older the shoot the more likely it is to initiate a flower bud in longday conditions (Furuta and Kiplinger, 1955).

Recently Cockshull (1975 and 1976a) has clearly shown that flower bud initiation in chrysanthemums in long days is inevitable. The time of initiation depends on the genotype and is related to an ageing process that occurs independently in each apical meristem. The number of leaves initiated before the flower bud is a sound measurement of this physiological age. However, environmental factors can modify the expression of the genetic information. For in-

stance, high light levels reduce leaf numbers prior to flower formation and increase the rate of leaf production. But despite this, Cockshull was able to show that some varieties always require to initiate more leaves before a flower bud can be formed in long days than other varieties. He used 12 varieties and found that, despite different environmental conditions for growth (apart from long days) the relative rankings of the varieties for leaf number prior to budding was always similar. Table 35 gives the figures for five of the varieties tested.

Budding in Short Days

Not only will budding occur inevitably after a certain physiological age in long days but chrysanthemums must reach a certain, but different physiological age before flower buds can be initiated by short days. Delworth (1941) stated that short days would not initiate buds when the period from pinching to shortday treatment was not of sufficient length, and this view was substantiated by Post (1945). Post's results also indicated that a certain amount of growth is necessary before buds can be initiated following a pinch, and the stem can develop to a certain length even though short days follow immediately after pinching.

He also found that varieties differed in the amount or period of growth needed before they became responsive to daylength for bud formation. Gold Coast and Arcadia required six to ten days of growth following a pinch before buds could be initiated by short days, whereas

TABLE 35 Numbers of Leaves and Bracts Initiated before the Flower on Five Varieties of Chrysanthemum Grown in Long Days (natural daylength plus 5-hour night break) (From Cockshull, 1975)

| Cultivar | Main axis of plant | | | | Lateral axis of plant |
| | Date of planting | | | | |
	13.6.73	10.10.73	29.5.74	Average	29.5.74
Tuneful	45·3	90·3	56·9	64·2	56·8
Gold Crystal	44·0	69·2	49·5	54·2	51·7
Polaris	33·5	56·1	40·8	43·5	45·3
Bluechip	29·9	48·4	33·8	35·4	37·5
Bright Golden Anne	20·3	34·3	18·4	24·3	25·3

Vesper, Valencia and Sunnyside needed 10, 15 and 20 days of growth, respectively.

Okada (1952) also recorded varietal differences in this respect, but gave his results as heights to which the plants must grow before they became photoperiodically reactive.

Year-round chrysanthemums are now almost exclusively grown as single stem flowering plants developed directly from rooted cuttings without pinching. Cockshull (1975, 1976a) was able to demonstrate that flower bud initiation in long days, following a measurable amount of growth, applied equally to all apical meristems whether they were developing on single stem or pinched plants. This is also true regarding the plant's reaction to short days. As reported above budding cannot be induced immediately following a pinch. In recent years, there has been increasing evidence that plants grown on single stems must reach a certain size before bud initiation can occur at the most rapid rate in short days. Plants require a longer period of short days to flower if fewer than optimum long days are given at different periods of the year (Anon., 1970, 1971, 1972). The variety Hurricane was used and Table 36 indicates that the plants which would have been the largest at the start of short days flowered earliest. They also generally produced the best quality flowers.

Machin's study of the varieties Heyday and Polaris (1973) has clearly shown that a large plant, measured either by number of leaves, stem length or total dry weight, will respond to short days more rapidly than a small plant. The

results suggested that, when daylength and temperatures are favourable for bud initiation, other factors which affect the size of the plant at the end of longday treatment have a quantitative effect on the response of the plant to short days. Table 37 shows the effect of four longday treatments on total plant dry weight at the end of long days (natural light in July)

TABLE 36   Effect of Longday Period on the Variety Hurricane

Flowering time	Weeks of long days	Response in short days (weeks)	Gross market return as percentage of middle treatment
May to Jun 1969	3	9	103
	$1\frac{1}{2}$	10	100
	0	10	98
Oct 1969	4	9	101
	$2\frac{1}{2}$	$9\frac{1}{2}$	100
	1	10	92
Feb 1970	6	12	102
	5	$12\frac{1}{2}$	100
	4	13	80
Jun 1970	3	$9\frac{1}{2}$	105
	2	$9\frac{1}{2}$	100
	1	10	91
Oct 1970	3	$9\frac{1}{2}$	106
	2	10	100
	1	10	79
Feb 1971	6	$10\frac{1}{2}$	96
	5	11	100
	4	$11\frac{1}{2}$	87

TABLE 37   Total Plant Dry Weight After Four Longday Treatments and Flowering Response in Two Light Levels in Short Days. Varieties Heyday (H) and Polaris (P) (from Machin, 1973)

Number of long days	Total plant dry weight after long days (g)		Number of short days to flowering			
			High light (1·26 MJ/m²/day)		Low light (0·54 MJ/m²/day)	
	H	P	H	P	H	P
10	0·28	0·33	83	78	101	101
17	0·36	0·49	70	70	88	83
24	0·46	0·58	69	69	88	78
31	0·74	0·84	66	66	77	69
LSD at P = 0·05	0·10	0·09	—	—	—	—

and the subsequent effect on flowering response in two levels of light in short days (growth room). Nutrition can also affect the response of the plant to short days. If inadequate nutrition leads to the production of small plants at the end of long days, flowering will again be delayed (Table 38).

TABLE 38 Length of Plant and Leaf Number after 21 Long Days Following Three Nutrition Treatments and Subsequent Effect on Flowering Response, Variety Heyday (from Machin, 1973)

Nutrition treatment in long days	Length of plant after long days (cm)	Leaf number after long days	Short days to flowering
High N : K₂O*	21·4	23·5	62·6
Medium N : K₂O	15·0	22·2	64·1
Low N : K₂O	7·9	18·5	71·8
LSD at P = 0·05			0·92

* N : K₂O = 1 : 1 in this and Table 39.

A further experiment showed that small plants produced by inadequate nutrition at the end of long days were delayed even more in short days than larger plants if light levels were low (Table 39).

TABLE 39 Effect of Three Nutrition Treatments in Long Days on Flowering Response in Two Levels of Light in Short Days. Variety Heyday (from Machin, 1973)

Nutrition treatments in long days	Short days to flowering	
	High light (1·26 MJ/m²/day)	Low light (0·54 MJ/m²/day)
High N : K₂O	62·4	72·3
Medium N : K₂O	62·9	74·6
Low N : K₂O	69·9	82·9
LSD at P = 0·05	1·3	2·5

Presumably a large or heavy plant contains a greater amount of phytochrome, or the enzymes or hormones which phytochrome activates during long nights, than a small or light plant.

Type of Bud

As Chan pointed out in 1950, there is some confusion regarding the terminology used to describe chrysanthemum buds. In North America, two bud types are referred to by both growers and scientists. 'Crown' buds are flower buds surrounded by vegetative shoots, and 'terminal' buds are flower buds surrounded by other flower buds. In Britain, the term 'break bud' is also used. This can be regarded as a special type of crown bud which is surrounded by vegetative shoots, but which rarely develops. Both crown and break buds are produced inevitably following a certain amount of growth in long days (Cockshull, 1976a).

Botanically, a terminal bud is a bud in a terminal position in relation to the main axis; under this definition, all three bud types mentioned should strictly be regarded as terminal buds.

Chan (1950) helped to clarify the present system of bud nomenclature. He found that from the standpoint of origin and subsequent development there is only one type of chrysanthemum bud. A crown bud is a normal bud which is arrested at a certain stage of development owing to environmental conditions. When crown buds do occur late in the season, that is when daylength is nearly short enough for bud development, development continues after only a brief suspension of growth and buds are formed on the lateral shoots as the days become shorter.

Crown buds consist of swollen apices or receptacles surrounded by bracts, but do not develop floret primordia because of prevailing longday conditions, which cause the growth of lateral vegetative shoots from axillary buds immediately below the apex of the stem. Crown buds result in a cessation of vegetative growth of the main axis and a subsequent loss of apical dominance. They can, and do, develop into flowers when the lateral vegetative shoots are removed and short days are given, provided the period of arrested growth has not been so long that abortion has occurred.

Terminal buds are similar in all respects to crown buds, except that owing to the prevailing shortday conditions, at no stage have they been arrested in development. Buds in the axils of leaves beneath the terminal bud are rapidly induced to flower initiation in short days (Cockshull, 1972).

If the present well-known terms for buds occurring during different stages of the growth of the plant are to be retained, it must be remembered that they are all anatomically similar at first except that:

(a) A break bud is permanently arrested in development, causing axillary buds to grow vegetatively;

(b) A crown bud is temporarily or permanently arrested in development according to subsequent daylength, axillary buds below the crown bud are vegetative;

(c) A terminal bud has not been arrested at any stage of development and is surrounded by axillary flower buds.

Flowering

The earlier, rather empirical experiments, although showing the overall effect of various daylength regimes on the time of flowering, did not differentiate between the various stages of flower formation, and consequently any effect of a given light regime on these various stages was not apparent. Post (1942) divided flower formation into three definable stages:

1 Flower bud initiation and the adjustments which preceded this stage to the time when the first primordia became evident;

2 Flower bud development from the first morphological change to the stage in which the bud is macroscopically visible;

3 Flower bud elongation and growth from the time it is visible to the time the flower is fully opened, that is, elongation of peduncle and growth of florets.

He suggested that a study of the effects of

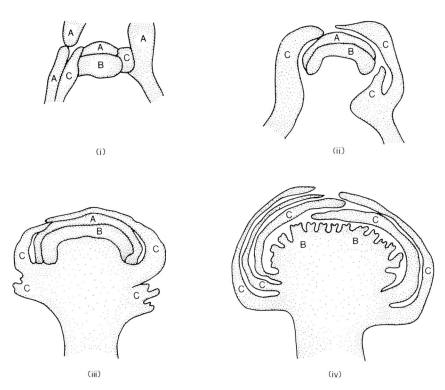

Fig. 56   Stages in the development of the chrysanthemum flower bud. (From Andrews and Watson, 1952): (i) Vegetative tip at commencement of shortday treatment. (ii) Transitional stage, after 18 short days. (iii) Young reproductive stage, after 27 short days. (iv) Older reproductive stage, after 36 short days. (A=tunica; B=upper corpus; C=bracts; D=foliage leaves.)

189

environmental factors on each of these periods of growth would be desirable.

FLOWER BUD INITIATION

Detailed and microscopic studies of bud anatomy at various stages during development have confirmed that the stages suggested by Post do in fact exist (Chan, 1950; Andrews and Watson, 1952; Doorenbos and Kofranek, 1953). The first visible symptoms of the transition from the vegetative to the flowering state (reproductive morphogenesis) occur with the disappearance of the cambial zone in the corpus and the simultaneous elongation of cells in the same area, which will later become the peduncle of the flower (Fig. 56). This is closely followed by an enlargement of the apex, which becomes in the first place more highly arched and globular, and later broader and flatter to form the receptacle around which several large bracts develop. At this stage, the receptacle bears no floret primordia.

The stages of flower bud formation described above have been generally accepted to constitute the period of bud initiation.

Bud initiation occurs when the light period decreases to 14 to $14\frac{1}{2}$ hours per day (Post, 1948). Since Borthwick showed that it is the length of the dark period which causes flowering, it may be more correct to say that bud initiation occurs when the dark period exceeds $9\frac{1}{2}$ to 10 hours.

Post's experiments at Ithaca, New York (latitude 42° N) show that days are naturally short enough for bud initiation from 1 September to 25 March, and that from 20 April to 15 August only vegetative growth occurs naturally. Periods when daylength may or may not be conducive to bud initiation, due to weather conditions, are from 15 August to 1 September and from 25 March to 20 April.

Experiments conducted by Vince (1955b) at Reading (latitude between 51° and 52° N) show that for certain mid-season and late varieties bud initiation begins about 22 August (Fig. 6). In a year such as 1954 when days were shortened earlier by cloud conditions, buds of the varieties Balcombe Perfection, Shirley Late Red and Indianapolis Pink, were initiated by 17 August.

Bud initiation can be induced by very few short photoperiods. Post and Kamemoto (1950) showed that one or two short days apparently caused no change from vegetative growth, but the onset of flowering was evident after three to five short days according to variety. This only occurred when the short days were given in succession, because Post (1959b) failed to induce initiation with six short days when no more than three of them were in succession, whereas four consecutive short days caused flower buds to be initiated.

FLOWER BUD DEVELOPMENT

The period of bud development is considered as the time from the initiation of floret primordia to the time when the bud is macroscopically visible. Chan (1950) could not detect floret primordia on the receptacles of chrysanthemums until the plants concerned had been given at least 14 successive short days. On the variety used by Doorenbos and Kofranek a similar stage was noticed after 18 short days had been given. Floret primordia first appeared as small protrusions on the outer edge of the receptacle and their formation progressed acropetally towards the apex until, on plants given 24 short days, the entire receptacle had become covered by primordia in both cases. At this stage receptacle and florets were enclosed entirely by at least

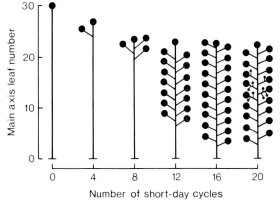

Fig. 57 The pattern of flower production in relation to the number of inductive short days received. Each 'flower bud' is represented by a closed circle. (From Cockshull, 1972.)

eight bracts and initiation of floral parts had occurred in the outer florets. In less than 24 short days the centre of the receptacle was bare of florets.

A later detailed investigation of each development stage in the flowering process in chrysanthemum was made by Popham (1963) using the variety Bittersweet.

Briefly, he found that the induction period for the receptacle was completed after five short days. The differentiation of bracts from leaf primordia had occurred after 12 short days when the diameter of the apex was twice that of a vegetative apex.

Cockshull (1972) studied reproductive morphogenesis in the pot variety Bright Golden Anne. Four short days led to receptacle initiation and after seven short days there was also a cessation of leaf production. After 12 short days a number of primary axillary meristems had irreversibly changed to the reproductive condition, and this stimulus had extended to some

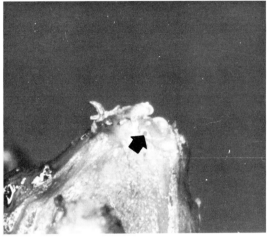

(a) A vegetative growing point in which the dome-shaped apical meristem (arrowed) has been exposed together with a few small leaf primordia.

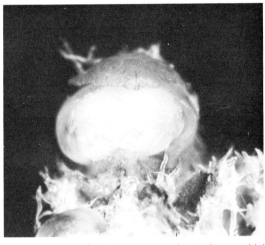

(c) Some bracts have grown over the meristem which shows the first signs of floret primordia.

(b) A young reproductive growing point showing how the meristem has enlarged and begun to form bracts.

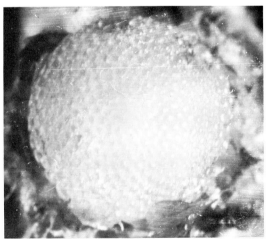

(d) The meristem has now enlarged considerable and florets have been initiated over almost its whole surface.

Fig. 58   Stages in the initiation of a chrysanthemum flower:

secondary axillary meristems after 20 short days (Fig. 57). A later study (Cockshull, 1976b) has shown that a vegetative meristem is 0·2 mm in diameter, florets are initiated when the receptacle reaches 1 mm and when floret initiation is complete the receptacle is about 2 mm in diameter (Fig. 58a–d). Schwabe (1959) gave a detailed account of reproductive morphogenesis in the variety Sunbeam. He illustrated the transition from the foliage leaves produced in long days to the bracts produced in short days via a number of leaves of intermediate type (shortday leaves). The time required to produce the bracts was much less than that required to produce leaves in long days, the plastochron being in the order of nine hours compared with two to three days.

With the variety Bittersweet (Popham, 1963), the first two rows of floret primordia were visible after only 10 short days and apical dominance had been lost by the top three lateral buds. Floret primordia covered 25 per cent of the receptacle after 16 short days, and after 24 short days the diameter of the receptacle was six times greater than that of a vegetative apex, and bract initiation was completed. The receptacle was full of florets after 26 short days and at 30 short days the diameter of the receptacle had increased to 12 times that of a vegetative apex.

Thus, although flower bud initiation occurs rapidly in optimum conditions (three to five short days), the development of the bud up to the end of floret initiation takes a much longer period. This explains the failure of earlier workers (Poesch, 1932; Post, 1932; Link, 1936; Okada, 1951) to obtain normal flowering when fewer than 30 shortday treatments were given.

Post (1948) found that for the varieties Arcadia and Goldsmith, the natural light period was short enough to induce bud initiation by 1 September, but not short enough for the most rapid development of the bud until 20 September. From these and other experiments (1947) he concluded that, although buds will initiate when the light period is 14 to $14\frac{1}{2}$ hours, rapid development does not occur until the light period is 13 to $13\frac{1}{2}$ hours. Most rapid development occurs in still shorter days.

Similar results have been recorded by Furuta (1954) using other varieties. The maximum photoperiod in which buds could initiate was an hour longer than the photoperiod needed for maximum rapidity of bud development (13 hours or less).

FLOWER BUD ELONGATION

Using Post's definition, the period of peduncle elongation and floret growth extends from the macroscopically visible bud to the fully open flower. During this stage, development of the floral parts is completed, and enlargement of the receptacle and elongation of the petals and peduncles occurs. It would appear from the anatomical work mentioned above that this stage commences after the plant has received about 24 shortday inductions.

The work of Okado and Post shows that this period of flower formation apparently has two phases regarding subsequent reaction to daylength. From the twenty-fourth to the fortieth day, the position is reversible in that longday treatment will inhibit further growth of the bud. After the fortieth day growth of the bud will continue to maturity in most varieties irrespective of subsequent daylength.

Schwabe (1950) found that the latest stage at which the oldest marginal florets of the receptacle could be arrested in development was at ovule formation. His work also showed that this stage occurred when the diameter of the bud was 2 to 3 mm.

Cockshull and Hughes (1968) found that, after approximately 42 short days, all assimilates from photosynthesis were used for the development of floral parts. It is now accepted that artificial shortday treatments for flowering can be discontinued after six weeks (Anon., 1973).

Clearly, the rate of reproductive morphogenesis, especially during the first few short days, is important to chrysanthemum growers because of its effect on the time taken for flowering in short days and on the quality of the flowering stem. The two major factors affecting the rate of bud initiation and development are the daily light integral and nutrition. This assumes, of course, that shortday conditions prevail and night temperatures are controlled at the optimum for the variety.

The time taken to reach a given stage of flower development increases as the amount of light for growth and flower development becomes more limiting (Schwabe, 1953; Watson and Andrews, 1953; Mason and Vince, 1962.) It is well known that a variety classified as having a 10-week response may flower after 10 weeks of short days in October but will require 11 or 12 weeks of short days for flowering during January or February in Britain. For June or July flowering, the same variety may require only nine weeks of short days.

Cockshull and Hughes (1971) investigated the effect of daily light levels on bud development in the variety Bright Golden Anne. Plants were grown in a constant light level of 1.25 MJ/m²/day, inducing flowering by giving daily cycles of eight hours of light and 16 hours of darkness. Transfer of some plants to 0.31 MJ/m²/day from the eighth to the fourteenth short day delayed receptacle formation in the apices of the shoots, and significantly more leaves were formed below the apical flower. Transfer to higher light (3.75 MJ/m²/day) for this period had no apparent effect. Transfer to low light at the onset of floret formation retarded their further development and reduced final flower size by reducing the total number of florets produced on the receptacle. Plants which were transferred to the low light treatment for periods of two weeks during shortday treatment had lower dry weights at flowering compared with plants at the constant light level.

Experiments using four different light regimes simulating light levels which can occur in southern England from October to March were also carried out (Hughes and Cockshull, 1971a).

The levels of visible radiation were:

0.31 MJ/m²/day = completely overcast midwinter day
0.63 MJ/m²/day = daily average for worst 12 weeks of the year
1.25 MJ/m²/day = daily average late October or mid-February

2.50 MJ/m²/day = daily average early October or early March

Bud development was extremely delayed by the lowest light level and substantially delayed at the intermediate levels, compared with the highest level.

In a further experiment, groups of plants were transferred from a constant light level of 0.63 MJ/m²/day to higher levels at the start of short days and at weekly intervals thereafter. After one or two weeks in the increased light regime the plants were returned to the lower light level for flowering. Flower induction began earliest if the transfer was made for the first two weeks of short days to a light level of 1.25 MJ/m²/day and the improved response was maintained until flowering.

Canham (1970b) has improved the flowering response of three spray varieties, from three to eight days according to variety, by the use of supplementary light for the first 14 short days.

Machin (1973) also found that plants grown in high light (1.26 MJ/m²/day) for the first 14 short days and thereafter in low light (0.54 MJ/m²/day) flowered earlier (seven days) than those grown in low shortday light throughout, using the spray variety Heyday. He found that 35 per cent more shortday leaves were formed beneath the apical flower bud in plants which had remained in low light, and he concluded that this was a good criterion for the study of the rate of reproductive morphogenesis. In further experiments on the effect of light and nutrition on bud initiation and development, both the number of shortday leaves produced and the time interval between each (shortday leaf plastochron) were used as measurements of the speed of the change from vegetative to reproductive growth.

Inadequate nutrition during the longday period of crops in which root systems are contained in a small volume of compost until short days (the direct shortday planting system) leads to flowering delay (Machin, 1973). This is due to the effect of low levels of nitrogen and potassium during the early period of reproductive morphogenesis. Some varieties are

TABLE 40 Effect of Nutrition During Long Days on Flowering in Short Days. Varieties Heyday (H) and Polaris (P) (from Machin, 1973)

Treatment	Period of Shortday leaf production (days)		Shortday leaf plastochron (days, calculated)		Short days to flowering	
	H	P	H	P	H	P
Low N : K₂O	17·0	10·5	1·9	2·1	70	68
Medium N : K₂O	6·5	5·0	1·2	1·1	63	66

delayed more than others. Specifically, the rate of shortday leaf production is reduced and the period of shortday leaf production is prolonged in starved plants compared with well-fed plants (Table 40).

In a further experiment he showed that low nutrition during long days can delay flowering (10 days) more than low light (6·5 days) during the first 14 short days (Table 41).

These results are interesting because they show that in certain conditions leaf primordia (developing into shortday leaves rather than bracts) can continue to be initiated below the enlarging receptacle for at least 17 days (Table 40). This poses the question when can the apex be regarded as definitely reproductive? As Schwabe has commented (1959), the actual moment when the apex is to be regarded as definitely reproductive might be defined differently according to the problem under consideration. Generally, it is satisfactory to define it

TABLE 41 Effect of Nutrition in Long Days and Light in Short Days on the Variety Heyday (from Machin, 1973)

Nutrition in long days	Number of short days to flowering		Mean nutrition
	High light	Low light	
Low N : K₂O	81·3	86·2	83·7
Medium N : K₂O	70·3	77·3	73·9
High N : K₂O	69·2	76·7	73·0
Mean light	73·6	80·1	76·9

LSD at P = 0·05 = 1·2
Light treatments high = 1·26 MJ/m²/day for first 14 short days; low = 0·54 MJ/m²/day for first 14 short days; low light was given until flowering.

as the point where any further development must be reproductive, that is when the change in anatomy, morphology and physiology of the apex is irreversible. Popham's view (1958) is that the anatomical differences which have resulted after between five and eight short days are irreversible even when long days, which will only delay the flowering process, are subsequently given. The changes at the apices of the plants of Heyday used by Machin, which were still producing leaves after 17 short days, could be regarded as irreversible since the receptacles had enlarged much earlier in the shortday induction period and apical dominance had been surrendered by the terminal apices.

However, cut flower growers are primarily interested in the length and quality of the flowering stem and in the total time needed for flowering in short days. For them, the best criterion for the time of transition from vegetative growth to flowering might well be the moment that leaf production ceases and floret initiation and development on the receptacle proceeds at the optimum rate. This is likely to be a different criterion from the presently accepted one.

FLOWERING STEMS

The quality of the flowering stem of spray varieties is directly related to the number of flowers developed from the lateral apices and on the length and character of the pedicels.

The number of buds initiated and developed per stem are directly related to the number of consecutive short days received by the plant.

Experiments conducted on several pompon varieties in 1932 (Post, 1934) showed that a period of five short days was sufficient to cause a few lateral buds to change to a flowering condition, 10 short days caused axils half-way down the stem to form flower buds, and treatment for 15 days caused flower bud initiation on almost all axils to the base of the stem.

On the varieties used by Hume (1941) no flower bud initiation was observed in the lower half of the stems examined despite the continuous shortday treatment, although flower buds formed quantitatively down the stem according to the number of short days received.

Cockshull (1972) has demonstrated the quantitative effect of continuous short days on flower bud initiation down the stem on the variety Bright Golden Anne (Fig. 57). He concluded that the number of lateral buds induced into a flowering condition is an estimate both of the flowering stimulus produced and of its duration.

Several workers have offered explanations for this flowering stimulus (Borthwick and Parker, 1938; Hamner and Bonner, 1938). They suggested that a diffusable hormone is produced in leaves under conditions favouring reproduction (short days) which moves first to the terminal growing point and later moves gradually downwards towards the lateral buds according to their position on the stem. Phytochrome is thought by some workers to activate the enzymes of these hormones. Others think that phytochrome controls flowering by regulating the permeability of cell walls and thus controlling the flow of water and diffusable hormones to different parts of the flowering stem. The number of buds per stem that will be switched into a flowering condition in a similar period of short days depends to a large extent on the variety used. In general, the number of flower buds initiated and developed per stem increases as the number of consecutive shortday treatments increase.

If conditions which delay flower bud initiation occur during the early part of the shortday period the flowering stem of spray varieties will tend to resemble the compound rather than the terminal form (Figs 27 to 30). These conditions include long days (Post, 1949b), low light levels (Machin unpubl.) low (Anon., 1974) and high temperatures (Furuta and Nelson, 1953) and low nitrogen and potassium fertilization (Machin, 1973). Clonal variations in some varieties (Heyday) will also cause either compound or terminal sprays to be formed, particularly in low light levels (Machin, 1973).

FLOWERS

The character of the flower is dependent to a large extent on the photoperiods which prevail during its development.

Plants which have been retarded by light treatment subsequently form flowers much more rapidly than those under normal environmental conditions, owing to the shorter days experienced during the period of bud development (Post 1948a; Vince, 1955b). This is one reason why flowers which develop late in the natural season are usually smaller than those which develop more slowly earlier in the natural season. Also, as suggested by Post in 1942, because high temperatures cause buds to develop more rapidly, the final size of the flowers might depend to some extent on this factor.

Theoretically, daylight hours should decrease in a steady orderly manner as the autumn approaches, but this rarely occurs. Light at sunrise and sunset is less than 530 lx (Post, 1948) but it is virtually daylight for plants probably for 30 minutes both before and after these times. Because light levels are so low during the early morning and late evening, atmospheric conditions and local obstructions may quite easily cause the actual length of day to be as much as 40 minutes shorter than the theoretical. Greulach (1942) found that the photoperiodically effective twilight in Ohio varied from 11 to 28 minutes.

Since the time limit between long and short-day conditions, according to the response of the chrysanthemum, is a very narrow one, alternating long and short photoperiods often occur naturally during the period of bud development. These conditions occurred markedly at Ithaca in 1947 and had noticeable effects on flower structure. An analysis of the environment of that season and its effect on chrysanthemums has been made by Post (1947). The days were shortened in mid-August, due to heavy cloud conditions, and buds were initiated and development began. This was followed by a period of clear weather and the normal longday conditions returned, causing a cessation of bud development and a tendency for the plants to make further vegetative growth. This was manifested by a lengthening of the peduncle and the formation of new growing points on the receptacle, resulting in the growth of a larger number of disc florets. Further development of the flower occurred only when shortday conditions returned. These physiological effects have been termed 'long necks' and 'bull heads' respectively. Such naturally occurring phenomena have been exploited with some success by Post and others, and it has been shown that pedicel length and petal number may be controlled by artificial long and short days.

Certain abnormalities in the flower have been attributed to very high temperatures combined with low light levels (Post, 1948). The variety Arcadia developed normally at 10°, but at higher temperatures the flowers contained many distorted and undeveloped petals. Plants of the spray variety Gold Coast appear as two distinct varieties under different temperature regimes, the petals being incurved at 15·6° but reflexed at 10°. This is also true for a number of standard varieties including Fred Shoesmith. Also, at low temperatures some varieties (Indianapolis Pink) tend to form an outer ring of tubular rather than normal flat petals.

High temperatures may increase the number of florets formed on the receptacle, in the same way as long days, and that this might lead to distorted blooms (Post and Lacey, 1951b).

Flower colour is adversely affected by high temperatures combined with low light levels (Post, 1953a), especially in pink and bronze varieties. This is because low light slows down the rate of photosynthesis and high temperatures increase the rate of food loss in respiration.

The daily radiation integral has a profound effect on flower quality, mainly during the last stages of flower growth (Cockshull and Hughes, 1971). They showed, for instance, that the ratio of flower dry weight to weight of vegetative parts was high when plants of a 10-week variety were transferred to high light after nine weeks of short days. This ratio was low when plants were transferred to low light at the same time. Low flower weight ratios occur when plants flower in poor light following good light during early growth. The highest figures are obtained when light levels at flowering are increasing rapidly following low light for vegetative and early reproductive growth. An average figure

Fig. 59   Despite our ability to control growth, the unexpected still occurs.

for flower weight ratio occurs when good light is available throughout the growing period (Machin, 1973).

Adequate nutrition (N and K_2O) during stock production and long days is essential for good flower quality. Adequate nutrition during short days cannot reverse effects on flower quality caused by inadequate nutrition during long days (Machin, 1973).

VARIETAL DIFFERENCES

There is normally a wide variation between flowering dates of different varieties of chrysanthemum. This indicates that varieties differ in their response to the environment and in particular daylength. A certain variety may need only eight weeks of shortday treatments before the flowers are fully open, whereas another requires a period of 12 weeks to reach a similar stage of development. In fact, all new year-round varieties raised are classified according to this response so that the timing schedule can be carried out correctly. The reason for this varietal difference to daylength is not known but it has been shown that the difference is most apparent during one particular stage of flower bud formation, and cannot be observed over the whole period of flower formation.

It could be suggested that in 10-week varieties bud initiation occurs at a daylength during which buds remain vegetative in later varieties. This is true to some extent, but Chan (1950) and Post and Kamemoto (1950) have shown that the differences between the numbers of short days required for bud initiation in a 10-week and a 14-week variety are very small. The former showed that a 10-week variety, Gold Coast, initiated flower buds after four short days, while five short days were needed for Vibrant, a 14-week variety. Quite obviously this small difference does not account for the much wider disparity in the natural flowering dates of these varieties.

To determine the actual stage during flower bud formation at which differences between these two varieties occurred, Doorenbos and Kofranek (1953) made critical anatomical studies over a long period of shortday treatments. During the period of bud initiation development (receptacle initiation and floret development, described previously, which ended after 24 short days), no apparent differences could be observed between the two varieties. From this stage to flowering much more time was required by Vibrant compared with Gold Coast.

The difference between these two varieties was therefore shown to be due to the rate of growth of the florets. The final size of the flower is not relevant because, although Vibrant was half as large again as Gold Coast, the difference in size was mainly due to the number of florets (the initiation of which occurred at the same time in both varieties) and the length of the petals (which was the result of expansion after the flowers opened).

Two well-known year-round varieties, Heyday (bred in the USA) and Polaris (bred in Britain), were compared in a wide range of environmental conditions (Machin, 1973). It was found that both could be grown successfully in Britain but some varietal differences were apparent. The most important of these differences are summarized in Table 42. This type of information is required for each variety by the year-round chrysanthemum grower and will be essential for efficient growing in the 1980's. These details, together with exact flowering responses at each season for each location should be supplied as 'production blue prints' by the raisers of new varieties.

TABLE 42   Differences in Vegetative Characteristics Between Heyday and Polaris in Summer and Winter (from Machin, 1973)

Season	Var.	Leaf number in cutting (50 mm)	Longday plastochron (days)	Leaves formed in long days	Leaf number at short day planting	Leaves formed in short days	Total leaf number	Mean internode length (mm)	Total stem length (cm)
Summer 21 long days	H	16	2·8	7·5	23·5	8·4	31·9	28	89
	P	15	4·8	4·4	19·4	6·2	25·6	34	87
Winter 28 long days	H	15	3·3	8·5	23·5	13·6	37·1	21	80
	P	14	7·1	3·9	17·9	8·4	26·3	29	76

APPENDICES

Varieties

CLASSIFICATION

The difference between a standard cut flower and a spray is essentially a simple one. In the former only the terminal or apical bud is retained and all smaller lateral buds are removed at disbudding time. With a spray variety, the large apical bud is removed (because it will flower slightly earlier than the other buds and may cause crowding at the top of the stem) and all lateral buds allowed to develop.

So far as flower characteristics are concerned, there are no limitations in sprays compared with standard form except in size of individual flowers. All types, forms and colours are possible.

The National Chrysanthemum Society (NCS) in the British National Register of Chrysanthemums lists four types under the heading 'Sprays':

> Anemones
> Pompons
> Reflexed
> Singles

The National Chrysanthemum Society for America also lists four main types:

> Pompons
> Singles
> Anemones
> Novelties (spidery, plumed, feathery and spoon)

These two lists are slightly different, but there are greater hidden differences so that some clarification is necessary. Singles and anemones are straightforward and need not be discussed. The NCS classification would be more complete if one further group, that is any other types, was to be added. This would include such forms as:

spidery long sometimes twisted petalloid tubes often with serrated tips;
quills straight petals in tubular form;
spoons quills with open ends to the tubes showing inner petal colour.

Furthermore, the word 'pompon' in common with some other words in the English language, has a different meaning on each side of the Atlantic. In the USA, all double flowers with normal flat ray petals (excluding spiders, etc.) are called pompons and are according to size sub-divided into:

large flowered diameter of flower 63 to 75 mm;
intermediate diameter of flower 38 to 63 mm;
baby or button diameter of flower less than 25 mm.

The NCS definition of the word 'pompon' seems more sensible because it is nearer to the true meaning of the word, a 'small and rounded object'. The majority of sprays with normal ray petals filling the centre of the receptacle (double flowers) do not fall into the NCS category pompon and are also wrongly described as pompon in the American classification. They are decorative in form and can be either incurving, intermediate or reflexed (as in the NCS Classification for decorative standards, Sections 13 to 15 in the Register). Thus, in this book, these types are grouped together as decorative rather than reflexed.

In the following list of spray varieties, we will use the following key for flower form, having extracted the best descriptions from the National Classifications;

a	anemone	q	quill
d	decorative	s	single
p	pompon	sp	spider
		spo	spoon

Standard varieties are classified according to the British Register of Chrysanthemums (NCS Publication) as follows:

Section 4   Reflexed Decoratives
        a) Large-flowered
        b) Medium-flowered

Section 5 Intermediate Decoratives
    a)   Large-flowered
    b)   Medium-flowered

There are nine other sections for late-flowering standards in the Register but they contain no varieties in use for year-round production.

PATENTED VARIETIES

Varieties with the suffix P (Plant Breeders' Rights) are sold under agreement, whereby the buyer undertakes not to part with the plants or any part thereof (other than the sale of the flowers and flowering pot plants) under any arrangement for propagation and resale, or for any other purpose. Cuttings of these varieties are sold only by authorized distributors, and on the sale of each cutting a royalty is paid by the distributor to the finder or raiser, as a contribution towards the cost of raising the new varieties.

RESPONSE GROUPS

The response (for example 9-week) represents the number of weeks to flower from the start of short days in a night temperature of 15·6° during average light conditions (autumn).

NOTES

1 Sports generally fall into the response group of the parent variety.

2 In the low light conditions of winter in Britain the number of weeks to flower may be greater for some varieties than shown above.

3 Some varieties in the 8-week and 9-week groups are partially temperature controlled and must be used with caution in year-round programmes.

Key to Colour Classification

B	Bronze	R	Red
LB	Light Bronze	S	Salmon
P	Pink	W	White
PP	Pale Pink	Y	Yellow
Pu	Purple	PY	Pale Yellow

SPRAY VARIETIES

9-Week

Apricot Marble	LB s	Imka	P sp	Yellow Marble	Y s
Apricot Winner	LB s	Judith	P s	Yellow Nimbo	Y s
Arctic	W d	Lara P	LB s		
Belair	P d	Melody	P s	**10-Week**	
Beloved P	P d	Memento	W s	Aglow	B s
Belreef	B d	Nanette	P s	Agneta	Y s
Bluechip	P d	Nicolette	LB s	Armelle P	W sp
Blue Marble	P s	Nimbo	W s	Bonnie Jean	W s
Blue Winner	P s	Pink Marble	PP s	Bronze Nero P	B s
Bronze Marble	B s	Pink Winner	P s	Deep Telstar	P d
Bronze Rosado	B d	Polished Marble P	LY s	Deep Tuneful	B s
Celebrate	Y s	Pride P	Y s	Fandango	Pu d
Cloudbank	W a	Rosado	P d	Flamenco	Pu d
Coral Marble P	S s	Rosechip	P d	Golden Crystal	Y sp
Dolly	P d	Sapphire P	P s	Golden Hurricane	Y d
Dramatic P	LB s	Snapper P	PP s	Golden Polaris	Y d
Flame Belair	B d	Southdown Chip	P d	Golden Sands	Y a
Florida Marble P	Y s	Sunbeam	Y s	Heyday	Y d
Garland P	W s	White Marble	W s	Hurricane	W d
Golden Winner	Y s	White Winner	W s	Improved Yellow	
		Yellow Arctic P	Y d	Hurricane	Y d
Horim	W s	Yellow Horim	Y s	Lemon Polaris	LY d

CHRYSANTHEMUMS

Orange Aglow[P]	LB s
Pink Gin[P]	P d
Polaris	W d
Pollyanne	PP d
Red Fandango	R d
Red Nero[P]	R s
Red Tuneful[P]	R s
Riviera Spider	P sp
Robeam[P]	Y d
Schneestern	W sp
Snowdon	W d
Snowstar[P]	W sp
Starlet Spider[P]	P sp
Super White	W sp
Super Yellow	Y sp
Tuneful	B s
Tune-up[P]	B s
White Sands	W a
White Spider	W sp
Yellow Agneta	Y s

Yellow Bonnie Jean	Y s
Yellow Hector[P]	Y d
Yellow Polaris	Y d
Yellow Sands	Y a
Yellow Snowdon[P]	Y d
Yellow Snowstar	Y sp
Yellow Spider	Y sp
Yellow Tuneful	Y s

11-Week

Apricot Illini Springtime	LB s
Divinity	W a
Golden Vedova	Y a
Illini Springtime	P s
Jubilee	Y d
Ranger	LB d
Souvenir	Y s
Taffeta	P d
Tan Vedova	LB a

Vedova	P a
White Illini Springtime	W s
White Taffeta	W d
Yellow Divinity	Y s
Yellow Illini Springtime	Y s
Yellow Taffeta	Y d

12-Week

Crackerjack	R s
Galaxy	B s
Red Galaxy	R s
Yellow Galaxy	Y s

14-Week

Cream Elegance	LY d
Cream Japanerin	LY sp
Elegance	W d
Golden Elegance	Y d
Japanerin	W sp

STANDARD VARIETIES

9-Week

Apricot Joanne	4b S
Escapade	5b PP
Promenade	5b P

10-Week

Bright Golden Anne	4b Y
Bronze Princess Anne	4b B
Cream Princess Anne	4b LY
Crimson Anne[P]	4b R
Gay Anne	4b LB
Giant Indianapolis White iv	5b W

Giant Indianapolis Yellow iv	5b Y
Goldburst Mefo	5b Y
Improved Mefo	5b W
Improved Yellow Mefo	5b Y
Lemon Princess Anne	4b LY
Purple Anne[P]	4b Pu
Red Anne	4b R
Regal Anne	4b P
Rocco[P]	5b Y
Snowdon	5b W
Sunburst Mefo	5b Y
Woking Scarlet	4b R
Yellow Snowdon[P]	5b Y

11-Week

Bright Yellow May Shoesmith	5b Y
Cassandra	5a P
Deep Champagne	5b P
Fred Shoesmith	5a W
May Shoesmith	5b W
Pink Champagne	5b P
Red Resilient	5b R
Resilient	5b B
Rivalry	5a Y
Yellow Fred Shoe-Smith	5a Y

POT VARIETIES

8-Week

Altis[P]	W d
Deep Louise	P d
Gay Louise	B d
Spic[P]	Y sp
(Plate 27)	
Windsong[P]	W d

9-Week

Always Pink	P d
Bard[P]	LY s
Copper Hostess[P]	B d
Distinctive[P]	PP d
Dramatic[P]	LB s
Garland[P]	W s

Hostess	P d
Illini Spinwheel[P]	W sp
Neptune	W d
Paragon	W d
Pride[P]	Y s
Rascal[P]	B s
Reaper[P]	Y's

Rory P	R s	Crimson Torch P	R d	Red Torch P	R d
Rose Hostess	P. d	Dark Maritime P	P d	Regal Anne	P d
Rufus P	R s	Deep Popsie P	P p	Royal Purple	Pu d
Wedgewood P	PP s	Gay Anne	LB d	Royal Trophy P	p d
Yellow Illini Spin-		Glowing Mandalay P	B d	Snow Crystal	W sp
wheel P	Y sp	Golden Crystal	Y sp	Sparkling Mandalay P	B d
Yellow Paragon P	Y d	Illini Trophy	P d	Stargold P	Y d
		Judith	P s	Sunny Mandalay P	LY d
		Lemon Princess Anne	LY d	Tuneful	B s
10-Week		Mandalay	B d	Tune-up P	B s
Aglow	B s	Maritime	PP d	White Anne P	W d
Armelle P	Y s	Mountain Peak P	Y d	White Popsie P	W p
Bonnie Jean	W s	Mountain Snow P	W d	Woking Scarlet	R d
Bright Golden Anne	Y d	Orange Aglow	LB s	Yellow Bonnie Jean	Y s
Bronze Popsie P	LB p	Orange Bowl	LB d	Yellow Delaware	Y d
Bronze Princess Anne	B d	Princess Anne Superb	P d	Yellow Hector P	Y d
Cerise Magnum P	Pu d	Proud Princess Anne P	P d	Yellow Mandalay	Y d
Cream Princess Anne	LY d	Purple Anne P	Pu d	Yellow Popsie P	Y p
Crimson Anne P	R d	Red Anne	B d	Yellow Tuneful	Y s

Leaflets

Advisory Leaflets concerned with chrysanthemum pests available* in Britain from the Ministry of Agriculture, Fisheries and Food:

AL   86   Glasshouse Whitefly
AL   115   Slugs and Snails
AL   224   Red Spider Mites on Glasshouse Crops
AL   286   Chrysanthemum Midge
AL   339   Chrysanthemum Eelworm
AL   484   Glasshouse Symphilid
AL   550   Chrysanthemum Leaf Miner
AL   555   Virus Diseases of Chrysanthemums
STL   110   Sciarids on Pot Plants
UL   Mediterranean Climbing Cutworm

Leaflets published by the Agricultural Development and Advisory Service on greenhouse construction:

STL   28   'Glasshouse Construction—Siting and design.'
STL   106   'Minimum standards for glasshouse construction—loading.'
STL   148   'Glasshouse Construction—Specifications for timber, concrete and foundations.'

STL   149   Glasshouse Construction—Glazing, roof water collection and disposal.'
STL   150   'Glasshouse Construction—Specifications for steel and aluminium alloys. Corrosion—its nature and prevention.'
STL   151   'Glasshouse Construction—Dimensions in relation to crop growing systems.'

Ministry of Agriculture Publications on greenhouse heating systems and associated equipment:

ML   14   'Boilers for nursery use.'
ML   27   'Greenhouse heating systems.'
ML   3   'Pumps and pipework for heating systems.'

References on ventilation:

ML   5   'Glasshouse ventilation.'
Electricity Council Grow Electric Handbook No. 3 'Ventilation for greenhouses.'

* Single copies may be obtained, free, from the Ministry of Agriculture, Fisheries and Food (Publications), Tolcarne Drive, Pinner, Middlesex HA5 2DT, England.

Nutritional Disorders

Disorder	Severity	Description of symptoms	Possible causes	Remedial action
Nitrogen deficiency	Mild	Leaves become pale green and growth may be checked.	Liquid feeding neglected, over-watering, undersized pot.	Feed at alternate waterings with 150 g sulphate of ammonia dissolved in 100 l water until normal colour and growth are restored.
	Severe	Plants stunted with pale yellow-green foliage; younger leaves are reduced in size and remain almost erect. Only the youngest leaves darken when buds become visible. Flowering delayed, flower size reduced and fewer flowers develop on sprays. In extreme cases leaf margins become yellow; reddish-purple tints may develop and lower leaves die prematurely.	Omission of nitrogenous fertilizer, particularly from soilless media or soils with a low nitrogen content. Use of unhumified organic material as soil conditioner without addition of a suitable nitrogen source.	
Nitrogen excess	Mild	Very dark green leaves; flowering delayed.	Overfeeding with nitrogen.	Water heavily to leach excess nitrogen. Supply only water until colour of new growth is normal.
	Severe	Cuttings suffer root damage, making poor growth; leaves very dark green and wilt prematurely.	Accumulation of nitrate due to overfeeding.	
		Older leaves remain very dark green but younger leaves become yellow, excepting the veins, which stay green. In extreme cases the symptoms appear identical with those of iron deficiency.	Excessive use of an organic nitrogen fertilizer which releases ammonia in the soil, hoof and horn, dried blood, urea; most damaging in calcareous or heavily limed media.	Flooding may not be effective until much of the ammonia has nitrified. Avoid waterlogging a closely retentive medium as this may accentuate the disorder.
Phosphorus deficiency	Mild	Growth checked, becoming spindly. New leaves dark green and reduced in size; lower leaves may develop a 'muddy' orange-green colour.	Undersized pot, overwatering of soilless media, inadequate base fertilizer.	Feed at alternate waterings with 30 to 40 g mono-ammonium phosphate dissolved in 100 l water; 5 applications should suffice. *or* Apply 30 to 60 g superphosphate per m² and water in.
	Severe	Plants stunted. Younger leaves become dark green, much reduced in size and almost erect. Lower leaves become orange; marginal browning develops rapidly and results in premature death of affected leaves. Flowering delayed, flower size reduced, fewer flowers develop on sprays and petals may suffer some loss of colour.	Omission of phosphatic fertilizer, particularly from soilless media or soils with a low phosphate content.	

Disorder	Severity	Description of symptoms	Possible causes	Remedial action
Phosphate excess	Severe	Certain micronutrient deficiencies may be induced, (iron, copper, manganese and zinc).	Excessive use of superphosphate or mono-ammonium phosphate. Not a common problem.	Water heavily to leach excess phosphate. Treat any identifiable micronutrient deficiency.
Potassium deficiency	Mild	Margins of lower leaves become yellow and rapidly turn brown.	Insufficient base fertilizer, undersized pot, overwatering of soilless media.	Feed at alternate waterings with 125 g sulphate of potash dissolved in 100 l water; 5 applications should suffice.
	Severe	Plants shortened. Leaves dark green and reduced in size. Marginal browning spreads up the plant and lower leaves die prematurely. Flowering delayed, flower size reduced, fewer flowers on sprays and keeping quality impaired.	Omission of potash fertilizers, particularly from soilless media or soils with a low potash content.	
Potassium excess	Mild	Leaves very dark green.	Overfeeding with potash.	Water heavily to leach excess potash and omit potash from the subsequent feeding programme. Treat with calcium or magnesium if specific deficiency symptoms develop.
	Severe	Growth may be checked and plants may wilt prematurely. Symptoms of magnesium deficiency are likely to develop. Calcium deficiency may develop if the rooting medium is too acidic.	Excessive use of potash as base fertilizer and in liquid feeds. Occurs most easily with soilless media.	
Magnesium deficiency	Mild	General loss of colour in lower leaves.	Overfeeding with potash.	Use a foliar spray for rapid control; dissolve 1 kg Epsom salt in 100 l water and add a wetting agent. Repeat after 10 to 14 days if necessary.
	Severe	Lower and middle leaves become yellow, the veins and margins remaining green at first. Reddish-purple areas may appear on older leaves; small brown interveinal areas may also occur. The rapid development of symptoms on established plants is characteristic. Flower size reduced and petals may be paler than normal.	Omission of magnesium from a soil or soilless medium with a low magnesium content.	
Magnesium excess	Mild	Leaves become dark green.	Excessive use of Epsom salt, not a frequent problem.	Water heavily to leach excess magnesium. Treat with potassium or calcium if specific symptoms are identified.
	Severe	Growth may be checked and plants may wilt prematurely. Deficiencies of potassium and calcium may be induced.		
Calcium deficiency	Mild	Youngest leaves become yellow. Short internodes reduce plant height. Flowers very susceptible to heat injury.	Omission of both lime and superphosphate from an acidic soil or peat; very rare.	Apply 60 g gypsum and 150 g finely ground limestone per m² and water-in heavily.

Disorder	Severity	Description of symptoms	Possible causes	Remedial action
	Severe	Yellowing of leaves and internodal shortening become very marked; upper leaves form a rosette. Small brown spots develop along the margins of upper leaves and coalesce into a marginal scorch; leaves distort and curl downwards. Buds or growing point die. Lower leaves, which remain a dull dark green, are stiff and brittle. Plants wilt easily.	Above condition exaggerated by high levels of potassium and/or magnesium in the medium.	Spray with a solution containing 200 g calcium nitrate dissolved in 100 l water; add a wetting agent. Treat the soil as above.
Calcium excess		Lime-induced deficiencies of boron, iron, manganese and copper. Growth may be limited by reduced availability of phosphorus.	Over-liming or highly calcarous soil.	Treat identifiable micronutrient deficiencies or phosphorus deficiency as appropriate.
Boron deficiency	Mild	Foliage normal. Petals become 'quilled', (fail to unroll properly or to reflex fully) and bruise easily.	Calcareous soil or heavily limed soilless medium.	Feed at alternate waterings for 3 to 4 weeks with 2 g borax dissolved in 100 l water.
	Severe	Leaves become characteristically brittle, closely spaced, and may be downcurled. Tips of middle to upper leaves may curl upwards and become pale green, yellow or even white, with purple tints at the margins. In some varieties the youngest leaves become yellow. Slight delay in flowering with some loss of colour; in acute cases the abnormal buds formed fail to open properly. Death of the growing point may result in multiple shoot formation.	Omission of boron from deficient soils and heavily limed soilless media.	
Boron excess		Tips of small upper leaves become scorched; brown margins develop on middle and lower leaves.	Overfeeding with borax or excessive use of a fritted trace element mixture. Occurs most readily in acid media.	It is difficult to remove excess boron during cropping; flooding may help.
Iron deficiency	Mild	Interveinal yellowing of rapidly expanding leaves; basal area remains green at first.	Highly calcareous soil, omission of iron from soilless media, overwatering.	Feed with 30 g iron sequestrene dissolved in 100 l water; repeat 7 to 10 days later if necessary.
	Severe	Youngest leave become pale yellow or cream; leaf size greatly reduced and growth stunted. Flowering may be delayed and petal colour paler than normal.	Excessive application of certain organic nitrogenous fertilizers to soil or soilless media. Omission of iron from a very deficient soilless medium. Damaged root system.	

Disorder	Severity	Description of symptoms	Possible causes	Remedial action
Iron excess		Deep red colouration develops in the veins of older leaves a few days after planting rooted cuttings.	Excessive application of iron sequestrene; most likely to occur in soilless media.	Flood well to remove some of the excess sequestrene.
Manganese deficiency	Mild	Leaves become lime green, making plants uniformly pale.	Calcareous soil. Omission of manganese from soilless media.	Spray with a solution containing 60 g manganous sulphate dissolved in 100 l water; add a wetting agent.
	Severe	Upper leaves reduced in size; plants spindly and stunted. Middle leaves develop yellow margins which spread interveinally; areas around the veins remain green. A netted appearance is characteristic in some varieties.		
Manganese excess		Small brown spots may develop on mature leaves and spread to the younger leaves.	Omission or inadequate addition of lime to a steamed soil of the brick-earth type. Excessive application of manganese to a soilless medium.	Feed with 60 g mono-ammonium phosphate dissolved in 100 l water if the growing medium does not contain a high level of phosphate. Then apply 150 g carbonate of lime per m² and water-in.
Copper deficiency	Mild	Leaves remain uniformly pale green. Lateral shoots of sprays tend to become highly branched. Flowering delayed, bloom size reduced and quality impaired.	Unlikely to occur in soil-based media, even if highly calcareous or heavily limed.	Spray once with a solution containing 35 g copper sulphate dissolved in 100 l water; add a wetting agent.
	Severe	Plants continue to make vegetative growth instead of budding. Middle leaves develop yellow interveinal areas and collapse as the plants mature. Terminal bud formation feeble and greatly delayed. Vegetative lateral shoots develop on sprays; buds formed fail to develop.	Omission of copper from a soilless medium; rare.	
		In extreme cases the plants are very stunted and the growing point dies; a few basal shoots may develop.		

From Scopes, 1975b. Reproduced by permission of the NCS.

Guides to Pesticides and Fungicides

PESTICIDE USAGE

Pesticide	Aphid (R)	Caterpillar (R)	Earwig	Eelworm	Gall midge	Leafminer (R)	Mirid (Capsid)	Red Spider Mite (R)	Sciarid	Slug	Stoolminer	Symphilid	Thrip	Whitefly (R)
aldicarb	2	–	–	2	2	2	I	2	2	–	–	2	2	2
Bacillus thuringiensis	–	2	–	–	–	–	–	–	–	–	–	–	–	–
carbaryl	–	2	2	–	–	–	2	–	2	–	–	–	–	–
cyhexatin	*–	–	–	–	–	–	–	2	–	–	–	–	–	–
DDT	–	2	2	–	–	–	2	–	–	–	–	–	2	2
demeton-S-methyl	*2	–	I	–	–	I	2	I	–	–	2	–	I	I
diazinon	2	I	2	2	I	2	2	I	–	–	–	2	2	–
dichlorvos	*2	2	2	–	–	I	–	I	I	–	–	–	2	2
dicofol	–	–	–	–	–	–	–	I	–	–	–	–	–	–
diflubenzuron	–	–	–	–	–	–	–	–	2	–	–	–	I	–
dimethoate	*2	–	–	–	–	2	–	I	–	–	2	I	2	2
dioxathion	I	–	–	–	–	2	–	–	–	–	–	–	–	–
HCH (BHC)	I	–	2	–	2	2	2	–	–	–	2	2	2	–
malathion	2	–	–	–	–	–	2	–	–	–	–	–	2	I
metaldehyde	–	–	–	–	–	–	–	–	–	2	–	–	–	–
methiocarb	–	–	–	–	–	–	–	–	–	2	–	2	–	–
methomyl	–	2	–	–	–	–	–	–	–	–	–	–	–	–
naled	I	–	–	–	–	–	–	I	–	–	–	–	–	I
nicotine	2	–	I	–	–	–	2	–	–	–	–	–	2	–
parathion	2	I	2	I	2	–	2	I	2	–	I	2	2	I
pirimicarb	2	–	–	–	–	I	–	–	–	–	–	–	–	–
pirimiphos-methyl	–	–	–	–	–	–	–	–	–	–	–	–	–	2
propoxur	–	–	–	–	–	–	–	2	–	–	–	–	–	–
pyrethrins	2	–	2	–	–	–	2	–	–	–	–	–	–	2
tetradifon	–	–	–	–	–	–	–	2	–	–	–	–	–	–
thionazin	2	–	–	2	2	–	I	–	–	–	I	–	–	–

2   should give good control
I   should give some control
–   no control or effect not known
*   risk of phytotoxicity
R   resistance prevalent

FUNGICIDE USAGE

Pathogen	Common name	benodanil	captan	carbendazim†	copper	dichlofluanid	drazoxolon	mancozeb	oxycarboxin	pyrazophos	quintozene	sulphur	thiram	triforine	zineb
Botrytis	Grey mould		√	√		√							√		
Didymella	Ray blight		√	√				√						√	
Fusarium	Wilt			√											
Itersonilia	Petal blight														√
Oidium	Mildew			√						√		√		√	
Phoma	Root rot*														
Phytophthora	Root rot		√		√		√						√		
Puccinia	Rust	√							√	√			√	√	√
Pythium	root and stem rot		√		√		√						√		
Rhizoctonia	Foot rot			√							√				
Sclerotinia	Stem rot			√							√				
Septoria	Leaf spot							√							√
Verticillium	Wilt			√											

* Control relies on soil sterilization.
† Examples of carbendazim-forming fungicides include
  benomyl and thiophanate-methyl.
√ = effective.
‡ Further reference; see Scopes (1975b).

Composts

JOHN INNES

The John Innes composts are made up as set out below.

Seed Compost

Part by volume	2 medium loam
	1 peat
	1 sand
to which is added per m³	1·0 kg superphosphate
	0·5 kg ground chalk

Potting Compost No. 1

Parts by volume	7 medium loam
	3 peat
	2 sand
to which is added per m³	2·5 kg John Innes base
	0·5 kg ground chalk

Potting Compost No. 2

Parts by volume	7 medium loam
	3 peat
	2 sand
to which is added per m³	5·0 kg John Innes base
	1·0 kg ground chalk

John Innes Base

Parts by weight	2 hoof and horn (13 per cent N)
	2 superphosphate of lime (18 per cent P_2O_5)
	1 sulphate of potash (48 per cent K_2O)

John Innes Liquid Feed

Parts by weight	15·0 ammonium sulphate
	2·25 mono-ammonium phosphate
	2·75 potassium nitrate and diluted 6·3 g/l of water

LOAMLESS

Loamless composts developed by the GCRI, Littlehampton, Sussex, England.

GCRI Seed Compost

Parts by Volume	1 sphagnum peat
	1 lime-free sand
to which is added per m³	0·75 kg superphosphate
	0·40 kg potassium nitrate
	3·00 kg ground limestone

GCRI Potting Compost 1

Parts by volume	3 sphagnum peat
	1 lime-free sand
to which is added per m³	0·40 kg ammonium nitrate
	1·50 kg superphosphate
	0·75 kg potassium nitrate
	2·25 kg ground limestone
	2·25 kg dolomitic limestone
	0·38 kg fritted trace elements (WM 255)

This compost contains inorganic nitrogenous fertilizers only, so it can be safely stored for a period before use.

GCRI Potting Compost II

If a compost with slow release nitrogen is required, the ammonium nitrate in formula 1 can be omitted and replaced with urea formaldehyde at the rate of 0·5 to 1·0 kg/m³.

Calculations of Cubic Capacity

CUBIC CAPACITY OF A GREEN-HOUSE
Even Span and Lean-to Houses

Calculate the average height

Average height =
$$\frac{\text{height to ridge} + \text{height to eaves}}{2}$$

Capacity = average height × length × width

Uneven Span Houses

Assume each side of the ridge to be a separate lean-to house (as above) and add the results.

CAPACITY OF RECTANGULAR TANKS

Measure in inches

$$\frac{\text{height} \times \text{length} \times \text{width}}{227} = \text{gallons}$$

Measure in feet

height × length × width × 6·23 = gallons

Measure in Centimetres

$$\frac{\text{height} \times \text{length} \times \text{width}}{1000} = \text{litres}$$

CAPACITY OF CYLINDRICAL TANKS

Measure in inches

diam × diam × height ÷ 353 = gallons

Measure in feet

diam × diam × height × 4.9 = gallons

Measure in centimetres

diam × diam × height ÷ 1274 = litres

Liquid Feeding

The weights of potassium nitrate (13·8 per cent N and 46·4 per cent K_2O) and ammonium nitrate (35 per cent N), in g/l of stock solution, to give various concentrations of N and K_2O in the *diluted* feed when applied at 1 in 200.

Fertilizer	ppm N					pp m K_2O
	100	150	200	250	300	
Potassium nitrate	45	45	45	45	45	100
Ammonium nitrate	40	70	95	125	155	
Potassium nitrate	65	65	65	65	65	150
Ammonium nitrate	30	60	90	115	145	
Potassium nitrate	85	85	85	85	85	200
Ammonium nitrate	25	50	80	110	140	
Potassium nitrate	110	110	110	110	110	250
Ammonium nitrate	15	45	70	100	130	
Potassium nitrate	130	130	130	130	130	300
Ammonium nitrate	5	35	65	90	120	

All feeds contained 200 N 30 P 150K ppm and were made with bore hole water containing 250 ppm equivalent calcium carbonate.

In winter, pH changes due to water quality and fertilizer composition are less marked.

1 All quantities have been rounded up to the nearest 5 g.

2 For dilutor settings other than 1 in 200, multiple these quantities (g/l) by the fraction $\dfrac{\text{dilution to be used}}{200}$

For example, if working at 1 in 100, multiply by $\dfrac{100}{200}$ or 0·5.

3 Urea can be used instead of ammonium nitrate, at three-quarters the rate shown for ammonium nitrate.

CALCULATIONS FOR LIQUID FEEDING

The concentrations of liquid feeds can be calculated as set out below.

Liquid Concentrates

ppm in diluted feed =

$$\frac{\text{per cent nutrient in concentrate} \times 10,000}{\text{dilution}}$$

Solid Concentrates

ppm in diluted feed =

$$\frac{\text{g(fert)/l stock solution} \times \text{per cent nutrient} \times 10}{\text{dilution}}$$

Stock Solutions

g(fert.)/volume (l) required =

$$\frac{\text{ppm required} \times \text{dilution}}{\text{per cent nutrient} \times 10}$$

APPENDIX 8
Metric and Other Equivalents

All measurements in this book have been converted to the metric scale.

LENGTH

0 to 10 centimetres (cm) are expressed in millimetres (mm).

10 to 100 cm are expressed in cm.

100 cm (1 metre) and above are expressed in metres (m).

Only one place of decimals has been used.

AREA

One place of decimals only has been used except in the calculations for determining the number of pots in a house of 0.2 ha (page 147).

Simplification here would have caused too great an error in the calculation.

TEMPERATURE

Temperature conversions have been made to the nearest whole number (for example, $60°F = 16°$), except that temperatures from recent research have been quoted to one place of decimals (for example, $60°F = 15.6°$).

LIGHT

Illuminance is measured in lumens per square metre.

1 lumen per square metre $(lm/m^2) = 1$ lux (lx)
1 lumen per square foot $= 10.764$ lx

To convert lux (illuminance) to watts per square metre (power) multiply by the corresponding conversion factor for each lamp given below and divide by 1000.

Lamp type	Conversion factor
Incandescent (GLS, 100 to 200 W)	4.3
Warm White fluorescent (40 to 125 W)	2.7
Mercury fluorescent (MBFR/U, 400 to 1000 W)	3.1
Low-pressure sodium (SOX, 180 W)	2.1
High-pressure sodium (SON/T, 400 W)	2.4

EXAMPLE

5000 lx from MBFR/U

$$\frac{5000 \times 3.1}{1000} = 15.5 \text{ W/m}^2$$

To convert power units (W/m^2) to units of daily energy $(MJ/m^2/day)$ proceed as follows:

a) Multiply Wm^2 by the number of hours the light is in use. Assuming the MBFR/U lamps were in use for 12 hours

$$15.5 \times 12 = 186.0$$

b) Multiply this answer by 3.6 to give the daily light integral in $KJ/m^2/day$ and divide by 1000 to give $MJ/m^2/day$

$$\frac{186.0 \times 3.6}{1000} = 0.67 \text{ MJ/m}^2/\text{day}$$

EQUIVALENTS
Length and Area

1 inch	=	25.4 millimetres (mm)
1 foot	=	30.48 centimetres (cm)
1 yard	=	0.919 metre (m)
1 square inch	=	6.45 square centimetres (cm²)
1 square foot	=	0.093 square metre (m²)
	=	929 square centimetres (cm²)
1 square yard	=	0.836 square metre (m²)
1 acre	=	0.4047 hectare (ha)

Volume

1 fluid ounce (fl. oz)	=	28·41 millilitres (ml)
1 pint = 20 fl. oz	=	568·0 millilitres
1 Imperial gallon	=	4·546 litres (l)
1 cubic inch	=	16·39 cubic centimetres (cm³)
1 cubic foot (= 1728 cu. in.)	=	28·32 litres (l)
1 bushel	=	0·0364 cubic metres (m³)

Weight

1 ounce	=	28·35 grammes (g)
1 pound	=	0·454 kilogrammes (kg)
1 hundredweight	=	50·8 kilogrammes (kg)

Pressure

1 atmosphere (British)	=	760 mm of mercury
	=	1·0332 kg/cm²

Heat

1 British Thermal Unit (BTU)	=	3412 watts (W)
		107·6 metre kilogrammes (mkg)
1 Therm	=	100,000 BTU

Power

1 horse power (hp)	=	1·0139 hp (metric)

PRACTICAL CONVERSIONS

1 oz/yd² = 303 lb/acre = 33·9 g/m²

1 oz/gal = 0·625 per cent w/v = 6·25 g/l

1 lb/100 gallons = 0·1 per cent w/v
$\qquad$ = 100 g/100 l

1 lb/acre = 1·12 kg/ha

1 g/1000 ft³ = 3·52 g/100m³ = 35 μg/l

1 oz/1000 ft³ = 100 g/100m³

1 oz/yd³ = 37 g/m³ =
$\qquad$ 40 ppm in potting compost

General Conversion Table

		To Convert	
		A to B	B to A
A	B	Multiply by	Multiply by
inches	centimetres	2·54	0·3937
feet	metres	0·3048	3·2808
yards	metres	0·914	1·094
miles	kilometres	1·609	0·621
square inches	square centimetres	6·451	0·255
square feet	square metres	0·093	10·764
square yards	square metres	0·836	1·196
cubic inches	cubic cm	16·39	0·061
cubic feet	cubic metres	0·028	35·317
bushels (bu)	cubic metres	0·036	27·47
cubic feet	litres	28·3	0·0353
cubic feet	gallons	6·23	0·1601
cubic yards	cubic metres	0·76	1·308
pounds (av)	kilogrammes	0·4536	2·2046
ounces (av)	grammes	28·35	0·0352
grains	grammes	0·065	15·43
cwt	kilogrammes	50·8	0·01968
tons	kilogrammes	1016·0	0·000984
gallons (imp)	litres	4·546	0·22
m.p.h.	k.p.h.	1·609	0·6214
metres/sec	ft/min	197·0	0·0508
oz/acre	g/ha	70·053	0·0143
lb/acre	kg/ha	1·12	0·89
fl. oz/acre	cc/ha	70·053	0·0143
pints/acre	lit/ha	1·4	0·71
imp gal/acre	lit/ha	11·23	0·089
cwt/acre	oz/sq yd	0·37	2·703
oz/100 lb	kg/100 kg	0·0624	16·033
fl. oz/100 gal	cc/100 litres	6·25	0·16
pints/100 gal	cc/100 litres	125·0	0·008
oz/100 gal	g/100 litres	6·25	0·16
imp gal	US gal	1·20	0·833
fl. oz	cc	28·35	0·0352
lb/yd³	kg/m³	0·593	1·687
oz/bushel	kg/m³	0·778	1·284

Temperature Conversion Table

°C		°F	°C		°F
−17·8	0	32·0	−11·7	11	51·8
−17·2	1	33·8	−11·1	12	53·6
−16·7	2	35·6	−10·6	13	55·4
−16·1	3	37·4	−10·0	14	57·2
−15·6	4	39·2	−9·4	15	59·0
−15·0	5	41·0	8·9	16	60·8
−14·4	6	42·8	−8·3	17	62·6
−13·9	7	44·6	−7·8	18	64·4
−13·3	8	46·4	−7·2	19	66·2
−12·8	9	48·2	−6·7	20	68·0
−12·2	10	50·0		*(continued overleaf)*	

°C		°F	°C		°F
-6.1	**21**	69.8	19.4	**67**	152.6
-5.6	**22**	71.6	20.0	**68**	154.4
-5.0	**23**	73.4	20.6	**69**	156.2
-4.4	**24**	75.2	21.1	**70**	158.0
-3.9	**25**	77.0	21.7	**71**	159.8
-3.3	**26**	78.8	22.2	**72**	161.6
-2.8	**27**	80.6	22.8	**73**	163.4
-2.2	**28**	82.4	23.3	**74**	165.2
-1.7	**29**	84.2	23.9	**75**	167.0
-1.1	**30**	86.0	24.4	**76**	168.8
-0.6	**31**	87.8	25.0	**77**	170.6
0.0	**32**	89.6	25.6	**78**	172.4
0.6	**33**	91.4	26.1	**79**	174.2
1.1	**34**	93.2	26.7	**80**	176.0
1.7	**35**	95.0	27.2	**81**	177.8
2.2	**36**	96.8	27.8	**82**	179.6
2.8	**37**	98.6	28.3	**83**	181.4
3.3	**38**	100.4	28.9	**84**	183.2
3.9	**39**	102.2	29.4	**85**	185.0
4.4	**40**	104.0	30.0	**86**	186.8
5.0	**41**	105.8	30.6	**87**	188.6
5.6	**42**	107.6	31.1	**88**	190.4
6.1	**43**	109.4	31.7	**89**	192.2
6.7	**44**	111.2	32.2	**90**	194.0
7.2	**45**	113.0	32.8	**91**	195.8
7.8	**46**	114.8	33.3	**92**	197.6
8.3	**47**	116.6	33.9	**93**	199.4
8.9	**48**	118.4	34.4	**94**	201.2
9.4	**49**	120.2	35.0	**95**	203.0
10.0	**50**	122.0	35.6	**96**	204.8
10.6	**51**	123.8	36.1	**97**	206.6
11.1	**52**	125.6	36.7	**98**	208.4
11.7	**53**	127.4	37.2	**99**	210.2
12.2	**54**	129.2	37.8	**100**	212.0
12.8	**55**	131.0	43	**110**	230
13.3	**56**	132.8	49	**120**	248
13.9	**57**	134.6	54	**130**	266
14.4	**58**	136.4	60	**140**	284
15.0	**59**	138.2	66	**150**	302
15.6	**60**	140.0	71	**160**	320
16.1	**61**	141.8	77	**170**	338
16.7	**62**	143.6	82	**180**	356
17.2	**63**	145.4	88	**190**	374
17.8	**64**	147.2	93	**200**	392
18.3	**65**	149.0	99	**210**	410
18.9	**66**	150.8	100	**212**	413.6

Examples

1 centimetre = 0.394 inches, 1 inch = 2.54 centimetres. 1 sq. metre = 1.196 sq. yds, 1 sq. yd = 0.836 sq. metres.

Centimetres		Inches	Sq. metres		Sq. yards
2.54	**1**	0.394	0.836	**1**	1.196
5.08	**2**	0.787	1.672	**2**	2.392
7.62	**3**	1.181	2.508	**3**	3.588
10.16	**4**	1.575	3.345	**4**	4.784
12.70	**5**	1.969	4.181	**5**	5.980
15.24	**6**	2.362	5.017	**6**	7.176
17.78	**7**	2.756	5.853	**7**	8.372
20.32	**8**	3.150	6.689	**8**	9.568
22.86	**9**	3.543	7.525	**9**	10.764
25.40	**10**	3.937	8.361	**10**	11.960
50.80	**20**	7.874	16.723	**20**	23.920
76.20	**30**	11.811	25.084	**30**	35.880
101.60	**40**	15.748	33.445	**40**	47.840
127.00	**50**	19.685	41.806	**50**	59.800
152.40	**60**	23.622	50.168	**60**	71.759
177.80	**70**	27.559	58.529	**70**	83.719
203.20	**80**	31.496	66.890	**80**	95.679
228.60	**90**	35.433	75.251	**90**	107.639
254.00	**100**	39.370	83.613	**100**	119.599

Metres		Yards	Square kilometres		Square miles
0.914	**1**	1.094	2.590	**1**	0.386
1.829	**2**	2.187	5.180	**2**	0.772
2.743	**3**	3.281	7.770	**3**	1.158
3.658	**4**	4.374	10.360	**4**	1.544
4.572	**5**	5.468	12.950	**5**	1.931
5.486	**6**	6.562	15.540	**6**	2.317
6.401	**7**	7.655	18.130	**7**	2.703
7.315	**8**	8.749	20.720	**8**	3.089
8.230	**9**	9.843	23.310	**9**	3.475
9.144	**10**	10.936	25.900	**10**	3.861
18.288	**20**	21.872	51.800	**20**	7.722
27.432	**30**	32.808	77.699	**30**	11.583
36.576	**40**	43.745	103.598	**40**	15.444
45.720	**50**	54.681	129.498	**50**	19.306
54.863	**60**	65.617	155.397	**60**	23.167
64.007	**70**	76.553	181.297	**70**	27.028
73.151	**80**	87.489	207.196	**80**	30.889
82.295	**90**	98.425	233.096	**90**	34.750
91.439	**100**	109.361	258.995	**100**	38.611

DOUBLE CONVERSION TABLES FOR WEIGHTS AND MEASURES

The central figures in heavy type represent either of the two columns beside them, as the case may be.

Hectares		Acres	Kilogrammes		Av. pounds
0·405	1	2·471	0·454	1	2·205
0·809	2	4·942	0·907	2	4·409
1·214	3	7·413	1·361	3	6·614
1·619	4	9·884	1·814	4	8·818
2·023	5	12·355	2·268	5	11·023
2·428	6	14·826	2·722	6	13·228
2·833	7	17·298	3·175	7	15·432
3·237	8	19·769	3·629	8	17·637
3·642	9	22·240	4·082	9	19·842
4·047	10	24·711	4·536	10	22·046
8·094	20	49·422	9·072	20	44·092
12·140	30	74·132	13·608	30	66·139
16·187	40	98·843	18·144	40	88·185
20·234	50	123·554	22·680	50	110·231
24·281	60	148·265	27·215	60	132·277
28·328	70	172·976	31·751	70	154·323
32·374	80	197·686	36·287	80	176·370
36·421	90	222·397	40·823	90	198·416
40·468	100	247·108	45·359	100	220·462

Litres		Gallons	Litres per hectare		Gallons per acre
4·546	1	0·220	11·21	1	0·089
9·092	2	0·440	22·42	2	0·178
13·638	3	0·660	33·63	3	0·267
18·184	4	0·880	44·83	4	0·356
22·730	5	1·100	56·04	5	0·461
27·276	6	1·320	67·25	6	0·535
31·822	7	1·540	78·46	7	0·624
36·368	8	1·760	89·67	8	0·714
40·914	9	1·980	100·87	9	0·803
45·460	10	2·200	112·08	10	0·892
90·919	20	4·399	224·17	20	1·784
136·379	30	6·599	336·25	30	2·676
181·838	40	8·799	448·34	40	3·569
227·298	50	10·999	560·43	50	4·456
272·758	60	13·198	672·51	60	5·353
318·217	70	15·398	784·56	70	6·245
363·677	80	17·598	896·68	80	7·137
409·136	90	19·797	1008·77	90	8·029
454·596	100	21·997	1120·85	100	8·922

Grammes		Ounces	Metric tons		Long tons
28·35	1	0·035	1·016	1	0·984
56·70	2	0·071	2·032	2	1·968
85·05	3	0·106	3·048	3	2·953
113·40	4	0·141	4·064	4	3·937
141·75	5	0·176	5·080	5	4·921
170·10	6	0·212	6·096	6	5·905
198·45	7	0·247	7·112	7	6·889
226·80	8	0·282	8·128	8	7·874
255·15	9	0·317	9·144	9	8·858
283·50	10	0·353	10·161	10	9·842
566·99	20	0·705	20·321	20	19·684
850·48	30	1·058	30·482	30	29·526
1133·98	40	1·411	40·642	40	39·368
1417·47	50	1·764	50·803	50	49·211
1700·97	60	2·116	60·963	60	59·053
1984·47	70	2·469	71·124	70	68·894
2267·96	80	2·822	81·284	80	78·737
2551·46	90	3·175	91·444	90	88·579
2834·95	100	3·527	101·605	100	98·421

US gallons (liquid)		Imperial gallons (liquid)	cc per 100 litres		Fluid oz per 100 gallons
1·200	1	0·833	6·24	1	0·16
2·401	2	1·666	12·47	2	0·32
3·601	3	2·499	18·71	3	0·48
4·802	4	3·332	24·94	4	0·64
6·002	5	4·165	31·18	5	0·80
7·203	6	4·998	37·41	6	0·96
8·403	7	5·831	43·65	7	1·12
9·603	8	6·664	49·89	8	1·28
10·804	9	7·497	56·13	9	1·44
12·004	10	8·330	62·36	10	1·60
24·009	20	16·661	124·72	20	3·21
36·013	30	24·991	187·09	30	4·81
48·017	40	33·321	249·45	40	6·41
60·022	50	41·652	311·81	50	8·02
72·026	60	49·982	374·17	60	9·62
84·030	70	58·312	436·53	70	11·22
96·034	80	66·642	498·90	80	12·83
108·039	90	74·973	561·26	90	14·43
120·043	100	83·303	623·62	100	16·04

cc per 100 litres		Pints per 100 gallons	Hecto-litres per hectare		English bushels per acre	Grammes per 100 litres		Ounces per 100 gallons	Kilogrammes per hectare		Pounds per acre
125	1	0·008	0·898	1	1·113	6·24	1	0·16	1·121	1	0·892
250	2	0·016	1·796	2	2·226	12·47	2	0·32	2·242	2	1·784
375	3	0·024	2·695	3	3·340	18·71	3	0·48	3·363	3	2·677
500	4	0·032	3·593	4	4·453	24·94	4	0·64	4·483	4	3·569
625	5	0·040	4·491	5	5·566	31·18	5	0·80	5·604	5	4·461
750	6	0·048	5·389	6	6·679	37·41	6	0·96	6·725	6	5·353
875	7	0·056	6·287	7	7·793	43·65	7	1·12	7·846	7	6·245
1,000	8	0·064	7·186	8	8·906	49·89	8	1·28	8·967	8	7·137
1,125	9	0·072	8·084	9	10·019	56·13	9	1·44	10·088	9	8·030
1,250	10	0·080	10·982	10	11·132	62·36	10	1·60	11·209	10	8·922
2,500	20	0·160	17·964	20	22·265	124·72	20	3·21	22·417	20	17·844
3,750	30	0·240	26·946	30	33·397	187·09	30	4·81	33·626	30	26·765
5,000	40	0·320	35·928	40	44·530	249·45	40	6·41	44·834	40	35·687
6,250	50	0·400	44·910	50	55·662	311·81	50	8·02	56·043	50	44·609
7,500	60	0·480	53·982	60	66·794	374·17	60	9·62	67·251	60	53·531
8,750	70	0·560	62·874	70	77·927	436·53	70	11·22	78·460	70	62·453
10,000	80	0·640	71·856	80	89·059	498·90	80	12·83	89·668	80	71·374
11,250	90	0·720	80·838	90	100·192	561·26	90	14·43	100·877	90	80·296
12,500	100	0·800	89·820	100	111·324	623·62	100	16·04	112·085	100	89·218

References

Adams, P. 1976 'Nutrition'. In *Chrysanthemums—the Inside Story*. National Chrysanthemum Society, London.

Adams, P., Graves, C. J. and Winsor, G. W. 1970 'Nutrition of year-round chrysanthemums in soil'. *Rep. Glasshouse Crops Res. Inst.* **90**, 1969.

Adams, P., Graves, C. J. and Winsor, G. W. 1971 'Nutrition of year-round chrysanthemums in peat and sand'. *Rep. Glasshouse Crops Res. Inst.* **102**, 1970.

Adams, P., Graves, C. J. and Winsor, G. W. 1975a 'Some effects of copper and boron deficiencies on the growth and flowering of *Chrysanthemum morifolium* (cv. Hurricane)'. *J. Sci. Food and Agric.* **26**, 1899.

Adams, P., Graves, C. J. and Winsor, G. W. 1975b 'Some responses of *Chrysanthemum morifolium* (cv. Hurricane) grown as a year-round crop in a peat-sand substrate to micronutrients and liming'. *J. Sci. Food and Agric.* **26**, 769.

Allard, H. A. 1928 'Chrysanthemum flowering season varied according to daily exposure to light'. *Year-book U.S.D.A.* 1928, 194.

Allen, P. G. 1965 'Chrysanthemums can follow straw bale grown tomatoes'. *Grower*, London **64**, 817.

Anderson, G. A. and Carpenter, W. J. 1974 'High intensity supplementary lighting of chrysanthemum stock plants'. *HortScience* **9**, 58.

Andrews, P. S. and Watson, D. P. 1952 'Stages in anatomical development of the flower head of *Chrysanthemum morifolium* Bailey. *Proc. Amer. Soc. hort. Sci.* **59**, 516.

Anon. 1970 *Rep. Efford Expl. Hort. Stn. for 1969.*

Anon. 1971 *Rep. Efford Expl. Hort. Stn. for 1970.*

Anon. 1972 *Rep. Efford Expl. Hort. Stn. for 1971.*

Anon. 1973 *Rep. Efford Expl. Hort. Stn. for 1972.*

Anon. 1974 *Rep. Efford Expl. Hort. Stn. for 1973.*

Anon. 1975 *Rep. Efford Expl. Hort. Stn. for 1974.*

Anon. 1976 *Rep. Efford Expl. Hort. Stn. for 1975.*

Anon. 1977 *Rep. Efford Expl. Hort. Stn. for 1976.*

Anon. 1978 *Rep. Efford Expl. Hort. Stn. for 1977.*

Ben-Jaacov, J. and Langhans, R. W. 1969 ' "After lighting" of chrysanthemums'. *Bull. N.Y. St. Flower Grs.* **285**, 1.

Ben-Jaacov, J. and Langhans, R. W. 1972. 'Rapid multiplication of chrysanthemum plants by stem-tip proliferation'. *HortScience* **7**, 289.

Borthwick, H. A. 1947 'Daylength and flowering'. *Yearbook U.S.D.A.* 1947, 273.

Borthwick, H. A. and Cathey, H. M. 1962 'Role of phytochrome in control of flowering of chrysanthemum'. *Bot. Gaz.* **123**, (3), 155.

Borthwick, H. A. and Parker, M. W. 1938 'Influence of photoperiod upon the differentiation of meristems and the blossoming of Biloxi soybeans'. *Bot. Gaz.* **99**, 825.

Bowen, H. J. M., Cawse, P. A. and Dick, M. J. 1962 'The induction of sports in chrysanthemums by gamma radiation'. *Rad. Bot.* **1**, 297.

Broertjes, C. 1966 'Mutation breeding of chrysanthemums'. *Euphytica* **15**, 156.

Broertjes, C., Roest, S. and Bokelmann, G. S. 1976 'Mutation breeding of *Chrysanthemum morifolium* Ram. using *in vivo* and *in vitro* adventitious bud techniques'. *Euphytica* **25**, 11.

Bunt, A. C. 1965 'Look for boron deficiency in peat–sand composts'. *Grower, London* **64**, 440.

Bunt, A. C. 1967 'Loam-less composts'. *Rep. Glasshouse Crops Res. Inst.* **1966**, 119.

Bunt, A. C. 1973 'Factors contributing to the delay in the flowering of pot chrysanthemums grown in peat–sand substrates. In Symposium on pot plants'. *Acta Hort., int. Soc. hort. Sci.* 1971.

Bunt, A. C. 1976a *Modern Potting Composts*. George Allen and Unwin, London.

Bunt, A. C. 1976b 'The growing medium'. In *Chrysanthemums—the inside story*. National Chrysanthemum Society, London.

Burges, H. D. and Jarrett, P. 1978 'Behaviour of moth larvae in glasshouse and their control with *Bacillus thuringiensis*'. *Bull. Ent. Res.* (In preparation.)

Butler, W. L., Norris, K. H., Siegalmann, H. W. and Hendricks, S. B. 1959 'Detection, assay, and preliminary purification of the pigment controlling photoresponsive development of plants'. *Proc. Nat. Acad. Sci.* **45**, 1703.

Butters, R. E. 1975 'Pot chrysanthemums; the effect of short-day treatment during the rooting stage'. *Expl. Hort.* **27**, 17.

Butters, R. E. and Wadsworth, G. A. 1974 'Nutrition of year-round spray chrysanthemums in beds of soil-less composts'. *Expl. Hort.* **26**, 17.

Cailachjan, M. H. 1945 'Photoperiodism of individual parts of the leaf; its halves'. *C.R. Acad. Sci. U.R.S.S.* **47**, 228.

Canham, A. E. 1962 'A new lamp for daylength control in horticulture'. ERA Report W/T 45.

Canham, A. E. 1964 *Electricity in Horticulture*. Macdonald, London.

Canham, A. E. 1966a *Artificial Light in Horticulture*. Centrex, Eindhoven.

Canham, A. E. 1966b 'The fluorescent tube as a source of night-break light'. *Expl. Hort.* **16**, 53.

Canham, A. E. 1970a 'Supplementary artificial light for pot chrysanthemums. A preliminary report'. *Electricity Council Research Centre* ECRC/R254 (1970).

Canham, A. E. 1970b 'Year-round chrysanthemum production'. *Gdnrs. Chron.* **168**, No. 18.

Canham, A. E. 1972 'Supplementary artificial light for pot chrysanthemums. A cultivar response trial and comparison of light sources'. *Electricity Council Rep.* ECR/R514 (1972).

Canham, A. E. 1973 Personal communication.

Canham, A. E. 1974 'Some effects of environmental factors on the rooting of cuttings'. *Applied Research Section, Dept. of Agric. and Hortic. University of Reading*, Feb. 1974.

Canham, A. E. 1975 'Supplementary lighting for spray chrysanthemums'. *Acta Hort.* **51**, 253.

Canham, A. E., Cockshull, K. E. and Hand, D. W. 1977 'Night-break lighting with low-pressure sodium lamps'. *Acta Hort.* **68**, 63.

Cathey, H. M. 1954a 'Temperature classification of chrysanthemums'. *Bull. N.Y. St. Flower Grs.* **104**, 1.

Cathey, H. M. 1954b 'Chrysanthemum temperature study. A. Thermal induction of stock plants of *Chrysanthemum morifolium*'. *Proc. Amer. Soc. hort. Sci.* **64**, 483.

Cathey, H. M. 1955a 'Temperature guide to chrysanthemum varieties'. *Bull. N.Y. St. Flower Grs.* **119**, 1.

Cathey, H. M. 1955b 'Chrysanthemum temperature study. D. Effect of temperature shifts upon the spray formation and flowering time of *Chrysanthemum morifolium*'. *Proc. Amer. Soc. hort. Sci.* **66**, 386.

Cathey, H. M. 1958 'Chemical produces compact mum plants retarding elongation without injury'. *Flor. Exch.* **130**, 13.

Cathey, H. M. 1969 '*Chrysanthemum morifolium.* (Ramat.) Hemsl.' In *The Induction of Flowering*. Macmillan Australia.

Cathey, H. M. 1970 'The next new chemical growth regulators for plants'. *Proc. 18 Int. hort. Congr.* **V**, 207.

Cathey, H. M. 1974 'Participation of phytochrome in regulating internode elongation of *Chrysanthemum morifolium* (Ramat.) Hemsl.' *J. Amer. Soc. hort. Sci.* **99**, 17.

Cathey, H. M. 1976 'Influence of a substituted oxathiin, a localized growth inhibitor, on the stem elongation, branching and flowering of *Chrysanthemum morifolium*. Ramat.' *J. Amer. Soc. hort. Sci.* **101** (5), 599.

Cathey, H. M., Bailey, W. A. and Borthwick, H. A. 1961 'Cylic lighting: a procedure for reducing cost of delaying chrysanthemum flowering'. *Flor. Exch.* **136** (42), 14.

Cathey, H. M. and Borthwick, H. A. 1961a 'Growth control by cylic lighting'. *Agric. Res. Wash.* **10** (1), 10.

Cathey, H. M. and Borthwick, H. A. 1961b 'Cyclic lighting for controlling flowering of chrysanthemums'. *Proc. Amer. Soc. hort. Sci.* **78**, 545.

Cathey, H. M. and Borthwick, H. A. 1964 'Significance of dark reversion of phytochrome in flowering of *Chrysanthemum morifolium*'. *Bot. Gaz.* **125**, 232.

Cathay, H. M. and Borthwick, H. A. 1967 'Action of phytochrome in controlling the flowering of *Chrysanthemum morifolium* Ramat., in response to prolonged exposures of artificial light'. *Plant Physiol.* **42**, (Suppl.) 9.

Cathey, H. M., Yeomans, A. H. and Smith, F. F. 1966 'Abortion of flower buds in chrysanthemum after application of a selected petroleum fraction of high aromatic content'. *Proc. 17 Int. hort. Congr.* 215.

Chan, A. P. 1950 'The development of crown and terminal flower, buds of *Chrysanthemum morifolium*'. *Proc. Amer. Soc. hort. Sci.* **55**, 461.

Chan, A. P. 1955 'Some factors affecting flower bud development of chrysanthemum'. *Rep. 14 Int. hort. Congr.* **2**, 1955.

Chan, A. P. 1966 'Chrysanthemum and rose mutations induced by X-rays'. *Proc. Amer. Soc. hort. Sci.* **88**, 613.

Cockshull, K. E. 1972 'Photoperiodic control of flowering in the chrysanthemum'. In *Crop Processes in Controlled Environments*. Academic Press, London.

Cockshull, K. E. 1975 'Premature budding in year-round chrysanthemums'. *Rep. Glasshouse Crops Res. Inst.* 1974, 128.

Cockshull, K. E. 1976a 'Flower and leaf initiation by *Chrysanthemum morifolium* Ramat. in long days'. *J. hort. Sci.* **51**, 441.

Cockshull, K. E. 1976b 'Flowers and flowering'. In *Chrysanthemums—the Inside Story*. National Chrysanthemum Society, London.

Cockshull, K. E. and Hughes, A. P. 1967 'Distribution of dry matter to flowers in *Chrysanthemum morifolium*'. *Nature, Lond.* **215**, 780.

Cockshull, K. E. and Hughes, A. P. 1968 'Accumulation of dry matter by *Chrysanthemum morifolium* after flower removal'. *Nature, Lond.* **217**, 979.

Cockshull, K. E. and Hughes, A. P. 1971. 'The effects of light intensity at different stages in flower initiation and development of *Chrysanthemum morifolium*'. *Ann. Bot.* **35**, 915.

Cockshull, K. E. and Hughes, A. P. 1972 'Flower formation in *Chrysanthemum morifolium*: the influence of light level'. *J. hort. Sci.* **47**, 113.

Crater, G. D., Kiplinger, D. C., Tayama, H. and Staby, G. 1973 'Ammonium versus nitrate nitrogen for standard chrysanthemums'. *Ohio Florist's Assoc. Bull.* **529**, 10.

Culbert, J. R. 1957 'Seeding spray type chrysanthemums'. *Nat. Chrys. Soc. Inc., U.S.A. Breeders Handbook* 54.

Delworth, C. 1941 'Production of quality blooms explained at Cornell Short Course'. *Flor. Rev.* **88**, 1.

Dicks, J. W. 1976 'Chemical restriction of stem growth in ornamentals, cereals and tobacco'. *Outlook on Agriculture* **9** (2), 69.

Dimock, A. W. and Post, K. 1944 'An efficient labour-saving method of steaming soil'. *Corne Univ. Agr. Exp. Sta. Ext. Bull.* **635**, 1.

Donald, C. M. 1968 'The breeding of crop ideotypes' *Euphytica* **17**, 385.

Doorenbos, J. and Kofranek, A. M. 1953 'Inflorescence initiation and development in an early and late chrysanthemum variety'. *Proc. Amer. Soc. hort. Sci.* **61**, 555.

Dowrick, G. J. and El-Bayoumi, A. S. 1966 'The origin of new forms of the garden chrysanthemum'. *Euphytica* **15**, 32.

Earle, E. D. and Langhans, R. W. 1974a 'Propagation of chrysanthemum *in vitro*. I. Multiple plantlets from shoot tips and the establishment of tissue cultures'. *J. Amer. Soc. hort. Sci.* **99**, 128.

Earle, E. D. and Langhans, R. W. 1974b 'Propagation of chrysanthemum *in vitro*. II. Production, growth and flowering of plantlets from tissue cultures'. *J. Amer. Soc. hort. Sci.* **99**, 352.

Emsweller, S. L., Stuart, N. W. and Byrne, J. W. 1941 'Using a short interval of light during night to delay blooming of chrysanthemums'. *Proc. Amer. Soc. hort. Sci.* **39**, 391.

Engelhard, A. W., Crane, G. L. and Mellinger, H. C. 1976 'Stem rot, a new disease on chrysanthemum incited by *Fusarium solani*'. *Plant Disease Rep.* **60**, 437.

Engelhard, A. W. and Woltz, S. S. 1973 'Fusarium wilt of chrysanthemum. Complete control of symptoms with an integrated fungicide–lime–nitrate regime'. *Phytopathology* **63**, 1256.

Furuta, T. 1954 'Photoperiod and flowering of *Chrysanthemum morifolium*'. *Proc. Amer. Soc. hort. Sci.* **63**, 457.

Furuta, T. and Kiplinger, D. C. 1955 'Chronological age of cuttings, a factor influencing the spray formation of pompon chrysanthemums'. *Proc. Amer. Soc. hort. Sci.* **66**, 383.

Furuta, T. and Nelson, K. S. 1953 'The effect of high night temperature on development of chrysanthemum flower buds'. *Proc. Amer. Soc. hort. Sci.* **61**, 548.

Gardner, R. 1966 'Effects of carbon dioxide enrichment on crops of tomato, lettuce and chrysanthemum as grown commercially on the N.A.A.S. Experimental Horticulture Stations in England and Wales'. *Proc. 17 Int. hort. Congr.* 347.

Garner, W. W. and Allard, H. A. 1920 'Effect of the relative length of day and night and other factors of the environment on growth and reproduction in plants'. *J. agric. Res.* **18**, 553.

Good, G. L. and Tukey, H. B. Jr 1966 'The leaching of metabolites from cuttings propagated under mist'. *Proc. Amer. Soc. hort. Sci.* **89**, 727.

Good, G. L. and Tukey, H. B. Jr 1967 'Redistribution of mineral nutrients in *Chrysanthemum morifolium* during propagation'. *Proc. Amer Soc. hort. Sci.* **90**, 384.

Graves, C. J. and Sutcliffe, J. F. 1974 'An effect of copper deficiency on the initiation and development of flower buds of *Chrysanthemum morifolium* grown in solution culture'. *Ann. Bot.* **38**, 729.

Green, L., Withrow, R. B. and Richman, M. W. 1932 'The response of greenhouse crops to electric light supplementing daylight'. *Purdue Univ. Agr. Exp. Sta. Bull.* **366**, 1.

Gregory, F. G. and Purvis, O. N. 1938 'De-vernalisation by high temperature'. *Nature, Lond.* **155**, 113.

Grouet, D. et Allaire, L. 1973 'La Rouille blanche du chrysanthème. Evolution et methodes de lutte'. *L'Horticulture Française* **30**, March 1973, 3.

Gurney, B. and Hussey, N. W. 1974 'Chemical control of the chrysanthemum leaf miner *Phytomyza syngenesiae* (Hardy) (Diptera: Agromyzidae)'. *Pl. Path.* **23**, 127.

Hall, R. A. 1975 'Aphid control by a fungus *Verticillium lecanii* within an integrated programme for chrysanthemum pests and diseases'. *Proc. 8th Brit. Insecticide and Fungicide Conf.* 93.

Hamner, K. C. and Bonner, J. 1938 'Photoperiodism in relation to hormones as factors in floral initiation and development'. *Bot. Gaz.* **100**, 388.

Hand, D. W., Cockshull, K. E., Hannah, M. A. and Horridge, J. S. 1977 'Air pollution: effect of propylene on growth, morphology and flowering'. *Rep. Glasshouse Crops Res. Inst.* 1976, 56.

Hassan, M. R. A. and Newton, P. 1975 'New light treatments for spray chrysanthemums'. *Commercial Grower*, March 7, 1975, 484.

Hellmers, E. 1958 *Four Wilt Diseases of Perpetual Flowering Carnations in Denmark*. E. Munksgaard, Copenhagen.

Hollings, M. and Stone, O. M. 1968 'Techniques and problems in the production of virus-tested planting material'. *Scient. Hort.* **20**, 57.

Hughes, A. P. and Cockshull, K. E. 1971a 'The effects of light intensity and carbon dioxide concentration on the growth of *Chrysanthemum morifolium* cv. Bright Golden Anne'. *Ann. Bot.* **35**, 899.

Hughes, A. P. and Cockshull, K. E. 1971b 'The variation in response to light intensity and carbon dioxide concentration shown in controlled environments at two times of year'. *Ann. Bot.* **35**, 933.

Hume, E. P. 1941 'The effect of short days upon the development of the fall blooming chrysanthemums'. *Proc. Amer. Soc. hort. Sci.* **38**, 665.

Hussey, N. W. 1969 'Differences in susceptibility of different strains of chrysanthemum leaf miner (*Phytomyza syngenesiae*) to BHC and diazinon'. *Proc. 5th Brit. Insecticide and Fungicide Conf.* 93.

Jackson, A. A. 1971 'Chrysanthemum breeding at Wye College'. *J. roy. hort. Soc.* **96**, 23.

Jank, H. 1957 'Experimental production of mutations

on *Chrysanthemum indicum* by X-rays'. *Der Züchter* **27,** 223.

Joiner, J. N. 1967 'Effects of P, K and Mg levels on growth, yield and chemical composition of *Chrysanthemum morifolium* "Indianapolis White" '. *Proc. Amer Soc. hort. Sci.* **90,** 389.

Joiner, J. N. and Pickhardt, G. D. 1970 'Chemical pruning and disbudding of *Chrysanthemum morifolium*'. *Proc. 83rd Annual Meeting Florida State Hort. Soc.* **83,** 461.

Joiner, J. N. and Poole, R. T. 1967 'Relationship of fertilization frequency to chrysanthemum yield and nutrient levels in soil and foliage'. *Proc. Amer. Soc. hort. Sci.* **90,** 397.

Joiner, J. N. and Smith, T. C. 1962 'Effects of nitrogen and potassium levels on the growth and flowering responses and foliar composition of *Chrysanthemum morifolium* "Bluechip" '. *Proc. Amer. Soc. hort. Sci.* **80,** 571.

Kiplinger, D. C. and Alger, J. 1948 'Interrupted shading of chrysanthemums'. *Proc. Amer. Soc. hort. Sci.* **52,** 478.

Kiplinger, D. C. and Rose, S. 1951 'Year around flowering of potted chrysanthemums'. *Proc. Amer. Soc. hort. Sci.* **58,** 347.

Kofranek, A. M. and Halevy, A. H. 1972 'Conditions for opening cut chrysanthemum flower buds'. *J. Amer. Soc. hort. Sci.* **97,** 578.

Kofranek, A. M. and Halevy, A. H. 1974 'Minimum number of short days for production of high quality standard chrysanthemums'. *HortScience* **9,** 543.

Kramer, P. J. 1934 'Effects of soil temperature on the absorption of water by plants'. *Science N.Y.* **79,** 371.

Langton, F. A. 1976 'Sports'. In *Chrysanthemums— the Inside Story*. National Chrysanthemum Society, London.

Langton, F. A. and Cockshull, K. E. 1976 'An ideotype of chrysanthemum. (*C. morifolium* Ramat.)'. *Acta Hort.* **63,** 165.

Laurie, A. 1930 'Photoperiodism—practical application to greenhouse culture'. *Proc. Amer. Soc. hort. Sci.* **27,** 319.

Lawrence, W. J. C. 1950 *Science and the Glasshouse.* Oliver and Boyd, Edinburgh.

Leiser, A. T., Sanborn, J. and De Rolf, L. 1966 'The effects of various potassium ratios and sources on growth of *Chrysanthemum morifolium* fertilized with magnesium ammonium phosphate'. *Rep. 17th Int. hort. Congr.* 1966, **1,** 476.

Lelliott, R. A., Billing, E. and Hayward, A. C. 1966 'A determinative scheme for the fluorescent plant pathogenic pseudomonads'. *J. appl. Bact.* **29,** (3) 470.

Lert, P. J. 1959 'Gibberellins on chrysanthemum'. *Calif. Agric.* **13,** 4.

Link, C. 1936 'Preliminary studies on flower bud differentiation in relation to photoperiodic response'. *Proc. Amer. Soc. hort. Sci.* **34,** 621.

Lockhart, C. L. and Swain, G. S. 1966 'Cold storage of chrysanthemum stool cuttings'. *Res. for Fmrs. Canada* **11,** (1), 6.

Lunt, O. R. and Kofranek, A. M. 1958 'Nitrogen and potassium nutrition of chrysanthemum'. *Proc. Amer. Soc. hort. Sci.* **72,** 487.

Lunt, O. R., Kofranek, A. M. and Oertli, J. J. 1964 'Some critical nutrient levels in *Chrysanthemum morifolium*, cultivar Good News'. *Plant Anal. and Fert. Problems* **4,** 398.

Maatsch, R. and Bachthaler, E. 1965 'Never on Sundays! Uninterrupted and periodically interrupted shortday treatment of chrysanthemums'. *Gartenwelt* **65,** 218.

Machin, B. J. 1955 'The effects of light and temperature on chrysanthemums'. Dissertation for B.Sc. (Hons.), University of Nottingham, 1955.

Machin, B. J. 1973 'Factors affecting the growth and flowering of *Chrysanthemum morifolium* Ramat. in a direct shortday planting system'. Ph.D. Thesis (unpubl.), University of Nottingham, 1973.

Machin, B. J. 1975 'Foliar feeding in relation to more conventional methods of nutrition'. *Nat. Chrys. Soc. Yearbook* 1975, 84.

Machin, B. J. 1976 *Chrysanthemum Nutrition.* National Chrysanthemum Society, London.

Machin, B. J. (unpubl.) Perifleur Ltd experimental programme.

Marousky, F. J. 1971 'Handling and opening bud-cut chrysanthemum flowers with 8-hydroxyquinoline citrate and sucrose'. *Marketing Research Report, U.S.D.A.* 905.

Marousky, F. J. 1973 'Recent advances in opening bud-cut chrysanthemum flowers'. *HortScience* **8,** 199.

Mason, D. T. and Vince, D. 1962 'The pattern of growth in chrysanthemum as a response to changing seasonal environment'. Advances in Horticultural Science and Their Application. *Rep. 15 Int. hort. Congr.* 1958, Vol. II. Pergamon Press, London, 374.

Massey, D. M. and Winsor, G. W. 1970 'Nutrition of year-round chrysanthemums in soil'. *Rep. Glasshouse Crops Res. Inst.* 1969, 93.

Massey, D. M. and Winsor, G. W. 1971 'Nutrition of year-round chrysanthemums in soil'. *Rep. Glasshouse Crops Res. Inst.* 1970, 104.

Massey, D. M. and Winsor, G. W. 1974 'The nitrogen nutrition of spray chrysanthemums (cv. Hurricane) grown as a year-round crop in soil borders'. *Expl. Hort.* **26,** 1.

Maw, G. A. and Kempton, R. J. 1973 'Methyl bromide as a soil fumigant'. *Soils and Fertilizers* **36,** 41.

McCoy, R. E. and Dimock, A. W. 1972 'Relationship of temperature and humidity to development of Mycosphaerella lesions on chrysanthemums'. *Phytopathology* **62**, 1195.

Menhenett, R. 1976a 'New growth retardant for pot mums has promise'. *Grower*, February 28, 1976.

Menhenett, R. 1976b 'Plant hormones and the modification of growth and development'. In *Chrysanthemums—the Inside Story*. National Chrysanthemum Society, London.

Miller, H. N., Miller, J. W. and Crane, G. L. 1975 'Relative susceptibility of chrysanthemum cultivars to *Agrobacterium tumefaciens*'. *Plant Disease Rep.* **59**, 576.

Ministry of Agriculture 1965 *Tech. Bull. No. 4*. 'The calculation of irrigation need'.

Morton, W. M. and Boodley, J. W. 1969 'The effect of mist-fertilizer propagation on the growth and nutrient content of *Euphorbia pulcherrima* and *Chrysanthemum morifolium*'. *J. Amer. Soc. hort. Sci.* **94**, 549.

Nichols, R. 1976 'The cut-flower'. In *Chrysanthemums—the Inside Story*. National Chrysanthemum Society, London.

Okada, M. 1951 'Studies on the crown bud of chrysanthemums. iv. On retardation of blooming by longday conditions afer flower bud differentiation (*Japanese*)'. *J. hort. Ass. Japan* **20**, 33.

Okada, M. 1952 'On the relation of stem length and leaf area to flower bud formation in chrysanthemums (*Japanese*)'. *J. hort. Ass. Japan* **21**, 174.

Okada, M. 1959 'On the rosetting of suckers and measures for breaking rosetting in chrysanthemums (*Japanese*)'. *J. hort. Ass. Japan* **28**, 209.

Okada, M. 1963 'Studies on flower bud differentiation and flowering in chrysanthemums'. *Mem. Faculty Agric. Tokyo Univ. Ed.* **9**, 63.

Parker, M. W., Hendricks, S. B., Borthwick, H. A. and Scully, N. J. 1946 'Action spectrum for the photoperiodic control of floral initiation in Biloxi soybean'. *Science N.Y.* **102** (1945), No. 2641, 152.

Parups, E. V. 1976 'Use of 2,3-dihydro-5,6-diphenyl-1,4-oxathiin for disbudding of standard chrysanthemums'. *Can. J. Plant Sci.* **56**, 531.

Paul, J. L. and Leiser, A. T. 1968 'Influence of sodium in mistwater on rooting of chrysanthemums'. *HortScience* **3**, 187.

Paul, J. L. and Smith, L. V. 1966 'Rooting of chrysanthemum cuttings in peat as influenced by calcium'. *Proc. Amer. Soc. hort. Sci.* **89**, 626.

Paul, J. L. and Thornhill, W. H. 1969 'Effects of magnesium on rooting chrysanthemums'. *J. Amer. Soc. hort. Sci.* **94**, 230.

Peerally, M. A. and Colhoun, J. 1969 'The epidemiology of rootrot of chrysanthemums caused by *Phoma* sp.' *Trans. Brit. Mycol. Soc.* **52**, 115.

Penman, H. L. 1949 'A general survey of meteorology in agriculture and an account of the physics of irrigation control'. *Quart. J. R. Met. Soc.* **75**, 293.

Penman, H. L. 1952 'Experiments on irrigation of sugar beet'. *J. Agric. Sci.* **42**, 286.

Poe, S. L. 1971 'Evaluations of pesticides for phytotoxicity on chrysanthemum flowers'. *Florida Flower Grower* **8**, 1.

Poesch, G. H. 1931 'Studies of photoperiodism of the chrysanthemum'. *Proc. Amer. Soc. hort. Sci.* **28**, 389.

Poesch, G. H. 1932 'Further studies of photoperiodism of the Chrysanthemum'. *Proc. Amer. Soc. hort. Sci.* **29**, 540.

Poesch, G. H. 1935 'Supplementary illumination from mazda, mercury and neon lamps on some greenhouse plants'. *Proc. Amer. Soc. hort. Sci.* **33**, 637.

Poesch, G. H. 1936 'Prolonging the flowering period of chrysanthemums with the use of supplementary illumination'. *Proc. Amer. Soc. hort. Sci.* **34**, 624.

Popham, R. A. 1958 'Cytogenesis and zonation in the shoot apex of *Chrysanthemum morifolium*'. *Amer. J. Bot.* **45**, 198.

Popham, R. A. 1963 'Developmental studies of flowering. Meristems and differentiation. (Brookhaven National Lab.)'. *Brookhaven Symp. Biol.* No. 16.

Popham, R. A. and Chan, A. P. 1950 'Zonation in the vegetative stem tip of *Chrysanthemum morifolium*'. *Amer. J. Bot.* **37**, 476.

Popham, R. A. and Chan, A. P. 1952 'Origin and development of the receptacle of *Chrysanthemum morifolium*'. *Amer. J. Bot.* **39**, 329.

Post, K. 1931 'Reducing the daylength of chrysanthemums for the production of early blooms by the use of black sateen cloth'. *Proc. Amer. Soc. hort. Sci.* **28**, 382.

Post, K. 1932 'Further results with black cloth for the production of early blooms of the chrysanthemum'. *Proc. Amer. Soc. hort. Sci.* **29**, 545.

Post, K. 1934 'Production of early blooms of chrysanthemums by the use of black cloth to reduce the length of day'. *Cornell Univ. Agr. Exp. Sta. Bull.* **594**, 30.

Post, K. 1936 'The determination of the normal date of bud formation of shortday plants'. *Proc. Amer. Soc. hort. Sci.* **34**, 618.

Post, K. 1939 'The relationship of temperature to flower bud formation in chrysanthemums'. *Proc. Amer. Soc. hort. Sci.* **37**, 1003.

Post, K. 1941 'The effect of light intensity on response of *Euphorbia pulcherrima* and *Euphorbia fulgens* to photoperiod and temperature'. *Proc. Amer. Soc. hort. Sci.* **38**, 663.

Post, K. 1942 'Effects of daylength and temperature on growth and flowering of some florist crops'. *Cornell Univ. Agr. Exp. Sta. Bull.* **787**, 1.

Post, K. 1947 'Chrysanthemum troubles of 1947'. *Bull. N.Y. St. Flower Grs.* **27**, 4.

Post, K. 1948 'Daylength and flower bud development in chrysanthemums'. *Proc. Amer. Soc. hort. Sci.* **51**, 590.

Post, K. 1949a *Florist Crop Production and Marketing.* Orange Judd Publishing Co. Inc., New York.

Post, K. 1949b 'Precision spray formation in pompons'. *Bull. N.Y. St. Flower Grs.* **46**, 4.

Post, K. 1950a 'Controlled photoperiod and spray formation of chrysanthemums'. *Proc. Amer. Soc. hort. Sci.* **55**, 467.

Post, K. 1950b 'Accumulation of photoperiodic stimuli in chrysanthemums'. *Proc. Amer. Soc. hort. Sci.* **55**, 475.

Post, K. 1952 'Temperature and flowering of ornamentals'. *Rep. 13 Int. hort. Congr.* 935.

Post, K. 1953a 'Shading carnations and chrysanthemums'. *Bull. N.Y. St. Flower Grs.* **93**, 3.

Post, K. 1953b 'It's a short night you want'. *Bull. N.Y. St. Flower Grs.* **99**, 3.

Post, K. 1953c 'Temperature and flowering of ornamentals'. *Rep. 13 Int. hort. Congr.* 935.

Post, K. and Kamemoto, H. 1950 'A study on the number of short photoperiods required for flower bud initiation and the effect of interrupted treatment on flower spray formation in two commercial varieties of chrysanthemums'. *Proc. Amer. Soc. hort. Sci.* **55**, 477.

Post, K. and Lacey, D. B. 1951a 'Interrupted short day improves standard chrysanthemums'. *Bull. N.Y. St. Flower Grs.* **70**, 2.

Post, K. and Lacey, D. B. 1951b 'High temperature produces longday effect on chrysanthemums'. *Bull. N.Y. St Flower Grs.* **76**, 4.

Potter, R. 1975 'New developments in chrysanthemum culture. "Culture in nutrient film" '. *Nat. Chrys. Soc. Bull.* **87**, 13.

Read, P. E. and Hoysler, V. C. 1969 'Stimulation and retardation of adventitious root formation by application of B-Nine and Cycocel'. *J. Amer. Soc. hort. Sci.* **94**, 314.

Roberts, R. H. and Struckmeyer, B. E. 1938 'The effects of temperature and some other environmental factors upon the photoperiodic responses of some of the higher plants'. *J. agric. Res.* **56**, 633.

Roest, S. and Bokelmann, G. S. 1975 'Vegetative Propagation of *Chrysanthemum morifolium* Ram. *in vitro*'. *Scientia Horticulturæ* **3**, 317.

Russell, E. W. 1973 *Soil Conditions and Plant Growth*, (10th Edition). Longman, London.

Ryugo, K. and Sachs, R. M. 1969 '*In vitro* and *in vivo* studies of Alar (1,1-dimethylaminosuccinamic acid, B-995) and related substances'. *J. Amer. Soc. hort. Sci.* **94**, 529.

Sachs, R. M. and Kofranek, A. M. 1963 'Comparative cytohistological studies on inhibition and promotion of stem growth in *Chrysanthemum morifolium*'. *Amer. J. Bot.* **50**, 772.

Salter, P. J. 1954 In *Plant Climate and Irrigation.* Chichester Press, Chichester.

Schwabe, W. W. 1950 'Factors controlling flowering in the chrysanthemum. I. The effects of photoperiod and temporary chilling'. *J. exp. Bot.* **1**, 329..

Schwabe, W. W. 1953 'Effects of temperature, daylength and light intensity in the control of flowering in the chrysanthemum'. *Rep. 13 Int. hort. Congr.* 952.

Schwabe, W. W. 1954 'Factors controlling flowering in the chrysanthemum. V. De-vernalisation in relation to high temperature and low light intensity treatments'. *J. exp. Bot.* **6**, 435.

Schwabe, W. W. 1959 'Some effects of environment and hormone treatment on reproductive morphogenesis in the chrysanthemum'. *J. Linn. Soc. (Bot.)* **56**, 254.

Scopes, N. E. A. 1969 'The potential of *Chrysopa carnea* as a biological control agent of *Myzus persicae* on glasshouse chysanthemums'. *Ann. appl. Biol.* **64**, 433.

Scopes, N. E. A. 1970 'Control of *Myzus persicae* on year-round chrysanthemums by introducing aphids parasitized by *Aphidius matricariae* into boxes of rooted cuttings'. *Ann. appl. Biol.* **66**, 323.

Scopes, N. E. A. 1975a 'The evaluation and use of predators for protected cropping'. *Ann. appl. Biol.* **80**, 123.

Scopes, N. E. A. 1975b *Pests, Diseases and Nutritional Disorders of Chrysanthemums.* National Chrysanthemum Society, London.

Scopes, N. E. A. and Biggerstaff, S. M. 1973 'Progress towards integrated pest control on year-round chrysanthemums'. *Proc. 7th Brit. Insecticide and Fungicide Conf.* 227.

Searle, S. A. 1954 *Plant Climate and Irrigation* Chichester Press, Chichester.

Searle, S. A. 1973 *Environment and Plant Life.* Faber and Faber, London.

Sheard, G. F. 1955 'Trickle irrigation and water requirement'. *Agriculture, London* **62**, 413.

Sheehan, T. J. and Sagawa, Y. 1955 'The effects of gamma radiation on chrysanthemum and gladiolus'. *Proc. Florida State Hort. Soc.* **72**, 388.

Spomer, L. A. and Langhans, R. W. 1975 'The growth of greenhouse bench *Chrysanthemum morifolium* Ramat. at high soil water contents; effects of soil water and aeration'. *Comm. Soil Sci. and Plant Analysis* **6**, 545.

Spurway, C. H. 1933 'Soil testing—a practical system of soil diagnosis'. *Mich. Agr. Exp. Sta. Tech. Bull.* **132**, 1.

Stewart, R. N. and Dermen, H. 1970. 'Somatic genetic analysis of the apical layers of chimeral sports in chrysanthemum by experimental production of adventitious shoots'. *Amer. J. Bot.* **57**, 1061.

Stobart, A. K. 1974 'Personal communication. Plant Cell Metabolism Laboratory', Dept. of Botany, University of Bristol.

Stuart, N. W. 1943 'Controlling time of blooming of chrysanthemums by the use of lights'. *Proc. Amer. Soc. hort. Sci.* **42**, 605.

Stuart, N. W. and Cathey, H. M. 1959 'Growth and metabolism of chrysanthemum as modified by nutrients and gibberellin'. *Plant Physiol.* **34**, 16.

Tayama, H. C., Kiplinger, D. C. and Staby, G. C. 1974 'Effects of high intensity discharge light on pompon and pot chrysanthemums: a preliminary report'. *Ohio Florist's Assoc. Bull.* **539**, 10.

Tincker, M. A. H. 1929 'The effect of length of day period of illumination upon the growth of plants'. *J. roy. hort. Soc.* **54**, 354.

Tsujita, M. J., Kiplinger, D. C., Tayama, H. K. and Staby, G. 1974 'The effects of nitrogen source, temperature and light intensity on standard chrysanthemums'. *Ohio Florist's Assoc. Bull.* **541**, 3.

Uhring, J. 1971 'Histological observations on chemical pruning of chrysanthemums with methyl deconoate'. *J. Amer. Soc. hort. Sci.* **96**, 58.

Vince, D. 1953 'Delayed blooming of mid-season and late-flowering chrysanthemums'. *Agriculture, London* **60**, 68.

Vince, D. 1955a 'Some effects of temperature and daylength on flowering in the chrysanthemum'. *J. hort. Sci.* **30**, 34.

Vince, D. 1955b 'Latest work on flowering of chrysanthemums'. *Grower, London* **43**, 437.

Vince, D. 1955c 'Temperature as well as light controls growth'. *Grower, London* **44**, 1174.

Vince, D. 1956 'Chilling will prevent rosetting'. *Grower, London* **45**, 33.

Vince, D. and Mason, D. T. 1959 'Low temperature effects on internode extension in *Chrysanthemum morifolium*'. *J. hort. Sci.* **34**, 199.

Wadsworth, G. A. and Butters, R. E. 1972 'The nutrition of A.Y.R. spray chrysanthemums in loam-less media'. Potassium Institute Ltd. *Colloq. Proc.* No. 2, 1972.

Watson, D. P. and Andrews, P. S. 1953 'The effect of light intensity on the flowering of chrysanthemum variety Gold Coast'. *Proc. Amer. Soc. hort. Sci.* **61**, 551.

Waxman, S. 1961 'Flashing lights cut lighting costs by 86 percent'. *Grower* **56**, 252.

Whittles, C. L. and Schofield-Palmer, E. K. 1951 'On pC, pS and pN as indicating functions of electrical soil conductivity'. *J. Soil Sci.* **2**, 243.

Wille, D. 1974 'Influence of nutrition on rooting capacity of cuttings'. *Mededelingen van de Faculteit Landbouwwetenschappen, Rijksuniversiteit, Gent* **39**, 1520.

Winkler, G. 1967 'The effect of different temperatures on chrysanthemum mother plants'. *Dtsche. Gartenb.* **14**, 325.

Winsor, G. W. 1968 'Nitrogen and glasshouse crops'. *Tech. Bull. Minist. Agric. Fish. Fd.* **15**, 118.

Winsor, G. W. and Hart, B. 1965 'Nutritional trials with glasshouse and other crops'. *Rep. Glasshouse Crops Res. Inst.* 1964, 65.

Winsor, G. W. and Hart, B. 1966 'Nutritional trials with glasshouse crops'. *Rep. Glasshouse Crops Res. Inst.* 1965, 80.

Winspear, K. W. 1977 'Thermal screens save fuel in protected cropping'. *ARC Res. Rev.* **3**, 1, 11.

Wott, J. A. and Tukey Jr., H. B. 1969 'Cutting size and nutrient mist effect rooting of chrysanthemums'. *Bull. N.Y. St. Flower Grs.* **284**.

Wyatt, I. J. 1966 'Insecticide resistance in aphids on chrysanthemums'. *Proc. 3rd Brit. Insecticide and Fungicide Conf.* 52.

Wylie, A. W., Ryugo, K. and Sachs, R. M. 1970 'Effects of growth retardants on biosynthesis #95 of gibberellin precursors in root tips of peas *Pisum sativum* L.' *J. Amer. Soc. hort. Sci.* **95**, 627.

Zacharioudakis, J. N. and Larson, R. A. 1976 'Chemical removal of lateral buds of *Chrysanthemum morifolium* Ramat.' *HortScience* **11**, 36.

Index